Contents

CONTENTS

PRIDE,
POP AND
POLITICS

PRIDE, POP AND POLITICS

MUSIC, THEATRE AND LGBT ACTIVISM, 1970–2021

DARRYL W. BULLOCK

OMNIBUS PRESS

For Dale, Norman and Ralph,
and for all of those who did their bit

A Note on Language

Of all the various initials different sections of the community now use, LGBT became the accepted standard in the 1990s, and it is that term that I have adopted for this work, unless quoting directly from other sources or using language in its correct historical context.

The word 'homosexual' was not coined until 1869; prior to this (as you'll see in the first chapter) the accepted legal term was sodomy or, occasionally, buggery: sodomy and buggery both refer specifically to anal sex, and historically buggery was also used to refer to bestiality. 'Lesbian', used in a sexual sense, as opposed to referring to the poets Sappho and Erinna having come from the island of Lesbos, appeared in 1732, but was not in general use to describe women attracted to other women until the 1920s. 'Gay' first began to be used as a slang term for homosexuality (both male and female) in the 1920s; it starts turning up in Hollywood movies from 1933 although it became more popular in the years after the Second World War, and by the mid-1960s was in common use. At the same time 'queer' was used, almost exclusively in a pejorative sense: it would be decades before the LGBT community would reclaim ownership of the 'q' word.

During the early years of the gay liberation movement, there was no distinction between gay men and gay women, although that would change as factions developed, each with their own individual issues and needs. LGB did not appear until the late 1980s in America (where, more commonly, the order was GLB), and again was not in common

ix

usage for several years. In the following decade this would morph into LGBT, to embrace the Lesbian, Gay, Bisexual and Trans communities, but again the term would not see common acceptance (i.e. use in the media) until the beginning of the new century. In more recent years, LGBTQ has entered into common usage, especially in the United States but, as this book is primarily about the British experience, we'll stick with the four initials for now.

A Note on Sources

Unless otherwise credited, all quotes from the following people are taken from interviews, conversations and correspondence with the author: John Aggy (October 2020), Charlie Beaton (March 2020), Andy Bell (November 2020), Richard Bolingbroke (July 2020), Phil Booth (September 2019), Theodore 'Ted' Brown (February 2021), Mark Bunyan (August 2020), Angela Cooper (September 2020), Gary Cosby (July 2020), Jayne County (October 2019), Josefina Cupido (September 2020), Gillian Dickinson (December 2019), Hifi Sean Dickson (November 2020), Stuart Feather (February 2021), John Grant (October 2019), Frankie Green (September 2020), Rupert Herries (February 2020), Ken Howard and Alan Blaikley (October 2018), Stephen Ireland (October 2019), Martin Isaacs (November 2019), Don Letts (November 2021), Lucia Lucas (February 2020), Horse McDonald (November 2020), Andy Polaris (October 2020), Alison Rayner (September 2020), Tom Robinson (November 2016), Melanie Rosatone (September 2020), Paul Rutherford (February 2017), Rosemary Schonfeld (May 2020), the late Norman Scott (April 2020), Peter Scott-Presland (August 2020), Lord Smith (Baron Smith of Finsbury, formerly Chris Smith, MP) (March 2020), Paul Southwell (May 2020), Oli Spleen (May 2018), the late Ralph Stephenson (March 2020), Steve Swindells (January 2020), Peter Tatchell (October 2019), the late Dale Wakefield (March 2020), and Ken and Dede Wilson (December 2019).

Introduction

'The last 50 years have not just been about gaining LGBT rights from straight society, it's also been about convincing LGBT people that they actually deserve rights.' – Peter Scott-Presland[1]

Over the last 50 years or so, the UK has made great strides towards equality for LGBT people. But prior to the implementation, in 1967, of the recommendations made by the 1957 Wolfenden Report, the equalisation of the age of consent, the adoption of same-sex marriage and all of the other changes that finally allowed members of the LGBT community to feel as though they were no longer being treated as second-class citizens in their own country, a war had to be won. In recent years, with the re-emergence of the right wing and the erosion of LGBT rights in many countries around the world, you could be forgiven for thinking that war had never been fought.

Music, and the arts, have had their own vital roles to play in that struggle: for decades clubs and concerts have provided safe spaces for queer people to meet and form lifelong friendships, and LGBT artists have used their positions and their creative abilities to highlight inequality. Music amplified the voices of protesters, offered support for the lonely and dispossessed, and supplied the soundtrack to celebrations. In the early days of gay liberation, when there was a need to raise both funds and awareness for the cause, it was LGBT people in the arts who performed for free, who rattled tins and who lent their names to the movement. During the 1970s and 1980s, when successive governments were trying to suppress LGBT rights and the time came to stand up and be counted, it was LGBT musicians, actors, playwrights and producers who were among the first to raise their heads above the parapet, to take to the streets and to lead the protests. Gay, lesbian, bisexual, trans and queer musicians, composers and performers have always been part of our community; for decades now their songs have documented the fight for LGBT civil rights, and their work has inspired successive generations to join the battle.

The laws that protect the rights of members of the LGBT community in various parts of the world are relatively new. The struggle for equality, for emancipation, has been similar to the fight for the rights of Black and Minority Ethnic (BAME) communities or for women the world over, but even today there are still 11 countries or territories where LGBT people can – and do – face the death penalty simply for existing: they don't have to fall in love, or have sex, or take part in any protest.* They simply have to *be*.

Let that sink in for a minute. As a gay man, a lesbian woman, a bisexual, trans or queer person, you can be hanged, beheaded or stoned to death just for daring to share the same air as a heterosexual. In more countries still, LGBT people are persecuted, publicly flogged and imprisoned for their so-called 'crimes'. In the heterosexual, gender-binary world you need to commit murder or rape to receive such drastic punishment, and even then, according to Amnesty International,[2] less than 20 countries around the globe still enact capital punishment for these most heinous crimes. Within 34 of the 53 member states of the Commonwealth of Nations, the remnants of the once-mighty British Empire, same-sex relationships are illegal, and of those three still enact the death penalty. In other regions, LGBT people are murdered by

---

* As of August 2021, according to the Human Dignity Trust, these are: Afghanistan, Brunei, Iran, Mauritania, Northern Nigeria, Pakistan, Qatar, Saudi Arabia, Somalia, the UAE and Yemen.

militia; in the Chechen Republic, LGBT people have been imprisoned, tortured and often have permanently 'disappeared', and in countries including Russia, Jamaica, Uganda and Kenya the authorities have turned a blind eye while LGBT people are taken from their homes, beaten and left for dead by gangs of vigilantes. Today, 69 countries still criminalise same-sex relationships, and this type of state-sanctioned hostility still provides cause for concern when artists consider the ramifications of coming out. 'I was surrounded by homophobia, which still exists today,' said Judas Priest singer Rob Halford when explaining his own concerns over coming out. 'There are places I can't go back to because I'll be stoned to death.'[3]

For decades, LGBT artists have had to weigh up the desire to be honest with their public against the opprobrium they might face from the media, from fans and even from the state. Yet in much of the ancient world, same-sex attraction was less of an issue. There are countless examples of what Oscar Wilde's lover Lord Alfred Douglas would later term 'the love that dare not speak its name' in the literature and art of Greece and of the Roman Empire, and even a military unit, the Sacred Band of Thebes, formed in the 4th century BC that was made up of 150 pairs of male lovers. Yet for centuries, a couple of sentences in the Bible have been widely interpreted as condemning homosexuality, influencing attitudes and policies around the world. However, the book of Leviticus condemns adherents to death should they wear mixed fibres, yet Britain's biggest supplier of clothing to the Church of England specialise in polycotton cassocks, and when was the last time you saw someone being thrown from the roof of Primark after spending an afternoon clothes shopping? According to the Bible, eating shellfish is an abomination, so why do we not see the warning 'not for consumption by Christians' on an Iceland fish pie? The biblical story of Sodom and Gomorrah, the source of the word 'sodomy', does not mention homosexual acts explicitly: whatever happened that caused God to destroy the cities is entirely up to interpretation, as is the loving relationship between David and Jonathan, the same-sex couple in the book of Samuel.

Rome was showing its influence over Britain a full century before the conquest of AD 43, and although there were laws passed in Rome that forbade sodomy, these appear to have been loosely implemented and the punishment varied depending on your status. When Hadrian visited the country – on the same tour of Roman provinces that saw the start of the construction of his eponymous Wall – the bisexual emperor was accompanied by a retinue of beautiful young men, and it is certain that high-ranking men in Roman Britain kept male lovers. According to 4th-century text the *Historia Augusta*, Hadrian's marriage to his wife, Sabina, was unhappy and, quite possibly, never consummated. Sabina may have been a lesbian, and it has been speculated that she enjoyed a relationship with her lady-in-waiting, a poet inspired by the works of Sappho. It wasn't until monotheism became the norm that the persecution of homosexuality began.

Passed by Parliament during the reign of Henry VIII, 'an Acte for the punishment of the vice of Buggerie', more commonly known as the Buggery Act of 1533, was the first time that male homosexuality had been targeted in law for persecution by the state in England. Prior to this, acts of sodomy between two (or more) males had been dealt with by the church, via ecclesiastical courts, at least officially. Henry was a well-educated man who would have known that a predecessor, Edward II, had been persecuted for his relationship with a man, but the Buggery Act, passed less than a year before the English church separated from Rome, completely outlawed sodomy, with any transgressions punishable by death. As first Wales, then Scotland, became part of Great Britain, they too adopted the Act. It is peculiar that the state wished to legislate against same-sex attraction when the theatre of the day was filled with men dressed as women, and poets including William Shakespeare and Richard Barnfield were writing about homosexuality, but other countries that became subject to British laws, including the member states of the British Empire, also implemented the Act. Apart from a 10-year period between 1553 and 1563, when the policing of homosexual acts was handed back to the church by Queen Mary, the law stayed on the statute books until 1861.

There is no definitive figure for how many men were convicted over the three centuries that followed the implementation of the Buggery Act, but state-sanctioned murder would continue unabated for centuries.

When moves were made to oppress or suppress LGBT people, there was little argument. However, in 1724, almost 250 years before Stonewall, Britain's LGBT community began to fight back.

For more than half a century now, the riots that took place in June 1969 at the Stonewall Inn, on New York City's Christopher Street, have been pinpointed as the beginning of the radicalisation of the LGBT movement. There is no denying how momentous those days and nights of conflict and demonstration were, but the Stonewall riots were far from the first time that LGBT people had taken a stand against a system that had oppressed them for so long; the road that led to Stonewall – and which presaged the establishment of the gay liberation movement and world's first Pride marches – was a long one.

Stonewall (or, as it was first known, the Christopher Street Uprising) is noted for Black and mixed-race activists – including trans woman Marsha P. Johnson and lesbian Stormé DeLarverie – becoming involved in the fight for gay rights; but Black, mixed-race and trans members of America's LGBT community had already proved their mettle in a stand-off with the police at Cooper Do-Nuts in Los Angeles in May 1959 and at Gene Compton's cafeteria in San Francisco in August 1966, after one trans woman, sick of the constant abuse and harassment, threw a cup of coffee in a policeman's face. In January 1967, following a particularly violent police raid on the Black Cat Inn in Los Angeles, placard-bearing protesters assembled outside the bar complaining about the escalation in police harassment. Almost three years before that, on 19 September 1964, the first organised gay political protest took place in New York, with a picket of the US Army's Whitehall Induction Center over their failure to keep gay men's draft records confidential. That picket was followed by an annual protest march which took place in Philadelphia on the fourth of July, and which continued until 1970, when it was superseded by the Christopher Street Liberation Day, the first recognisable Pride march.

However, over two centuries before these events took place, in December 1724, up to 40 men and women we would now embrace as gay, trans or queer fought off a raid by constables (more than 100 years before Sir Robert Peel would establish a full-time, professional police force) at one of London's 'Molly' houses. The customers of the house, on Covent Garden's Hart Street, were attending a private masquerade, the precursor of the drag ball. They were arrested for 'misbehaving themselves and obstructing and opposing the Peace Officers in execution of their duty' and carted off to a number of jails in the vicinity.[4] That's right: the first recorded instance of members of the LGBT community standing up to and actively opposing oppression took place not in New York or San Francisco, but in London.

1

Before Stonewall

'I suppose your regular readership are a selection of society's misfits: homos, lesbians, transvestites, prostitutes, junkies, unmarried mothers, in fact all the kinky types under the ruddy sun! But you are the most despicable of all; you cash in on the perversions of such people as male homosexuals by offering them by way of ads a pile of pornographic piss which these poor abnormals will lap up like vultures around a bloody corpse. To hell with the lot of you, you bleeding bastards and bisexual cunts.' – International Times[1]

By the beginning of the 1700s, Molly houses, a nickname given to taverns, coffee shops and private residences that acted as covert meeting places for homosexual men, were springing up across London. The men who frequented Molly houses would dress as women, call each other by female-sounding nicknames and act out traditionally female roles. A few of these venues sold liquor, and if they were not licensed the owner would often bring in beer and wine from a nearby tavern. Entertainment was sparse, if there was any: harpsichords and spinets had been around for a while, while pianos were a relatively new, and expensive, invention. Few Molly houses could boast of employing musicians to entertain. Instead, the men who met there would indulge in ceremonies such as a 'birthing', where one man would pretend to give birth to a doll, aided by others acting as midwives. Mock-marriages, where two men would enter a hastily rigged-up 'chapel' in the house and hold a commitment ceremony before moving on to their bridal chamber for the night, were another regular feature.

Molly house owners were either active participants in the shenanigans or more than happy to provide space for their paying customers, and they became a soft target for local law enforcers. In 1707, in one of the first reported cases of a raid on a Molly house, a group of at least 40 men, who frequented a house near the Stock Exchange, were arrested. Three of the accused committed suicide while awaiting trial, and a 14-verse ballad, entitled 'The Woman-Hater's Lamentation' was published shortly after, promising that 'Unnat'ral deaths attend unnat'ral lusts in you.'[2] Two years later nine men, the members of 'a notorious gang of sodomites', were apprehended in a brandy house on Jermyn Street, London.[3] In 1721 the *Ipswich Journal* reported on a 'Club of Sodomites discovered in [a] Leicester Square' coffee house, where up to 50 men would meet nightly: 'those abominable wretches publicly call one another by the name of Dolly, Molly, Betty, Bridget, Grace, et cetera, and perform such beastly actions in that lude house, as is not fit to mention.'[4] In December 1723, the High Constable of Holborn and his men raided a public house on Hare Street, the Two Blue Posts, and arrested '25 persons belonging to a club who have met frequently in Masquerade Habits to perpetrate, as is supposed, the heinous sin of sodomy; several of those taken, 'tis assured, have stood in the pillory for such practices'.[5]

The Molly house in Hart Street (now known as Floral Street), Covent Garden, where the December 1724 raid took place, was well known to authorities, who had visited previously. A few days after this particular raid, a number of the men and women who had been arrested, some still in drag, were hauled before the courts, fined and made to 'promise not to resort to such places anymore'.[6] It's doubtful that many, if any, kept their vow; several of the men charged had already been pilloried for similar crimes.

The Hart Street regulars were lucky: none of them were put to death for their crimes, although one, Samuel Roper – known to his friends as Plump Nelly – would later die in prison (the colourfully named Poultry

Compter, in Cheapside), while awaiting trial for running his own Molly house on Giltspur Street. But men would continue to run the risk of execution should they be found guilty of being sodomites (the word 'homosexual' had not yet been coined), although more often than not the punishment would be a fine, a session at the pillory and a spell in jail. While standing at the pillory (a wooden frame on a post, usually in the centre of the town or village, that a prisoner's hands and head would be locked into), the public would hurl abuse, rotten vegetables, mud and stones at the felon.

On 26 July 1726 Margaret Clap, known to the customers of her Molly house as Mother Clap, was pilloried for the crime of 'keeping a disorderly house for the entertainment of sodomites'.[7] Clap had fallen victim to entrapment: her house, on Field Lane, Holborn (a street notorious for stalls selling stolen goods), had been raided in February and around 40 people arrested after a customer turned police informant, taking an officer to Mother Clap's and introducing him as his 'husband'. The officer, Samuel Stevens, first visited the house the previous November: it is unknown why it took him more than three months to arrange for the house to be raided, although he did admit in court that he 'went to the same house on two or three Sunday nights following and found much the same practices as before'. Having attended the place on several occasions, he must have taken part in at least some of the activities there. On that first visit, in November 1725, he witnessed men 'hug, and play, and toy, and go out by couples into another room on the same floor to be married, as they called it'.

'The company,' Stevens told the court, 'talked all manner of gross and vile obscenity... and she [Clap] appeared to be wonderfully pleased with it.'[8] As well as standing in the pillory in Smithfield, Clap was fined 20 marks (roughly £15) and jailed for two years.* One of the men arrested at Mother Clap's that night was William Griffin, who would later hang at Tyburn Tree, on the site of what is now Speaker's Corner. Griffin and his lover, Thomas Newton, had lodged with Mother Clap for almost two years, but, as Stevens alleged, Griffin had thrown 'his arms

---

* Mother Clap's story would inspire the 2001 musical drama *Mother Clap's Molly House* and the 2017 Broadway musical *The Mollyhouse*.

around my neck and hugged and squeezed me, and would have put his hands into my breeches'.[9] Newton absconded, leaving his 43-year-old partner to face the charges alone, but not before giving evidence against another of his lovers, Thomas Wright, who ran a small-scale Molly house of his own, from rooms in a house on Beech Lane. Wright, 32, would hang alongside Griffin.

London was rife with similar establishments: in 1726 there were 20 Molly houses known to the authorities, and no doubt many more escaped detection. The authorities may have wished to eradicate them from the city, but some of the men who frequented such establishments were beginning to become more bold, unashamedly wearing female attire in public and, apparently, accepted (to a degree) within their local community. In 1732 the country learned of John Cooper, known to friends as Princess Seraphina, who had been robbed at knifepoint by a man who threatened to reveal that Cooper had attempted to bugger him, an accusation often used to elicit blackmail. After recovering from the ordeal, Cooper went to the police and the attacker was arrested. In court it was revealed that Cooper ran errands for men who frequented Molly houses, was understood to be a sodomite by people in the local community and was accepted as a trans woman, referred to by friends and acquaintances as princess, highness and, throughout the trial, as 'her'. Uniquely, although the jury acquitted the attacker, Princess Seraphina was not charged with any wrong-doing.

Princess Seraphina was lucky: she lost no more than some items of male clothing and a few pennies, but many of those caught using Molly houses would face tougher sanctions, and even if most escaped with a fine, an afternoon in the pillory and/or a prison term, death sentences would continue to be handed out with alarming frequency. In 1806 alone, more men were hanged in England for sodomy than for murder, and many of these cases were eagerly described by the newspapers of the day in lurid detail. In one of the most widely reported cases, two men were hanged and a further six sent to the pillory after a raid on the White Swan in London's Vere Street in 1810. The house, run by Thomas Cook (not the travel writer), 'was furnished in a style most appropriate for the purposes it was intended. Four beds were provided in one room – another was fitted up for the ladies' dressing-room, with a toilette, and every appendage of rouge, &c &c. A third room was called the Chapel, where marriages took place, sometimes between a "female grenadier", six feet high and a "petite maitre" not more than half the altitude of his beloved wife! There marriages were solemnized with all the mockery of "bridesmaids" and "bridesmen"; the nuptials were frequently consummated by two, three or four couples, in the same room, and in the sight of each other. The upper part of the house was appropriated to youths who were constantly in waiting for casual customers, who practiced all the allurements that are found in a brothel.'[10]

A total of 23 men were questioned by Bow Street magistrates. The six men (including Cook) who were sent to the pillory, after they were found guilty of attempted sodomy, were subjected to an extraordinary level of violence from a crowd outside the Old Bailey, with men, women and children throwing 'mud, dead cats, rotten eggs, potatoes, and buckets filled with blood, offal and dung' as they processed to the Haymarket.[11] Cook was also attacked with a whip. So vicious was the crowd that a guard of 200 armed constables, half on horseback, was brought in to protect the men from even worse mistreatment. After their humiliation, the six were imprisoned for between two and three years each. A seventh man, Robert Aspinal, escaped the pillory but was jailed for a year. The other two, Thomas White (16 years old) and John Newball Hepburn (42), were hanged at Newgate Prison the following March, having been found guilty of 'having mutually committed an abominable offence'.[12] White, a drummer in the Guards, was not present during the raid but was noted as 'being a universal favourite... very deep in the secrets of the fashionable part of the coterie of which he had made a most ample confession in writing'. Hepburn, an ensign in the Eighth West India Regiment, met White through another young drummer, James Mann, whose testimony about the goings-on at Vere Street was enough to have both condemned to death.

On 12 March 1823 three men were sentenced to be hanged in Lincoln and a song, 'A Doleful Dirge on the Wicked Men', was composed to mark their fate. Army lieutenant William Arden, Benjamin Candler (former valet to the Duke of Newcastle), and joiner John Doughty had been

5

arrested after a confession from a fourth member of their group. Arden was believed to be the head of an underground group of homosexual men, and letters were found in his lodgings from a number of men 'of rank in society, even from Ministers of the established church, demonstrating the most depraved and disgusting associations'.[13] Their crime, the judge announced after a 12-hour sitting, 'was too dreadful to reflect upon; it was of so horrible a nature, that in every page of the law it had been designated as an offence not to be named among Christians. It was of so deep a dye, of so damning a character, that the Almighty had destroyed whole cities for its commission.'[14] Like the good judge, 'A Doleful Dirge on the Wicked Men' also compared Britain to Sodom and Gomorrah, suggesting that the same fate would befall our green and pleasant land should Arden and his contemporaries have escaped punishment.

Little changed for the men and women we would now recognise as LGBT until, on 28 November 1835, at eight o'clock in the morning, James Pratt and John Smith became the last men to be executed in England for sodomy. The pair had been hauled into court two months earlier, where a jury heard that Smith, of Christchurch in Surrey, 'feloniously, wickedly, diabolically, and against the order of nature, had a venereal affair with one James Pratt, and did then and there, feloniously, wickedly, diabolically, and against the order of nature, carnally know the said James Pratt, and with him the said James Pratt did then and there feloniously, wickedly, diabolically, and against the order of nature, commit and perpetrate the detestable, horrid, and abominable crime (among Christians not to be named) called buggery, to the great displeasure of Almighty God, to the great scandal of all human kind'.[15] The judge told them that he 'could hold out little expectation of mercy to them', for 'without offending the ears of the audience dilating upon the enormity the offence, he would implore them to seek mercy from God, as they stood upon the brink of eternity, guilty of offences which could hardly excite a tear of pity for their fate, and in consideration of which in a British country mercy ever had been stranger'.[16] William Bonill, the man who rented the room in which Pratt and Smith were alleged to have had sex, and whose landlord had reported the men to the authorities after he broke into their room and caught them *in*

6

flagrante, was sentenced to be transported to a penal colony for 14 years. Sentencing took place in Brighton, at a session attended by King William IV, of a number of 'prisoners who were capitally convicted at the September and October Sessions of the Central Criminal Court, all of whom his Majesty was graciously pleased to respite'[17] – apart from Pratt and Smith, that is.

On the day of their execution, which took place before a small crowd in front of Newgate Prison, Pratt was in such a state that he had to be dragged to the hangman's noose, and 'both denied their guilt until the last moment'.[18] A salacious tract which was widely circulated after the execution purported to include a letter written by Smith while in prison in which he admitted to his guilt, blaming 'the baneful effects of liquor and bad company, which must have rendered me void of every feeling of decency'.[19]

Although no man would be sent to the gallows for having sex with another man again, the death sentence would stay on the statute books until 1861 in England and Wales (and the introduction of the Offences Against the Person Act, when the death penalty for sodomy was replaced by a minimum of 10 years' imprisonment), and 1889 in Scotland. But although homosexuals would no longer face the noose, the powers that be did all they could to stamp out such immorality, and to make scapegoats of any transgressors. When two men were discovered dressed as women while on a night out at the theatre in April 1870, what should have been a simple case dealt with by the local magistrates became a national scandal.

Had London's Molly houses still existed, there's little doubt that Thomas Ernest Boulton and Frederick William Park would have been regular frequenters. Following their arrest, at the Strand Theatre, the two – known as Stella and Fanny respectively – were charged with 'conspiring and inciting persons to commit an unnatural offence', one of those persons being former Liberal MP Lord Arthur Pelham-Clinton, who lived with Stella as man and wife from 1868 onwards: Stella signed her letters to Clinton, 'affectionately yours, Stella Clinton'.[20] Encouraged by her mother, Stella Boulton had dressed and acted as a girl from an early age, and in her late teens met Park, by now styling herself Fanny Winifred. The two became friends, began a successful music hall act and played for private audiences in the provinces. Both acted in female roles, and Stella was also a talented pianist.

Men impersonating women, and women impersonating men, was nothing new as far as the theatre went, and for gender-fluid people the stage provided useful camouflage. However, Fanny and Stella were not content to confine their true selves to box-office hours; they attended drag balls at Haxell's Hotel on the Strand, exhibited themselves at the Oxford and Cambridge boat race, would go on dates with young men while dressed in their finery and were said to be part of a group 'which numbers nearly thirty of these foolish young men'.[21] When they were arrested, their male companions claimed to believe that they were women who dressed as men for a lark, rather than the other way around, although the court heard that the two had been living as women for the last few years. One of their friends, 'who belonged to a different class of life, was known by the name of Lady Jane Grey'.[22] The pair referred to each other as sisters, and in letters Fanny would refer to Arthur as her brother-in-law. Lord Clinton died of scarlet fever the day after he was subpoenaed to appear in court, although the gossip of the day suggests that he took his own life rather than face being questioned about his role in the scandal. Over a year from their initial arrest and after several appearances in front of both judge and jury, the first in their finest silk dresses, Boulton and Park were finally acquitted, as the prosecution failed to establish that they had anal sex (the legal definition of buggery), or that appearing in public wearing women's clothing was in any sense a crime, despite the court branding them and their circle 'a plague which, if allowed to spread without check or hindrance, must prove a serious contamination of our national morals.'[23]

Following the trial, the duo moved to New York where they continued to appear on stage, blurring gender lines a century before Boy George, Marilyn and Pete Burns had been heard of. While the pair were wowing audiences in America, back in England a further scandal erupted when 47 men were arrested at a fancy dress ball in Hulme, Manchester. Police had been tipped off about the immoral shenanigans taking place at the Temperance Hall, and of those arrested (including a dance teacher and a singer) 22 were found to be dressed as women. When the group appeared in court later that day, the public gallery erupted in laughter as at least eight of the men were still in their ball gowns.

The Stateside fame enjoyed by Fanny and Stella would be short lived. Fanny died, aged just 34, in 1881; Stella outlived her by 23 years, returned to England and continued to perform under the name Ernest Blair. Published the same year as Fanny died, *The Sins of the Cities of the Plain*, a scandalous biography supposedly written by infamous male prostitute Jack Saul, went into graphic detail about the lives of Fanny, Stella and their circle. The book is one of the earliest works of homosexual pornography printed in Britain, though it's almost certainly not the biography it claimed to be: Saul was just 12 years old when Boulton and Park were arrested and did not arrive in London until after the pair had left the country.

The book may have been fiction, but Saul was all too real. Described as 'an effeminate, but very good looking young fellow',[24] he was later caught up in the 1884 Dublin Castle Scandal, when government employees were accused of frequenting male brothels and of holding homosexual orgies at the British government's administrative seat in Ireland, and in the notorious Cleveland Street Scandal. The latter involved a male brothel frequented by Lord Henry Arthur George Somerset (the manager of the future King Edward VII's stables), Henry FitzRoy, Earl of Euston, and Edward's son, Prince Victor, then second in line to the throne. The ensuing court case saw Saul defiant in the dock, refusing to deny or to apologise for his homosexuality; Lord Somerset fled the country, living in self-imposed exile in France with his boyfriend, James Neale, until his death in 1926.

Six decades after the deaths of Pratt and Smith, and a quarter of a century after Boulton and Park were prosecuted, Oscar Wilde was convicted of gross indecency and sentenced to two years' hard labour. The country's leading playwright had been forced to face in court the Ninth Marquis of Queensberry,* who also happened to be the father of Wilde's lover, Lord Alfred 'Bosie' Douglas, after Queensberry had sent Wilde the misspelled note 'To Oscar Wilde posing Somdomite.'

---

* Although the title Marquess of Queensberry is the accepted form, John Sholto Douglas used the spelling 'Marquis' on his calling card.

Offered the choice of ignoring the slur or suing for libel, Wilde unwisely chose the latter, protesting his innocence and perjuring himself in the process.

For years Wilde acted as if he cared not if he were discovered, and he was often lampooned in the press for being effete. But this was a time when the lines between sex and sexuality were becoming more blurred, thanks partly to the fame of performers such as Vesta Tilley, who had become a huge star performing in full male drag on the stages of music halls around the country. A certain amount of eccentricity was tolerated from painters, writers and performers, and the music halls provided both an income and an audience for a number of cross-dressers, performing such sexually suggestive songs as 'Any Old Iron' ('iron' being rhyming slang for a homosexual: iron hoof – poof) and 'Hildebrandt Montrose', a song about an exceptionally effeminate young man who 'looks just like a Christmas toy underneath his silk umbrella'.

A close friend to members of the peerage, Wilde probably thought that his connections made him immune from prosecution, but the evidence against him was overwhelming. Douglas was not the only young man that Wilde had become intimate with (another acquaintance, Robert Cliburn, apparently told Wilde that he had successfully blackmailed Henry FitzRoy) and Queensberry's solicitors amassed handwritten witness statements confirming Wilde's dalliances with rent boys and the like. There were those who demanded that Wilde, like Pratt, Smith and countless men before them, should face the rope.

Wilde was released from Reading Gaol, where he spent the majority of his prison sentence, in May 1897, around the same time that his friend George Cecil Ives established the Order of Chaeronea, the UK's first homosexual social group. That same year, Magnus Hirschfeld founded the Scientific Humanitarian Committee in Berlin, now recognised as the first LGBT rights organisation. The world of music was fostering the talents of LGBT composers including Tchaikovsky and Britain's own Dame Ethel Smyth, and forward thinkers like German lawyer Karl Heinrich Ulrichs and English poet and philosopher Edward Carpenter began to lobby for a change in attitude towards homosexuals, or 'Uranians' as both liked to term people of this supposed third sex. At the time Wilde was sent down, Carpenter was living openly with his lover George Merrill; the two men were together for almost 40 years, would die within 18 months of each other and would be buried together. Although Ulrichs died two months after Wilde was incarcerated, he had been fighting for equal rights since the early 1860s and, in August 1867, pleaded for the repeal of anti-sodomy laws at the Congress of German Jurists in Munich. Two years later, Austrian writer Karl-Maria Kertbeny coined the word 'homosexual'.

Although persecution would continue, many LGBT people found comfort in the growth of a new underground social network. The 1920s and 1930s saw the rise of a number of entertainers who, through necessity, had to remain in the closet as far as the general public was concerned yet allowed their audience a glimpse into their lives through their acts. In America, where Black queer jazz and blues artists were openly celebrating their sexuality, newspaper columnists coined the phrase 'the Pansy Craze' to notify readers of the cafés and nightclubs hosting outlandish performers like Gladys Bentley in full male drag and Jean Malin, whose outrageously camp show delighted audiences right up until his untimely death in a freak car accident. The cabarets of Paris, Vienna and especially Berlin provided homes to a burgeoning new homosexual scene, and in Britain Noël Coward made no bones about his sexuality when he wrote 'Mad About the Boy', although he was forced to tone down several of his more outré lyrics before they could be performed in public. Coward's friend Douglas Byng – who began his career as a light comic actor before moving into cabaret and specialising in female impersonations and bawdy songs – refused a contract with the BBC, then Britain's only broadcaster, when they insisted on censoring his act. Byng was the first man to perform the Cole Porter song 'Miss Otis Regrets' on stage and, in 1938, presumably having been forgiven by the BBC, became the first man to appear in drag on British television. Music hall comedian and popular recording artist Fred Barnes was arrested several times for dalliances with young servicemen and was notorious for parading around London in white plus fours and pink stockings, with a pet marmoset on his shoulder, or for cruising the streets in his white Rolls-Royce, looking for trade.

Known as 'the male Vesta Tilley', he was jailed in 1924 for being drunk in charge of a motor vehicle while in the company of a half-naked sailor.[25] Three years later he took part in a sham marriage for publicity purposes: a photograph of the bride and groom appeared in the press under the headline 'A Queen's Portrait'.[26]

Barnes was not the only homosexual man constantly at odds with the law. In December 1932 more than 50 men were arrested at a private party in Holland Park Avenue, after undercover officers had watched them dancing and, they claimed, having sex dressed as women. Two years later, in August 1934, more than 100 people were arrested at queer-friendly club the Caravan after locals complained of it being 'frequented by sexual perverts, lesbians and sodomites'. Branded 'a vile den of iniquity which was corrupting the youth of London', two of the men involved – Jack Neave and club proprietor William Reynolds – were sentenced to 20 months and a year's hard labour respectively.[27] Seventy-six other men and women had the charges against them dropped, including musician Charles Lewins, who told the court that he was engaged to play the accordion at the club, on Soho's Endell Street. 'My mind was on my music,' he explained. 'The accordion is an instrument which requires a lot of concentration.'[28] That same year, the Forty Five Café in Hanover Street, Liverpool, a favourite with homosexuals and prostitutes, was raided and a number of arrests made. Police had been keeping the café under observation, and one officer, Constable Robert Banner, had visited several times (shades of the raid on Mother Clap's 190 years earlier), finding it full of 'drunken men, loose women, and men of a description and class which we do not often have to meet in these courts. They are persons who have been described by [proprietor] Colin Arthur Browne... as "pansies." The police call them men of an effeminate kind. They appear to be persons who in public powder their faces, paint their lips, colour their fingernails, like to be called by the Christian names of women, and who address one another as "dear," "darling," and so forth in a public cafe.'[29] Banner, who told the court that he had 'heard men of an effeminate type addressing each other as "Gertrude", "Sybil" and "Doris"', had no trouble fitting in with the men who 'met together, passed certain jokes, danced together and indulged in indecent gestures', although the arrests were only made after a second officer, Constable Plank, had gone to the Forty Five wearing face powder and lipstick, attempting to inveigle his way into café patrons' confidence.

In 1936, when the Prince of Wales, whose own sexuality was much gossiped about despite his highly publicised relationship with American socialite Wallis Simpson, took over the throne, US singer and piano player Judd Rees issued the salacious and audacious 'The King's a Queen at Heart', a song immediately banned from the airwaves not just for suggesting that Edward VIII preferred the company of men, but for the use of the word 'homosexual'. Edward's brother, Prince George, Duke of Kent, was rumoured to have had affairs with, among many others, Noël Coward. 'We had a little dalliance,' Coward would later tell biographer Michael Thornton. 'It didn't last long. We were both very young at the time. He was absolutely enchanting and I never stopped loving him.'[30] Coward was inconsolable after Prince George's death, the result of a military air crash in 1942.

The end of the Second World War precipitated an era of change around the world. If women, BAME people and homosexuals had made valuable contributions to the war effort, why should they go back into their respective boxes in peacetime? Even before the war, we had votes for women, the first female members of Parliament had taken their seats, towns and cities around the country were getting used to the idea of Black councillors and Battersea in London saw its first Black mayor in 1913. Accepting women and people of colour in positions of power had not brought about the end of the Union. Why should homosexuals be treated any differently?

History was made shortly after the end of the War when the world's first successful female-to-male gender reassignment took place, in Bristol. Michael Dillon's 14 operations began in 1946. Five years later the same pioneering surgeon, Sir Harold Gillies, performed the country's first male-to-female transition, on racing driver and spitfire pilot Roberta Cowell. Were we embarking on a new era of tolerance and understanding? Hardly. The World Health Organization published its first list of mental illnesses and classified homosexuality as a sexual deviation, the result of an underlying personality disorder. Meanwhile, as the Cold War era began and Western governments became spooked by the thought of their secrets being passed to Moscow, they were positively apoplectic at the idea that those communist sympathisers might also be homosexual. In America in the 1950s, the persecution of homosexuals by the FBI was inextricably linked to the ever-present fear of communist infiltration: Reds were not only under the bed but in it too – and J. Edgar Hoover's paranoiac henchmen could not wait to pass on their concerns to their British colleagues. When, in 1951, Donald Maclean and Guy Burgess defected to the Soviet Union, the world became aware of the misdeeds of the infamous Cambridge spy ring. The fallout would continue for years as further members, including Kim Philby and Anthony Blunt, revealed themselves. The British press leapt on any opportunity to portray these men as sexual pariahs. The truth was far more mundane. Burgess lived with dancer Jack Hewit for more than 14 years before his defection, and Blunt – who confessed to being a spy in 1964 but had been granted immunity, rising to the rank of Surveyor of the Queen's Pictures – spent the last three decades of his life with former Irish Guardsman John Gaskin.

In May 1953 a magazine called *One* was brought to the attention of the FBI. Established the previous December, *One* was a monthly magazine affiliated to the Mattachine Society, founded in Los Angeles in 1950, and one of the earliest gay rights organisations in the United States. British-born professor Harry Hay, one of the Society's co-founders, was a fully paid-up member of the Communist Party of the United States of America, and lost his job at the University of California for refusing to sign the school's recently instigated anti-communist loyalty oath. It did not take much to persuade the authorities that his co-founders were not only friends of Dorothy, but also friends of Marx, Lenin and Stalin too.

In Britain, bigger scandals were still to come. In May 1953 the British media got wind of a story about a member of the peerage up to no good, and, soon after, Lord Montagu of Beaulieu fled the country. His recent engagement was called off, and although his family claimed that he was recuperating after picking up a bug, a warrant was issued for his arrest. A second warrant was issued for his friend, film director Kenneth Hume, with both men accused of having committed indecent

14

assault. The bisexual Montagu was eventually acquitted and the case against Hume was dropped. Montagu insisted that he had been set up, but three weeks later the law came for him again: Montagu, his cousin Michael Pitt-Rivers and *Daily Mail* correspondent Peter Wildeblood were charged with 'conspiracy to incite certain male persons to commit serious offences with male persons'. Montagu protested his innocence, but this time he was jailed for a year, with his co-defendants receiving 18 months each. Also that year, Labour MP Bill Field was arrested for cottaging and fined £15 despite one of the policemen involved in the arrest perjuring himself in court. At his appeal hearing, Field was ordered to pay a further 30 guineas in costs. Actor Sir John Gielgud was also fined £10 after pleading guilty to 'persistently importuning male persons for immoral purposes' in a public convenience in Chelsea.[31]

There were 320 convictions for gross indecency in 1938, but by 1953 that figure had jumped to 1,686. The publicity surrounding such high-profile cases as those of Montagu and Field would eventually cause Home Secretary Sir David Maxwell Fyfe to establish the Departmental Committee on Homosexual Offences and Prostitution in Great Britain, headed by the vice-chancellor of the University of Reading, Sir John Wolfenden. The Report of the Departmental Committee on Homosexual Offences and Prostitution (aka the Wolfenden Report), published in September 1957, stated that the continued criminalisation of homosexuality impinged on civil liberties, but despite MPs on both sides of the house lobbying for change, for now the government refused to act.

The Homosexual Law Reform Society, and its charitable arm, the Albany Trust, was established in early 1958 to help promote the findings of the Wolfenden Report; in March the *Times* printed a letter signed by 33 eminent men and women, including members of the Society, Robert Boothby MP and writers including Bertrand Russell and J. B. Priestley, calling for the implementation of the report's recommendations. But within months British newspapers were gloating that the government had no intention of legalising homosexuality, stating that the then-current Home Secretary Richard Austen 'Rab' Butler 'believes the nation is not ready to relax the complete ban on homosexuality... if anybody tries to force the government's hand in a bid to get the law on homosexuality changed, Mr. Butler will get tough. He will clamp down on the Tory whips to make sure that any amendment is thrown out.'[32] The country's newspapers were right: in November up-and-coming Tory MP and junior government minister Ian Harvey was arrested after being caught 'acting in a manner likely to offend against public decency' with a Coldstream Guards officer in the bushes of St James's Park in London: 'A young guardsman in uniform passed me at a slow pace and I knew what that meant. I turned and caught up with him and we went together into the park. Had I been more alert I would have known from past experience that the place where we went was regularly patrolled before midnight.'[33] The Under Secretary for Foreign Affairs, who had tried to escape from arrest and then given a false name, was forced to resign from his post, although a further charge of gross indecency against Harvey and 19-year-old Guardsman Anthony Plant was dropped. Both men were fined £5, and a contrite Harvey paid both penalties: 'I felt it was the least I could do,' he wrote later.[34] The scandal badly affected the bisexual Harvey's marriage and sent him into a downward spiral of depression and alcoholism, although he would re-emerge in the early 1970s as vice-president of the Campaign for Homosexual Equality.

In the same month that Harvey was arrested, the MP for Belfast North, Harford Montgomery Hyde, became one of the most vocal proponents for implementing the recommendations of the Wolfenden Report. The barrister – and author of the book *The Trials of Oscar Wilde* – was deselected by his party, the Ulster Unionists, shortly after arguing in favour of the decriminalisation of homosexuality during a House of Commons debate. In an underhand move, the decision to deselect him took place while he was out of the country, but he would continue to advocate equal rights for LGBT people.

But the disenfranchised wanted more than recognition; they wanted equality. In 1963, after six years of government intransigence, the Homosexual Law Reform Society set up a number of regional assemblies and, the following year, the Campaign for Homosexual Equality (CHE) was born, originally as the North Western Homosexual Law Reform Committee, founded by gay rights activist Allan Horsfall. The group held its first public meeting in October 1964, in Church House, Manchester, and soon began to push for law reform. 1963 had also seen the birth of the Minorities Research Group, Britain's first lesbian rights lobby group. Founded by a group of five women including journalist Esme Langley and run from a small office above a bookshop in Bloomsbury, the MRG 'changed the lives of a number of previously most unhappy people', according to an article written by Montgomery Hyde for *The People*, through 'counselling and heart-to-heart discussion of the average lesbian's basic difficulties'.[35] These early groups were vital, if somewhat respectful, thorns in society's side, campaigning at a time when being visible carried serious consequences.

Introduced as a Private Members' Bill by Leo Abse, a long-time advocate for homosexual law reform, the Sexual Offences Act was eventually passed on 4 July 1967 after a bad-tempered, all-night debate in the House of Commons that saw accusations of a number of MPs being homosexual flying across the despatch boxes: 'There is quite a percentage of people in this country who practise homosexual acts,' announced Harold Gurden, the Tory MP for Selly Oak. 'It would be a strange thing indeed, in a place of 600 members if there were not some MPs in this house.'[36] Abse had tried to get the law changed two years earlier without success, but finally the House accepted that the British public were ready for change.

Upon winning the day, Home Secretary Roy Jenkins announced that 'this is an important piece of legislation', although in the very next breath he referred to homosexuality as a 'disability', and that 'those who suffer from this carry a great weight of loneliness, guilt, shame and other difficulties'.[37] Jenkins' words summed up the feeling of many in the Labour government, including its leader, Harold Wilson. This Labour government has a reputation for liberating the country and ushering in the permissive society in the years following their election in October 1964. Under Wilson, homosexuality and abortion were both legalised, theatre censorship came to an end, the divorce law was reformed and the death penalty was abolished, yet the prime minister himself was not that interested in granting gay rights, and this 'important piece of legislation' only went as far as to decriminalise consensual homosexual acts in private, so long as only two men were involved and both were over 21 years of age. Members of the Armed

Forces and the Merchant Navy were excluded, and the legislation only applied to England and Wales; it would be several decades before Scotland and Northern Ireland would offer homosexuals the same legal status as the rest of the United Kingdom.

Ten days after the bill came into law, during a debate on abortion, Conservative MP Hugh Fraser spoke for the old guard when he bemoaned that it was 'a rather sad commentary – but accurate – that after a thousand days of this Government there should have been no extension of freedom except to the bugger and the abortionist'.[38] Fraser's words would make the front cover of underground newspaper *International Times*, beneath a photograph of two naked men.

The change in the law was not marked with street parties and demonstrations, but in LGBT venues around the country gay men celebrated the notion that their lives were about to improve. 'I turned 21 a few weeks before the act made homosexuality legal,' says Ralph Stephenson, then moonlighting as a pirate radio presenter while also working for the BBC in Nottingham. 'It wasn't that my gay life started then, but it took away a lot of the threat. It wasn't nirvana overnight, but it was one heck of a solid contribution. It was a major difference and coincided with my being able to be part of a community that, in large proportion, hadn't seen itself as a community up until then.'

Yet instead of being liberating, the authorities used the law as an excuse to double down on homosexual activity: arrests for importuning in public toilets, or 'cottaging', increased, and plain-clothes police officers took to hanging around gay-friendly pubs, ingratiating themselves with local rights groups and procuring arrests through entrapment. The spurious reason for limiting the age of consent to 21 was to protect young males from being corrupted by older men; however in March 1968, less than a year after the implementation of the Wolfenden Report's recommendations, four youths were remanded in custody by police in the West Midlands following an intensive investigation into homosexual acts in the region. No older men were involved: all four had admitted to having had consensual sex, but sadly all were under the age of 21 and therefore fair game for the police. The 'Potteries Purge', as it became known, resulted in one of the youths hanging himself while in custody.

The law had changed, but clearly there was still a long way to go, and it would take years for everyone in a position of authority to deal with their long-standing prejudices. 'When I was in the third form at school, during sex education classes it was explained to me that normal human beings go through five stages of development,' recalls cabaret singer and gold medal-winning gymnast Mark Bunyan. 'Homosexuality was just a phase. "One day you will grow out of this; you will touch a girl's hand, and everything will be different." I had been wanking over pictures of [professional bodybuilder and actor] Steve Reeves since I could remember, but it was obvious that this was a terrible, terrible thing and that I had to get away from it. I was horrendously in the closet, and I just kept waiting for it to change.

'In 1968, in my second year at the University of St Andrews, I started to suffer from depression and made a minor attempt at suicide. I ended up being sent to a mental health institution, a gothic, baronial building outside of St Andrews. While I was there I heard the words "I'm a homosexual" come out of my mouth for the first time in my life and I immediately burst into tears. There was a clinical psychologist who kept asking me, "What sort of men are you attracted to?", and I remember saying to him, "You must not tell anyone else." "Oh no," he said. "This is all completely in confidence." So, I went to see the university psychiatrist and the first thing he said was "Doctor so-and-so tells me that you're experiencing certain homosexual fantasies." His advice was, "Why don't you get married and think about it later?" And his last line was, "Never forget! Oscar Wilde was a happily married man with two kids, you know!" I tell people that now and it gets a huge laugh, and of course it is funny, but it is not so funny when you're being told that as a 19-year-old being torn to pieces.

'He put me on all of these drugs, just gave me what was in the cupboard. I was on Librium, Valium and Imipramine, eight pills a day for three months. When I went home, I told my father; all he said was, "For God's sake, don't let your mother know." I cannot forgive that: do not have a child and say that to your child. Everything was about making my mother's life perfect... and she did not want a gay son.'

Bunyan, like hundreds of thousands of LGBT people before and after him, had discovered that a change in law did not necessarily mean

19

a change in attitudes. The passing of the Sexual Offences Act was not a magic bullet. Britain's lawmakers may have finally concluded that homosexual men should not be prosecuted for simply being gay, but anything close to equality for LGBT people was still decades away.

2

Sowing the Seeds of Liberation

"'We've listened to you long enough," said a bearded homosexual called Konstantin, running around the hall in a bright red dress. "We're fed up with being told we're sick. We're gay and proud."' – Black Dwarf[1]

In 1967 the majority of Britain barely acknowledged the implementation of the Wolfenden Report, and life for LGBT people went on much as before. However, on the other side of the Atlantic, the fight for civil rights was gaining pace. Following the success of the Black rights movement, the first women's liberation groups had been set up in cities around North America and Canada. Within two years, they would be followed by the country's first gay liberation groups, which formed in the immediate aftermath of the Stonewall riots, in June 1969.

Homosexuality was still illegal in all but one state (Illinois), and New York state Liquor Authority regulations prohibited the sale of alcohol to homosexuals on the basis that gay people were disorderly. Consequently, the Mafia-owned Stonewall Inn, which had been operating as a gay bar since 1967, only managed to stay open thanks to weekly kick-backs to the local police. The regulars were used to police harassment, it was a fact of life. Just a few days before the riots the NYPD had raided the bar and taken the names and addresses of anyone inside assumed to be homosexual. But when officers returned on the weekend of 28 June, the Stonewall regulars decided that they had had enough of the constant persecution. 'I was there for all three nights of rioting, but the third night was actually very low-key,' says singer Jayne County. 'The first night was the worst – or the best, whichever way you look at it – and the second night was very good because that's the night we all marched down Christopher Street screaming "Gay power! Gay power!" The third night there was a lot of trash-can burning, things like that, but not hundreds and hundreds of people out in the street rioting. They usually call it three days of rioting, but I always say there were only about two and a half!

'I was on my way to the Stonewall; I'd been hanging out there. But when I got there, the doors were locked, and there were burn marks all over the door. People had tried to set fire to the door, I don't know why because there were still gay people and drag queens and the like inside! People were already rioting in the street, and I gleefully joined in. There were people who had been inside but who had been ejected. The police interviewed certain people, some were arrested, and others were just let out onto the street. The police put the drag queens behind the bar and then took them [to the bathroom] one by one. If you decided to go out dressed as a drag queen or whatever – people didn't use the word 'transgender' back then – a policewoman would take you to the ladies' bathroom, and you would have to reveal your genitals to prove what sex you were. It was called a "sex search": they were quite common during that era.'

Part of the reason that the Stonewall Inn had become popular with the local LGBT community is that it had a small dancefloor where same-sex couples could dance together. The music played on the Stonewall jukebox was a mix of recent hits, soul favourites and the occasional camp anthem, such as the Connie Francis hit 'Where the Boys Are'. The then-closeted lesbian singer Lesley Gore featured prominently, as did Judy Garland, whose funeral took place in New York the day before the riot kicked off. There were no out acts or singers making pop records at that time, at least none that would have encouraged the Stonewall patrons to part with a hard-earned quarter to hear. The LGBT-themed songs that were being recorded were marketed as novelties and sold through magazines or under the counter in sex shops.

Press reports stated that 13 people were arrested in the early hours of that Saturday morning, including folk singer and political activist Dave Van Ronk, and at least three policemen received minor injuries. Van Ronk, a major influence on Bob Dylan, had just finished dining with friends at a nearby restaurant, the Lion's Head, when the riot broke out. 'I was passing by and I saw what was going down,' he said, 'and I figured, they can't have a riot without me!'[2] Joining in the fight against oppression, Van Ronk was dragged inside the Stonewall by three policemen, handcuffed to a radiator and beaten senseless. He was later charged with assault after it was claimed that he had thrown a heavy object at one of the officers. He would plead guilty to the lesser charge of harassment.

It would take more than a year for the reverberations of the Stonewall riots to be felt in Britain. However, the civil unrest that was being expressed around the world was starting to make waves among Britain's queer youth. At the very same time, a revolution was also taking place in musical theatre: on the West End stage, a US musical that documented hippie culture and the sexual revolution, *Hair*, was grabbing headlines, and providing a training ground for a generation of British LGBT musicians including Peter Straker, Richard O'Brien and Joan Armatrading. Young British men and women, many not even teenagers when the Beatles first stormed the charts, were throwing themselves wholeheartedly into this new permissive society.

'In July 1969 I ran away from school to go and see the Rolling Stones in Hyde Park,' says artist and Gay Liberation Front activist Richard Bolingbroke. 'This was not long after the Paris Riots, with the Sorbonne burning, and the assassinations of Martin Luther King and Bobby Kennedy. The world was in turmoil and for a 17-year-old it felt amazing. It was absolutely mind-blowing. I'd had a pretty sheltered life up until then: I went to an English public school that was great if you were a stupid, rich Englishman, but not great if you were fairly smart, which I guess I was. At school we watched *Top of the Pops* and shows

23

like that, and the Beatles and all those other groups were always on TV, but then I heard about the free concert.

'Seniors were allowed to wear their own clothes, and I had this black-and-white striped shirt, turquoise bell-bottoms and a purple jacket... so that's what I wore to London. As I approached Hyde Park, I could see this cloud of smoke. It was the first free concert I had ever been to, and looking back it was ridiculous. They had a tiny stage, there was almost no security and it was packed. Every tree was filled! I crawled up into a tree and got stoned. I remember King Crimson coming on for what was their major debut; Mick Jagger came on – this was right after Brian Jones had died – and read a poem by Shelley, and then someone else opened this box full of white butterflies. Jagger was wearing this very campy white outfit, like a dress, and that caused a big stir in the newspapers with people questioning his sexuality, but that androgynous look was fascinating to me. The concert absolutely blew my mind, and I decided then and there: "This is where I want to be."'

News of the Stonewall insurrection continued to trickle across the pond. 'I remember reading about the Stonewall riots and doing cartwheels and feeling very, very excited,' gay rights activist Ted Brown recalls. On the first anniversary of the Stonewall riots, international headlines were made when gay rights protests were held in New York (the Christopher Street Liberation Day), Chicago, Los Angeles and San Francisco. Pride as we know it today was born, although the word had first been used in relation to LGBT people in May 1966, when a Los Angeles gay rights organisation began issuing the *Pride Newsletter*. In August 1967 *Pride Newsletter* would become *The Advocate*, now the longest-running LGBT magazine in the world.

As more people became aware of the seismic events taking place in America, Britain's media began to take notice of the queer community on its doorstep. In January 1970 the publishers of a British underground newspaper, *International Times*, were hauled into court to answer charges of conspiracy to corrupt public morals 'by inducing *IT* readers to resort to homosexual acts and also conspiring to outrage public decency by publishing lewd, disgusting and offensive matter'.[3] Their offence: to carry contact advertisements in their small ads section for gay men looking to meet other gay men. Since its first issue, in 1966, *IT* had carried small ads, but over the previous 12 months or so more and more of the magazine's back pages were given over to contact ads, mostly from men seeking men, as well as advertisements for pornographic photos, magazines (including *Jeremy*, Britain's first over-the-counter gay magazine) and contact groups. After five days of arguments, during which 15 men who had either placed or replied to ads were asked to explain what was meant by words and phrases such as 'versatile', 'well-hung', 'passive gay' and 'well equipped', the case was committed to trial. A defence fund was set up to raise money to cover legal fees, estimated at around £2,000, win or lose, and a benefit concert held in Manchester, featuring poet John Cooper Clarke, plus local bands Greasy Bear (whose members would go on to form seventies hitmakers Sad Café and Alberto y Los Trios Paranoias) and Stack Waddy.

This media attention may have been welcomed in some quarters, but the prurience was inescapable and few outside of the gay community showed any interest in equality. Three years after the passage of the Sexual Offences Act 1967, the age of majority – the legal age at which a minor becomes an adult – was reduced from 21 to 18. The age of consent – the age at which you can legally have sex – had been 16 since 1885, but for gay men sex would remain illegal until you reached your 21st birthday. Luckily for women, sex between females had never been legislated for, and for lesbians the age of consent remained at 16.

British media had become fascinated with the emergent, and as yet unnamed, LGBT community, and stories involving homosexual men and lesbians continued to attract attention throughout 1970. In the summer, during a half-hour documentary aired as part of ITV's *World in Action* series, British television viewers were first introduced to a quirky Soho character by the name of Quentin Crisp. Not everyone who viewed the programme, in which Crisp admitted he 'definitely would have liked to have been a woman', found his candour palatable: the *Daily Mirror*'s television reviewer, Mary Malone, described him as 'a pathetic scrap of human flotsam who doesn't fit in.'[4] His willingness to talk about his life unapologetically made him an icon, and the community celebrated his refusal to conform.

Despite the grumblings of Ms Malone and her colleagues, change was in the air. In September 1970, shortly after Britain was introduced to Crisp, singer Dusty Springfield, then living with her partner Norma Tanega, came out as bisexual to journalist Ray Connolly, and in doing so became the first major British pop star to open up about their sexuality. Her revelation would have little immediate impact: Dusty's career was already all but over in Britain (she would not have another major chart hit until she teamed with Pet Shop Boys in 1987), and not long after she would flee to America. At the very same time as Dusty was packing her bags, a young, out and politically aware singer was becoming a regular face on early evening television. With a British mother and a Nigerian father, Labi Siffre, who had recently issued his eponymous debut album on Pye Records, would have caused a stir in certain households even if they had not been aware that he had been openly living with his partner (and, later, husband) since 1964. In November 1971 Siffre would score his first chart hit, 'It Must Be Love', becoming the first openly gay singer to have a Top 20 hit in the UK charts.

From the outset, music was an integral part of the gay liberation movement. Within months of the first groups forming in America, the Gay Liberation Front (along with a dozen more local community groups, each with their own agenda) became involved in New York Pop, a three-day festival which took place on Randall's Island in July 1970. Believing that promoters were making big bucks from the counterculture, they insisted that the event employ local people, give stage time to local acts, and invest in regeneration projects in the area. It was a utopian dream that quickly went wrong: after more than 30,000 gate crashers managed to get in over the first two days, organisers simply opened the gates for the final day and let everybody in for free. Indian sitar maestro Ravi Shankar refused to play because of the chaos and many of those that did perform, including Jimi Hendrix, Ten Years After and Little Richard, did not get paid.

On 13 October 1970, less than four weeks after Dusty made her couched revelation, and spurred on by their counterparts in the United States, 19 men and women met in a basement classroom at the London School of Economics (LSE), in a building constructed on the site of the White Swan, the infamous Molly house where 23 homosexual men had been arrested back in 1810. Two of the men, former LSE students Bob Mellors and Aubrey Walter, had encountered each other earlier that year in Philadelphia, at the Revolutionary Peoples' Constitutional Convention. Others present included Walter's partner David Fernbach, Elizabeth Wilson and her partner Mary McIntosh, and Bev Jackson, who had run for election to the Students' Union under the slogan 'Bev the Lez for Prez'.

Mellors and Walter had become politically charged by witnessing the work of New York's Gay Liberation Front, and by meeting with representatives of the Black Panthers, the US revolutionary organisation described by FBI Director J. Edgar Hoover as 'the greatest threat to the internal security of the country'.[5] It was at the Revolutionary Peoples' Constitutional Convention that Panthers' co-founder Huey P. Newton urged fellow Black revolutionaries to 'form a working coalition with the gay liberation and women's liberation groups'.[6] On returning to London, Mellors and Walter set about setting up their own group, and by the end of that October evening, the first British chapter of the Gay Liberation Front (GLF) had been formed.* Two weeks later, the LSE's Students' Union newspaper, *The Beaver*, reported on the fledgling GLF's first action, a protest against the misogyny and homophobia displayed in an article in student paper *The Sennet*: 'our sisters and brothers painted slogans over the building to make certain that the people at "Sennet" know that we are not going to take this anymore.'[7]

Although those early meetings were 'characterised by stormy political differences', within weeks, thanks to a highly successful leafletting campaign, hundreds of people were turning up to the Wednesday evening meetings.[8] 'In August 1970 I moved to London. I found a place to live, in Hampstead, and my local pub was the King William IV,' artist and early GLF activist Richard Bolingbroke explains. 'I wasn't out, and didn't know anything, I was this nervous, intellectual kid: I used to sit in the corner with a notebook and write poetry! One

---

* Around the same time, similar groups sprang up in France (le Front Homosexuel d'action Révolutionnaire, or FHAR) and West Germany (Homosexuelle Aktion Westberlin, HAW).

day someone came up to me and said, "We're having a party. You should come." So, I went, and I met a group of people who embraced me. Aubrey Walter and Bob Mellors had just come back from the United States, and before long I was going to the meetings at the LSE.'

Intent on fighting 'gay oppression by whatever means necessary',[9] the use of the word 'gay' in the group's name was significant. Every word used by the media to describe homosexuality had medical or legal connotations, and all were oppressive. Taking ownership of the 'G' word and using it proudly and defiantly was a political act meant to attract attention. Jim Anderson, the art editor of underground magazine *OZ*, had been encouraging people to do something similar for the past six months, writing in *International Times* back in April that it was 'time to be proud of making it with other guys, time to get out of the guilt-ridden ghettoes of the gay world,' and 'join the Gay Liberation Front'.[10] Veteran human rights campaigner Peter Tatchell, himself an early participant, calls the GLF, 'Britain's first direct action human rights movement of openly lesbian, gay, bisexual and transgender people'.

Gay Black rights activist Theodore 'Ted' Brown was an early convert to the cause. 'We had lived in a small house in Deptford,' he explains. 'At that time the National Front were becoming much more prominent. We had dog mess posted through our letterbox, obscenities painted on our walls. Our windows were broken so often that we just left them boarded up.' The son of Jamaican parents, whose mother had been involved in the civil rights movement in the United States before she was deported as a troublemaker, Brown had faced both racism and homophobia from an early age. 'I told my mother that I thought I was homosexual in 1965,' he says. 'She cried and I cried, but I knew that she would support me, and she understood.' Brown's mother knew gay civil rights leader Bayard Rustin, the confidante of Dr Martin Luther King Jr who helped plan the 1963 march on Washington. 'She told me that the civil rights movement was not just campaigning for Black rights, but for women's rights and for homosexual rights and various other issues. We knew that these things were all related. Partly because of my experiences as a Black person, I never felt any inferiority or shame about being gay, but I did feel fear for what the future held.

'Around November 1970, I went to see the film *The Boys in the Band*, and there were people outside leafletting against it, for the way it portrayed gay men as these sad stereotypes. And it turned out that they were from the Gay Liberation Front. They had not long started meeting at the LSE, and I dashed along to the next one.'

Yorkshire-born artist and activist Stuart Feather began attending meetings around the same time as Ted Brown. 'I had seen an article in the *Sunday Times*, just a paragraph or two about events in America that mentioned the Gay Liberation Front, and I was very curious. I knew about things like the Palestinian Liberation Front, about nationalities trying to reclaim their territory, but that was all. Then the friends I was sharing a flat with told me they had seen a leaflet about the meetings at the LSE and that they were going, so I said, "Well, count me in!" I imagine that must have been the third meeting that they had held there.'

There were no members: the GLF was not a club and people did not subscribe. Everyone, every brother and sister, as they referred to themselves, was supposed to be equal. 'It was a grassroots organisation,' says Brown. 'We had no formal membership, and we never had a director or a CEO. We did everything spontaneously: if you had an idea you just shared it with others. There was no hierarchy: we were deliberately rejecting that idea. Joining meant going to the meetings and agreeing to the principles.'

It is no coincidence that, at the same time as the GLF coming together, Britain's Women's movement was also gaining traction. Women's Liberation had already established several regional bases, and at a conference that year delegates formulated the 'Four Demands' for liberation for women: equal pay, equal education and opportunity, 24-hour nurseries and free contraception and abortion on demand. Like the Four Demands, the original GLF manifesto was pithy and to the point: it demanded an end to discrimination and to police harassment, the immediate cessation of the treatment of homosexuality as a disease and full equality for gay people. In the years before the initials LGBT became the norm, it was understood and accepted that 'gay' applied to both male and female homosexuals: although the GLF manifesto did not specifically mention trans, bisexual or queer people, it was tacitly

29

understood that the GLF would represent anybody of any gender who did not identify as heterosexual. The GLF manifesto also encouraged gay brothers and sisters to come out. 'Coming out was really important to me,' says Richard Bolingbroke. 'It meant that I could do what the hell I wanted with my life. I did not have to be who my parents wanted me to be. That was a huge revelation, and much more important than the sex.'

Having formed action groups to tackle everything from catering and finance to education and the medically approved use of barbaric electroshock therapy, the GLF took part in their first demonstration just six weeks after their foundation, following an escalation in the number of arrests for importuning on popular gay cruising ground Highbury Fields. In August 1970 journalist and former chair of the Young Liberals Louis Eaks was arrested there and charged with 'committing an act of indecency' with another man. He pleaded not guilty, telling the jury at his trial that 'I can get all the sex I want from my girlfriend, and I am not a homosexual.'[11] The jury disagreed, fining him £60. His companion had run off after pushing one of the two arresting officers to the ground and had not been seen since.

On 27 November 1970, two days after Eaks was found guilty, the first ever gay political protest in Britain took place, when up to 150 GLF supporters gathered for a torchlight demonstration on Highbury Fields. 'This was a very exhilarating moment for homosexuals in Britain,' Aubrey Walter (who, in 1979, would found publishing house Gay Men's Press) would later recall, 'to actually be banded together in public for the first time, holding hands and shouting our "Give us a G" slogan. Burning torches were distributed, and we kissed warmly and perhaps a little dramatically for the press. We all felt so tremendously high.'[12] Eaks, a passionate campaigner for Palestinian rights who had previously been the publicity organiser for homeless charity Shelter, would be arrested again in Hyde Park the following year for the same crime. Found guilty and fined £100, he would once more protest his innocence.

The first few weeks of the GLF's existence saw a flurry of activity, and shortly before Christmas another milestone was passed when, on 22 December, Kensington Town Hall became the venue of the first ever GLF dance. Three weeks earlier, on 4 December, the brothers and sisters of the GLF had held their own disco at the London School of Economics (LSE), but this would be the first time in British history that a dance, advertised as a gay event and open to all, would be organised by gay people for gay people. Prior to this, Britain had not had a club night exclusively geared towards LGBT people. There were clubs, such as Soho's Le Duce, the Catacombs in Earl's Court, the Moulin Rouge in Bristol or Manchester's Picador, where the management would turn a blind eye while gay couples danced together, but anyone daring to touch another person of the same sex while dancing risked arrest should the club be raided. Now the GLF intended to host its own, fiercely out events. 'More than 700 homosexuals, lesbians and their "straight" friends packed the old town hall,' according to a report in the *Sunday People*. 'Another 500 had to be turned away.'[13] Everyone who came was given a free copy of the mimeographed GLF journal, *Come Together*, a further 100 copies (cover price five new pence) were sold within an hour to the crowd outside. Street selling was an important tool, as one of *Come Together*'s editorial team explained: 'Half the point in street sales is to talk to people, to try and persuade them to come out. You may end up giving the paper away. "Come out" means to be open about being homosexual – at work, in your home, wherever you go.'[14] Co-organiser Peter Urbach heralded the event as 'the most important night in the history of homosexuality in Britain'.[15]

Because few artists had come out publicly, organisers were obliged to use whoever would play for them. Hawkwind, the Pink Fairies and the Edgar Broughton Band, all groups with a strong connection to the underground scene, were approached about playing the gig (Broughton had a concert in Newcastle that night), but blues-rock cover band Hot Ice, a group more used to playing the working men's club circuit around Gateshead and Newcastle than for the sexually liberated metropolitan elite, has the distinction of being the first band to perform at a public function organised by the GLF in Britain.

Unlike the more respectful Campaign for Homosexual Equality, the GLF was a rabble of radical rowdies, anarchists who wanted to shake things up and were tired of waiting for the rest of the world to catch up. Many of them adopted radical drag as their very obvious calling card, but unlike the glossy, primped and preened stage drag that had made stars of people like Danny La Rue, the GLF's dragsters wore full beards and sports shoes with their frocks. 'Danny La Rue was very Las Vegas,' says Stuart Feather. 'He was very glamorous, wore lots of diamante and false breasts and was pretending to be a woman although he was obviously not one. We were not into the glamour and had no intention of trying to parody women at all. But some of the people in GLF were not happy; they thought we were letting the side down, giving a bad impression. We made a whole bunch of enemies within the GLF, but that was good in a way. It challenged the Marxists and the socialists and the Maoists in GLF, and it made us think about our own masculinity and machismo, and the attitudes that we had. When you're in drag you are constricted, by the clothes, the shoes and in the way people respond to you. In a very small way, we were learning something about how women felt.'

The brothers and sisters of the GLF had been inspired by the wave of student protests that took place in France and in America, by the anti-war lobby and by hippie free-love culture. The attitude of the CHE was more in line with the suit-and-tie-sporting members of the Mattachine Society in the US than with these anti-establishment, freakishly attired rebels. Significantly, the CHE failed to attract many women to the cause: female membership of the CHE was a lowly 8 per cent whereas, initially at least, more like a quarter of those attending GLF meetings were women. That's not to say that the CHE did not have its moments: in Burnley in August 1971, at a public meeting to discuss opposition against the local Co-operative Society renting out one of their buildings for a new gay club, CHE founder and former Labour councillor Allan Horsfall invited all of the homosexuals present to stand up and be identified. Horsfall's plan was for a series of gay social clubs (called Esquire Clubs) across the country, and he needed to show that there was a need for such an establishment locally. Over a hundred people rose to their feet in what is now regarded as one of the first mass coming-out demonstrations in the UK. Still, throughout the two groups' existence, the CHE and GLF were often at loggerheads over the best way forward for the cause.

'I left Melbourne in 1971 at a time when male homosexuality was totally illegal and when there were no LBGT organisations, no campaign groups, not even any helplines or counselling services,' Peter Tatchell explains. 'All that we had was two unattractive gay bars. Arriving in London, sex between men had been partially decriminalised in 1967, the Gay Liberation Front was several months old and there were more than a dozen gay bars and clubs. The atmosphere here was much more open and liberal. It was a great personal liberation, and with the GLF activism, very exciting politically. In contrast to the CHE, the GLF was much more radical and visionary. It had a wider LGBT focus than gay law reform, sought to transform society rather than assimilate into it, and was allied to other social movements working for women's, Black, Irish and working-class liberation.'

'The GLF has attracted more attention,' says CHE member, theatre director and author Phil Booth. 'Its activities were generally far more glamorous and headline-grabbing. But the CHE was a worthy complement to that kind of campaigning. Local activism is slow and often tedious; I didn't always want to turn out on a cold January night with my stack of newspapers and sit with the few hardcore members in a draughty pub hoping that someone else might eventually show up, and we faced our fair share of abuse and threats of violence.'

Following a meeting in Leeds on 18 June, dubbed the 'national come-together', a loose umbrella body, the National Federation of Homophile Organisations (NFHO), was set up to bring all of the disparate groups within the gay liberation movement – including the CHE, the GLF, the Albany Trust and the Scottish Minorities Group (SMG), which had formed in Glasgow in January 1969 – under one banner, but there seemed little that the individual groups could collectively agree on. With the Leeds Gay Liberation Society taking the lead, a national newsletter, simply called *Broadsheet*, was founded, containing reports from local groups around the UK. The GLF soon withdrew support, and the NFHO folded after little more than a year. Ego, the desire for power and personality clashes made co-operation difficult. Michael Launder, writing in *Gay News*, likened the situation to 'a ten ton truck being driven by a herd of demented elephants on a glacier'.[16]

33

The CHE saw its role as continuing to lobby, respectfully and within the limits of the law, for equality; the GLF was not prepared to be so polite. 'The two were not easy bedfellows,' says former CHE member Charlie Beaton. 'GLF was a lot of heat, not a lot of light, a small group who were quite hysterical about what we needed to be doing. CHE as a movement was very plodding in comparison, but it was the organisation that changed things for people in the seventies, with a network of groups across the country doing mundane things, like a social once a week and little talks.'

Across the country, thousands of men and women were drawn to local CHE and GLF groups. 'I grew up with a strong sense of fairness and unfairness,' says Phil Booth. 'I had a fairly conservative upbringing, but once I had come out as gay, using that as a kind of prism to see how society worked, I could see this constant build-up of examples of unfairness, the dice being loaded towards the system. The GLF produced a lot of pamphlets; it was like a return to 17th- or 18th-century tracts. I read a lot of those when I was first in London, in places like Compendium Books [on Camden High Street], and they were very important in radicalising me. I moved to London after university, and music was the goal, but I'm a bit of a small-town boy, and then the opportunity came to move to Hereford. I was there for seven years. I immediately got involved with the CHE; that was much more about practical politics, and the people who came to that helped shape my ideas because they had had experiences that I had never even dreamed of. It was a very immersive thing. When you are in the capital, with a large number of gay people around you, you can think in broad categories. We were trying to deal with people individually in a context where there wasn't that much structure to help them out. We were the structure, and that pushed me to see how much people need to do for themselves. The collective was not going to back up a small minority, such as the LGBT population of Hereford, especially when half of the lesbians and gays had gone to London! You've got to do it for yourself.'

While the CHE were forming groups around the country, the GLF established several commune-like bases – often little more than glorified squats – in London, a city that, at that time, still had a plentiful supply of cheap, run-down property. From strongholds in

Notting Hill and King's Cross, the brothers and sisters coordinated events around the capital, in church basements, town halls and any pubs that would allow them. Far from the affluent, gentrified place it is today, Notting Hill was then a bohemian, multicultural enclave where being different was the norm, but the local police were having none of it. 'From the first, the police made us aware of their presence,' Stuart,* a GLF spokesperson, explained to journalist Maurice McKee. 'They tried to get the message to us that we were not welcome. We tried to get the message to them that we were here to stay.'[17] He claimed that GLF supporters were frequently arrested for spurious reasons, including obstruction (two young women, one a housewife, were arrested at a GLF demonstration on the King's Road, Chelsea, for 'wilfully obstructing the highway' in April 1971; both were fined £8 each), and that the GLF was working with the National Council for Civil Liberties (NCCL, now known as Liberty), collecting statements from 'people arrested on various charges which come down to being gay. We are convinced that there is also entrapment... we will confront the police with the results of this inquiry.'[18] The NCCL was no stranger to run-ins with the police over their support of Britain's homosexual community: in January 1970 NCCL General Secretary Tony Smythe received a visit from two detectives while he was investigating claims 'from homosexuals in Britain that their overseas letters were being intercepted'.[19] The tone of the police during that early morning call was tantamount to intimidation, and he wrote to then-Home Secretary James Callaghan to complain about his treatment.

As had happened with the CHE, GLF enclaves soon began to spring up outside of London. One of the first was established by a lesbian couple, Angela Cooper and Luchia Fitzgerald, who first met in a bar in Manchester, drawn together by the similarities in their upbringing. Both were the children of unmarried, working-class Irish mothers; both had been born in Catholic-run institutions. Angela had been lucky and was adopted by a loving family; aged just 15, Luchia ran away from an abusive home life in Ireland and wound up in Manchester, where she

---

* Not Stuart Feather: 50 years on no one can recall who this particular Stuart was, but Feather denies that it was him.

found a new family within the city's LGBT community. 'Luchia was out on the gay scene,' Angela recalls. 'I was a hippie who had become politicised as a student. The first meeting I ever went to was at the University of Manchester, and I can still remember putting my hand on that doorknob and thinking, "My life will change when I go through this door" and I walked into a Campaign for Homosexual Equality meeting.

'In a sense, I found my people in that setting, but I couldn't relate to everything that they were doing because I was quite radical politically, and some of them were Tories! But I met these two hippie guys there, and we three believed that massive social change was possible; we believed *anything* was possible. I always feel really grateful that I was born when I was, because before that there was not much to latch onto. Then came *The Female Eunuch* [Germaine Greer's groundbreaking feminist text], and suddenly everyone was going on about how we all wanted to burn our bras. I had read *The Female Eunuch* and was being drawn down that road, and Luchia was working in the Union pub. We did not use the word "gay" then, but we were starting to hear it, coming from what was happening in the States. I never felt confident enough to go into that pub and "come out", but I came out through my politics, and my interest in the women's movement. My friend Sue and I felt it was our mission to go into these awful places, take our leaflets and liberate these terribly oppressed people. It makes me laugh to think about it now – we were like the gay Salvation Army!

'It's pretty hard for people to realise what it was like at the beginning of the seventies for gays and for women. There was no Rape Crisis, there were no phone lines, there was just the scene and the nascent women's movement... It was very different, and it was pretty grim. We were in one of these places, the Picador Club – you had to knock on the door and a little hatch would open and someone would look at you to decide whether you could come in or not – probably being very loud and trying to tell people about gay liberation but nobody was interested. Luchia was on the next table and her ears pricked up. "I've been saying this for years," she said, and of course Sue and I were delighted because we had found a convert. And because Luchia worked at the Union, she was able to ask the landlord if we could hold the first

Manchester Gay Liberation Front meeting there.' They would not have realised it at the time, but Angela and Luchia were about to embark on a lifetime of fighting for equal rights, and their work would help Manchester establish itself as a major hub for gay people in the north.

3

Dancing with the GLF

'It is very difficult for homosexuals to persuade people to take a serious interest in their predicament... but the fact is that most of them are highly-intelligent, pleasant, personable individuals who have just as much right to be themselves as the rest of us have.' – Jean Austin[1]

From a basement office in Housman's Bookshop on Caledonian Road in North London, the GLF offered support, information and advice to anyone who needed it. A young musician called Rupert Herries, who had witnessed police intimidation first-hand, needed legal advice, and where better to find it than the GLF's Islington stronghold. 'I was 17 and I got into trouble,' he explains. 'In retrospect I now understand that I had walked into a trap. I went to the loo at Victoria Station and found myself amongst a load of cruising men. A new experience for me, and I was fascinated, but I didn't do anything. This guy next to me was displaying, if you like, and I thought I had better get out. I started making my way up the stairs, and these two butch policemen grabbed me and said, "Right, you're coming with us." I was questioned for a long time, which was a terrifying experience. They said, "We saw what you were doing", and they kept asking me if I was a member of this new organisation called the GLF. I didn't know what that was. They told me that I was in serious trouble because I was underage. Then a statement was typed out in front of me; I was really frightened, so I signed the bloody thing. My eldest sister was called, and she collected me. She was furious that I had signed the statement, but we did not know what to do. There was a chap living at her house who said, "Well, why don't we take you to the GLF offices?" They drove me to Caledonian Road that evening, and I met Ralph Stephenson, who phoned everyone he knew, telling them that "one of our brothers has been arrested for cottaging, I want you all to be at the court." He started this campaign to support me and get as many as possible to attend my court appearance.'

Stephenson, the former BBC radio DJ and one of the founders of Radio Free London, had thrown himself wholeheartedly into the day-to-day running of the GLF office on Caledonian Road. 'I felt this magnetic pull towards the GLF,' he explains. 'At that point I was something of a refugee from the good life and was quite dangerously adrift, and I met a man who took me along to my first full-on involvement with the GLF. By then they had established weekly meetings each Wednesday at All Saint's Hall in Powis Square. I dived in: I became involved in campaigning and the office, and by the December I was fully involved in all aspects of the GLF community. It became a bit of a lifestyle I suppose; there were newsletters, there was the paper we produced, Come Together, there were the groups and open meetings... What a special, cherished thing those Wednesday evening groups became... all those new, real friends.

'It was a kind of structured anarchism. There was an exhilaration in the freedom and flexibility of it all. It was real; it had truth. I'd managed to create my own role within the office, joyfully reactivating my sadly neglected skills in communication and media relations, and it was the most enjoyable place to spend time constructively, with a sense of warmth – even though the office in the basement of Housman's was draughty – and family. There were the meetings, and the paperwork, and the deskwork, and the phones... The phones were the forerunner of Gay Switchboard, although Gay Switchboard had a number of phones but the GLF office only had one! So much came from that and I was delighted to contribute.'

The GLF phone line, salvation for many gay people who needed to hear a friendly voice or gain advice on legal matters, was followed in 1972 by Friend (later London Friend), founded by members of the CHE as a befriending service, as well as providing support, advice and help for people dealing with coming out. Other similar volunteer-run helplines followed, including Manchester Friend (1973), the London Gay Switchboard (1974, taking over the GLF office and phone line at Housmans) and, in 1975, the West Midlands Lesbian and Gay Switchboard, Bristol Lesbian and Gay Switchboard, Oxford Gay Switchboard and Brighton and Hove Switchboard.

Stephenson had first heard about the GLF when living in Brighton in late 1970. 'We didn't have social media, the forerunner was the underground press which by 1970 was very prolific, and that's how I picked up on the early news of the formation of the GLF at the London School of Economics. One of the prime sources of information in Brighton was the Unicorn Bookshop... The frontage of the shop [painted in a mural, much like the Beatles' Apple Boutique on Baker Street] fascinated me. I used to go there to pick up my copies of *OZ*, *Ink*, *Black Dwarf* and numerous other fascinating alternative publications – and I was inspired to start contributing to some of them. The longer-established parts of the alternative society were slightly askance of the new wave, the arrival of embryonic gay campaigning, gay politics, gay rights, but the majority had no problem adapting or accepting. Gay rights became a useful slide rule to measure hypocrisy or integrity, open-mindedness or intent.

'Whenever I was in London I attended the meetings at the LSE. I signed up fully to this dawning possibility of solidarity and everything that followed. It was a very clear-cut, straightforward situation: one of the clearest campaigns you could think of. The meetings were primarily about planning demonstrations. I could not commit as much as I wanted to, because of where I was living, but then regional GLFs began to proliferate. Very soon we were seeing the people from the LSE meetings on the TV news, with their banners, and hearing about them in the papers and on the radio. I think there might have even been a couple of short items about early GLF protests in newsreels, which were still being shown at the cinema. Like so many other people, I was amazingly heartened, and as soon as I possibly could I became committed to the aims and intentions of the GLF. By now I was living part time in London. I'd go to the meetings, but that was the best that I could do... That intention, that urge, that desire to be involved, that semi-stillborn commitment was still there, but I didn't feel I had learned enough to be useful. I felt like I needed to find a role.

'I had spent three or four years as a bit of an edgy pirate radio personality, although by 1970 the majority of offshore broadcasting had finished. I wanted to do more reporting and was working for BBC Radio Brighton [later to become BBC Sussex] and making regional programmes for Radio 4. It was getting difficult to proportion time for gay campaign activities, which were just evolving, although the fuse had been lit... I knew that it would not be long before I was more fully involved.'

Although petrified, Rupert Herries dutifully turned up for his court appearance, and Ralph Stephenson was there to accompany him. Herries' father came too, advising his son to take off the many gay lib badges he was wearing. '"You don't need to label yourself, for God's sake," he said. "You're just you!" I was advised to plead not guilty, but at the last minute I was given a different solicitor who advised me to plead guilty, which caused a bit of a fracas. At one point, the magistrate turned to my father and said, "Do you think your son needs psychiatric treatment?" He lost his temper and shouted, "No! He needs to be left alone!"' The public gallery was filled with what Herries describes as a host of 'amazing, outrageous people', who accompanied his father's outburst with cheers and cries of 'right on!' Herries was charged with 'perpetually importuning for immoral purposes' and given a three-year conditional discharge with a fine.

'In between the arrest and the court case, I had been going to GLF meetings, which blew my mind,' Herries adds. 'They were really big meetings, with people getting up and making speeches, and I remember thinking, "Wow... this is absolutely amazing." They were organising demonstrations, and I went on several. On one I suddenly found myself walking hand in hand with a young Australian guy called Peter Tatchell, and through him I met another young guy, also called Peter, who I fell in love with. He was 16, I was 17, so in the eyes of the law what we were doing was illegal.'

Herries and his newfound friends in the GLF often went on sorties to known cottages to warn others of the methods the police

41

were employing. 'I was going around with Peter Tatchell and a whole group of people, with leaflets and stickers. We would go down into the cottages, the ones we knew people were cruising in. People would be standing there at the urinals and we would put a sticker on the wall in front of them, "police entrapment practised here!" Peter would stand outside, handing out leaflets encouraging people to join the GLF, to come along to meetings. We were at risk of being arrested for doing that, but we didn't give a shit!'

Herries would soon become a regular at GLF dances and fundraising benefits, often performing solo as support to rock act the Half Human Band, but his first brush with live performance had been as a callow 15-year-old at David Bowie's Beckenham Arts Lab, held at the Three Tuns public house on Beckenham High Street. 'My cousin ran Beckenham Arts Lab with Bowie before he became really famous,' he explains. 'Bowie offered me a spot one evening, but he forgot, leaving me waiting to come on. He apologised to me afterwards, but I think it was a good thing that it happened because I could hardly play at that point!' After a short fallow period following the release of 'Space Oddity', Bowie, who had recently moved into a rundown gothic pile, Haddon Hall, with new wife Angie, was starting to make headlines – not for his music, but for the startling way he dressed. Embracing the new decade's promise of sexual liberation, Bowie could often be found wandering around Beckenham wearing men's dresses from British fashion designer Michael Fish; the *Daily Mirror* in particular made great sport of this, publishing a full-page photograph of the couple walking their new-born baby Zowie (later Duncan), under the heading 'Right Then, Which One's Dad?'[2]

Bowie would wear one of his Mr Fish dresses on the front cover of the British release of his album *The Man Who Sold the World.* Despite the record being issued with an altogether less threatening cover in America, Bowie still ran into trouble there, according to the *Mirror*: 'He got to Texas to find himself staring down the barrel of a gun and a hunky rancher snarling at him, "If it wasn't against the law I'd blow your brains out, you fag. Quit town."'[3] 'I get all sorts of abuse showered on me,' he told reporter Don Short. 'It doesn't worry me anymore what people say. I get called a queer and all sorts of things...'[4]

Despite the fact that few, if any, out-gay acts could be found to play (leading to complaints over the sexist attitudes and lyrics of some of the performers), GLF dances would continue, usually with a rock band or two, a solo singer and a disco and light show. 'I'd often play between two very loud rock bands,' says Rupert Herries. 'At one dance in Kensington Town Hall, there was a particular band who were very macho, and a lot of the feminist lesbians who were in the audience got up on stage to mimic their singer. It was amazing. Those dances were one of the highlights of my life. I'd been living a bit of a double life, and up there, just me on my own, I felt completely liberated.'

In February 1971 all 550 tickets for the second GLF People's Dance, at Kensington Town Hall, were sold in advance, and on the night 700 were allowed inside. Rock band Patto, who had released their debut album two months earlier on the progressive rock label Vertigo, played to a packed hall, supported by Nigerian percussionist Ginger Johnson and his band. Johnson had also appeared on stage with the Rolling Stones at their infamous Hyde Park show in 1969 and with Pink Floyd, the Soft Machine, Yoko Ono and others at the legendary 14 Hour Technicolour Dream. In the spirit of the times, many ticket holders brought organic food and drink to share out.

A week before, 15 GLF supporters were arrested while handing out leaflets outside the Gateways Club in King's Road, Chelsea. The previous week two women had been thrown out of the club while trying to sell tickets for the dance, and their leaflets claimed that the management of the Gateways thought lesbians were sick: in fact the lesbian couple that ran it – Gina and Smithy – simply preferred that their patrons remain discreet about their sexuality and leave the politics at home, something that was entirely at odds with the GLF's mission to encourage people to come out.

Opened in 1931, in its early years the Gateways Club was often in trouble with the law for allowing gambling on the premises, but five years later the place became a members-only club, frequented by gay men, lesbians and other minorities. Visionary record producer Joe Meek had been a member; an urban legend has it that the Frankie Vaughan hit 'Green Door' was written about the club, which for years

was hidden behind an anonymous-looking, green-painted front door.*
In the 1960s, as most of the club's male patrons moved on to Soho
and Earl's Court, it became almost exclusively lesbian; the UK's first
lesbian rights group, the Minorities Research Group, was established
by members in 1963 and held many of its meetings there. The
Gateways Club became known nationally after it featured in the BBC
documentary *Consenting Adults* in 1967, part of the *Man Alive* series,
and internationally when, the following year, it appeared in *The Killing
of Sister George* starring Beryl Reid and Susannah York, one of the
earliest mainstream films to feature lesbianism. 'I remember going to
see *The Killing of Sister George*,' says jazz musician Alison Rayner. 'I
would go to anything I could find that had anything to do with lesbians,
but my God, that was a depressing film! You would want to come out
of the cinema and slash your wrists! It was somewhere like Orpington
in the afternoon: there were only about 10 people in there but nine of
those were men in macs! It was a bit gross...'

Around the same time that the GLF dances were becoming
established, Paul Southwell, a gay teenager with aspirations to become
a professional musician, said goodbye to his family in the Lancashire
town of Accrington and decamped to London. 'I was 19. I moved
because I wanted to be a musician, and there wasn't much going on
up north; you needed to be in a centre like New York or London,' he
explains. 'So, I moved to London, principally for that reason, but also
because I wanted to be open about my homosexuality. I came out when
I moved. I wasn't remotely political before, but as soon as you started
living a gay lifestyle in those days you needed to make a choice: you
became political pretty quickly or you needed to remain in the closet,
and I wasn't going to do that. I like honesty; I simply did not want to
pretend to be heterosexual. So, I needed to get political.'

Because they were publicly advertised, GLF dances became an easy
target for the police. In January 1971, at a GLF disco at the Prince of
Wales pub in Hampstead Road, a few dozen people were happily enjoying
themselves, until the police arrived. Claiming that they had evidence of

---

* It was not: the lyrics to 'Green Door' were composed by American songwriter Marvin
  Moore who had no connection with the Gateways Club at all.

drugs being on the premises, the officers made the men line up against one wall and the women line up opposite while they searched everyone. No drugs were found that night, but the police took details of many attendees' names and addresses and made it clear to the landlord that these events would not be tolerated. Before long, the People's Dances would also begin to attract the attention of gangs of queer bashers.

Despite these occasional setbacks, GLF dances were an overwhelming success. Taking inspiration from them, in July 1971 former public health inspector Richard 'Tricky Dicky' Scanes would launch London's first regular gay disco, in the upstairs room of a pub in Camberwell. 'I had heard that the governor of the Father Red Cap was gay,' he later explained to *Gay News.* 'I phoned him and said, "I am gay; I'm a DJ", and he gave me the chance to get started.'[5] Soon Tricky Dicky was working six nights a week, taking his mobile disco (Dick's Inn, where 'gays dance close together') to Southend-on-Sea, as well as to gay-friendly pubs in Bethnal Green, Soho, Brighton and on gay cruises along the Thames.

Manchester's Gay Student Group – which had only been formed in March – was also encouraged by the success of the GLF dances and, after a couple of low-key gay discos held in the University of Manchester Students' Union bar, the group booked a hall at nearby Salford University for their inaugural Gay Ball. 'We wanted to do something never before attempted,' organiser Glenys Parry explained. 'Hold an openly gay dance in a provincial town and make a splash.'[6] Sadly, despite the booking being accepted, the university was forced to withdraw permission after interference from the local council.

The Manchester ball may not have happened, but in other parts of the country things were taking off and, in the summer of 1971, at a country house in the Cotswolds, Britain got its first gay festival: a weekend-long outdoor event with bands, film shows, dance troupes and theatre. Luckily, it was a more peaceful, smaller and successful event than the one that had taken place on Randall's Island in the US the previous July. One of the acts booked to perform at the Cotswolds weekend was folk band the Solid British Hat Band, as member Ken Wilson recalls: 'It was extraordinary: gay festivals are ten a penny these days, but nothing like this had happened before.'

Postlip Hall, a 50-room mansion set in 14 acres near Cheltenham, Gloucestershire, had been sold the previous year to a commune, originally consisting of four families and their friends, for £20,000. When the families moved in, the Jacobean house was in a sorry state, with no working kitchen and few, if any, amenities, but the folk involved slowly created their own community, dividing the Hall into individual housing units with shared areas for eating and drinking, art classes, meetings, parties and so on. One of the residents of the community, Alan Baker, decided that he wanted to use the grounds to hold a weekend-long, open-air gay festival, which other residents helped him organise. 'We went down there to play,' Wilson says. 'There were probably 300 people there. It was the most amazing event; we had played a couple of times outside but never to an audience as big as that. It was fantastic to be on stage in front of 300 people. [Group member] Michael Klein had been working with a guy called Alan Wakeman; they had a band called Everyone Involved, and they'd written this thing called "A Gay Song", which we performed at Postlip.' 'Postlip Hall was amazing,' adds fellow band member Gillian Dickinson. 'It had a minstrels' gallery and everything! I remember that very clearly because it was so opulent, that place, just beautiful.'

The Solid British Hat Band was a four-piece folk group made up of teachers and students from four different countries who had recently released their debut album, *Mr Monday*. Wakeman, an early convert to the gay liberation cause, was also an English teacher who had devised a much-used language course, *English Fast*. He had been involved in the GLF group working out of the Caledonian Road office for some time, and was good friends with Denis Lemon, who would go on to edit *Gay News*. 'It was an overwhelmingly powerful experience, being there,' says Wilson. 'In the early days of the gay liberation movement it was dangerous for gay people to walk through the streets, but here we were in Postlip Hall. Alan came up to my wife Dede and me sitting on the grass, just enjoying the atmosphere and said, "How does it feel to be the odd ones out?" He could be kind of provocative like that, but it was great, to see all this... It was a very memorable time. I had just learned the bass line for "A Gay Song", and I had a nightmare trying to remember it, so I was staring at the guitar all the way through the performance. When the song finished, I thought, "Well, I fucked that up completely", but the place erupted. It was a very moving experience.' Sadly, life at Postlip was not fulfilling Alan Baker's needs. Described in *The Listener* magazine as 'a young bachelor of private means'[7] and by author Andrew Rigby as 'a loner' with 'real problems of identity' who 'found it difficult to relate to the other members',[8] Baker left the community in 1972 and moved to Australia where, according to Joy McMillan, one of the Postlip community's founding members, he was later murdered.

Shortly after the Postlip weekend, on 12 July 1971 the Solid British Hat Band played the inaugural Gay Lib Drag Ball, held at Chelsea Town Hall. Drag Balls had been held annually in Chelsea since the late 1960s, but this would be the first time that the GLF had been involved with its organisation. 'That was quite extraordinary,' the Solid British Hat Band's Gillian Dickinson recalls. 'It was the first time, I think, where queens felt they could just be who they were, and they dressed up to the nines. It was the most beautiful spectacle, these guys parading themselves around the room, looking absolutely stunning... It was wonderful. I remember being accosted in a booth by three girls who said, "Have you ever had a gay experience?" I told them "no", to which they said, "Well, how can you sing a gay song then?" I thought that was interesting, to see that prejudice works both ways. "You can't sing a gay song if you haven't had a gay experience!" So, I said, "Listen. I would be very happy to have a gay experience; I just haven't met a woman I fancy!"'

Jim Anderson, the art editor of *OZ* magazine, was part of the Notting Hill GLF. Arrested and tried for obscenity along with co-founders Felix Dennis and Richard Neville, Anderson had been sentenced to a year in prison for his part in the notorious 'schoolkids issue' of the magazine, which had appeared in 1970 and carried what he described as 'naked blue lesbians artfully going at it on the cover and Rupert Bear fucking Gipsy Grannie inside'. To help raise funds for the court case, John Lennon and Yoko Ono wrote, produced and performed on the single 'God Save Us' backed with 'Do the Oz', credited to the Elastic Oz Band and issued on the Beatles' Apple label in June 1971. 'I knew Richard

Neville; I'd met him when I was a student and I'd bumped into him a few times when I was living in London,' says Ken Wilson. 'Dede and I were quite good friends with Felix Dennis too. Jim Anderson and Richard Neville were both educated guys, and Felix was a secondary modern schoolboy who just loved working in odd places. He got himself involved, but at the trial, when the judge was summing up, he said, "and you, Dennis, because you're not as well educated as the other two, I'm going to send you to prison for a shorter period of time".' A suitably chastised Dennis would go on to found his own hugely successful publishing house. 'Felix didn't need a rocket up his arse to become a millionaire,' Wilson adds, 'But if he had, then that was it.'

As news of the severe sentencing reached the protesters assembled outside the court – Neville was jailed for 15 months and, as an Australian citizen, was recommended for deportation; Anderson was jailed for a year and Dennis for nine months – the previously peaceful scene erupted. An effigy of the presiding judge was set on fire and, as police attempted to disperse the crowd, a smoke bomb went off. In the ensuing fracas, both protesters and police sustained injuries. Eleven people were arrested, charged with a variety of offences from obstruction to being in possession of an offensive weapon. The *OZ* editors served four months of their sentences before being released on appeal after the trial judge was found to have misdirected the jury on dozens of occasions. It's hardly surprising then that just days after his release from prison, at a children's Christmas party given by GLF activists in December 1971 at All Saints Church Hall, Anderson took part in a sketch that featured the joke 'what's blue, smells and has flat feet? A dead copper!'[9]

The party, a GLF spokesperson explained, 'was held... to try and break down that hoary old myth linking homosexuals and children in the most suspicious way – this is where homosexuals are most suspect in the public eye. We hope to demolish the fear and paranoia about gay people.'[10] The 100 or so children were also treated to a puppet show, Graham Chapman of *Monty Python's Flying Circus* attempting a conjuring act, and a performance from the No Blame Street Theatre Group. According to contemporary reports, the Solid British Hat Band also played at the party, although it is more likely that this was an early outing for Wakeman's musical collective, Everyone Involved, as Ken and Dede Wilson have no recollection of performing. 'We were expecting our first child by then,' Ken explains. 'It's possible that Michael Klein played with other musicians.' The fourth member of the band, Gillian Dickinson, agrees: 'Michael and I did a few gigs at that time, but the whole band? Not really.' Wakeman, who helped organise the party, claimed that he had played that night: he was never a member of the Solid British Hat Band, but he worked with Klein and Dickinson in Everyone Involved, and he would later co-found Britain's first professional LGBT theatre collective, Gay Sweatshop.

Needless to say, elements of the event did not go down well with everybody. Len Adams, a journalist on tabloid the *Sunday People*, fairly foamed at the mouth, accusing the vicar of All Saints, the Reverend Peter Clark, and the GLF of wanting to 'shove anti-police propaganda at the kids'.[11] Wakeman and Denis Lemon penned a letter to local newspaper the *Kensington Post*, claiming that the entertainment 'was no more anti-police (and no less) than the traditional Punch and Judy show,' and insisting that 'the kids loved it'.[12] 'That was not an official GLF party,' Stuart Feather explains. 'Wakeman did not have the support of others in the GLF, and he was trying to promote these straight country music singers [the Solid British Hat Band] as representing the GLF. He wanted them to become figureheads; it was absurd. We had all of these people who thought that they were going to make a name for themselves through appearing with the Gay Liberation Front. Many of them were straight, and they all thought that we couldn't handle a revolution ourselves: they were there to do it for us. There was no support in the GLF for this Christmas party: why was everyone suddenly getting sentimental about children? It was very odd.'

The following year Wakeman's band, Everyone Involved, issued their only album, *Either/Or*, limited to 1,000 copies and given away free to anyone who wanted one. *Either/Or* featured the first studio recording of 'A Gay Song'; with backing vocals provided by GLF volunteers including Ted Brown, 'A Gay Song' became the first recording by a British act to explicitly discuss homosexuality in a positive way. Covering themes such as ecology, world peace and free love, the album also included a second gay-themed tune, 'A Sad Song', with vocals by the Solid British Hat Band's Gillian Dickinson. 'I felt enormously proud to be involved in that. It was a magical time.' she explains. 'There were various different people, which is why we called it Everyone Involved. There was Freya Hogue, who was in Sunforest, an all-female band; Arnolpho Lima Filho, the bass player of Brazilian rock band Os Mutantes, who is now one of South America's top producers; and James Asher, the cousin of Jane and Peter Asher, on drums. Everyone played for free. We gathered everyone together and had to make the entire album in three days; the idea was to give the album away... We had been given the studio time free, but we did have to pay to get it pressed. There were lots of different protest songs, and part of the protest was that the wrong people were making the money: that's why we wanted to do everything for free. None of the musicians had really worked together apart from Michael and me, and Alan was writing the words and helping to organise it, because he was very good at that.'

Everyone Involved released one further 45, a Wakeman-Klein song protesting the gentrification of Piccadilly. In January 1973, this loose collective of gay and heterosexual musicians headlined a GLF dance at Fulham Town Hall before going their separate ways. 'We were terribly idealistic and young, but it was a wonderful thing,' Dickinson adds. Protest had paved the way for the hugely successful GLF dances, and people were beginning to produce pop music specifically aimed at the LGBT community. Now came the opportunity for other artists, writers and performers to make their mark.

4

The Festival of Lies

'Moral pollution needs a solution' – Festival of Light banner[1]

The GLF continued to attract singers, actors and artists, and soon established its own street theatre group. 'All these groups started up quite quickly after GLF was founded,' Stuart Feather remembers. 'I went along to the media group meeting where they were putting together *Come Together*, but I couldn't see myself getting involved in that. Then there was an announcement that a street theatre group was going to form. I had been involved in amateur dramatics as a teen and had a role in a play in York, so it seemed like this was something I could do.' CHE had its own theatre group too (as did the women's movement), but as in everything else, the antics of the GLF Street Theatre Group would be far more radical than those of their CHE contemporaries.

Theatre would play an enormous part in the British LGBT experience, and for good reason, as playwright, producer and gay theatre activist Peter Scott-Presland explains: 'No one had a clear concept of what gay theatre could do at the start of the seventies – you had to articulate it as you went along and modify it according to your own experience. But there are lots of things you can use gay theatre, or gay performance, for. One is propaganda, for putting across a political argument; another is to politicise a gay audience. The last 50 years have not just been

51

about gaining LGBT rights from straight society, they've also been about convincing LGBT people that they actually deserve rights. We started from such a low place of oppression in the early 1970s and it took maybe 20 years before people realised that, yes, we deserve these rights. Part of gay theatre was building up self-esteem, building self-confidence, part of it was to address problematic issues within the LGBT community. You can put things into a play and explore them in a way that if you did in a polemic would become difficult. Theatre can break taboos.'

Stuart Feather was part of a commune, based in Notting Hill, that would also give birth to radical drag troupe Bloolips, formed by cabaret star Bette Bourne – brother of sixties pop star Mike Berry – and Lavinia Co-op. Other GLF communes soon popped up, including one in Hackney, where a squat in Abersham Road morphed into a gay centre, with open meetings every Tuesday evening. The Street Theatre Group would provide entertainment for gay days (picnics where men and women were encouraged to flout the law by holding hands and kissing, and that were inspired by the hippie 'be-ins' of 1967), attend protests in costumes and masks and generally make themselves heard. One of their earliest outings, or zaps, just a few weeks after the GLF came into being in Britain and before the theatre group even had a name, took place at the Royal Albert Hall on 21 November 1970, in support of a Women's Liberation Movement campaign against the televising of the annual *Miss World* contest. Host Bob Hope faced smoke bombs and ink pellets, and protesters held their own *Miss Used* contest outside the venue; however most of the newspapers the following day were more concerned with allegations that the results of the contest had been rigged than by any of the actions of the protesters. The following February, the now fully formed GLF Street Theatre Group would demonstrate outside Bow Street Magistrates' Court during the trial of the women's liberation protesters.

'Stuart was a brilliant organiser,' says Street Theatre Group member Richard Bolingbroke. 'We would get dressed up in our heels and our frocks, but this was not an attempt to be a woman, it was a way to shock people. Ten of us walking down the street kicking up our heels was quite a sight! We were not really into drag, because a lot of the drag performers were straight and the ones that were not thought that gay rights were not that important, but it was very entertaining.'

Although many of them were gay themselves, the biggest drag stars of the era were often dismissive about homosexuality: as late as 1987, Danny La Rue, who lived with his partner Jack Hanson for 40 years, announced that he was to marry an Australian millionairess, telling the press that, 'There are lots of people who think that any man who puts on make-up in the theatre must be a poof. I don't expect people to think I'm a heavyweight boxer, but my act wouldn't have worked if I were gay.'[2] The Canadian-born, London-based Mr Jean Fredericks was one of the few who openly supported the gay scene of the time, organising regular drag balls at Porchester Hall, near Paddington, and penning a regular column on gay and drag nightlife for short-lived monthly magazine *The Drag Queens*. Fredericks even attempted to form his own leather-clad gay rock band, the Iron Boys.

'We used to go out in drag a lot,' Richard Bolingbroke explains. 'The police didn't arrest us much; we were fairly good at escaping, or at keeping it together as a group. The idea was not necessarily to get arrested: if you got arrested it cost money, it was annoying, and nobody wanted to get a record.'

'It causes confusion,' explains Stuart Feather. 'People are really put on the back foot. Drag is immediately confrontational: "Why are you wearing women's clothes? Why are you behaving like that?" It was personal. It wasn't just about discussing the lofty ideals of the GLF, you were grabbing people by the short and curlies, and they were offended and challenged. You really felt like you were getting through to people, and I could see the power of that.'

As well as organising regular 'gay days' in London's parks, demonstrations became the GLF's stock-in-trade. In August 1971, around 400 members of the GLF's youth group and their friends took to the streets of London to protest the lack of parity in the age of consent between heterosexuals and homosexuals. Occasionally (and erroneously) referred to as Britain's first Pride event, supporters of the GLF also wanted to protest against a number of public houses who had refused to serve LGBT people – especially those leaving the weekly GLF meetings in Notting Hill. Three pubs in particular – Henekey's Wine

Bar on Portobello Road, the Pembroke Castle and the Duke of Norfolk – had closed early, deployed police outside the premises or simply banned anyone wearing GLF badges or assumed to be homosexual.

The day began with a gay day in Hyde Park, where people shared food, smoked a few joints and passed around copies of *Come Together*, before protesters took to the streets to march to Trafalgar Square, accompanied by Ginger Johnson's African Drummers. Once there, they held a public kissing session, asking members of the public to decide which of those involved were older or younger than 21. In many cases, they chose incorrectly. Estimates of the size of the event vary, with the fiercely anti-gay *People* newspaper claiming just 200 demonstrators and *Time Out* suggesting there were upwards of 1,000 people involved.

'I was a novice in terms of politics,' explains Richard Bolingbroke. 'I was a bit of a troublemaker and a rule breaker, and I wasn't particularly close to my family. When gay lib came along a lot of the discussions at the LSE went way over my head; it was very deeply political and very Marxist, and I did not understand what that had to do with 'liberation'. I learned a lot along the way, but I was more concerned about what it could do for me on a personal level.

'By now the LSE meetings had moved to the church hall in Notting Hill Gate. We knew that the priest there was gay because he always had a new gown on every week, fabulous dresses she would wear! From the start there were factions forming: there was a very out-gay faction, then there were people who were much more mainstream, who didn't want to rock the boat. But as far as I was concerned if you were in the GLF you *had* to rock that boat. You wanted to get noticed. At these meetings I met a number of people: Bette Bourne, Stuart Feather, Michael Lyneham, many others. I made a lot of friends and we started getting involved with stuff, taking LSD and developing deeper, more meaningful relationships within that community. And one of the events we went to was where we were dressed as nuns.'

On 25 September 1971 members of the GLF, alongside their counterparts in the Women's Liberation Movement, took part in a demonstration against the Nationwide Festival of Light, the religious organisation headed by campaigner Mary Whitehouse, which was holding rallies in both London and Liverpool. In the capital, the Festival of Light's followers, whose crusade saw them battling everything from pornography and the permissive society to the lowering of standards in public life and the use of four-letter words on television, marched from Trafalgar Square to Hyde Park, where they were met by GLF demonstrators, some – including Richard Bolingbroke (then known by his given name, Timothy) – dressed as nuns, eight years before the Sisters of Perpetual Indulgence first began wearing ecclesiastic costume on the streets of San Francisco.*

'We had already formed the Street Theatre Group, which Stuart Feather was a major member of, and we went there,' Bolingbroke adds. 'We didn't have a lot in the way of drag but we found some material to make nuns' habits out of, and we all brought large cucumbers with us which we were vigorously insulting people with.' Feather remembers that day well: 'The police in Trafalgar Square were verging on brutal,' he recalls. 'They grabbed [GLF activist] Michael Lyneham, who was on the plinth, and dragged him off head first, banging his body into the granite below.'

The Nationwide Festival of Light, founded just weeks after the first meeting of the Gay Liberation Front, had been targeted by the GLF from the outset: their inaugural rally, held on 9 September in Westminster Central Hall, was brought to an abrupt end when GLF members, some in drag, turned off the lights and caused pandemonium by sounding horns and releasing mice into the auditorium. 'I was at Westminster Hall when these nuns released the mice,' says musician Steve Swindells. 'That was absolute genius. I was in hysterics; it was a masterstroke of civil disobedience but very funny as well. All the screaming women standing on chairs... it was fabulous!' As the mice ran amok among the 3,000-strong audience and the born-again journalist Malcolm Muggeridge attempted to wrest control of the chaos from the stage, a

---

* Mrs Whitehouse and her friends (around 45,000 people congregated on Hyde Park for the gospel concert, less than half of the predicted 100,000) should have realised that their god was not on their side when a nationwide beacon-lighting programme, timed to take place the night before the rally, became quite literally a washout. Despite high-profile Christians like television-talking-head Malcolm Muggeridge and pop singer Cliff Richard taking part, many of the beacons failed after parts of the country were drenched in heavy rain following a three-week drought.

chorus line of five GLF 'nuns', clad in blue-and-white habits, danced the can-can in front of the stage. 'Mary Whitehouse was a real threat,' Stuart Feather recalls. 'But it seemed like it was only us, the queens, who saw it. When it came to demonstrating against the Festival of Light at that inaugural meeting, it was only GLF Street Theatre Group and Women's Liberation Street Theatre who got involved. The GLF and Women's Liberation often came together to demonstrate because these things affected us both. One of the main tenets of the GLF was that there could be no gay liberation without women's liberation.'

Several further arrests were made in Hyde Park: Nicholas Bramble, dressed as 'the Spirit of Porn' was charged with assault after the diamante bracelet he was wearing scratched one of the police officers. Feather, dressed as Mary Whitehouse, and Bolingbroke were among those carted off to the cells. 'We were arrested for causing a breach of the peace,' adds Bolingbroke. 'We were thrown into Hyde Park jail. We ended up going to court and paying our fines and getting the magistrates very uptight; he was insulted by our looks and our behaviour.' At the ensuing trial – which Feather attended in his Mary Whitehouse costume – the magistrate told the accused that 'if men wish to dress as women or comic policemen that is not insulting, but men dressed as nuns at a Christian gathering is a different matter'.[3] But with 'queer bashing' incidents on the rise, this provocative stance was important. By being a visible part of society, and by being open about their sexuality, the GLF believed that gay people were less likely to be dismissed or ignored, and the hypocrisy of the Festival of Light was later exposed when one of its leading members, Nigel Goodwin, an advocate for gay 'cure' therapy, was arrested and fined after he was caught committing gross indecency with a French chef in a men-only sauna in Kensington. Goodwin and Jacques Morel were among 12 men arrested at the sauna after two officers, who were prowling the sauna dressed in towels, observed them in bed together, masturbating each other. One of the arresting officers, Sergeant Facey, was known to his colleagues as 'Bubbles'.

Queer bashing was nothing new, but attacks on suspected homosexuals had become more frequent and increasingly violent, and it seemed as if the police were unable – or unwilling – to protect LGBT people. In September 1969 solicitor's clerk Michael de Gruchy was murdered near Wimbledon Common by a gang of 14 youths – including two 15-year-old girls – after their original prey, two gay men, escaped. The gang, from the nearby Alton Estate, pounced on de Gruchy as he emerged from a subway under Kingston Road, attacking him with sticks, forcing him to the ground and kicking him in the head. He died in hospital hours later from multiple fractures that left his skull, according to the pathologist, looking 'like a broken vase'. Geoffrey Hammond, the butcher's assistant who admitted to kicking de Gruchy in the head, was given a life sentence; three other members of the gang (aged 15 and 16) were detained indefinitely, and the rest were committed to a youth detention centre for conspiracy to assault and for being in possession of offensive weapons. Afterwards, a youth from the same estate boasted that: 'when you're hitting a queer, you don't think you're doing wrong. You think you're doing good. If you want money off a queer, you can get it off him – there's nothing to be scared of from the law, 'cause you know they won't go to the law.'[4]

In February 1970 the body of Albert Cox had been discovered, bound and gagged in his bedsit in Victoria. Police believed that he had been murdered by a man he had picked up at Victoria Station, and they appealed to other gay men who used the station as a pickup place to come forward. 'The extent of homosexual activity there is staggering,' said Detective-Chief Inspector Brian Smith. 'There is a real danger this man could strike again. We particularly want to hear from anyone who has been robbed in similar circumstances. They can rest assured anything they tell us will be treated in confidence. Queer-rollers, as they are called, are very ruthless, dangerous men and it would be in the interests of anyone who knows anything about their activities to come forward. There must be someone, somewhere, who knows what he has done.'[5] Bank clerk Anthony Lawrence was murdered in January 1971, stabbed through the heart after being chased by a gang of skinheads near the Spaniards Inn, a pub next to popular cruising ground Hampstead Heath.

These acts of violence were not limited to the metropolis: in Gloucester a man was beaten with what the judge called 'disgusting brutality' simply because his two assailants assumed that he was homosexual. Patrick Dobson, a 30-year-old gay man from Brighton, was stabbed and beaten with a lump of wood by a seven-member gang aged between 14 and 16. In July 1971 three teenage thugs were convicted of assault in Nuneaton; their victim spent four days in hospital after they beat him with a piece of wooden fencing. That same month, a gang of four teens attacked several gay men in Stratford-on-Avon, leaving one with a broken collarbone. In Maidenhead that November, another gang of four attacked and robbed a 55-year-old man in a public toilet. In July 1972 photographer Leonard Bestwick was murdered in a public convenience in Chester after two queer bashers attacked him with a claw hammer and a knife. Sixteen-year-old James Marquis and 22-year-old Alexander Main were both found guilty of murder after prosecution told the jury that the pair had purposely chosen to 'rob a man with violence, preferably a homosexual, the idea being that he would be less likely to report the crime'.[6] These brutal acts of violence would only increase as Britain's LGBT community became more voluble and visible.

The clashes between the GLF and the Festival of Light were widely reported in the press, and one young man in particular was paying close attention to the Street Theatre Group and their antics. Known to his friends in the GLF as Barry and to his parents as Farrokh Bulsara, he had recently adopted the stage name Freddie Mercury. 'By October 1971 I was at the Caledonian Road office almost daily,' his friend Ralph Stephenson recalls. 'Barry was around almost as much, and his usual morning encouragement to me, zonked after a phone helpline night shift, was saying – in that high-energy way later to fuel Queen performances – "Cheer up, Ralph, here's a good cuppa!", as he'd put an arm round me and place a massive steaming mug before me. He'd follow that up with buying bacon sandwiches and salad rolls all round, which he'd go and get from an art deco workman's cafe across the road.'

Like many gay men at the time, Mercury was leading something of a double life. To his friends, including Queen drummer Roger Taylor, who shared a stall in Kensington Market with him, he was camp but, as far as he knew, straight; he had had a couple of steady girlfriends and was now living with Mary Austin, who he would later declare to be the love of his life. In 1976 the now-world-famous Freddie Mercury would admit to Mary that he thought he might be bisexual. 'No Freddie... I think you are gay,' Mary replied.

It was the time of free love, of sexual experimentation, and Barry/ Freddie took full advantage. It was also around this time that the superstar began to emerge from his shell. After a spell in Liverpool-based band Ibex (later to change their name to Wreckage), Freddie teamed up with Taylor and guitarist Brian May who, alongside Freddie's art school chum Tim Staffell, had played as the three-piece group Smile. When Freddie joined the band, and in June 1970 changed their name to Queen, he drew on his art school training, taking an active interest in their image and staging. Mercury, May and Taylor played their first gig, billed as the Queen, with 17-year-old bass player Doug Bogie, at Hornsey Town Hall Assembly Rooms in February 1971; advertised under the banner 'Gay Times', the event also featured the Pink Fairies and the Pretty Things. After one more gig, this time supporting Yes and having dropped the definite article from their name, Bogie was out. By the time they next played in front of an audience, in July 1971, they had recruited John Deacon and the classic Queen line-up was complete.

But little work was forthcoming: over the next 18 months Queen would play just nine concerts, all in London or the surrounding area, leaving Freddie plenty of time to hang around the Caledonian Road office. 'He would often chat with me for hours, picking my experience of the technical comparisons of microphones that were best for stage work and such,' says Stephenson. But Ralph's friendship with Freddie was not limited to discussions about amplification and the occasional bacon butty: the singer also got involved with GLF campaigns, joining in wholeheartedly with their regular demonstrations. As Stephenson explains, 'He was someone who got what GLF was and what GLF did. He was a great kind of up-lifter and unifier... There were a whole bunch of main activists, but he always seemed central to things and was one of the warmest people, almost overwhelmingly so. As we'd prepare for going out on the latest picket or to join main marches and demos or prepare our latest guerrilla sudden swoops – the raid on Foyles bookshop notably – he'd say, "Come on, Ralph. Let's go get 'em!" I never saw anger from him, unless it was righteous anger of a very positive kind at events, actions, or protests. He was a larger-than-life, large-living personality. It was a surprise to me, when Queen arrived on the scene, that he had had anything to do with music at all. When I used to see him, it was more about performance, but I could see how the two blended later on. I didn't associate it with any sort of star charisma at the time, but nevertheless he was such an energetic, warm, inspirational character, and it was the general guarantee of warmth and bonhomie and cheerfulness and humour that is my long-lasting memory.'

The Foyles demonstration that Freddie was so keen on taking part in was held in October 1971 to protest against the paperback publication of David Reuben's 1969 international bestseller *Everything You Always Wanted to Know About Sex* (*But Were Afraid to Ask)*. Reuben's book was filled with outdated stereotypes of gay men and lesbians and their sexual habits, with claims that 'most homosexuals... transform themselves into part-time women',[7] and that 'if a homosexual who wants to renounce homosexuality finds a psychiatrist who knows how to cure homosexuality, he has every chance of becoming a happy, well-adjusted heterosexual'.[8] Reuben's imagination ran riot when he conjured up images of a woman with an 'unusually large clitoris which reaches as much as two or more inches in length when erect... Lesbians with this anatomical quirk are in great demand', but he was particularly damning of the S&M scene, claiming that 'those who combine homosexuality with sadistic and masochistic aberrations are among the cruellest people who walk this earth. In ancient times they found employment as professional torturers and executioners. More recently they filled the ranks of Hitler's Gestapo and SS.'[9] With the GLF trying to encourage people to come out, this hazardous rhetoric was in danger of sending gay people permanently back into the closet. However, the worst was reserved for his lurid descriptions of abortion, then still illegal in the majority of the USA, with exceptions in certain states in cases of rape, incest or where pregnancy would lead to permanent disability. Peter Tatchell stood outside Foyles on London's Tottenham Court Road, holding a placard that declared the book as 'inaccurate anti-homosexual propaganda'. The Street Theatre Group came along too, performing a mock coat-hanger abortion in front of a large crowd of protesters. A GLF handout described the book as '361 pages [of] recipes for despair and suicide'.[10] Reuben's obscene depictions of thalidomide victims as 'cheerfully flipping their flippers, totally unaware that all children aren't that way',[11] and his shocking accounts of DIY abortions using coat hangers brought many of the women and feminists in the GLF out to a second protest on the doorstep of Pan, the publishers of the paperback, to demand the book be withdrawn. At the demonstration outside the Pan offices, shocked onlookers were greeted by the sight of Denis Lemon, future editor of *Gay News*, being rogered by an eight-foot papier-mâché cucumber.

A committee was set up within the GLF, arguing that the ideas promulgated by medical professionals like Doctor Reuben were seriously outdated. The Counter-Psychiatry Group became one of the most active of all of the GLF's sub-groups, regularly disrupting medical seminars and protesting against the still-current use of electroshock therapy, which one GLF member, Jim Scott, described in detail to a reporter from left-wing newspaper *7 Days*: 'I sat in a comfortable armchair in a warm darkened room, equipped with an automatic slide-projector which I controlled, and a screen. My bare feet were placed on a sackcloth mat, embroidered with wires, and placed on a lino floor to encourage the feet to sweat (and thus facilitate conduction). Behind a screen — out of my vision but within earshot — a nurse controlled the supply of current. I was encouraged to masturbate while looking at the photos I had supplied, and the shocks came randomly, or whenever it was thought I might be having an orgasm... The shocks were increasingly painful.'[12]

Similar examples of direct action occurred frequently. When, on 22 September 1971, a GLF group arrived at the Chepstow pub in Westbourne Grove, London, they found police barring their entrance. Two weeks later, after issuing a press statement warning the media and the police of their intent, 200 GLF supporters descended on the pub demanding to be served. When they refused to leave, the landlord had them forcibly evicted by the police, but with little room to manoeuvre, the constables had to physically carry demonstrators out one by one. By strange coincidence, a couple of years later, the same pub would take over hosting the monthly women-only get-togethers organised by *Sappho* magazine after the women had been evicted from both the Museum Tavern and the Euston Tavern. *Sappho* would also run a monthly women-only disco at the Sols Arms, Hampstead Road.

The GLF was determined to be seen and to be part of the local community, and when the landlord of another pub, the Colville on Portobello Road, refused to serve members of the Notting Hill group after one of their weekly open meetings at All Saints Church Hall (where Pink Floyd and Hawkwind played some of their earliest gigs), they turned up waving placards and creating a fuss. Landlord Tony Carty had persuaded other publicans in the area to bar the GLF not 'because of the badges they wear but because of what they are and what they do,' he told reporter Maurice McKee. 'They were allowed in in the past, after their Wednesday meetings, but the hand-holding and kissing is putting my customers off.' Sadly, landlords were quite within their rights to refuse to serve people based on their sexual preferences: a piece of legislation that would remain in place until the Equality Act of 2010. As a spokesperson for the GLF said at the time, 'It is time gay people were treated just as people, not freaks.'[13]

'The "no kissing" thing was big,' artist Richard Bolingbroke recalls. 'It was still an offence to show public demonstrations of affection, so we would have "kiss-ins", which was an easy thing to do. You would be out with a friend, standing on a corner then as soon as you saw a policeman you would start kissing, which obviously annoyed them and the people passing. People were doing that all over the place.' These minor acts of insurrection were central to the GLF ethos, as was the idea, promulgated in the manifesto, that one had to 'come out'.

Sedition was integral to the GLF philosophy, and on 20 January 1972 Michael Lyneham became the first of the GLF's brothers to be sent to prison for refusing to pay a fine (of £10 plus a further £5 costs) imposed 'for importuning for immoral purposes'.[14] At his committal, the judge told Lyneham that he was 'sympathetic to people of your feelings but I feel that homosexuals are a nuisance – like parked cars'. Predictably, Lyneham's friends in the GLF organised a demonstration outside HM Prison Brixton.

Although the GLF was little more than 18 months old, serious fissures were beginning to appear. In reality, the cracks had been there from the beginning: women in the group felt that the men were exercising too much control and that chauvinism was alive and well within the GLF. 'There were a variety of reasons,' as percussionist Frankie Green describes it, 'and women had different positions on it. Women were in a minority in the GLF, and Black women and men even more so. Lesbians and gay men, though having some issues that overlapped, needed to focus on different political priorities. Most of us were increasingly involved in the women's liberation movement, and many of us left the mixed GLF organisation as we had come to view lesbian oppression as part of women's oppression generally, so we felt our place was within the women's movement. There was the issue of sexism within the gay movement also and some women felt a pressure from some men for us to leave. Autonomous political organising was recognised as important; we set up our own group and became active in many different aspects of subsequent political activism. In the New Year, a GLF women's group "think-in" was held at All Saints Church Hall, which decided that the women would split from the GLF.'

It would take a while for this fracturing to affect other GLF groups around the country. The only form of instant communication at that time was the telephone, and no one in London bothered to inform local GLF groups of this momentous development. 'We just had a payphone on the wall,' Manchester-based activist Angela Cooper recalls. 'We didn't always know what was happening in London. There was a sort of split in Manchester around that time because we were very keen on our politics and our feminism; the gay men were on a very different page. Our sexuality expressed itself in different ways, and I think that the gay men had male attitudes, and there was some misogyny. We realised that we only had a certain amount of time and energy, and we wanted to put that into our lesbian group and into our women's movement. That was our focus at the time, to try and understand what it meant to be "us".

'It was a pretty destructive scene, lots of drink and drugs... Luchia and I both wanted out of that. I hadn't met very many "real" lesbians; I'd had a few relationships, but it was all a bit "am I bi-, am I what?"

Luchia and I became a couple, and then we were invited to live in the women's centre. We lived there for five years; we had Manchester's first lesbian meeting in that building.

'I'd always felt like an outsider because I'd been adopted: you're different, you know something about yourself that other people don't know. I was a Catholic until I was 19, and through my teens I had a really conflicting time. It's bad enough being a teenager, but if you think that you have to confess to some old guy behind a screen that you might have these feelings when you're not allowed to have sexual feelings of any kind, let alone gay or lesbian ones, or, as they would have called us, queer, bent or whatever... So, I suppose I was primed to find my people, to find my tribe or somewhere that I could be the me that I couldn't express in the family I found myself in. I think that gives you a real motor, an energy inside, to want to make changes.'

'There was so little information around at the time,' says jazz musician Alison Rayner, 'but things were filtering over from the States about gay liberation, and I had read a little book called *Alternative London* [by Nicholas Saunders, first published in 1970], which was about how to find vegetarian restaurants, hippie stuff... and there was a section, about two-and-a-half pages, on gay London. So, I read this, and read this, and read this.... the Gay Liberation Front had been going for a little while and they were having these group meetings, and there was one group that used to meet at the Forester's Hall in Kentish Town, which was next door to the Forum [a former cinema, which later became the Town and Country Club before being renamed the Forum in 1993]. My bus home from college used to go past there. Week after week I went past but would not get off the bus, until eventually one week I thought, "I have to get off!" I didn't know anybody else who was gay, but I went along, and it was a bit strange because there weren't any other women there. It turns out that all the women had just left the GLF!

'When I met Frankie many years later, she told me, "Oh yes, all the women had walked out because they got so annoyed with the men," but I joined about three weeks after that. They were very welcoming, incredibly welcoming, and I think a little relieved that a woman had joined because they realised it wasn't very cool to have just men there.

I did feel a little alienated because they all lived in communes and called each other "she" and spent all of their time shopping for frocks... Well, it felt like that to me at the time! I remember thinking, "This is just not me." But they were very kind, and said, "Oh you must meet this very nice woman who comes, Pauline," and I went for a few weeks and then Pauline turned up. I think she may have been transgender, but I was not very clued up and didn't really know, not that it mattered. She had a little group round her house every week for women to go to, and I went to that, and that's where I met my American girlfriend.'

'Gay Women's Liberation began meeting at the Three Wheatsheaves pub in Upper Street, North London,' Frankie Green explains, 'and then in South London, when Lesbian Liberation set up in a women's centre. The exciting times of the late sixties and early seventies brought a burgeoning of creativity in the women's liberation movement and I was lucky to be in the right place at the right time. I had made my way to London in 1971 with a desire to get more involved in radical politics and was given a copy of the GLF paper when I was working at a waitressing job one night. I went along to the next meeting, joined the women's group, and moved into a communal house shortly afterwards. I wasn't in the GLF for long, but it was an important stage for me: it changed, and maybe saved, my life. It was an exciting whirlwind time of meeting people, ideas, discussion, activism in a context that was international; a time of great change, hopefulness and inspiration that included women's liberation, the civil rights movement, Black Power and anti-colonial struggles.'

The cracks that had formed within the GLF could not be papered over. Despite that, for many of those involved life would never be the same again.

5

Subversives in Sequins

*'My son is eight years old and, though this may seem foolish, I
am beginning to fear that he is growing up to be homosexual.
He never joins in the rough-and-tumble games of other boys and
seems much more drawn to the interests that attract his older
sister. Physically, he seems quite normal.' – The People*[1]

Since its inception, there had been an ongoing issue within the GLF
over sexuality: some of the brothers and sisters – especially those
who had adopted radical drag – wanted to promote a new, alternative
lifestyle free of the constraints of monogamy, something more akin to
the hippie ideals of free love, while others simply wanted the world
to recognise same-sex relationships as the equal of heterosexual ones.
In an attempt to take control, the less-radical office collective, still
operating from the basement of Housmans Bookshop on Caledonian
Road, put out an unauthorised edition of the GLF newsletter, *Come
Together*, which did little more than help speed up the schism. *Come
Together* had, up until then, been compiled by the media workshop,
often working from Aubrey Walter's flat. The remaining issues would
be produced from GLF hubs in Manchester and Birmingham, as well
as from different GLF communes in London. 'There was a lot of
infighting, in those days, in the GLF and probably in the CHE as well,'

Paul Southwell explains. 'The lesbians fought with the gay men, the gay men fought with them... Looking back and analysing it that should never have happened, but it did.'

Having extracted themselves from the infighting within the GLF, in Manchester Luchia Fitzgerald and Angela Cooper, now running a women's centre from a squat, were caught up in the heady euphoria of the times. 'This was a walk on the wild side for me, this former Catholic schoolgirl,' Angela reveals. 'Luchia is always quite defensive of the gay scene because it was her salvation when she turned up in the city as this little homeless 15-year-old trying to make her way, but these pubs and bars were places I probably wouldn't have gone if I wasn't gay. There were women who were on the game, there were women who were pimps, there was petty crime – all sorts. One night I was in the Picador, and on the dancefloor I saw my old schoolteacher, who I'd had a thing for when I was at school! It was fascinating, how we were all thrown together – there was nowhere else for us to go, so you would have all the different classes mixed in together.

'I'd go into the Union, then after Luchia had finished work we would go to the Picador, have a few more drinks and sometimes on to one of the all-night places, where there were butch lesbians and Black guys dancing and smoking dope. It was fun. [One night] I had my mother's car and this pot of yellow paint; we just thought, "What can we do?" So, we set off in this car with this big pot of paint, then got out and started daubing "Lesbians are everywhere", and at some point the paint tin tipped over... I had to give the car back to my mother with bright yellow paint all over the black carpet! We did things to entertain ourselves. We used to go into pubs in a mixed group, so I'd be sitting next to my friend Alan, and the other people would assume we were a straight couple, then I'd turn to the woman on the other side of me and we'd start kissing. It was a happening, agitprop, a bit like theatre. Sometimes we'd do things like that at these anti-abortion rallies, things that might make people think and that would give us a feeling of "we are here". We were making ourselves known and charging up our own sense of self-esteem. Because we weren't shut away in closets and we could do mad things like paint "Lesbians are everywhere" all over the town centre.'

For many within the GLF, squatting provided not just a roof over their heads but an instant family of like-minded and supportive comrades. 'I was spending a lot of time with Bette Bourne in his place in Colville Terrace,' explains Richard Bolingbroke. 'He had a boyfriend, a tall, ginger-headed Australian called Rex Lay, a brilliant artist. It was a lot of free love, a lot of smoking grass, taking LSD... There weren't a lot of other drugs around, maybe a few pills, but no ecstasy, no speed; there was heroin, but nobody really did that. We used to do Thai Sticks [cannabis cigars], and I soon got this reputation for passing out at parties! I'd be in the middle of the dance floor and just crash, and then wake up hours later when everyone had left!'

After a short time squatting with Bourne and Lay, members of the Brixton commune and others from GLF's street theatre troupe found a home in nearby Colville Houses. 'We found an old film studio, abandoned, just a block or so away from All Saints Church,' Bolingbroke continues. 'You had to go down a side street and then down this little alley and through the garden to get to the door. It was not huge, maybe 30 or 40 feet wide and a hundred feet or so long, but you had a little ante room and a kitchen, then the main place which was basically a warehouse. The back was divided off, and then there was a mezzanine level with two more rooms. About 20 of us moved in, very quickly, brought our mattresses, got the kitchen working... One of the upstairs rooms became our make-up room, and in the back we had a communal wardrobe.

'A group of people in the squat had a stall on the Portobello Road, just under the flyover. That was one of the communal sources of income; I used to go down there to help. We had a teapot on top of one of the bookshelves, by the art deco designer Clarice Cliff, so naturally the teapot was christened Clarice, and the idea was that if you earned any money then you put it in the teapot, and if you needed money you took it out. It was an amazing attempt at communal living, and for a while it worked. Every weekend we would drop acid together and make big bowls of jelly in these glass film development jars, which we'd eat afterwards. We collected a serious wardrobe. We'd get a gown in and everybody would want to wear it; there would have to be a list of who was going to get it next. Then somebody would sell it on the stall, get 20 quid and put that in Clarice! That was our life: nothing was permanent. I had a little part-time job in a clothes store off Baker Street to supplement what I got, but I was one of the few people who actually worked; the main feature of our lives was going on demonstrations.

'In the commune, for the first time I felt part of a family, my adoptive family, my chosen family. It was an amazing time, and for me it was the epitome of what Aubrey [GLF founder Aubrey Walter] and the other folk had been trying to do. They were always talking about the communist ideal of communal living, but we were actually doing it. It was messy and challenging – who was going to cook, who was going to buy the food, who was going to do this – but we always figured it out. We had been there for about nine months. I remember waking up one morning and there were coppers standing in the living room, banging their truncheons, going, "Get out!" and we just got up and fled: that was it.'

Several of the radical queens would move on from Colville Houses to Bethnal Green Road, where they would begin squatting in the former Agitprop Bookshop. From this enclave the group, now calling themselves Bethnal Rouge, would organise their own events, beginning with a dance featuring the Half Human Band and Rupert Herries and his new band, Kork, held in the gym of the University of London. Herries would soon become resident musician at the Little Theatre in St Martin's Lane, writing and performing songs on a daily basis to please the lunchtime audience. 'I used to have to write a song and sing it before the play started,' he recalls. 'People would come in from their offices with their sandwiches and sit down and watch a play. It was all very experimental!'

GLF dances continued, with the cream of Britain's emerging progressive rock scene happy to provide music for the brothers and sisters to get their groove on to. A new group from Guildford, Camel, played one of their earliest shows at a GLF-sponsored St Patrick's Day People's Dance at Hammersmith Town Hall on 17 March 1972, supporting Monksilvar, a band fronted by singer/songwriter John Kerruish. In April Warm Dust, a progressive rock band that included keyboard player Paul Carrack, who would go on to sing with hit acts Ace and Mike and the Mechanics and tour as part of Ringo Starr's All-Starr Band, played a GLF benefit at Fulham Town Hall, supported by folk duo Brierley Cross. Carrack has since dismissed Warm Dust as 'a dreadful, Frank Zappa-inspired band [that] thought that we were in the forefront of modern music',[2] but there can be little doubt that the band's overtly political stance – their second album, *Peace for Our Time*, interpolated anti-war speeches between eight original jazz-rock pieces that were 'symbolic of past wars and conflicts' and also 'showed the complete futility of war'[3] – helped them get the gig.

Squidd, a rock band from Bristol, played a GLF dance at Fulham Town Hall on 7 July, having already performed at a GLF-promoted Cosmic Carnival at Seymour Hall the previous December. Support included a band called Uncle Dog, which featured bass player John Porter, who would go on to play with Roxy Music before establishing a name for himself as a producer, working first at the Beatles' Apple studio in Savile Row and later on several albums for Bryan Ferry and the Smiths. Squidd's keyboard player, Steve Swindells, remembers the Fulham Town Hall gig clearly. 'I played my organ wearing a retro silk dress, Afro wig, Doc Martens and a Moroccan cape,' he laughs. 'It marked a big turning point for me because my life changed thereafter.' The keyboard player would soon discover that being young, inexperienced and gay could lead you down some very dark alleyways.

Swindells had first encountered the GLF in April 1971, at a CND rally, the Festival of Life (not to be confused with Mrs Whitehouse's Festival of Light), in London's Alexandra Park. 'I used to hitchhike up to London and sometimes sleep under the trees in St James's Park' he explains. 'I was slowly getting to know a few people, hanging around with all of these gay hippie, counterculture types. I met some people from the GLF at that festival, and not long after they asked me if I would chair a GLF meeting in All Saints Church Hall. I was still only 18. That was great fun!' The young musician had only recently come out. 'I stood up on a chair at my 18th birthday party and said, "I've got an announcement to make, and if you don't like it you can fuck off! I'm bisexual... and thanks for coming." The only person who fucked off was my then-girlfriend. Never saw her again!

'I had been jamming in a disused cinema in Bristol with local musicians like Manny Elias, who went on to join Tears for Fears, and

Andy Davis and James Warren who would form Stackridge and have huge success with the Korgis,' the musician, who grew up in Saltford, near Bath, explains. 'I saw an advert in a magazine from a group looking for a keyboard player; that's how I joined Squidd. I had a Farfisa organ, and the drummer, Rodney Matthews, had a lovely set of vibes, which I also learned how to play. We played rock versions of classical pieces like "The Sorcerer's Apprentice" and *The Planets*. I was a big fan of Keith Emerson and the band was heavily influenced by the Nice; they regularly played at the Pavilion in Bath, where I saw other bands like the Who play too. I had no idea at the time that Roger Daltrey would record four of my songs later! Squidd were using a local agency, Plastic Dog,* who got us some amazing gigs. We supported Deep Purple, Wishbone Ash... We were booked to support Bowie during his Ziggy Stardust period, at the Rainbow Pavilion in Torquay, but our van broke down, and when we finally arrived at the venue it was too late for us to play. We did, however, get to see the show, and I remember watching him on stage performing "Starman".

'I would hang around places like Housmans. [The GLF] had a piano there, so I was happy. One day, someone said, "Aren't you in a band? We're doing a benefit; would you ask the band if they'll do it?" I asked the band and they said, "Sure. Let's see if we can get another London gig to make it worth our while." I was out; the guys in the band knew I was gay, and it was never an issue. I had already appeared on television back in Bristol with Squidd wearing fishnet tights, sequinned knickers, an Afro, football boots and my Moroccan cape! Rodney went on to become really successful as an illustrator, but when he was with Squidd he used to look like Frank Zappa and would smash toilet bowls on stage and burn effigies of skinheads... It was all very provocative! We knew what we were doing was political, but we were also having fun. The media was relentlessly evil when it came to gay people... If they were short of news it would be the pervy vicar stories or ridiculous stories connecting gay people to paedophiles, so what I was doing was

---

* Plastic Dog was co-run by Squidd's drummer Rodney Matthews, who would later become one of Britain's most influential album sleeve designers, working on covers for Rick Wakeman, Asia, Thin Lizzy, Hawkwind, Nazareth and dozens more.

deliberate: it was gender-confusing. It wasn't traditional drag: there was no make-up involved, I just liked the idea of challenging people's assumptions.'

It was at that GLF dance on 7 July that Swindells met the man that would become his manager, former BBC cameraman and co-founder of the independent Eyemark label, Mark Edwards. Abuse was rife, and if you were a teenager trying to break into the business, you were easy prey, as Swindells can attest. 'He came up to me afterwards, looking like Gandalf,' he says. 'He had produced Curved Air's hit album, *Air Conditioning*. He approached me with some nonsense, like "I'm going to get you a record deal and make you a star." Well, he didn't make me a star, but he did get me a deal. First, he got me a publishing deal with Chappell, but the abuse and violence were already happening. He took everything going. The drug of choice in those days was Mandrax, the British version of Quaaludes. You'd take them because they were great for sex, but you would wake up the next day covered in bruises because you'd fallen over... or worse. When Mark wasn't drunk he was charming, and he made sure that I moved in with him in Battersea, rent free. He was a complete snob: he would scream abuse at our very working-class neighbours, who were complaining about him playing super-loud music, and he ran up a bank loan based on the fact that I had a record deal. He used to attack me in public places like [Earl's Court gay pub] the Coleherne, and managed to get me into bed once by drugging me. I should have reported him to the police, but I thought, "Well, he got me my record deal," you know?'

The casting couch may well have originated in Hollywood, but in Britain Edwards was just one of a number of homosexual men in the record industry who were not above using their positions of influence to cajole young men into bed, just as there were a number of young men who would sell their souls, and their bodies, for a shot at stardom. With the legal age for gay sex still set at 21, several of these men would eventually find themselves in trouble with the law.

Sadly, the regularity of the GLF dances held at Fulham Town Hall made them an easy target for queer bashers, and it was becoming increasingly obvious that the Metropolitan Police had no intention of arresting the yobs involved. 'I remember after one GLF dance we were warned that were a lot of gay bashers waiting for us outside,' Rupert Herries recalls. 'They may have been National Front, who were quite big at the time and had been marching through London. Well, they took one look at us "weirdos" as we left en masse, some dressed in drag and others as nuns et cetera, and they fled! It was hilarious!' The far-right National Front had been subjecting homosexuals to abuse from day one, having been established in the same year that the Wolfenden Report was adopted into law, sometimes with unintentionally comical results. In 1969, 20 NF agitators who turned up to cause trouble at a staging of gay-themed play *The Staircase* in Richmond Green were seen off by an 80-year-old usherette, who drove them out of the theatre and into the arms of the police. Unfortunately, the thugs would not always be so easily intimidated, and on occasion it appeared that the police were on the side of the aggressors, not their victims.

Arrests continued: police were accused of overstepping the mark, of taking suspected homosexuals in for questioning without notifying their legal representatives or, in the case of minors (anyone under the age of 18), without the knowledge of their legal guardians. On one utterly ludicrous occasion, Julie Frost, a member of the *Gay News* editorial collective, was stopped and questioned by police while on his way home from a GLF dance – one of the officers took umbrage with Frost's 'Glad to be Gay' pin badge and snatched it off his jacket, telling him that he was confiscating an offensive weapon. Harassment was not limited to the streets of London: in May 1972 the Gay Liberation Society at Keele University announced that the local police had spent eight months compiling a dossier on the activities of all known homosexuals in the area. After raising a formal complaint with authorities, the number of arrests increased. Between 1967, when the Sexual Offences Act was passed, and 1972, convictions for gross indecency in England and Wales increased by 160 per cent.[4] Home Office figures showed that virtually all of the increase came from two areas: those covered by the Metropolitan Police (32 boroughs of London) and the Lancashire Constabulary. It is no wonder that LGBT people in those areas were questioning why they were being targeted.

Police harassment became part of daily life for LGBT people, and arrests at well-known cottages and cruising spots increased. In the seaside town of Scarborough, a dance school and club owned by a judge on popular BBC TV show *Come Dancing* was raided by two dozen policemen and forced to close. The local authorities claimed that they had searched the club because they had heard it was serving alcohol after hours, but owner Ken Parkes knew the real reason. The police acted after a tip-off that roughly a quarter of the club's clientele were homosexual. 'The justices based their reasons on the fact that a number of gay people attended these premises,' he said. 'They could come somewhere to relax and have a drink with normal people. I never had any complaints at all.' The 'normal' people included several married women, who explained that they had never seen any 'indecent behaviour' at the club.[5]

Injustice was rife. In Stockwell, London, a 46-year-old gay man, Kenneth Fairhurst, was murdered, stabbed 22 times with a twin-pronged carving fork by a young man he had picked up in a local pub the previous evening. His assailant was given just two years in prison by the court, after the judge found he was 'provoked' by the older man's advances. At a GLF dance on 30 June 1972, on the eve of the capital's first Pride march, two men leaving hand-in-hand were jeered and had missiles thrown at them. The pair decided to give chase, brandishing milk bottles as weapons. The youths involved scarpered, and the two men returned the bottles to their crate, only to be arrested for being in possession of offensive weapons. The following week, further attacks left one man in hospital, the police again doing little or nothing to disperse the gangs of youths and arresting a friend of the injured man after he accused the police of laughing and joking with the attackers. Tony Reynolds, who had co-organised the first Kensington Town Hall dance, was charged with using threatening behaviour. In court, Sergeant Mervyn Sault claimed that Reynolds had shouted obscenities and raised his arm with his fist clenched, threatening the group of youths. This was denied, not only by Reynolds but also by three independent witnesses to the event. Reynolds admitted to magistrates that he had shouted, 'Look, there's one of them. He's laughing and joking with them – British justice,' and, with the police unable to deny that they had been laughing and joking with the queer bashers, they were forced to withdraw a charge of using threatening words. Reynolds was still fined £5, which was paid by one of the many well-wishers who filled the court's public gallery. At the GLF dance held on 28 July, there was no trouble outside, but inside a crowd of youths who had forced their way in were thrown out after a scuffle by the volunteer stewards and a roadie for one of the bands playing that night. 'You people are no trouble at all,' a member of town hall staff commented. 'It's just these kids with nothing to do. They think they're being big.'[6]

Squidd did not encounter any trouble at the GLF dance that they performed at because so few turned out to see them. 'There were only about 30 people,' Swindells explains. 'It felt like a soundcheck, not a gig. I remember feeling embarrassed that I'd made the band do this.' With queer bashing reaching epidemic proportions, the relentless attacks did a lot to put LGBT people off going out. But like the regulars of the Stonewall Inn, some were prepared to fight back. In November 1970 a company director, John Wetter, was attacked by a gang of four young men in a cottage in Leicester. Unfortunately for one of the gang, Wetter was the head of a precision tool-making company and carried a small knife with him; the following month a court found that Wetter had acted in self-defence when he stabbed 20-year-old unemployed labourer Peter Hope in the heart, killing him.

Unlike Squidd, many artists seemed to enjoy playing GLF fundraisers. Martin Isaacs, founding member of the Half Human Band, recalls that 'no one in the band was gay, nor has come out since, but we generally liked supporting outsider or underground causes, and playing as many gigs as possible was a way to get exposure and attract interest.' The Half Human Band played at least six GLF dances in London between 1972 and 1974, as well as shows for other gay groups, including the Wimbledon School of Art's Gay Society. 'We played Lord knows how many benefits – for [anti-racist political group] the White Panthers, fundraisers for the Windsor and Watchfield Free Festivals – as well as the larger free festivals going,' Isaacs explains. 'We looked forward to playing the GLF gigs because the audience always really threw themselves into dancing, cheering and general mayhem – just our sort of crowd!' At a dance held in St Pancras Town Hall in October

1971, headliners Pink Fairies (an apt name, although none of the band were queer at the time) were supported by Hawkwind. Like the Half Human Band, both acts were happy to play any benefit they were asked to, as John 'Twink' Alder, the Pink Fairies' drummer, recalled: 'The cultural vision was simply to share our gift for free with who we felt were deserving.' Hawkwind's Nik Turner had cause to regret his band's decision to play the gig after he was accidentally electrocuted on stage. 'I used to wear this shirt with bits of metal, sequins, on it,' he said. 'I had this saxophone with a pick-up, and it went through a 100-watt amplifier and a big speaker cabinet or two. I went up to the microphone to say "good evening", and I was blown over backwards by the full force of 10,000 watts coursing through my body... I had really bad burns all over my hands. I was rushed to hospital, but I came back and finished the show. I just thought it was a laugh!'[7]

That was not the first time that Hawkwind, Pink Fairies and the GLF had come into each other's orbits. Eight months earlier, both bands had played at a peculiar event under a flyover. The Dwarves Carnival was held to announce the establishment of a new political party, based on the Dutch environmental anarchist group Kabouters (which translates as Gnomes or Dwarfs, though the members were not necessarily height challenged), but the event ended in chaos after members of the GLF stripped to their underwear, and the police were enjoined by stallholders from the nearby Portobello Market to break up the impromptu festival.

The Half Human Band, Pink Fairies and Hawkwind may have been 'straight', but in the same month that the latter two bands played St Pancras, a genuine queer star headlined his one and only GLF benefit. On 4 October 1971 David Bowie performed a solo acoustic set at a fundraiser in Seymour Hall in Marylebone, less than a fortnight after his first gig with all three members of the band who would become the Spiders from Mars: Mick Ronson, Woody Woodmansey and Trevor Bolder. Bowie had built up a small but loyal following amongst London's LGBT concert-goers, and a brace of gigs at Hampstead's Country Club that July and August had brought a large gay contingent out to see him perform. They caught him at a pivotal point in his career. Earlier that year, he had hooked up with a young gay fashion designer called

Freddie Burretti (born Fred Burrett) after seeing him dance at gay nightclub El Sombrero. Bowie would attempt to turn Burretti into a star, and, in turn, the designer would help turn the hippie spaceman into something altogether more startling and androgynous. The next time Bowie stepped onto a stage, on 29 January 1972, he would unveil Ziggy Stardust to an incredulous audience – an audience partly made up of people who, just a week earlier, had read an interview with their hero in which he announced, 'I'm gay, and I always have been.'[8]

'I went to all of those dances,' says Paul Southwell. 'All of them. The gay scene in the early seventies was either the GLF events or the "normal" gay scene, which had been around for years, long before it was legal: clubs where you knocked on the door and they opened a little hatch and checked if you were gay and either let you in or not. It was all a bit seedy, and I hated it. I knew that I was gay, and I knew that there was nothing wrong with being gay. I didn't want to hide it so the GLF dances were great. I liked the atmosphere and the politics of it; I related to the people I met there, the activists, and I became quite political.

'I thought it was a bit weird that the bands playing were very heterosexual, but I soon realised that there were a lot of gay people in music and the music business, but they all kept it quiet. They didn't embrace gay liberation or the GLF; they wanted to stay in the closet and keep it all secret. The people from the sixties were still running the business in the early seventies: you had all those gay impresarios that were still involved, but they were not "out". Their friends and people in the business knew they were gay, but they didn't actually talk about it or do anything to help gay people or attempt to change the world.'

Since the beginning of the rock 'n' roll era, the British music industry had been run by gay men. Few of them were out, but it was an open secret within the business that many of the era's top managers, label heads, radio DJs and songwriters had helped create a safe, protective space for homosexual artists – so long as they, in turn, did not rock the boat. But by the time the seventies came along, some artists were beginning to question the status quo. Ballad singer Long John Baldry, whose band once included a young piano player named Reggie Dwight, had long given up pretending to be anything other than his outrageous self, and Dusty Springfield had already proved she had more balls than most of her male contemporaries. A new market was emerging, and some record companies, managers and songwriters, notably the team of Alan Blaikley and Ken Howard, began to take more risks. Blaikley and Howard – who would soon team up with Steve Swindells' manager Mark Edwards to make pop music TV shows for international distribution – had been writing songs from a gay perspective ever since their first hit, the Honeycombs' 'Have I the Right' in 1964. 'Having lived through the Second World War, the bleak and buttoned-up fifties, the "peace and love" sixties and the permissive decades that followed, in a catalogue of hundreds of songs, we have covered a very wide range of subjects. Some were simply melodic pop, designed be catchy "earworms", others reflected, and sometimes anticipated, momentous changes in social and sexual mores,' says Alan Blaikley.

Dusty's revelation had passed by with barely the bat of a heavily mascaraed eyelid, but when, in January 1972, the married-with-a-kid David Bowie announced to the world, through the pages of *Melody Maker*, that he was gay, people started to take notice. Before long it seemed as if everyone was jumping on the gay bandwagon; glam rock and glitter pop began to dominate the charts, and bands which had little success previously were now chalking up hit after hit. Embracing androgyny, but often looking like dockers in drag, bands like the Sweet, who had been issuing singles since 1968 and managed to score a couple of novelty hits in 1970, were feted as glam-rock stars simply through smearing a little eyeshadow on their faces and stitching a few sequins to their clothes. Slade – a band from the Midlands with a similar history – also hit pay dirt when they adopted glam rock, after a brief attempt to embrace first psychedelia and then the bovver-booted skinhead look. As Sweet guitarist Andy Scott explained, 'We elaborated on the make-up and clothes, and it has all got a bit out of hand. But the kids like it and expect it. We know where we are at.'[9] Both of these acts, along with Roxy Music, Gary Glitter, Mud and countless others, owe their signature looks and successful careers to the radical drag of early GLF adherents and to genuine LGBT pop stars like Bowie and Marc Bolan, both of whom were making just as many headlines for their choice of clothes and make-up as for their chart-topping discs.

In September 1972 the *Daily Mirror* ran a double-page spread on Bolan and T. Rex percussionist Mickey Finn that went into great detail about their – and their peers' – preferred brands of lipstick and face powder. 'Curly-haired Bolan... says he has been wearing eye make-up since he was fourteen... Other Glam Rock idols who have resorted to paint and powder include Mick Jagger, who took a make-up man with him on his recent tour of America and often wears make-up in public. Eno, of Roxy Music, is also painted and powdered. He wears Mary Quant eyeshadow, eyeliner, pancake make-up and nail varnish.'[10] The same article commented that the average Bolan audience was 'a mixture of hysterical girls and camp-looking boys, many of them wearing sequins on their faces because their pop idol did'. 'The record which seems to have lasted with me all my life is T. Rex's "Get It On",' musician and DJ Hifi Sean reveals. 'It looked really cool and subversive, but it had a kind of cheeky wink, with the playfulness of the groove and the words. I suppose that's something that has gone deep into my psyche, as I would like to think that, in some ways, I have achieved that mix with a few of my own records.'

Bolan admitted to the man from the *Mirror* that on many occasions he had been verbally assaulted for his looks, with men calling him '"you little poof". I just tell them to eff off. This stuns them. They usually come back with: "you talk like we do". After two minutes you could have a green face and they wouldn't care about it.' A few months later, it was Bowie's turn in the spotlight, *Mirror* reporter Deborah Thomas calling him 'the gentleman with the make-up and the hair-do reminiscent of a bright orange lavatory brush', and 'the Glam Rock idol [with] an image as camp as a row of tents'. Talking about his on-stage look, a candid Bowie told Thomas that 'I'm not an innovator. Everything has been done before. I'm just a photostat machine that puts out what has already been fed in.'[11]

With glam or 'fag' rock grabbing headlines, several major American labels made an attempt to capitalise on the trend, signing LGBT artists including the Bowie-influenced Jobriath and out singer/songwriter Steven Grossman. This would be the first time that any major record company would try to market out-LGBT artists to a mainstream audience, but despite both acts receiving positive reviews on both sides of the Atlantic, and Jobriath grabbing headlines as rock 'n' roll's 'only true fairy',[12] neither would reward their companies (Elektra and Mercury respectively) with the kind of sales their media coverage promised. Outside of the mainstream Alice Cooper, Jayne County (then fronting the group Queen Elizabeth) and the New York Dolls began to make headlines for their gutter glam, gender-defying look. Despite being dismissed by British reviewers for being 'representative of a new wave of New York groups who have picked up on Marc Bolan, Slade, Elton John [and] David Bowie in a big way', and playing 'faggot rock',[13] the stateside acts were unique in their levels of hedonism and theatrics. In New York, Jayne County was 'fucking himself with [a maraca] in his artificial cunt and waving the other above his head as he jumps about the stage in some kind of awful climax... He confronts himself with a huge double ended limp rubber penis which he sucks, drools over, swings like a baton while strutting across the stage, stuffs between his legs, leers at the audience with and beats on the floor.'[14] The Dolls, whose androgynous stage gear predated the dangly earrings and satin culottes of Mud's Rob Davis by two years, were dismissed as Rolling Stones copyists: 'a hard rock, camp prissy 100% homosexual group in black tights posturing and imitating all of Mick's stage gestures and leaps.'[15] Their infamy had been cemented in November 1972 when original drummer Billy Murcia died in a bath in a Kensington flat on the last night of their British tour.

'Fag rock' may have been meant as an insult, but Britain's music papers and underground press were full of stories about the country's own glam stars as well as these American usurpers. 'The attitude of the press was very mixed,' Jayne County explains. 'Julie Burchill [then writing for the *New Musical Express*] absolutely adored me, she always gave me great reviews, but one person from *Melody Maker* said that I wasn't much different from Danny La Rue, which was rude – I'm totally different! Danny La Rue would come out in these great glamorous gowns and furs, but I was coming out with holes in my clothing and my stockings, and safety pins pinning my clothes on. They just didn't like me, I guess! It wasn't totally negative, but it was kind of, "Oh, well, we've seen this before."

'No one was doing it; no one was that outrageous and doing real raw rock 'n' roll. Years later, people copied a lot of my act, but at the time it was totally new. The audience loved it: they went absolutely crazy. Some people didn't get it though.

'No one knew what to call it in those days: drag rock, shock rock, whatever. People never said anything around me. I guess they were afraid I'd end up brawling with them if they got on my nerves! That was the reputation I had, but it wasn't real. It came from a big fight I had with [US punk rock singer] Dick Manitoba: I clocked him with a microphone stand [Jayne hit Manitoba after he climbed onto the stage during her performance at CBGB, breaking his collar bone]. People got a little bit afraid of me, and they were a bit afraid of the stage act too.'

Inspired by the freedom of sexual expression that glam rock appeared to allow, struggling actor Richard O'Brien began writing a musical that would exploit the glam-trash aesthetic while also having a laugh at the expense of terrible 1950s B-movies. By the time *They Came from Denton High* reached the stage, in June 1973, it had a new title. *The Rocky Horror Show*, a camp, comic tale of 'mad mutants, tame transvestites and musclebound monsters',[16] proved to be an immediate success, winning the *Evening Standard* Theatre Award for Best Musical that year. Record producer Jonathan King saw the show on its second night and rushed to sign up the company for an original cast album. By August, the show had transferred from the Royal Court's 63-seat Theatre Upstairs to the 230-seat Chelsea Classic Cinema (the first time a live show had ever been staged there), before moving to the 500-seat King's Road Theatre, where it would set up home for almost six years. The look would have a direct impact on up-and-coming artists such as Paul Southwell, who was putting his first band together around the time of its release. 'We were influenced by anything that was cutting edge and outrageous. We wanted to be outrageous,' he explains. Southwell's group, a three-piece he decided to call Handbag, would quickly become an integral part of London's expanding gay scene.

Caked in glitter and lipstick, glam rock allowed gay men to hide in plain sight, and also allowed musicians to write and sing songs about something other than boy meets girl. Like many others, Bowie and his friends (and collaborators) Marc Bolan and Lou Reed would embrace this queer aesthetic, although all three would flip-flop about their own sexuality and their influence on the LGBT community. When Reed announced that he might 'come out with an anti-gay song, saying, "Get back in your closets, you fuckin' queers!"', fan Tom Robinson was disheartened.[17] 'For those of us involved with Gay Liberation, this was disappointing at best and at worst, downright betrayal... Had Lou been a heterosexual impostor all along, only in it for the money?'[18]

'In those days I really did think that we needed to change the world,' says Paul Southwell. 'We'd just had [gay sex] legalised, and things needed to change. We needed a revolution, and I soon realised that if I didn't get involved and do something then it wouldn't happen. If you just sit there and ignore it and pretend it's not happening, or you live in your own little world and pretend that it's all okay, nothing will change.

'I jumped in with both feet. It didn't help my career, but I am glad I did it, and I can rest easy because I was honest! I liked some of those prog rock bands that were playing at the time, but the only one of them I knew was gay was Robert John Godfrey of the Enid; there were not a lot of others who were out. Pink Fairies, what a great name, but they weren't gay. The Pretty Things had Phil May, who was bisexual, but he hadn't come out of the closet. You had to be in the know to know, you didn't talk about it in the press.'

May may not have been ready to talk to the press about his sexuality, but he was not above switching lyrics around to reflect his own interests; he had already included a song about a man coming to terms with his emerging homosexuality – 'Deflecting Grey' – on the Pretty Things' classic psychedelic album *S.F. Sorrow*. Godfrey had been employed as musical director for progressive rock band Barclay James Harvest but would later claim he had been ousted from his role because he was gay. Signed as a solo artist to Charisma by gay impresario Tony Stratton-Smith, Godfrey issued one album, *Fall of Hyperion*, before forming the Enid in 1974. He took his concept for a new album, based on the Tarot, to Stratton-Smith who decided not to finance the project, although shortly afterwards another Charisma signing, former Genesis guitarist Steve Hackett, issued a similarly themed album using the same title Godfrey had suggested, *The Voyage of the Acolyte*. The Enid's debut, now renamed *In the Region of the Summer Stars*, would eventually appear on Decca imprint BUK.

Like Paul Southwell, Tom Robinson was one of a new generation of politically aware singers and songwriters who were beginning to take their first tentative steps into the music industry. From the start, Robinson wanted the songs he was writing for his group to reflect his own life. 'I sang in the church choir,' he says, 'but when I was 13 the Beatles arrived and erupted into all of our lives. I became a big fan of the new beat music that was being made from '63 and '64 onwards, and that's continued for all of my life.

'Around that time, I fell in love with a boy at school, and my attraction to other people of the same sex was happening simultaneously, but I couldn't connect the two. My "straight" contemporaries at school could relate to the "boy meets girl" songs in pop music, but for me there was, on the one hand, pop music that seemed to be about somebody else but was very appealing, and on the other hand my emotional experience which was completely undocumented in music. When I was in my early 20s and I set out on a career in music, that was a continuation of my fandom of the early beat era, and it was only really after discovering the music of David Bowie that music was suddenly about me instead of about somebody else.'

With Bolan and Bowie providing fodder for the press, it looked like queer had gone mainstream. But equality was a long way off yet. At a time when civil rights activists like Angela Davis could be arrested and charged with kidnap and murder despite not being at the scene of the crime, and when the government thought that the solution to the troubles in Ireland was to put more troops on the streets of Belfast, the brothers and sisters of the GLF made sure that they were part of the protest. On 30 January 1972, Bloody Sunday, when British soldiers shot 28 unarmed civilians during a protest march in Bogside, Derry, and 13 people were killed (a fourteenth died later from his injuries), GLF groups across London amassed on Hyde Park to protest. 'How long must this continue?' they asked. 'Irish today: blacks and gays tomorrow.'[19] Alan Wakeman had been arrested the previous November at a Remembrance Sunday memorial in the grounds of Westminster Abbey, after laying a cross with a GLF badge attached to it in an attempt to highlight the many homosexual people who had died in Hitler's concentration camps.* People were indeed angry: the police, they claimed, were 'mounting a campaign against GLF members, with the object of driving them back into the ghetto'.[20]

By now, glam had reached its apogee, and with a band calling themselves Gay Weak End currently doing the rounds of London's nightclub scene, it seemed the time was right to move on. In October 1973 Bolan had announced that 'glam rock is dead',[21] cut his hair and swore off the sequins. That same month, Tom Robinson attended his first gay dance, at Surrey Halls in Stockwell, which had been organised by the South London GLF. 'It was just like all the rural village hall discos I'd known as a teenager,' he explains. 'Loads of shy people sitting round the outside of the room in the semi-dark and somebody playing records. The crucial difference was that men were dancing with men and women were dancing with women. For the first time ever in that innocent non-predatory environment, it was okay to just go up to a man you fancied and ask if he fancied a dance... It may sound banal nowadays, but back then it was a huge liberation. For me, dancing had been one of those things from schooldays – like football – that I'd never really got the point of. That night, thanks to South London GLF, the penny dropped. Afterwards, on the way out, I bought a "Come Out" badge, a GLF badge and a copy of *With Downcast Gays: Aspects of Homosexual Self-Oppression* by Andrew Hodges and David Hutter. It completely changed the way I thought about queer sexuality.'[22]

---

* In Islington in 1986, Labour Party activist Bob Crossman became the UK's first openly gay mayor. A former member of the Inner London Education Authority, Crossman got into trouble on Remembrance Sunday 1986 when his partner, Martin McCloghry, laid a wreath of poppies surrounding a pink triangle motif at Islington's war memorial – an echo of what had happened to Alan Wakeman in 1971. In June 2021 McCloghry unveiled a plaque in Islington, celebrating Crossman's time as mayor there.

6

Have You Heard the News?

'I don't know whether I am against or for Gay Lib. I understand
that they want to have people to be with, so that they're not on
their own. I know that feeling so well. But on the other hand, to
put that many people all together at once is perfect, perfect meat
for the papers to pick upon and ridicule. When you're all together
like that, you can be stamped on immediately.' – David Bowie[1]

As 1972 progressed, it must have felt as if the world was being turned
upon its head. In Britain, unemployment had almost doubled in
just two years, and strikes caused Prime Minister Edward Heath to
declare a state of national emergency. Soon Idi Amin would expel
50,000 Asians from Uganda, despite their contributing 90 per cent
of the country's tax revenue, and Richard Nixon would be re-elected
President of the United States, even though he was already fighting for
his political career as the Watergate scandal continued to unfold. But
amongst all of this turmoil, something quite extraordinary happened:
in the summer of 1972, the first issue of *Gay News* hit the newsstands.

Selling for 10 new pence (the country having gone decimal 15
months beforehand), this tabloid-sized publication was just 12 pages
long, yet for many it carried all the heft of the Bible. Here, for the very
first time, was a publication written for and by LGBT people that was

not sold under the counter in sex shops or could only be purchased by mail order.

There were plenty of LGBT publications before *Gay News*: the muscle mags of the fifties and sixties; *Arena Three*, a groundbreaking magazine for lesbians which first appeared in 1963, and the Gay Liberation Front's own *Come Together* among them, but these were only available to subscribers or, in the case of the latter, at GLF meetings, events or from street sellers. Then, at the start of 1969, *Jeremy: The Magazine for Modern Young Men* appeared. *Jeremy* was the first magazine aimed at homosexuals that was available over the counter at newsagents – the scant few that would stock it, at least. Advertised extensively in *International Times* and similar underground newspapers, *Jeremy* was a conundrum: many of the covers featured artful photographs of barely clothed young men and the word 'gay' prominently, but it lacked the political awareness and confrontational attitude of *Gay News*, and poor distribution meant that few people got to see it. *Jeremy* carried an early interview with David Bowie (set up by his then-manager, Kenneth Pitt, explicitly because he wanted to market Bowie to a gay audience) in which he skirted around the issue of his own sexuality, telling interviewer Tim Hughes that 'I don't feel the need for conventional relationships', without quite coming out.[2]

'I had been volunteering at the GLF office,' says Richard Bolingbroke. 'I used to go in there regularly and there was always stuff to do. I was helping with *Come Together* and I remember *Gay News* coming along. I remember thinking, "This is cool," but getting a magazine like that together was a lot of work. Putting *Come Together* together proved that: you needed dedicated staff and some money. *Come Together* was all mimeographed.'

In the months before *Gay News* debuted, *International Male Advertiser* (which would soon change its name to *Spartacus*) offered gay men a taste of what pubs, clubs and sex shops existed in other parts of the world. *Sappho*, a new magazine for lesbians put together by a 12-strong women's collective, arrived at the same time as *Gay News*, and was available both via subscription and through radical bookshops.

Like *Sappho*, which was founded and edited by broadcaster and lesbian rights activist Jackie Forster and her partner Babs Todd, *Gay*

News was resolutely out and proud, and produced by a collective of gay men and women. 'Some of the homosexual groups like Gay Lib produce their own news sheets,' Suki Pitcher, one of the women involved in the magazine's launch, told the *Daily Mirror*, 'but we want to produce a national newspaper for gay people. We want to avoid any commercial overtones, and will certainly carry no porn.'[3] Suki, her partner David Seligman and the other members of the collective originally wanted *Gay News* to become a registered charity; when that move failed, allies with deep pockets had to be found. With financial support from some high-profile LGBT people, including Monty Python star Graham Chapman and his partner David Sherlock, Roger Baker, the press officer of the Campaign for Homosexual Equality, and Anthony Grey, former secretary of the Homosexual Law Reform Society, the first issue appeared that June, the same month that feminist monthly *Spare Rib* debuted.

From an office sandwiched in between a porn shop and a public house, the *Gay News* collective attempted to produce a fortnightly newspaper that would 'belong to the whole of the gay community. It's for gay women as well as gay men. For transexuals [sic] and transvestites, for anyone with a sexual label but who we like to call "gays of all sexes".'[4] This small band of brothers and sisters were adamant that gay people should be able to purchase copies of *Gay News* wherever they lived, and sent copies to bookstores, newsagents and other outlets around the country. They would often encounter fierce resistance: Britain's biggest newsagents, W.H. Smith and John Menzies, refused to stock the publication. The owners of the Edinburgh Bookshop wrote a terse letter admonishing the collective and telling them that, 'We have no intention whatever of displaying or selling this publication here, and if you cannot arrange to collect these copies from us, they will be dumped with other refuse.'[5] Luckily, other outlets would stock the paper, including branches of Virgin Records, the first of which had opened on Oxford Street in 1971. '*Gay News* was the main purveyor of news,' Paul Southwell explains. 'Most of what was going on was promoted by *Gay News;* that's how we knew that there were meetings or there was a dance or a gig.'

Yet opposition to gay rights continued: in July, Weymouth Town Council announced that it had refused a licence for the CHE's first annual conference, originally scheduled for the following spring. CHE had expected up to 500 people to attend, but the burghers rallied against the initiative, initially endorsed by the town's entertainment committee. 'It seems to be the desire of the committee to get money any way it can, regardless of the standing of the town or the feelings of the people,' former mayor of Weymouth, Wilfred Ward, told the *Daily Mirror*. 'It is a disgusting lead to set, and I feel there are limits below which we should not fall.' 'This will bring in a lot of morbid sightseers who will want to see a crowd of queers,' added councillor John Knight.[6] Not waiting to be given permission to address an audience, that same week brothers and sisters from the GLF took to the stage at a Festival of Light conference in Newcastle, 'frightened a few people when the significance of Gay Lib badges was realised, involved ourselves in a few pointless arguments and then went home'.[7]

From its earliest days, *Gay News* carried news and reviews of the latest record releases, live concerts and film appearances by recognised LGBT icons and musicians known to be gay-friendly. Appearing just a few short weeks after David Bowie's seismic performance of 'Starman' on *Top of the Pops* had angered one generation but enthralled another, the launch issue featured record releases by bisexual movie star Marlene Dietrich and *diva du jour* Liza Minnelli; issue two carried a review of Bowie's latest opus, *Ziggy Stardust and the Spiders from Mars*, and the third issue reviewed Alice Cooper's *School's Out*, the singer and his band causing an uproar on both sides of the pond as purveyors of what the US music press was terming 'fag rock'. *Gay News* was an early champion of Bowie: issue six carried a fulsome review of his August 1972 concerts at the Rainbow in Finsbury Park ('If you didn't see David Bowie at the Rainbow, you missed a remarkable performance by a truly original artist. Whether the gay aspects of his act are just part of the show, or a real part of the world of David Bowie, are unimportant. His defiance of accepted social conventions and the purity streak that runs through all levels of society, including the young and the supposedly aware and informed, does much to break down the barriers that stop so many from accepting and understanding. David Bowie is just what the World needs'),[8] and Bowie would feature as issue 22's cover star. Yet, despite the newspaper championing gay and gay-friendly acts, no record company would dare offer financial support until, in November 1972, RCA took out a half-page advertisement for a concert and album, *Private Parts*, by actor/singer Peter Straker, that Denis Lemon had called 'one of the most important releases of 1972'.[9]

Written by songwriters and producers Ken Howard and Alan Blaikley, the record 'reflected a life passing through various stages of personal and sexual identity,' Howard explains. 'By this time, homosexuality was [becoming] a prevalent topic [and] record companies were not afraid to release material with a gay or bisexual subtext – if indeed they were aware of it! So, songs such as Starbuck's "Do You Like Boys" [written by Howard and Blaikley and issued in 1973] encountered no opposition.' Shortly afterwards, GM, a new record label set up by Rod Stewart's 'flamboyant' (to use one of British tabloids' favourite euphemisms) manager Billy Gaff, began taking ads in *Gay News* for its releases, beginning with the new albums by the Gaff-managed gay singer John Baldry, and former Herd member (and future Status Quo keyboard maestro) Andy Bown.

The newspaper tried to stay independent of the ongoing squabbles between the different factions of the gay lib movement, but nevertheless often found itself involved. Born out of a meeting of GLF supporters, many there were concerned that the paper would be too lightweight for this radical new movement. 'Each of the groups had different politics and agendas,' explains civil rights activist Peter Tatchell. 'Though we did all join forces to organise Pride from 1972 onwards.'

In the first issue, almost hidden among the stories of gay-bashings, the BBC's refusal to participate in discussions with representatives from the CHE, calls to equalise the age of consent, and tales of lesbians being refused service in a gay club in Manchester, was an important announcement: 'The London Gay Liberation Front is planning a week-long series of events as part of this year's celebration of Gay Pride. Theme of the activities will be both an assertion of Gay Pride and two concrete demands: repealing of all anti-gay laws and full civil rights for gay people.' Beginning on 23 June, continuing until 2 July, and marking the third anniversary of the Stonewall riots, London was about to get its first proper Pride, and the city's various gay rights groups would work together to make it happen.

Much of the organising committee came from within the ranks of the GLF, including many who were below the age of consent. The plan was for a series of events across the capital, culminating in a 'Gay Pride Carnival' that would begin with a march and end in one of London's public parks where 'there will be music, food, fun and surprises'.[10] Things did not quite go to plan: on the first night, around 50 members of the GLF were forcibly ejected from both the Coleherne and the Boltons in Earl's Court while trying to sell copies of *Come Together*, although three gay days, a torchlit procession across Clapham Common, performances by the GLF Street Theatre Group, a fancy dress party and a couple of gay discos – where Top 40 hits, Tamla Motown and glam sounds were replacing the prog and heavy rock – fared better.

'We decided to organise a Gay Pride march to combat the invisibility and denigration of queer people,' says Tatchell. 'This was a radical departure from the norm. In those days, nearly all LGBT people were closeted, and many felt ashamed of their sexuality.' Tatchell participated in the organisation of that first event and has been on every Pride march in the capital since then. In 1972 there were no motorised floats, no sound systems, no sponsorship, and no cost to enter; but everyone joining the march knew that they were engaging in an act of political defiance. 'Only 700 people turned up,' he remembers. 'Many of my friends were too scared to march. They thought everyone would be arrested. That did not happen, but we were swamped by a very heavy, aggressive police presence. They treated us like criminals. It was quite scary. But despite this intimidation, we were determined to have a fun time and make our point. The march was a carnival-style parade, which went from Trafalgar Square to Hyde Park. There were lots of extravagant costumes and cheeky banners poking fun at homophobes like Mary Whitehouse. We got mixed reactions from the public – predominantly curiosity and bewilderment. Most had never knowingly seen a gay person, let alone hundreds of queers marching to demand human rights.'

Many of those brave enough to join the march carried placards, declaring 'we demand the right to show affection in public' and insisting on 'total equality now!' Groups from other parts of the country, even sedate little Georgian theme park Bath, joined in and, flanked by police, the 700 snaked their way to Hyde Park. 'By then, most of the women had split away from the GLF, but some of us felt it important that there be lesbians at that protest,' says Frankie Green. 'It was far from what Pride was later to become: it was quite scary, there was a lot of abuse, there was a heavy police presence and there were just a few hundred of us. But it was groundbreaking. There is a carnivalesque aspect to such events when people who are supposed to not be seen, stay powerless or have no rights, claim the streets as theirs. Taking up space and insisting on being out in the world, rather than banged up in prison or psychiatric institutions, or pretending to be heterosexual and staying married in order to keep your job, home or kids. Turning the world upside-down, disrupting the status quo: the GLF turned shame into Pride. That seems light years away from the way Pride, at least in London, has become a depoliticised, commercialised event, which many now view as corporate and co-opted, and you have to register or pay to take part!'

'Unlike nowadays, there was no festival or entertainment after the march – just an impromptu gay day,' Tatchell adds. 'Everyone brought food, booze, dope and music. It was all shared around. We played camped-up versions of party games like spin the bottle and drop the hanky. I won one of the games and my prize was a long, deep kiss with a gorgeous French gay activist. But it was more than good fun. Because we were same-sex kissing in public, which was an arrestable offence in those days, it was also a gesture of defiance. In 1972 homosexuality was still viewed as an illness; lesbian mothers had their kids taken off them, and the police were at war with the gay community – with thousands of gay men arrested for consenting behaviour.'

'Somebody who worked with my father saw me on one of the marches,' Richard Bolingbroke recalls. 'I'm not sure how he knew me, because we all wore make-up, and I had this big fur coat, but they told my father who was completely freaked out – he knew I was gay, but he didn't want someone to see me looking like that. I remember my mother telling me, "Darling, I'm fine with what you are, but don't wear your make-up when you come to see me", but my father said "I don't want anything more to do with you. I'm done." That was it.'

91

On 12 August 1972, just as the fifth issue was being put to bed, Denis Lemon was arrested while taking photographs for *Gay News* near the Coleherne. He was charged with 'wilfully obstructing the passage of the footway of Wharfdale Street' and released on £10 bail. He appeared at Great Marlborough Street Magistrates' Court two days later and, after pleading not guilty, was remanded until later that month.

The real reason Lemon was arrested was for taking photographs of police openly hounding the pub's clientele. The Coleherne was one of London's best-known gay cruising establishments, and police harassment had been increasing in recent months, with a number of people arrested on tenuous charges and claims of excessive force being used by police. After an article in the *Times* linking the GLF to the Angry Brigade, a far-left terrorist group responsible for a series of bomb attacks in England, the police felt justified in denying the GLF places to gather.*

'One of the things we did regularly was go down to Earl's Court and hand out flyers outside the Boltons or the Coleherne,' Richard Bolingbroke explains. 'The Coleherne was the leather bar: people would come down with a bag with their leather gear in, go into the toilets and get changed. Our thing was the same thing that [San Francisco-based gay politician] Harvey Milk was saying: "Come out". Wear your leather, wear whatever you want, but come out and join us. But they hated us! We regularly got beer thrown at us, got pushed over in the street – not by the police but by the guys using those pubs. They did not want their cosy lives disturbed, but we were very "in your face": very, very persistent. We'd throw flyers – with the GLF mission statement and phone number – all over the place and some people would start coming to the meetings... Some people were easily drawn into what we were doing in the GLF, but after a while I think it kind of hit its capacity. The meetings were wild, there was very little moderation going on and there was a lot of dissent about what path we should be taking: often it felt like there were many different groups meeting in this one space, all with different ideas. It must have been quite difficult

---

* Angie Weir, accused of being a Brigade member, was also involved with the GLF, and took part in the first Pride march. Years later, as Angela Mason, she would become chair of LGBT rights charity Stonewall.

to get a foothold in there if your previous experience had just been drinking in the Coleherne, especially for these middle-aged guys who probably had wives and kids at home.'

Lemon – one of the co-founders of the paper and the only one of the original collective to last out the first year – documented his run-in with the law through the pages of *Gay News*; it did not make edifying reading. 'What might interest you is some of the comments the police made whilst I was their guest: "It's bad enough that there are places (The Coleherne) like that"; "Soon all you homosexuals will be driven out of sight again"; "The public has had enough of hearing about your sort"; "If you took a picture of me I'd knock your head off"; "There are 195,000 people in Kensington who would like to see homosexuality stopped"... Most of these comments came from the Station Sergeant at Kensington Police Station, who, on various occasions throughout my two hour stay with them, informed me that I was a "pervert", "a queer", and "an abnormality that had to be stamped out". He also said that he did and always would refer to black people as "wogs", and that they didn't mind, and it was "too bad if they did".'[11]

In court, Lemon admitted that he 'took photographs of police activity because of the number of allegations we have received of police harassment outside the pub. I took a photograph of two policemen coming towards me and the flash-cube accidentally fell off my camera. I stooped to pick it up, without stopping, and they cautioned me to move on. I walked about 30 or 40 yards up the road to take pictures of the activity outside a coffee bar up the road to help us build up a dossier.

'I crossed the road and took more photographs and then I crossed back again to outside the Coleherne and I was standing on the pub's steps to take more photos, and the police warned me again. I walked around the corner in Coleherne Road to take more pictures, and then I moved into Wharfdale Street and began to talk to about four people who were standing there, about the police activity.'[12] Despite his plea, Lemon was found guilty of wilful obstruction and fined £5, paid for by a *Gay News* supporter.

The country's mainstream political parties started to take notice of these noisy young gay people. Perhaps surprisingly, it was the Tories, in the guise of the Greater London Young Conservatives, who first attempted to get gay rights on their party's agenda. At their annual conference in Blackpool, former junior minister Ian Harvey, whose career ended after he was caught with a 19-year-old guardsman in St James's Park in London in 1958, addressed a Young Conservatives fringe meeting at the conference. Now vice chair of the CHE, Harvey had no luck in persuading the party to adopt gay rights, but his appearance marked a noticeable shift, and the UK's political parties would begin to take more notice of the LGBT voter.

Yet if political parties were starting to pay attention, the country's police forces and law courts were not, and police officers around the country continued to use entrapment to secure easy arrests. In October 1972, at the annual CHE conference (which, that year, took place in Brighton), vice president Michael de la Noy told delegates that, 'local authorities all over the country are keeping open public lavatories which they and the police know perfectly well are used as nothing but haunts for those homosexuals who wish to make contacts in such places. The lighting in these lavatories is often non-existent, they are frequently situated so as to be of little use to the general public, and no member of the public ever complains to the police about their use by homosexuals, or claims to have been in any way annoyed. They simply serve as a lucrative source of income for the local courts.' He continued to express his disgust at a court system where a man who 'stole no less than nine motorcars was fined £10. But fines of £50 for an act of indecency in these so-called public lavatories is now commonplace... The patrolling by police officers of public lavatories to entrap homosexuals and often actually procure an offence constitutes a disgraceful misuse of police manpower.'[13]

Dirty tricks were being employed by the police to drive LGBT people back into the closet, but many were spurred into action by this constant abuse of power. 'It was a political issue, to stand up and be counted,' says Phil Booth. 'At the time you could not see yourself in the public sphere – anywhere – and it was vital to stand up and be seen. That was the first thing that you did, and that was a political act. It was the way to begin to change things: if nobody did then nothing would change.' There were no positive images of LGBT people in the media, no portrayals on television, and none in the cinema, where a gay man or a lesbian was inevitably portrayed as a maniac, an object of pity or a figure of fun, and joining a Pride march could feel like taking your own life in your hands.

'I went on all the marches from about 1974 onwards,' says Paul Southwell. 'I was absolutely petrified, frightened to death – I honestly thought that I would be shot or stabbed or something, which when you look back sounds ridiculous. Once I got there and saw other people, including my friends in solidarity, chanting, "We're here, we're queer, get used to it", it was great. But there wasn't the big kind of festival at the end in those days. When we got to Hyde Park or wherever it was, there would be someone with a megaphone doing speeches before everyone dispersed to go home and get ready to go out again later, to discos in King's Cross or Stockwell. There wasn't much music: Tom Robinson would have done a few songs, but I can't remember anything else.'

'I would have thought that everybody there thought that Pride was a political act, not an afternoon out,' says Phil Booth. 'I wasn't frightened or worried about being seen, and to some extent I put that down to naivety, because at that stage I'd not encountered any serious anti-gay feeling. There was the usual low-level prejudice but certainly not violence, the unwanted attentions of the police or anything like that.' Frankie Green agrees: 'Everything we did was political. We were angry, and we wanted to change the world. So pretty much everything we did expressed our politics.'

Sadly, while many LGBT people were enjoying their first chance to express themselves freely, the GLF commune in Brixton was forced to close after repeated attacks by students from the local comprehensive school. In one particularly violent incident, the front door was kicked down, and one member of the commune had a milk bottle broken over his head. An attempt by the GLF to talk to the school was abandoned after the headmaster called the police, and they had to leave their Tulse Hill home and move to alternative accommodation in Notting Hill.

'I moved down to Brixton at one point; it didn't last long, and we got the hell out of there,' says Richard Bolingbroke. 'I remember getting bricks thrown through our window – it was not exactly friendly territory. We moved there to back up the GLF office, give them some extra manpower, but it was too scary. There were lots of kids around who thought that bashing peoples' heads in was a good thing to do, so we left.'

The following March, South London GLF would establish a new home in Brixton – then one of the city's most deprived and crime-riddled areas – squatting in an abandoned shop at 78 Railton Road. Converting the upper floors into accommodation, and the basement into a venue for discos and meetings, the group quickly established the South London Gay Community Centre. Handily positioned next door to one of the two women's centres on Railton Road, the members of the collective wasted little time in making their presence known, launching a regular disco night at Lambeth Town Hall, offering counselling and health advice via a telephone helpline, a dance workshop and even their own South London Gay Liberation Theatre Group, which would later become the Brixton Faeries.

GLF enclaves outside of London began to supplement their regular discos with dances featuring live bands. In Newcastle, a local but now-forgotten band luxuriating in the name Karl Mary Marx, entertained the brothers and sisters and, like the live music nights, it would not take long for Pride to spill out to the provinces too. Gay days had already become a regular part of the calendar in GLF strongholds such as Brighton and Manchester, and in Birmingham a hastily arranged Pride weekend took place, complete with an impromptu march and a small rally outside the city's council house, a week after London. In May 1973, ahead of London's second Pride, Oxford became the first city outside of the capital to hold its own Gay Pride Week, organised by the city's Gay Action Group. The week included a Pride march, discos, a drag show and a picket of the local branch of W.H. Smiths, targeted for its refusal to stock *Gay News*. Brighton followed suit in July, despite the fact that the local branch of the GLF had been banned from holding any events in venues owned by the town council.

Oxford had already provided the venue for the first British Women's Liberation Conference (held in February 1970), so perhaps it is not surprising that there was support in the city for a Pride festival. 'Quite a lot of straight organisations wanted to be part of it: trade unions and things like that,' Peter Scott-Presland – who had been on that first Pride march in London – recalls. 'We had very good relationships with the trade unions and the women's movement, so there were a few hundred people marching. We assembled near the roundabout on the other side of the river, came up the High Street, turned into Cornmarket Street and ended up outside Carfax College, but there was nothing after it. We didn't have any big speeches or entertainment.'

One year earlier, the Oxford Gay Action Group had staged the Pride Punt, probably the first organisation – and Oxford the first city – to use the word Pride for a gay event in Britain. 'In May 1972 we had 10 or perhaps a dozen punts, one of which had an Oxford Gay Action Group banner on the front of it, and we punted up the river to a place called Parson's Pleasure, a nude male bathing spot above a weir,' Scott-Presland explains. 'You had to pull your punt up rollers to get to the bathing pond, and women had to go around the outside, quite a long way round, but we thought, "Sod this for a game of soldiers!" We got our punts up the rollers and the women lay down in the punts so you couldn't see them, and we punted into Parson's Pleasure and then, in the middle, we put the banner up, the women leapt up and we chanted "Out of Parson's Pleasure and onto the streets". Parson's Pleasure was a well-known gay cruising ground, and these middle-aged dons looked on in absolute horror, covered their genitals and ran away like headless chickens... all except one, who instead of covering his genitals covered his face!'

A gay life was developing in towns and cities around the country. Not everyone could afford, or had the inclination, to go to London every weekend, and regional groups – including those set up by the CHE and GLF – provided social and political support for men and women in their own communities. 'I started the first gay discos in Oxford, in a pub called the Cape of Good Hope, fundraisers for Oxford's Gay Switchboard,' Scott-Presland adds. 'I think part of the reason that first Oxford Pride happened is that we had one of the first gay switchboards. Certain types of organisations give you a sense of solidarity, of identity, and switchboards are one of those, just as *Gay News* was as a publication. And also we had three separate socio-political organisations in Oxford at the time: the CHE, which had two branches, the town branch and the university branch; the GLF; and the Oxford Gay Action Group (OGAG), which I was involved in, which was basically made up of people who did not want to be involved with either CHE or GLF, but who wanted to forge an independent path. A lot of people came out through the OGAG.'

While the provinces were discovering that it was possible to enjoy gay-themed entertainment on their own doorsteps, back in London, Tricky Dicky's gay disco nights had become so popular over the last two years that the management of the Father Red Cap asked him to do more. As he was already working six nights a week and offering a 'straight' disco for weddings on Saturdays, Richard Scanes could not help. The pub carried on regardless, bringing in other DJs to fill the empty spots and running a women-only disco on Fridays. But same-sex couples dancing together was a provocative and political act, one the law sought to put a stop to. In June 1973, over a period of eight days, plain-clothes police made a number of arrests at the Father Red Cap, charging pub manager Alf Carmody, owner John Adams and DJs Tricky Dicky and Solly Mead of 'permitting a disorderly house'.[14] The fourth and final raid took place on the eve of London's second Pride march.

One of the arresting officers would later tell the court that he had seen around 40 people one night and that 'the men appeared to be effeminate... wearing perfume and tight-fitting clothes. There were two males and six females dancing and they were all closely embraced and fondling each other's private parts.'[15] According to Carmody, the police objected to 'Men dancing together in close contact, groping each other with hands in trouser pockets,' and they intended to invoke a Victorian law to ensure that such wantonness would not continue. 'I've been running the club for two years and never had any trouble,' Carmody told Gay News. 'Then last Thursday night about 10 policemen went steamrolling upstairs. They stopped the music dead and began asking for names and addresses. A few of the boys said flatly that they wouldn't give them the information. I spoke to one of the policemen in the kitchen, and he said to me, "You're running a club for poofs and lesbians." He said they had kept watch on the disco for four particular nights – they had plants up there – and they believed I was running a disorderly house.'[16] Almost 250 years after the raids on London's Molly houses, the police were still using the same tactics to entrap gay people. Carmody continued to run disco nights but told punters that they would not be allowed to dance closely together. 'We explained it over the microphone to the boys, and they were terrific about it. I know all the regulars that come in, and they weren't angry with the hotel, they were angry with the men in blue.'[17] Shortly after the raid, the pub had its supply of alcohol cut off by the brewery; a new licensee was brought in, who demanded an end to the drag and the discos, and Tricky Dicky was forced to move to the nearby Sun and Doves in December 1973.

The raid on the Father Red Cap certainly infected the mood of the Pride march: Gay Pride Week 1973 saw the factions that already existed within the organising committee split apart. The more radical, politically motivated GLF continued to organise events around the anniversary of the Stonewall riots, which would usually end in a picnic where those who had joined the march were encouraged to bring food to share and instruments to play, while the CHE would wind up organising their own week of Pride celebrations. All of these events would be dutifully documented in the pages of *Gay News*. The nationally circulated fortnightly offered LGBT people outside of the capital a tantalising window into queer life in the metropolis, and its pages of small ads, community listings and directories of local CHE and GLF groups gave readers around the country the comfort of knowing that they were not alone.

7

Taking a Stand

'Despite the explosion of permissiveness and the exploitation of sexual susceptibilities, homosexuality has remained a dirty word. The homosexual has, perhaps, in the public image, been translated into a caricatured "camp" figure but, in reality, remains a "sick" being, condemned to a twilight zone of loneliness and guilt.' – Aberdeen Evening Express[1]

More than a decade before the miners' strike would highlight the interaction between unions and the LGBT community, as depicted in the hit 2014 film *Pride*, there was already a move to gain support for gay rights from the trade union movement. As early as February 1971, the various groups within the GLF came together to demonstrate alongside the TUC (Trades Union Congress) against the government-backed Industrial Relations Bill, legislation to curb the power of the unions. Over 140,000 people marched through London, the biggest public gathering in Britain since the celebrations that followed the end of the Second World War. Bob Mellors, one of the co-founders of the GLF in Britain, was among the 100 or so GLF activists taking part. 'Gay liberation is part of wider issues such as the oppression of blacks, of women and of the workers,' he told reporters, while handing out leaflets that proclaimed that 'nearly a million trade unionists are gay'.

'We are calling into question the whole idea of sexuality, of stereotypes which put even straight people into strait jackets,' he added.[2] Those wider issues also included the ongoing protests against the Vietnam War, with the brothers and sisters of the GLF encouraged to join vigils outside the American Embassy in London.

'I wanted to change the world!' laughs Lord Smith, then young Labour party activist Chris Smith, now Baron Smith of Finsbury. 'I grew up in the 1960s; it was a time when we were all optimistic. We thought that it was possible to bring about change and it was possible to do that by democratic means: campaigning and persuading and arguing and making the case and convincing people.

'It took me quite a long time to come to the personal realisation that I was gay, so when that first bit of decriminalisation happened it sort of passed me by. Of course, I rapidly came to realise just how important it was. I didn't get involved with the GLF, but I was aware of them partly because I was heavily involved in Labour politics. I went on quite a number of marches and demonstrations wearing my Labour movement hat and noticed people from the GLF marching in solidarity. I remember thinking, "Oh, that's rather good", but partly because I was still coming to terms with my own sexuality, I didn't go over and say, "Can I come and march with you?"'

In September 1972 an out-gay man, and an unapologetic member of the GLF, had been elected as a city councillor in Durham. Sam Green, a psychiatric nurse, won the Crossgate ward on behalf of the Liberal Party, defeating a former mayor who had been on the council for 14 years. Green offered to stand down the following year after objections from other members of the council that his story was attracting the wrong kind of interest – including from the makers of the television documentary series *World in Action*. Some of his fellow councillors denounced him on screen: 'Can't homosexuals be cured by pills or treatment,' said one, while a second added that he 'wouldn't actually go out with Sam for a drink'. Green proved to be a popular and effective councillor, although sadly his status as a local celebrity did not protect him from becoming victim to a gay bashing by a pair of 17-year-old youths. A few months after he took up his seat on the council, the Liberal Party fielded another out-gay man, CHE member Michael

Steed, in a by-election in Manchester. Although Steed came second to the Labour candidate, he became the first openly gay man to stand for election to the House of Commons.*

The campaign by certain British tabloids against the encroaching homosexual menace continued unabated throughout 1973. In January the *People* reported that Mike Roberts, singer with *Opportunity Knocks* winners the Pleasuremen, had decided to quit showbiz as 'the homosexuals in the business really turned me off. One fellow in Brighton said he was in love with me and wanted to marry me. Others used to mince up to me and say I was a lovely mover. Ugh!'[3] The police continued to infiltrate safe spaces: in April and December 1973 raids took place on the Paint Box, a club in Marylebone, with the management and owners fined because drinks were being served after hours, contravening the club's licence. The police, who made several visits before making their arrests and taking details from the club's customers, found that the clientele was 'predominantly male, and several of them were dressed in female clothes. Men were dancing together'.[4]

Gay News employed street sellers, supporters of the newspaper who would go into venues frequented by LGBT people to sell copies and promote subscriptions, but even that could lead to arrest: in Glasgow, where homosexuality was still a criminal offence, a street seller was arrested for breach of the peace. Back in London, a man selling copies in the Boltons was stopped and searched by three plain-clothes policemen. When he arrived at his home address later that evening, the same three police were sitting in an unmarked car opposite the entrance to his flat.

Peter Tatchell had been conducting a survey, on behalf of the GLF, into the lives of Britain's LGBT community, soliciting participants through fortnightly advertisements in *Gay News*. 'This was coordinated with the National Council for Civil Liberties, and the support of CHE,'

---

* In December 1976 Green was selected by his local constituency as a prospective Liberal candidate for the city in the upcoming general election. He lost out in the selection process to Chris Foote Wood (brother of the late writer and comedian Victoria Wood), who came third at the election.

he explains. 'Our aim was to document and publicise the then-unknown scale of police harassment, in order to pressure the police to change and to provide evidence that the handful of sympathetic MPs could cite when pushing for further legal reforms. The survey feedback was self-selected and therefore not a proper randomised UK-wide survey, but the replies revealed many outrageous examples of police victimisation. We demonstrated that the police were institutionally homophobic.'

Alongside attacks from the mainstream press and the continual police raids, it seemed that some in the underground were falling out of love with the push for LGBT equality: even the formerly supportive *International Times* went on the attack, calling gay poet Allen Ginsberg an 'old fairy' on their front page and attempting to shock readers with sensational tales of the outrageous exploits of those involved in 'fag rock'.[5] 'I think its dwindling circulation had something to do with that,' says Paul Southwell. Courting controversy, the floundering paper took to printing photographs of a naked Jackie Kennedy Onassis[6] and, in a bizarre move, images of a cast of film director Roman Polanski's penis that bisexual jazz singer George Melly was shopping around.

Meanwhile, morals campaigner Mary Whitehouse climbed upon her high horse once again. Backed by *Guinness Book of Records* co-founder Ross McWhirter – now a household name thanks to being co-presenter, with twin brother Norris and entertainer Roy Castle, of BBC TV kids' show *Record Breakers* – she took umbrage with ITV's plans to broadcast a documentary film about gay US artist Andy Warhol. Despite a judge initially siding with the pair, in mid-February the decision was overturned: the documentary was screened by ITV, and McWhirter was ordered to pay half of the court costs.*

---

* McWhirter, who, along with his brother, was co-founder of the right-wing lobby group the National Association for Freedom, was assassinated by the IRA in 1975. He had lobbied for years for the British government to take a tougher stand on Irish terrorism, going so far as to suggest that it should be compulsory for all Irish nationals in Britain to register with the local police and to provide signed photographs of themselves when renting flats or booking into hotels and hostels. Prior to his death he had offered a reward of £50,000 out of his own pocket for information that might lead to the arrest of an IRA cell carrying out a bombing campaign in London.

If the media would not support gay rights, then it was up to LGBT people themselves to continue to press for action. In January, at a general meeting of the University of Bristol's Students' Union, a motion was passed – without opposition – which called for trade union support for homosexuals who had been dismissed from their jobs simply for being gay, a perfectly legal process at that time. Similar motions were passed at other universities around the country, showing a promising growing support for LGBT people in Britain's places of learning, yet all the while the GLF continued to splinter. At a 'think-in' held at the University of Leeds in mid-February 1973, the Scottish GLF group announced that they felt neglected by groups in England and Wales who had no concept of the difficulties faced north of the border, where gay sex was still illegal; *Gay News* was accused of being sexist and *Come Together* of being too London-centric; and the Notting Hill GLF group were charged with demanding that every male member cross-dress, insisting that any man who refused to do so was a chauvinist pig. Delegates left the weekend feeling that little had been achieved, apart from an agreement to produce future issues of *Come Together* outside of London.

The seaside town of Morecambe was the venue for the Campaign for Homosexual Equality's first national gay rights conference, in April 1973. Jointly organised by the Scottish Minorities Group, the conference was a call to arms to local CHE groups to start working together for change nationally, and the three-day event resolved to demand an end to all laws that 'showed distinction between people on the grounds of their sexual orientation'.[7] This followed two years of sustained political schmoozing: while the GLF was barracking in the streets, members of the CHE had been talking to the Select Committee on Discrimination in the House of Lords, which culminated in an apology from Lord Longford 'for disparaging remarks about homosexuals contained in his report on pornography', the 520-page *Longford Report* which had seen the Mary Whitehouse supporter dubbed 'Lord Porn' by *Private Eye*. The GLF held its own national 'get together' in Brighton in October 1973, sponsored by the gay society of the University of Sussex, that featured a disco, arts festival, talks and a dance. To mark its first anniversary, in

June 1973 *Gay News* ran its own survey, conducted by CHE member John Gough, into various members of Parliament's attitudes towards gay people. The Brighton branch of the CHE took umbrage in his sharing such information with *Gay News* and censured Gough.

That November, at the annual National Union of Students (NUS) conference, representatives from the University of Reading and Lanchester Polytechnic (now Coventry University) tabled a motion on sexual freedom, calling for an end to the harassment of gay people, the lowering of the age of consent to 16 and demanding that the laws covering homosexuality in Scotland, the armed forces and the Merchant Navy be brought in line with those covering England and Wales. The NUS, which represented hundreds of thousands of students across the country, became the first member of the TUC, and the first Labour-affiliated union, to pass a policy in favour of gay rights.

The move to work alongside the unions cut both ways. Using the then-widely accepted figure of at least five per cent of the population being homosexual, it was estimated that there were around a million trade union members who would identify as gay or lesbian, and many of those were under constant threat of losing their jobs should they dare to come out in the workplace. Simultaneously, many union jobs were under threat from the Conservative government and its recently introduced austerity measures and public sector pay caps. Inflation was out of control, thanks partly to an embargo on oil from the OPEC countries, which was immediately followed by industrial action by Britain's coal miners. With most of Britain's electricity coming from coal-fired power stations, in December 1973 Prime Minister Edward Heath introduced a three-day week in an attempt to conserve energy and, shortly after the New Year, called a general election, putting the blame for the current crisis on the unions. The public disagreed: Heath lost his majority in the House of Commons and, with no offers of support to form a coalition, was forced to concede the role of Prime Minister to Labour's Harold Wilson.

In the run-up to the election, activists from CHE London sent questionnaires to candidates, asking their opinions on subjects including homosexual equality and the age of consent. Very few bothered to answer and, of those that did, fewer still would officially endorse the CHE's position on such sticky subjects. One of the new Labour MPs entering Parliament in March 1974 was Maureen Colquhoun, representing Northampton North. The following year – after her sexuality was made public by the press – Colquhoun would become Britain's first openly lesbian MP, having left her husband (and father of her three children) for Babs Todd, co-publisher of *Sappho* magazine, who she met while campaigning for women's rights. Colquhoun gained a reputation, first as a town councillor and then as an MP, for her outspoken views, and was regularly referred to in the press as a 'gasbag'. Although she had been accustomed to being censured by her local branch of the Conservatives, she soon faced opposition from within her own party. Two weeks before Colquhoun took her seat, Todd, addressing a symposium in Belfast, talked about how both she and her unnamed partner had previously been married for several years and that both had children who now lived with them and who accepted their mothers' lesbianism, 'without any apparent emotional or psychological upset'. She went on to tell the 100 or so delegates that, in order to change attitudes towards homosexuality, homosexuals themselves had to change first: 'Those of us who have been so conditioned to hide, to be ashamed, to feel guilty and to lead double lives... It is difficult for us to change. We have to face the possible loss of jobs, of friends, of support from parents and even the vilification from our own gay brothers and sisters who feel threatened by our openness.'[8]

Demanding the right to be referred to as 'Ms' in the House of Commons, Colquhoun's own party refused to support her due to her 'obsession with trivialities such as women's rights'.[9] Her constituency party chairman, Norman Ashby, wanted to deselect her because, he said, 'She was elected as a working wife and mother... This business has blackened her image irredeemably.'[10] That vote was overturned, and very few people outside of Parliament paid much attention until *Daily Mail* columnist Nigel Dempster outed her and Babs in the press after gatecrashing a housewarming party. In the aftermath of the revelation, the pair became targets for the press and for homophobes: after Colquhoun's London home was broken into twice in the space of a few months, she raised concerns that the house was being bugged by the police.

A vocal supporter of women's and LGBT rights, Colquhoun spoke in Parliament on subjects including sexual equality, appeared at pro-abortion rallies, supported Northern Ireland's Women's Peace Movement and campaigned to encourage other MPs to come out. 'My sexuality has nothing whatever to do with my ability to do my job as an MP,' she rightly said, but in 1979 she lost her Northampton seat to Tory Tony Marlow, who opposed gay rights and claimed campaigners were seeking to 'legalise the buggery of adolescent males'.[11]

In April 1974 the Belfast Gay Liberation Society, run by student volunteers from an office at Queen's University, began offering an LGBT information service; within two weeks, they were receiving 100 calls a day from towns and cities across Northern Ireland and were forced to look for other premises after jamming the university's telephone switchboard. That same month, the first annual National Lesbian Conference took place in Canterbury, 15 years before a similar event would take place in the United States, and they would continue for a number of years. 'It was an exciting time,' remembers Frankie Green. 'It was a very buzzy event, and to have live music for dancing was something lots of women enjoyed. The van we had arranged to hire to transport our equipment from London fell through as the company refused us when we turned up, a bunch of scruffy women musicians. We thought we'd have to cancel, but when we went back to the Women's Liberation Workshop, women there who were heading off to the conference offered to take our instruments, which were carried off in a variety of cars and minibuses and were reunited with us later. There was great goodwill of that kind.'

At the beginning of May 1974, local elections took place across the UK. A few weeks earlier, at their annual conference, the Young Liberals had passed a resolution calling for sex education in schools to include positive depictions of gay and lesbian couples, and for a reduction in the age of consent for homosexual men. Typically, the newspapers of the day saw this as a call to arms for paedophiles, zoophiles and for children as young as five to be taught about same-sex relationships: 'How stupid of the Young Liberals wanting to teach children about homosexuality. Next it will be bestiality or the like.'[12] Agony aunt Marje Proops, writing in the *Daily Mirror*, was one of the few voices of reason: 'I applaud the Young Libs' stand for a more open-minded attitude to those members of society who are still made to feel ostracised by those who call themselves "normal". The time to direct children's thinking in decent, human terms is when they are very young... Many schoolchildren who go through the homosexual stage, which is common to nearly everyone, worry about their sexuality... Such children need to be told that most youthful homosexual passions fade as puberty directs them to the opposite sex. Or that if it doesn't they are not doomed monsters. They need to be reassured, to be helped to lead full lives, whatever their eventual sexual preferences.'[13]

In the London constituency of Tulse Hill, South London, the GLF fielded three candidates: Malcolm Greatbanks, Alistair Kerr and Michael Mason. The trio stood on a platform that demanded better housing, education and social services for local people, and made themselves popular by forming bonds with women's groups, the local BAME community and with groups representing squatters, the homeless and the poor. In a country where libraries refused to carry copies of *Gay News* but were happy to offer members the opportunity to peruse the latest issue of *Spearhead*,* the paper of racist political group the National Front, it was, perhaps, unsurprising that none of the three candidates were elected. Greatbanks would later stand on behalf of the GLF in the October general election; on the evening of the poll count several of his supporters turned up at Lambeth Town Hall in drag, raising more than a few eyebrows in the process. Also in October, the annual CHE conference took place at the Winter Gardens in Malvern. Whereas GLF dances had been marked by their promotion of prog rock acts, the entertainment offered to CHE delegates came in more sedate forms, such as the lesbian nightclub singer and actress Polly Perkins performing songs from her latest album, *Polly Perkins –*

---

* At a council meeting in May 1974 the committee in charge of Harrow libraries took the decision not to stock publications including *Gay News* and the left-wing daily *Morning Star*; however they decided to keep *Spearhead* on library shelves 'for a further six months' trial'.[14] The National Front also lobbied libraries in other parts of the country (including Gateshead in January 1975) to make *Spearhead* available.

Liberated Woman, singer-songwriter (and, later, lawyer) Gideon Wagner and classical pianist Peter Katin, who was also the president of the CHE Music Group.

Despite having achieved so much in such a short space of time, by late 1974 it seemed as if it were all over for the Gay Liberation Front. The initial excitement and energy had all but dissipated; the third annual Pride march was a lacklustre affair, and those that did join were subjected to abuse from onlookers. 'It wasn't very big,' Alison Rayner concedes. 'We eventually hooked up with a few people in Trafalgar Square, but I remember that there was a certain amount of unpleasantness from some of the people who saw us along the route.' No new issue of *Come Together* had appeared in over a year and the constant infighting had become too much. The GLF all but disappeared with little more than a whimper, but in its short, tempestuous life it helped lead LGBT people out of the ghetto and into the mainstream; by the end of 1974, many of Britain's major cities had gay bars, regular gay discos, LGBT switchboards and social groups to nurture and support their own, local scene.

The all-London weekly meetings ceased to be, and many of the city's GLF offices, collectives and communes were disbanded. The Caledonian Road office was taken over by the newly formed London Gay Switchboard, and the South London Gay Community Centre remained one of the few GLF enclaves in the capital. Switchboard, the UK's only national LGBT helpline, is still running today, offering a vital service, as Scottish singer Horse McDonald, a patron of the charity, recognises: 'It means that no matter who you are, or where you are, you've got someone to talk to. That's incredibly important. Had Switchboard been around when I was growing up, I would have been on the phone. I would have been a bit nervous, but I would have done it.' In April 1976 the South London Gay Community Centre would be forced to disband, evicted by the building's owners, but by then a lack of funding (several applications had been made to Lambeth Council, but all had been met with disdain) had seen most of their good works come to an end. The building was sold to the council which, rather than investing in redevelopment, knocked it down.

But it was not all bad news. Although the different LGBT rights groups were finding it impossible to work together in the capital, in other parts of the country people were much more willing to find common ground. In Manchester a Gay Alliance, including the local GLF, CHE, the Manchester Gay Women's Group, the Lesbian Collective, and the university's Homophile Group, formed and opened a gay information centre and helpline, available seven nights a week. The Alliance found support from the local Quakers, who allowed them to use the Friend's Meeting House for events and organised picnics, discos and coach trips to other events around the country.

Despite the passing of the Wolfenden committee's recommendations some seven years earlier, there was still massive inequality, not least in the age of consent. In November 1974 the CHE held what they claimed was the first rally of its kind ever seen in Britain, in an effort to gain parity. In truth many of the gay lib rallies that preceded had featured men and women carrying banners and placards demanding an equal age of consent, and the GLF had been openly protesting this disparity since August 1971, but this would be the first time that a group as large as the CHE, which then boasted a paid-up membership of around 5,000, had asked its members to assemble in one place to demonstrate and to publicly out themselves. Coaches were booked to carry members – and their friends and supporters – from CHE strongholds around the country to converge on Trafalgar Square.

There were other demands too: the CHE wanted the government to consent to allow gay men and women the right to public displays of affection; they wanted to lift the ban on gay people in the armed forces and Merchant Navy, and they wanted the laws covering homosexual activity in England and Wales extended to Scotland and Ireland, where homosexual acts were still outlawed. In short, full parity. 'The law is full of ridiculous anomalies,' CHE secretary Howarth Penny told reporter Bob Phillips. 'In Scotland and Northern Ireland, for instance, acts between men of all ages are illegal, but between women they aren't. In England, homosexual acts are illegal if one or both males is under 21, but they're legal for women of all ages.'[15] The CHE, along with the Scottish Minorities Group and Union for Sexual Freedoms in Ireland (USFI), had been lobbying for change in Scotland and Northern

PUBLIC MEETING

SOCIETY AND ITS HOMOSEXUALS: WHY THE LAW MUST BE CHANGED

Speakers:
HUMPHRY BERKELEY
ALAN FITCH, M.P.
ANTONY GRAY

Chairman:
THE DEAN OF MANCHESTER
THE VERY REVEREND ALFRED JOWETT

FRIDAY, 11th NOVEMBER 1966, AT 7-30 p.m.
HOULDSWORTH HALL, 90 DEANSGATE,
MANCHESTER.

Meeting sponsored jointly by the North-Western Homosexual Law
Reform Committee, 460 Bridgeman Street, Bolton and the Diocese of

▲
Flyer advertising an open
meeting of the Homosexual Law
Reform Society, Manchester 1966.
Author's collection

Flyer for the GLF newspaper
Come Together, 1971.
LSE Hall-Carpenter Archives
▼

▲
GLF protestors in
Trafalgar Square,
August 1971.
***LSE Hall-
Carpenter
Archives***

David and
Angie Bowie,
with son Zowie
(Duncan Jones),
June 1971.
Mirrorpix
▼

The GLF ►
Manifesto
booklet,
1971.
***Author's
collection***

london 1971   10p

**gay
liberation
front
manifesto**

Ted Brown, Noel Glynn and Peter Tatchell at the first Gay Pride in 1972.
Photo courtesy of the Bishopsgate Institute
▼

▲
The Coleherne, Earl's Court, mid-1970s.
Mirrorpix

OPPOSITE
Poster for the Northern Women's Liberation Rock Band, 1974.
Image courtesy of the Women's Liberation Music Archive ►

◄ Campaign for Homosexual Equality conference, Malvern 1971.
Alamy

Peter Tatchell and ► members of the GLF stage a sit-in at the Chepstow, Notting Hill, October 1971.
Photo courtesy of the Peter Tatchell Foundation

Festival of Light protest, Hyde Park, September 1971. *Mirrorpix* ▼

GLF at the ► Women's Lib march, March 1971. *Mirrorpix*

GLF ► supporters on the streets of London, October 1972. *Getty Images*

The Northern Women's Liberation Rock Band perform in Edinburgh, 1974. *Image courtesy of the Women's Liberation Music Archive* ▼

Advert ► for Steve Elgin's single in *Gay News*, 1974. *Author's collection*

▲
Publicity photo for
Handbag, 1978.
Paul Southwell

Marc ▶
Bolan, 1975.
Mirrorpix

Jam Today, 1977.
**Photo courtesy of the Women's
Liberation Music Archive**
▼

OPPOSITE ▶
Tom Robinson on
stage at Pride, 1978.
Getty Images

Frankie Green at the Women's ▶
Festival, Amsterdam, 1977.
**Photo courtesy of the Women's
Liberation Music Archive**

◄ Pride marchers take a break, June 1977. *Mirrorpix*

Protestors march against the convictions handed out in the *Gay News* blasphemy trial, 1978. *Mirrorpix* ▼

◄ Jayne County at the premiere of Derek Jarman's *Jubilee*, 1978. *Mirrorpix*

▲

Steve Strange struts his stuff at
Global Village, 1979. **Getty Images**

◄ Mark Bunyan,
circa 1979.
**Photo by
Larry Brown,
courtesy of
Mark Bunyan**

▲

Maureen
Colquhoun,
the UK's first
openly lesbian
MP, April 1980.
Mirrorpix

Marilyn ►
and Andy
Polaris, 1981.
Shutterstock

ALISON RAYNER - BASS   FRAN RAYNER - SOUND ENGINEER   TERRY

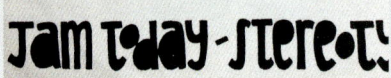

Jam Today - Stereoty

▲

Jam Today's EP, *Stereotyping*,
1981. **Author's collection**

Bloolips go to America, 1981. ►
Author's collection

Divine live
on stage at
Heaven, 1981.
Getty Images

TOP RIGHT
Freddie
Mercury,
New Orleans,
1981.
Mirrorpix

Pat Fernandes,
George Michael,
Norman Scott
and Divine
at Bolts, 1983.
*Photo courtesy
of Norman
Scott*

◀ Pride march,
June 1983.
Mirrorpix

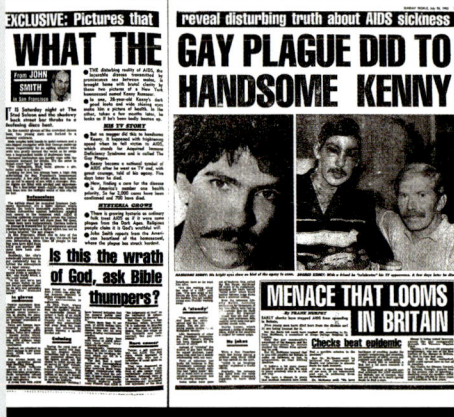

▲

The *Sunday People* covers AIDS, July 1983.
Mirrorpix

▲

Poster for *Pits and Perverts*, December 1984.
Author's collection

Frankie Goes to Hollywood, October 1984.
Mirrorpix

▼

◄ Jana Runnalls and Rosemary Schonfeld, Ova, 1984.
Photo courtesy of the Women's Liberation Music Archive

Ireland for years and, in 1975, the three groups pulled together a draft Sexual Offences Bill in an attempt to reform the law and bring the punishments meted out for indecency and soliciting in line with those of England and Wales. The laws would remain unchanged for now, but one tiny step forward was achieved when the CHE phone line, London Friend, supported by Islington Council, secured an Urban Aid Grant from the Home Office: the first ever government grant to a gay-led organisation in Britain.

Students from Queen's University in Belfast travelled to London for the demonstration, and activists marched from their meeting point to the Northern Ireland Office, the Scottish Office and on to Downing Street, just three weeks after the re-election of Labour's Harold Wilson. In all, around 2,500 people turned out for the demonstration, which the CHE hailed as 'the biggest ever gathering of British homosexuals' and the largest gay demonstration in Europe.[16]

8

Sisters Are Doing It for Themselves

'The stereotyped lesbian is of muscular build, wears a plain felt hat, cropped hair, a collar and tie and flat-heeled shoes. Nothing could be further from the truth. The majority of lesbians are constitutionally quite like other women.' – Brenda Maguire[1]

Although glam was dominated by male acts, the early 1970s saw several female artists – including Suzi Quatro, lesbian singer-songwriter Joan Armatrading and four-piece rock band Fanny (which include both lesbian and bisexual members) – start to make headway too. Their success inspired other women to explore the possibility of a career in pop music.

'Some women I had met in the GLF who I had gone to a Women's Liberation Movement conference with suggested getting together to make music,' percussionist Frankie Green recalls. 'They knew I had played drums in a group before. We invited women to join us through a notice in the London Women's Liberation Movement Workshop newsletter and rehearsed there, at a squat in Covent Garden and in council flats and other squats. Loads of women were interested and eventually a group emerged, the London Women's Liberation Rock

Band; other bands formed in similar ways, such as the Northern Women's Liberation Rock Band. We endeavoured to create our own music that reflected our politics and ideas. Culture is integral to political movements and feminism is no exception. In the Women's Liberation Movement, there was a great proliferation of art forms: music, drama, dance, painting, pamphlets, posters, poetry, novels, film, et cetera.

'We wrote songs about feminist issues: the struggles and campaigns for women's control of our own bodies; housing; relationships between women; solidarity.' Self-penned songs included 'Male Chauvinist Oink' and 'Equal Pay Blues'; the group's manifesto railed against a world where 'Pop lyrics present women as sex objects for men... Men think nothing of singing about women as "baby", "doll", "my girl", in other words, as their playthings, their possessions.'[2] 'We also played cover versions or changed lyrics, as in "Street Fighting Women",' Frankie continues. 'We saw skill-sharing as important, and doing everything ourselves, organising our own events. A basic premise was that of putting politics into action, to complement debates and theory. That band was majority lesbian, as were subsequent ones I played in; all-lesbian groups also formed, such as the Harpies, Newcastle's Friggin' Little Bits, and many others.'

The London Women's Liberation Rock Band made their live debut in October 1972, at a Women's Liberation Conference in Acton Town Hall. 'It wasn't so much a gig as a workshop,' Frankie adds. 'We set our instruments up in the hall during the lunch break and handed out lyric sheets so that women could join in. It was chaotic fun. We wanted to encourage women to be a part of it, and not to have a separation between audience and performers – we were all a part of the movement.' Inspired by the same ideals, in late 1973 Luchia Fitzgerald and Angela Cooper, the instigators of Manchester's GLF group and now running a women's centre in the city, founded a new act, the Northern Women's Liberation Rock Band.

'Luchia had a background in music,' says Angela. 'A lot of Irish people do. She used to be in a showband when she was little and was singing all the time. I had been in the school choir, but that was the limit of my experience and aspirations. I didn't think that I had a good voice, but there were a few people that we knew... We had a bit of a pool I guess. The women's centre acted as a sort of hub, so there were a lot of women coming in and out and dozens of groups going on; there was a cross-fertilisation of ideas, and out of that mix came this idea of forming a band. We wanted to have our own things. A lot of the music of the time reflected male, sexist attitudes – "Brown Sugar", for example.

'We felt like we could do anything,' Angela adds. 'We had this clear objective to prove that women could do it. We didn't know anything about PAs and amps though, so I went to ask some musician friends [future members of post-punk act the Durutti Column]. Manchester was like a little village then; everybody knew everybody. They were really helpful. We bought these massive speakers (which weighed a tonne and had to be carted about) and a valve amp, microphones and stands, and we had to figure out what plugged into what. I don't think any of us had played any electric music before that; the guitars had been acoustic, I'd never sung using a microphone, and we had to balance that against the drum kit... We were all learning.'

In June 1974 around 900 women came together in Edinburgh for the sixth national Women's Liberation Conference. Chief on the agenda were new demands the movement sought to adopt, including legal and financial independence for women, and 'an end to all discrimination against lesbians, and the right of all women to a self-defined sexuality'. 'There was this big conference happening,' Angela continues, 'and the idea grew: "What if we got a band together and played?" There were no women's bands; you might occasionally see a woman playing an instrument on *Top of the Pops*, but that was it. We had about six months to get it together, so we started to meet in the front room of the Women's Centre and try a few things. As I recall somebody looked at me and said, "Can you sing?", and I said that I didn't know, but I had a go and apparently I could, so I became the lead singer! But it was all about our desire to sing for the movement, it was not "I want to be a pop star". We were trying to think of what songs we could do that you could dance to... a bit of reggae, a bit of soul, a bit of Tamla, and we were writing some of our own stuff about what was happening.' The songs the band rehearsed for their Edinburgh debut included Jimmy Cliff's big chart hit 'You Can Get It if You Really Want' and 'Marge's Song' from feminist singer-songwriter Susan Straight Arrow. By now news was reaching Britain of a new American record company, run entirely by women and issuing records by women about their own lives and experiences. 'We had heard about this record company, Olivia, in the States, so we started listening to what they were doing and that inspired us,' Angela explains. 'We couldn't think of a name that everyone would agree on, so we ended up with one that nobody particularly liked! But it said what it was on the tin.

'We were playing a hall in this big university building in Edinburgh. It was hot, and Luchia decided to take off her T-shirt and put her waistcoat back on again, but the women started shouting, "Leave it off!" So, she took her top off and hundreds of women in this room all started taking their tops off too. There was this security guard in a peaked cap at the back of the hall who couldn't believe what was going on. It's an indelible moment in our history. Presumably for the women in the audience that was an incredible moment where they, with hundreds of other women, could dance to a women's band, throw their tops off, throw their bras off too, if they wore one. There are women who are grandmothers now who can still recall that moment. It was a great experience to have had.'

All across the country, women recognised that rock and pop could be used as tools to combat oppression and express political ideas. Shortly before Christmas 1974, during a wide-ranging conversation in their London squat, Caroline Gilfillan, Marion 'Benni' Lees (both former students from the University of York) and Nony Ardill decided that the time was right to start their own women's rock band. Benni and Caroline were classically trained and had performed in a band while at university, and Nony was a talented guitar player, but none had played rock music in a band before. After only a few weeks of rehearsals, they played their first gig on Valentine's Day 1975 as the Girl Guides; by April they had expanded to a six-piece, with singer and saxophone player Ruthie Smith (another University of York alumni), Sharon Nassauer on keyboards and drummer Susy Hogarth, and now calling themselves the Stepney Sisters after the location of the squat. Although they initially identified as heterosexual, within a short space of time at least two members of the band would begin lesbian affairs, causing the

Stepney Sisters to reassess their previously heteronormative approach: their song 'The Sixth Demand' was a plea for individuals to be able to define their own sexuality. 'We all think it is a crucial issue, [a] feminist and general political issue,' Gilfillan told *Spare Rib*'s Marion Fudger. 'To have your sexual freedom is very important.'[3]

'The Women's Liberation Workshop had a building in Earlham Street, in Covent Garden which, at the time, was very run-down,' Alison Rayner explains. 'There were squats all along Earlham Street, and I went along to some meetings there. I got involved with the committee that was organising a "women's bop" for International Women's Day, in March 1975. I knew that there was the London Women's Liberation Rock Band that I later discovered Frankie Green had been in, but I don't think I had seen them or the Northern Women's Liberation Rock Band. But I had seen the Stepney Sisters, and we booked them to play at Conway Hall. I remember seeing them and thinking "I have to do this! I have to be in a band!"' That same month, alongside an article on discrimination against women in orchestras, feminist monthly *Spare Rib* carried a copy of the Northern Women's Liberation Rock Band manifesto. In it, Angela, Luchia and the group railed against a music industry that kept women in their place, and that was 'controlled by a gang of male, profit-hungry parasites' who 'take away the power of people to express themselves through music and turn music into a power over them'.[4]

Rayner's ambition to be part of a group began before she hit her teens. 'By the time I was 11 or 12, I was playing guitar a lot. All the boys were in bands, but it was really hard as a girl to get into a band. I persuaded my parents to buy me an electric guitar and an amp for my 13th birthday, as by then I was at boarding school and I'd found a couple of kindred spirits to play with. One girl had a drum kit and the other managed to get a bass; we must have been terrible, but I loved it!'

Alison realised early on that she was not heterosexual, but pressure to conform was immense. 'I was a bit confused about it all. I'd had boyfriends; it was the thing you did. Everyone assumed you were straight. I had these very intense emotional relationships [with women]; I suppose you would call them romantic friendships which never became physical. I knew that what I was feeling was so much

116

more than what I felt when I was with my boyfriend. In my last year at school, I had my first sexual relationship with a girl who was a year older than me, and it suddenly went "ding!" in my head! I remember thinking, "Oh, my God; I'm queer." And queer in those days was an insult; it had very negative connotations. I remember thinking, "I don't know anybody like me." I felt alone. A couple of months later, I left school. The relationship didn't work out: she had a boyfriend anyway and she said to me, "I can't hack this... it's too stressful. It would freak my parents out." We're talking about 1969, it wasn't a great time to be gay.' The following autumn, Alison enrolled at art school. 'I didn't study music. You couldn't study popular music at a higher level: you could do classical music, but that wasn't my thing. I carried on seeing guys for a couple of years but I kind of knew something was going to shift.

'I spent some time living in Washington DC, and that's where Olivia Records started. I was at one of the first concerts that Olivia Records put on, with Meg Christian and Cris Williamson. I quite liked it, but it really wasn't my type of thing. Around about the same time, there was an album out, *Lavender Jane Loves Women,* by Alix Dobkin [with Kay Gardner and Patches Attom]. The American scene was ahead of us, they had more money, there were more of them; it was all a little bit more sophisticated,' says Rayner. A completely separate women's music scene was developing in the United States. It had always been difficult for women to break into the mainstream: if your face did not fit, or your sound was not what the men running the industry imagined that consumers wanted, there was little likelihood of getting signed. Female musicians, songwriters, producers and audio engineers began to establish their own labels, their own distribution network and their own tours. Selling through bookshops, through adverts in the women's press and at concerts, lesbian and bisexual artists were finally being given a platform, and lesbian singer-songwriter Cris Williamson's album *The Changer and the Changed* would go on to become one of the biggest-selling independent albums in American history. Britain's female artists could not help but be inspired by the American scene. 'We were definitely directing our music towards women,' adds Rayner. 'And we did want to be very independent. We bought our own PA very

117

early on, got our own van... We wanted to drive ourselves everywhere, carry all of our own gear... We did not want to be seen as weak or feeble in any way. We perceived that sound engineers had a lot of control, and we wanted to be the ones in control of our own sound. We did not want to be shut away.'

Gay men may have had to watch out for harassment from the Old Bill, but gay women had the added imposition of trying to establish themselves in a world where all women, not just lesbians, were routinely treated as second-class citizens or objectified sexually. 'We all dealt with homophobia and sexism on an almost ordinary, day-to-day basis,' says Rayner. 'Particularly being young women, you constantly got comments – and if you were women doing stuff without men that could attract a lot of unwelcome approaches. Some of the time we were in a slightly exclusive environment because we played a lot of women-only gigs: women's liberation conferences, Women's Day events, lesbian dos. However, we also did a lot of other general political stuff. There were lots of benefits for abortion rights, and while many weren't women-only, they were mixed crowds of men and women who were supportive, who wouldn't give us a hard time. But we did play colleges and more general gigs, and there you could get groups of young guys who just couldn't handle it and were a bit unpleasant.'

'We had a really great time. I've had a great time with all of the bands I've been in, but in [Rayner's subsequent all-women band] Jam Today we were constantly arguing and discussing – we probably talked almost as much as we played! We discussed everything we did to the nth degree because it all got questioned anyway. If we played very rocky music, we were questioned about why we were playing 'cock rock'. We were questioned about what we wore: should we be getting dressed up? What does that say? Should we be on a stage: does that mean we're putting ourselves above other people? There were arguments about why we should be paid for playing – we were paid a pittance, it would barely cover our expenses, but there were a lot of women telling us that we should be playing for free... Initially there were about eight of us in the band, with a trumpet player and a sax player, two guitars, piano, bass, drums and a singer... and my sister, who became our sound engineer. It was very exciting, but we argued

118

too, about politics, working-class politics, socialist politics. There were lots of strikes and demonstrations happening in the seventies and we played many benefits to raise money for these causes... We played on the backs of lorries at some of those demonstrations in London and in Birmingham. It was a really intense time.'

One of the other women in the band, Anglo-Spanish/Polish percussionist and vocalist Josefina Cupido, remembers that these were exciting, heady days for political and feminist music and theatre. 'It was fantastic creatively, and I felt more at home with my sexuality,' she says, 'but it was also hugely confusing politically. I felt there was a real tug of war between radical lesbianism and the separatist feminist movement emerging.' In the late 1960s she had been a dancer, working in a flamenco troupe on cruise liners, where she became fascinated with rhythm, drums and percussion instruments, before moving to London in 1970. 'The glitz blinded me! And although it was wonderful, I was thrown into a different glamorous world which was either very heterosexual or very camp; it was all very unreal for a 16-year-old. I could hardly understand how to put make-up on or wear a dress, and it was very disconnected from, say, growing up and learning music skills from weekly lessons, or at music college or on the jazz circuit at that time.

'I met Betty Smith, a fantastic jazz saxophone player, on my first voyage on the Cunard Liners when I was 16. She was the first woman instrumentalist I had come across: most jazz players I met were men and the women were, in my experience, singers. I was very influenced by her and her husband, Jack Perdie, a composer and arranger who was part of the emerging UK jazz world. They took me under their wings and influenced me to play drums. As soon as I arrived in New York, I bought a pair of sticks, a practice pad and the book – *Buddy Rich's Modern Interpretation of Snare Drum Rudiments* – that I am still studying to this day. I fell in love with the drums and improvisation.' Josefina describes her well-meaning stepmother telling her to 'take off those Doc Martens and grey socks; take that dress, put it on, find a man and don't tell your father you're a lesbian! It will kill him!' She told him anyway, and he lived to be 101. 'It was very difficult as a lesbian woman to bring together all the different threads that were emerging

119

at that time and know which one to catch hold of for self-development,' she explains. 'There was a crazy, amazing explosion of events going on, with Vietnam, nuclear disarmament and, later, the class struggle during the Thatcher years all influencing me. You had to balance that with a woman's image of women in music, the industrialisation and commercialisation of a woman's image and women's socio-political history, feminism, lesbianism social politics, heterosexual feminism, radical feminism coming in from the USA... Incredible but also confusing times too. At that time, I felt that there was no love lost between gay men and lesbians, despite the need to unite. I hope we have learnt from that!'

While the women's music movement continued to develop and provide a comfortable and nurturing environment for new lesbian and bisexual female artists in America, in Britain lesbian bands were struggling in an industry dominated by men. Few solo women performers were openly out, the most notable exceptions being singer and actress Polly Perkins, who had for a short time been one of the presenters on hip sixties TV show *Ready Steady Go!* and now ran her own cabaret bar in London, and jazz singer Shirley Kent, who funded her own lesbian-themed folk album *Fresh Out*, issuing it in 1975 under the name Virginia Tree, and selling copies via *Sappho* and *Gay News*. Joan Armatrading's career was gaining momentum, but she was still some way from achieving mainstream fame: it would be more than a year before 'Love and Affection' would become her first Top 10 single, in November 1976.

At Hammersmith Town Hall on 20 September 1975, the Stepney Sisters played a benefit for London's Gay Switchboard, supporting Handbag, who earlier that year had been signed to Jet Records: the first out-gay rock band in Britain to win a recording contract. That particular gig was interrupted, and finally abandoned, after two bomb scares, a regular occurrence in British cities at the height of the 'Troubles' in Ireland, but during their career the Stepney Sisters became fixtures of the fledgling feminist music scene, playing dozens of benefits for women's charities around the country, and often crossing paths with the Northern Women's Liberation Rock Band. 'We got to know the Stepney Sisters really well,' says Angela Cooper, 'and there was a little bit of a romance between one of their group members and one of the women in the Northern Women's Liberation Rock Band! The two bands – and all our gear – went up to Bentham, in the countryside near Lancaster, and spent a weekend talking, exchanging music and playing together in a barn.'

Although the band split in 1976, the two singers fronting the Northern Women's Liberation Rock Band continued to perform together, and went on to establish Manchester's radical printing company, the Amazon Women's Press. The London Women's Liberation Rock Band also split up but, like Angela and Luchia, Frankie Green was not through with music yet. 'Every week the Women's Liberation Workshop would produce a newsletter, and Frankie put in a notice along the lines of "women wanted to get together and play music or form a band",' Alison Rayner explains. 'I knew who she was, because some time before her flatmate had been selling a van and I went down to see it, and I heard Frankie playing the drums... They had a garage or a shed at the back, and I heard this drumming and thought, "Oh, my God! That is fantastic!" When I saw her name on the ad I thought, "I have to do this", so I rang her up and said I wanted to come. I went down to her place, her shed in Peckham, and two or three other women went along, one of whom was Terry Hunt. It was Terry, Frankie and I who formed Jam Today out of that first meeting. I took my guitar, but Terry was already a really good guitar player. What we really needed was a bass player, and I thought that maybe I could do that... So, that's why I started playing the bass! I loved singing, but I really didn't have the voice or the confidence to be the singer, but bass was such a cool instrument.

'I wouldn't ever consider that we were separatists, although there were a lot of women who were. They only wanted to engage with women, but I've never really wanted to be in a ghetto, and I always felt like that when it came to being gay or being a lesbian and being a woman. Of course, it was very reassuring to be playing amongst all women. We all listened to a lot of music, and all of my musical heroes were men; I was hardly aware of any women who played instruments. I remember in the sixties the Honeycombs had a woman drummer, and the Applejacks had a woman guitarist, but that was it. I didn't know, at that point, about people like Carol Kaye; I didn't know that I was actually listening to her on all of those American chart hits, because as a session player her name was never mentioned. I think a lot of the women that we played to really appreciated these events where music was being made by women for them. Though there was also a certain amount of aggro... There was quite a big working-class lesbian movement who would have seen us as being a bit middle class and privileged, even though we were a very mixed group. It was intense. There was a lot happening.'

The aggravation that Rayner experienced was not just class-based: media hostility and the threat of physical violence was ever present, and if heterosexual society had their knives out for LGBT people, on occasion the community gave them ammunition. Over the last weekend of February 1976, around 500 women descended on Bristol for the third annual National Lesbian Conference. The Moulin Rouge, once the city's plushest gay club (closeted actor Patrick Cargill had visited when in Bristol, accompanied by several underage young men) but now very much on its uppers, had been hired out by conference organisers for their exclusive use; however the management of the venue decided not to tell their regular clientele or their door staff. Conference attendees were enjoying an evening of entertainment, including live music from local Bristol musicians, a play put on by women from Bradford and a disco, when a scuffle broke out between some of the women and several men who were told – in no uncertain terms – that their presence was unwanted. At least four women were injured, including one who had her jaw broken and another who was knocked unconscious. All of the workshops that were due to take place on the Sunday were cancelled, and a committee was convened to handle the fall-out from the affair. The altercation helped the local police force – who had raided the club on several occasions, fining managers and owners for serving alcohol to underage punters and for not adhering to the rules stipulated for members-only clubs – get the place closed down permanently. In October the Moulin Rouge's application to have its licence renewed was turned down.

It would take the happenstance meeting of a Briton residing in France, and a recent émigré to London, to really kick-start the lesbian music scene here.

In 1976 Canadian-born musician Rosemary Schonfeld, then fronting four-piece folk-rock band Rockwood and living in a squat in Kentish Town, met British-born musician Jana Runnalls. 'Jana had been living in Paris working as a bilingual secretary for a literary agent,' Rosemary explains. 'She was also a successful street singer and had a recording contract with a French record label. Her main genre was blues, but she extracted herself from the contract when it turned out they wanted her to sing everything in French. Jana was already identifying as bisexual, and I met her while she was visiting a friend who lived in a group of communal squats near me.' The two quickly became a couple. 'I had finally reached a point where I could acknowledge to myself that I was attracted to women. Jana was my first lesbian relationship. She left Paris to come and live with me early in 1976.' Those first few weeks together were blissful, then one night their drunken neighbour and a few of his friends decided to lay into the two women, violently attacking them. After spending the night on a friend's floor, the pair were taken in by another friend, Jamie Hall, a violinist who lived in a gay commune in Brixton – the Brixton Faeries.

It was while they were living in the commune that Rosemary went to her first lesbian bar, Vauxhall's Festival Inn. 'It blew our minds,' Rosemary laughs. 'We had never been around so many dykes before! Two of the men in the squat had befriended a lesbian living in Scotland, through GRAIN, a rural gay network, and she came to visit them while we were there. She took us to the Festival Inn. With hindsight, it was a life-changing experience.' Not long after, Jana and Rosemary's band was born, initially named the Dykier Than Sky High Forever Band, before, in an homage to *Monty Python's Flying Circus*, settling on the rather more user-friendly Lupin Sisters. 'I've no idea where that first name came from,' Rosemary admits. 'No doubt we were stoned when we came up with it. Something to do with being open and proud dykes forever reaching for the sky, I guess. Everything happened very fast: I don't think we did that many gigs with that first name.'

The politically charged atmosphere at the squat introduced them both to new perspectives, and Jana and Rosemary soon found that their songs were becoming more and more political. 'The political perspective helped make sense of our personal experiences,' Rosemary explains; early releases included 'The Lesbian Fighting Song' and 'Self-Defence', with its provocative opening line, 'One day I'm gonna kill a man in self-defence'. 'Being singer-songwriters, we naturally started writing about what was happening in our lives. The gay, lesbian and feminist movements were taking off, and our politics and music became inextricably linked. We tried not only to be political with our lyrics, but with our lifestyles and work.

'We realised that there was a real hunger for political songs written and performed by lesbians. We all shared the burning desire to play, create and develop our music in a safe environment. Women were still not allowed the freedom of forming and leading bands. It was a fight to be allowed to be anything other than the eye-candy singer fronting a load of men – or you could play the flute.' Within a year or so, the Lupin Sisters would become Ova, one of Britain's first recording groups consisting entirely of out-lesbian and bisexual women.

Alison Rayner and Terry Hunt, bass and guitar players respectively with Jam Today, were inspired by the US women's music movement to set up their own label, Stroppy Cow Records, Britain's first independent, lesbian-run record company. 'There were three incarnations of Jam Today,' Rayner explains. 'People left for different reasons, and Terry and I really wanted to be independent and out of the music industry. [The band] started before punk, when there weren't that many independent labels or recording studios around.

'After the first band folded, Terry and I wanted to keep going, so we formed a quintet, but at the same time we thought that we really needed our own record label. The name Stroppy Cow came about because the Women's Film Group had got some money from the BFI [British Film Institute] to make a film, different takes on the story of Rapunzel [*Rapunzel Let Down Your Hair*, released in 1978]. In one of them, Rapunzel was a singer/songwriter, and she meets a women's band, and we were the band! We had to record some pieces for the soundtrack, so we went into a studio and we met Sarah Greaves, who was learning how to be a sound engineer with Tom Newman, who had produced the Mike Oldfield album *Tubular Bells*. There was another guy in the studio, and he made some reference to one of the women being a bit of a stroppy cow, the usual kind of insult to women, so we thought that's what our record label ought to be called.

'Jam Today coalesced around Terry and me. We started up this record label, and then recorded the *Stereotyping* EP. Around the same time, we got to know Rosemary and Jana of Ova, and we did an album with them: Josefina and I came in together to add bass and drums. We had all kinds of grand notions of having a record label just for women to record for, and although it did not continue very long it was great while it lasted.' Although it would never reach the heights of its US counterpart, the women's music movement in Britain introduced feminist ideas and political commentary into music, theatre and the arts, and would inspire female musicians for decades to come.

9

Queer Things Are Happening

*'I was astounded to learn that certain young Liberals have urged
that homosexuality be included in sex education in our schools.
One can only guess at the untold mental damage that could result
if these trendy people have their way. Are these young Liberals
totally irresponsible by encouraging the young to enter the twilight
world of the homosexual?' – Coventry Evening Telegraph*[1]

Much of what passed for LGBT culture during the first half of
the 1970s was imported from the States. The discs that Tricky
Dicky was spinning – just like those played by his compatriots around
the country – came predominantly from Black American artists. The
music that was filling dance floors was soul, from the Motown and
Philadelphia stables, and a newly emerging hybrid: disco. It was the
imported sounds of George McCrae (whose 1974 single 'Rock Your Baby'
was the first disco single to top the UK charts), the Hues Corporation
and similar acts that people were dancing to; the only domestic sounds
being played came from glam rock artists, until Indian producer Biddu
linked up with Jamaican-born singer Carl Douglas in London to produce
Britain's first big disco hit, and worldwide smash, 'Kung Fu Fighting'.

Soon singles by out-gay and gay-friendly artists would find their
way onto the decks of Britain's professional DJs, including Valentino's

1975 release 'I Was Born This Way', marketed via the pages of *Gay News* as the world's first gay disco single. Despite the best efforts of gay songwriters and producers Ken Howard and Alan Blaikley, with their new duo Starbuck (and the 1973 release 'Do You Like Boys'), or Steve Elgin with his self-written 1974 single 'Don't Leave Your Lover Lying Around (Dear)', no out British artist would enjoy chart success until 1978. Elgin's management would accuse the BBC of banning his disc, having dropped it from the station's playlist after initially showing interest in making it 'record of the week' on Radio 1's David Hamilton show.

The success of Tricky Dicky's travelling gay discos caught the attention of brewery chain Bass Charrington (owners of both the Boltons and the Coleherne), who approached the DJ and offered him a regular weekly spot at Fangs, the vampire-themed disco in the basement of the Great Western Royal Hotel, opposite Paddington railway station. 'I'm very pleased about it,' he told *Gay News*. 'I've always had to make the first approach in the past, but this time they've come to me and asked if I'd like to do it.'[2] Sadly, although the night proved popular, Dicky's disco only lasted for six weeks, after which the venue's owner, the British Rail-operated British Transport Hotels, pulled the plug. 'We have very carefully considered the situation regarding the Tricky Dicky operation,' they told the brewery, 'and regret to inform you that we must ask you not to renew their agreement when the six weeks contract is lapsed. There are many factors affecting our decision and I think you will understand that there are certain risks which we do not feel justified in taking. This therefore presents us all with a challenge to find an equally lucrative replacement.'[3] Reputation, it seemed, was more important than financial reward: Tricky Dicky had filled the 600-capacity venue for the few weeks he was there, but hundreds of homosexuals descending on Paddington Station every Monday night was too much for British Rail to handle.

For the majority of society, homosexuality was still anathema and, sadly, homosexual victims of crime were still treated with disdain by the media, even if they were one of their own. On the afternoon of 6 December 1974, after they had been contacted by several of his friends, police discovered the bloody, battered body of journalist, radio

127

producer and former Conservative councillor Donald Willcox at his Kensington Home. Willcox, who was known to frequent the area's many cottages and cruising grounds, had been beaten to death with the casing of a WWII artillery shell, which he had been using as a doorstop. Police were convinced that Willcox had been the victim of a queer bashing, and that he probably knew his murderer. The coroner at his inquest concluded that Willcox was 'an active homosexual and his life from all indications was a promiscuous one'.[4] The inference was clear: homosexuals danced with danger and deserved what happened to them. After years of campaigning for better treatment by the media, absolutely nothing had changed.

That same evening, Handbag played a GLF dance in King's Cross. 'We were doing the pub circuit then, lots and lots of gigs in London,' Paul Southwell, who truncated his surname to South while in the band, explains. 'We got one at the Prince Albert in King's Cross. I had been going to their gay discos, and one night they decided to put us on. We went down a bomb. It was a great little gig. Everybody liked us, and that's where I first met Tom Robinson. We knew of each other because of *Gay News*. We'd had little articles in there, and I used to put our gigs in *Gay News* and *Time Out* and all of those publications that would list gigs, so he must have been aware of Handbag just as I was aware of his band, Café Society. He came along to the show and stopped to introduce himself.' Not long after, Handbag signed their first recording contract, to a company owned by the notoriously gangster-like Don Arden who, in 1982, would become father-in-law to Black Sabbath singer Ozzy Osbourne. 'We signed to Jet in '75,' says Southwell. 'As a band we were really tight by this point: we were as tight as a duck's arse! We used to play two, three, maybe four nights a week, so we had all these original songs, with all the harmonies sorted; it was a good little band.' Despite assurance from Arden's son David that Handbag were going to be the next big thing, Jet would drop the act the following year, and the album that Handbag recorded for the company remains unissued to this day.

In February 1975 Marc Bolan announced, via the pages of the *Record Mirror*, that he was 'bisexual, but I believe I'm more heterosexual, 'cos

I definitely like boobs. I always wished that I was 100 per cent gay, it's much easier.'[5] Given Bolan's days as a major contender for chart success were behind him – he would only score two further Top 20 hits in his lifetime – the timing of Bolan's admittance hinted at a desire to still appear relevant. But the revelation was nothing new to the people who knew him, from his first manager Allan Warren, who shared his home and his bed with the star when he was still Mark Feld, to his mentor Simon Napier-Bell, who confirmed in a 2006 interview that Marc 'was completely bisexual. I slept with Marc. But he also liked girls. Privately he was never discreet about it, or careful.'[6]

Rather than bandwagon-jumping, it may have been the more accepting public atmosphere and his recent relocation to Los Angeles that gave Bolan the confidence to be more honest with his fan base. In any case, his revelation was a bit old hat: no one had heard the phrase 'gender fluid' in the mid-seventies, but the concept of androgyny was nothing new, and bisexuality had become so fashionable that pop royalty including David Bowie, Lou Reed and Elton John had all already declared themselves to be sexual switch-hitters, and Alice Cooper had admitted that, if he had the choice, he would have liked to have been either bisexual or, preferably, pansexual: 'The prefix "pan" means that you're open to all kinds of sexual experiences, with all kinds of people. It means an end to restrictions, it means you could relate sexually to any human being, it means an end to unreal limits. I like that idea.'[7] Eleven months earlier, Freddie Mercury had attempted to come out, telling the *New Musical Express* that 'I am as gay as a daffodil, my dear', although drummer Roger Taylor had immediately dismissed his posturing, telling the *NME*'s Julie Webb that 'Freddie's just his natural self: just a poof really.'[8] Guitarist Brian May had been equally as keen to declare, via the pages of *Melody Maker*, that 'we're worried that the name Queen will give people the wrong impression'.[9]

Musicians may have been happy to talk about their sex lives in the pop press, but in the real world being LGBT still made you vulnerable to attack, either from the authorities or from psychopaths. Throughout the summer of 1975, police in London were on the hunt for a serial killer. After solicitor Michael Shepley was found murdered, 'with his head battered and throat cut'[10] in his flat in Pimlico, they quickly associated the horrific crime with another murder, that of accountant Thomas Bradford Wilson, three months earlier. Wilson, who also lived in Pimlico, had died from similar injuries and his flat had been robbed. At least three more serial killers would prey on London's gay community over the next two decades, yet instead of courting the local LGBT community in their hunt for the killers, raids on London's gay venues continued unabated.

The police's prurient interests were not limited to those who frequented the city's gay pubs. Country Cousin, a cabaret bar and restaurant situated above an antiques market at 533 King's Road, Chelsea, was popular with the capital's gay glitterati and was known locally as 'Rod's Club' after one of the boyfriends of owner Chris Hunter. Although the place had a star-studded clientele, prices were reasonable (a three-course meal, with coffee for £3; wine – just two on offer, red or white – at £2.10 a bottle), allowing diners on a budget to rub shoulders with the famous and the infamous. At midnight one hot July night, just half an hour after food service had finished and the first of the night's acts had taken to the stage, three coach loads of police turned up and turned everybody out. Demanding patrons divulge their names, ages and addresses, the police – whose number was estimated at between 60 and 80 – left without making a single arrest.

The following night a similar number of police (one person present estimated around 100 officers were involved, half in plain clothes, half in uniform) pulled the same stunt at the Boltons. Claiming that they were looking for drugs, officers blocked the exits before telling drinkers to stand with their arms folded. Many were subjected to searches, and several 'were taken apart. They went through all their pockets and possessions, checked for false heels in their shoes.'[11] That night around 20 people were arrested, while the rest were ordered out of the pub and told they could not return to finish their drinks. Two West End clubs popular with LGBT customers, Napoleon's and Louise's, were also raided, along with several well-known cruising areas, leading to accusations of a witch hunt in an attempt to clean up London during the busy tourist season.

For many years, the CHE would compile a monthly digest of arrests to highlight the inequalities faced by gay men in the media and in the courts; it does not make for edifying reading. Police complained that they were 'fighting a losing battle' against cottaging and gross indecency, especially in certain parts of London, where 'before they made it legal there was only the odd dirty old man in a toilet... now it's like a disease.'[12] In 1976 the disparity in the way upholders of the law treated gay men was brought into the spotlight when 32-year-old Bill Walker was sent to prison in Manchester for 18 months for having consensual sex with his 16-year-old partner when, in the same city, a 50-year-old man was fined just £25 for having unlawful sexual intercourse with a 15-year-old girl. According to research by the Oldham branch of CHE, annually around 400 men over 21 were charged with having consensual sex with girls aged 14 or 15. The maximum sentence for the crime was two years in jail, yet only a fifth of these men ended up in prison, with sentences tending to be between six and nine months. Each year only 30 men over 21 years old were charged with consensual sex with youths aged between 16 and 21, the homosexual age of consent, but the maximum penalty here was five years in prison.[13] That November Oldham CHE delivered a petition to the Home Office, signed by more than 2,000 people, that demanded Bill Walker's release.

The inequalities in British society meant that gay men, lesbian women, bisexual or trans people in the public eye had to think very carefully about how they were portrayed in the media, and many would go to great lengths to shield their true nature from the prying eyes of the press. In January 1976 the public first became aware of a scandal that had been brewing at the heart of the political establishment since the late 1960s. In a court case heard in Barnstaple, Devon, 35-year-old former groom and one-time male model Norman Scott (real name Norman Josiffe) was being charged with dishonestly obtaining state benefits when he suddenly blurted out that he was being 'hounded by people the whole time just because of my sex relationship with Jeremy Thorpe'.[14] Liberal Party leader Thorpe immediately issued a denial that they had had any kind of relationship, and Scott's ex-wife told reporters that her former husband had a 'fixation' about the politician, had once 'taken a gun to the House of Commons to kill Mr. Thorpe' and that he had 'a history of mental illness and a tendency to distort and wildly exaggerate things'.[15]

Thorpe's sex life was an open secret in Parliament. As early as 1971 the Liberal Party held an internal enquiry into the affair, interviewing Scott and his landlady at the Houses of Parliament before quietly dismissing his allegations. Prime Minister Harold Wilson had been aware of the situation for some time, but Wilson and Thorpe were old friends: it was partly because Thorpe refused a position in a coalition cabinet under Tory leader Edward Heath that Wilson had reclaimed the premiership in 1974, and to many it seemed that he intervened to try and protect Thorpe. A statement that Scott had given to a Chelsea policeman back in 1962, going into great detail about the relationship, mysteriously vanished, along with letters and other documents. But when the affair finally became public knowledge, Scott's allegations threatened to bring Thorpe's career – and his marriage – to an end. Not only had the Liberal leader lied to his family, friends and party members, the two men were supposed to have begun an intimate relationship 10 years before the Sexual Offences Act came into being, when Scott was still just 17.

It was a scandal that the establishment could not countenance, and in late 1975 Thorpe decided to try and silence Scott once and for all, paying airline pilot Andrew Newton to eliminate him permanently. Unfortunately, Newton was a useless assassin, shooting Scott's Great Dane, Rinka, instead of Thorpe's former lover. Newton was sent to prison for two years, and on 10 May 1976 Thorpe resigned the party leadership, his position untenable.

For a while the story died down: the newspapers seemed less interested in Thorpe's sex life now he was no longer in a position of power, and there were plenty of stories of kinky gay sex, dodgy queer vicars and potential paedophiles to fill the pages. If you were a tabloid reader, it must have appeared as if the gates of hell were about to open, revealing a crowd of gay men desperate to drag your poor, innocent soul inside. Once Newton was released from prison he went to the press, admitting 'I was paid to kill Scott. I accepted the job for money and it was a contract to murder... the Liberals were terrified that his story of a homosexual relationship with Thorpe would be disastrous.'[16] Thorpe continued to deny that there had been any plot, and although he was charged with conspiracy to murder Scott in August 1978, he would be acquitted the following year.

The farcical aspects of the Thorpe case would later cause the media to treat the whole thing as a bit of a joke, but at that time there was no way a politician of Thorpe's standing could have come out in Britain. Despite the courage shown by Maureen Colquhoun, it would be another eight years before a serving Member of Parliament would openly admit to being homosexual.

With the police and the press treating LGBT people as pariahs, it is perhaps no wonder that so few people in the public eye felt able to come out. But with record buyers apparently less fazed by a performer's perceived sexuality, Britain's record companies continued to make tentative steps towards embracing queer musicians. Although – like their American counterparts – Britain's female artists would have to plough their own furrow for a good while yet, major labels were finally starting to see the potential in signing out-gay male artists. After being snatched away from Squidd by Mark Edwards, Steve Swindells signed to RCA for his debut album, *Messages*. 'The A&R guy at RCA at the time was gay,' he explains. 'RCA had high hopes for me and had a launch party for the album in the penthouse at their very swanky offices in Mayfair. I was gobsmacked to see my old music teacher walk in. It turned out that he was working for my music publisher.' With all the songs written by Swindells, and production credited to Edwards, the sleeve of the album features Steve in a number of different guises, including bewigged judge and young leather-clad hustler. 'That cover was my concept – I'm amazed I got away with it. They said, "We'll let you have your concept on the front cover, so long as we can have a picture on the back of you looking pretty!" It's me being the judge of gay stereotypes; I was only 21, and that was pretty intellectual! The songs are pretty out there: "I Don't Like Eating Meat" has nothing to do with being vegetarian if you read the lyrics!' The album, sadly, did not sell well despite the high production values and stellar cast of session musicians including Caleb Quaye, John Gustafson, Doris Troy and Danny Thompson, and a follow-up was abandoned when Edwards threw a drunken fit in the studio, causing RCA to drop Swindells immediately.

'I ended up joining Pilot in 1976,' Swindells, who played keyboards on the hit group's 1977 album *Two's a Crowd*, explains. 'My friend [and

133

former Bay City Roller] Billy Lyall had been their keyboard player, but he'd left. He had written their big hit, "Magic", and later died of AIDS.* He actually told the band that I should be their keyboard player. So, suddenly I was in Abbey Road's Studio Two, where the Beatles had recorded and where the "Long and Winding Road" piano was. I was there for six weeks, every day. Alan Parsons was the producer, and Pilot – without me, much to my chagrin – were absorbed into the Alan Parsons Project. I did lots of TV shows, so I had a taste of this whole pop star thing, the screaming girls and all that, but I was still living in a basement bedsit with an outside toilet, even though I was on £60 a week, and I got an extra £1,100 for the album sessions. They were driving me around in limos, and I remember deliberately slamming the door of this stretch Daimler really loudly so that all of my neighbours would see. Another time, David Paton, the singer from Pilot, was sitting in front of me and all these girls were banging on the window. David turns around and in his heavy Scottish accent asks, "How's it feel to be a pop star, Steve?" I said, "Well, it's alright, it's fun", but I wasn't seduced by it.'

Paton had also been a member of soon-to-be superstars the Bay City Rollers before he and Billy Lyall formed Pilot in 1973. At the time Paton and Lyall were involved, the Rollers were just another struggling pop group, albeit with a fanatical local following, but no one, not even manager Tam Paton (no relation), could have guessed that they would become one of the biggest teenybop acts of the seventies. Tam Paton would end up behind bars in 1982 after pleading guilty to committing indecent acts with males under the age of consent, two teenage boys aged 16 and 17, although he had originally faced 10 charges involving 25 teenage boys between 1977 and 1982.

The question of the unequal age of consent was a constant problem for gay rights activists, one that would be exploited mercilessly by organisations lobbying for more than simply equality. In October 1975, a National Union of Students (NUS) Gay Rights conference at

---

* Billy Lyall – who went on to play keyboards for acts including early eighties hitmakers Dollar – died on 1 December 1989, but because of the hysteria surrounding AIDS his family were unable to hold a funeral until 5 January the following year.

the University of Warwick was poorly attended, but raised the thorny issue of paedophilia, debating whether paedophiles were, like gay men, lesbians, bisexual and transgender people, an oppressed minority or if they were simply exploiting the gay liberation movement for their own ends. Wanting to be seen to be accepting, groups including the Paedophile Information Exchange (PIE) and Paedophile Action for Liberation (PAL) were invited to give presentations to LGBT groups around the country as they sought ammunition in the fight to equalise the age of consent. 'In the early seventies, there was a lot of discussion about paedophile groups which was taken quite seriously not just by gay organisations but by people like the NCCL and MIND [formerly the National Association for Mental Health],' Peter Scott-Presland explains. 'People were being invited along to conferences so that delegates could hear the paedophile point of view. People advocated for the right of these organisations to exist on civil liberties grounds, but what was not understood then was that the issue of consent was a lot more complicated than was assumed, and so much more [related to] power dynamics: we know now that surface consent cannot be seen as real consent, for example.' It was 'an opportunistic attempt by a group of child abusers to jump on the bandwagon of gay liberation,' as Frankie Green describes it, and it would add weight to a series of homophobic articles in Britain's newspapers that equated homosexuality with child abuse.

With gay rights finally being discussed by politicians, and LGBT people making headlines in the media, it was inevitable that music which embraced LGBT themes would start to gain more traction. Pop had been flirting with LGBT characters for a while now – even major artists such as the Beatles (in 'Get Back'), the Kinks ('Lola') and Lou Reed ('Walk on the Wild Side') had included non-binary subjects – and, in August 1976 Rod Stewart, an artist better known for the misogyny of some of his lyrics and his playboy lifestyle than for his support of the LGBT community (despite being the man who brought the New York Dolls to Britain for their first tour), issued a new single. Taken from his recent album *A Night on the Town*, 'The Killing of Georgie' was based on a true story, and told the tale of a gay man, a friend of Faces keyboard

135

player Ian McLagan, who is rejected by his parents, is forced to leave home and finds a new life in a new city before being killed on the streets of New York. He did not think it particularly groundbreaking to write a song portraying a gay man sympathetically because, as Stewart explained, 'I was surrounded by gay men at the time. I had a gay manager and a gay PR guy. Long John Baldry, who discovered me, was gay.'[17]

Despite an initial ban by the BBC, the single spent 10 weeks on the UK singles charts, reaching number two – the same chart position that the Kinks' 'Lola', with its theme of gender fluidity, had peaked at six years before. Eight years after 'The Killing of Georgie', a London-based trio called Bronski Beat would reach number three in the charts with a similar tale, 'Smalltown Boy'.

It seems odd that, at a time when some acts (even heterosexual ones in Stewart's case) were happy to be aligned with the new, permissive attitude, others were scurrying back into the closet. Elton John came out as bisexual via the pages of *Rolling Stone* magazine, but the once defiantly queer Freddie Mercury – whose group was now being managed by Elton's manager and boyfriend John Reid – was telling the press that, even though he boasted of having a girlfriend, 'It is inevitable with our name that we attract some fans who look on us as a bunch of queers or transvestites. Okay, I have a lot of gay friends, but they don't influence my sexual habits.'[18] It is highly likely that Reid had taken Freddie to one side and told him to cut back on the campery, as Elton's career Stateside hit a 15-year slump following his admission.

While Stewart's single was rising up the charts, Bowie once again decided to talk to the press about his sexuality. This time he told Cameron Crowe, writing for *Playboy* magazine, that he no longer thought of himself as gay, but admitted that 'It's true — I am a bisexual. But I can't deny that I've used that fact very well. I suppose it's the best thing that ever happened to me. Fun, too.'[19] He went on to tell Crowe that things had come a long way since his infamous *Melody Maker* interview: 'Sex was still shocking. Everybody wanted to see the freak. But they were so ignorant about what I was doing. There was very little talk of bisexuality or gay power before I came along.' Bowie explained that, when he gave that interview at the beginning of 1972, he felt that British fans understood what he was trying to achieve: his biggest battle had been with the American media. 'Nobody understood the European way of dressing and adopting the asexual, androgynous everyman pose,' he said. 'People all went screaming, "He's got make-up on and he's wearing stuff that looks like dresses!" I wasn't the first one, though, to publicise bisexuality.' Although he would flip-flop on the subject of his sexuality over the years, Bowie's level of fame offered him a platform to talk openly about his own particular brand of gender-fluidity and, three decades on from his *Melody Maker* interview, he would admit that 'I'm quite proud that I did it.'[20] He was one of the lucky ones: most LGBT people would find 1970s society far less accepting.

10

Britain's Stonewall

'The police in London were completely out of hand... They were able to swan in and make easy arrests in Earl's Court because they figured that gay men in that climate and at that time were very unlikely to contest an arrest in court.' – Tom Robinson

Back in August 1974, the *Evening Standard* had carried a story, 'Debauched Life of Ex-choir Boy', that revealed details of the private sexual habits of a 26-year-old man, Peter Wells. This case had everything a tabloid could possibly wish for, and soon the public were lapping up the tales of 'sadism and debauchery' taking place within the membership of a Croydon church choir.[1] Wells was hauled into court for having enjoyed S&M sessions with two men aged 18 and was sent to prison for two-and-a-half years, despite his insistence that the sex had been consensual. As *Gay News* put it, 'the adults in question were 18 years old, entitled to drink, smoke, enter legal contracts, marry, arrange mortgages, vote, make Hire Purchase agreements – but not make love'.[2]

The following year, Wells's appeal to have his sentence commuted was turned down, even after the court learned that he had been kept in solitary confinement after attacks by other prisoners. The judge, Lord Justice Widgery, noted that prison had not yet had the desired effect: 'It was not a case where Wells hoped to change his ways. In fact, he maintained that he intended to continue indulging in homosexual practices.'[3]

Wells was released in 1976 after serving 20 months inside, a period in which he had 'attempted suicide twice, been beaten up on nine occasions, been raped and scalded by boiling water, had lost four stone and heard another prisoner die while awaiting trial in the next cell'.[4] He was angry, politically engaged and soon became a member of the Croydon branch of CHE. It was only after his release that the whole story came out: how he had learned that he was to be arrested and so voluntarily attended his local police station, contacted legal representation but still had the police turn up on his doorstep, threatening to smash the door down. It was the mother of one of the 18-year-olds who had raised her concerns with a church rector, and the rector who had informed the police. Wells's story deeply affected singer-songwriter Tom Robinson, and he included a verse about how he was 'arrested and dragged to the cells for being in love with a man of eighteen' in a new song he had been writing, 'Glad to Be Gay'.

Robinson had formed his first group, Café Society, with friends Hereward Kaye and Raphael 'Ray' Doyle, in 1974. Café Society were not a gay group: both Doyle and Kaye had female partners, but they had no issue with Robinson's sexuality or with performing his gay-themed songs. They looked very much like a folk group, three men with jumbo acoustic guitars, and sounded like any one of a number of bands doing the London pub circuit, but Kinks main man Ray Davies saw something there and signed them to his own Konk label. The ensuing album, *Café Society*, was a perfectly good record which featured the talents of some exceptional sidemen, including three-quarters of the Kinks, but has none of the swagger of Bowie or his contemporaries. By the time *Café Society* hit the stores in 1975, Bowie had already moved on to his next incarnation, but there is no denying that his particular brand of androgyny provided succour to hundreds of young people questioning their own sexual identity, including Robinson. Although copyrighted by Davies's own music publishers, one song that did not make the album was a gay-themed love song that Robinson had debuted at a *Gay News* benefit gala in October 1974, 'Kum Back'.

Café Society rehearsed at the Troubadour, a café-bar and live music venue on Old Brompton Road in Earl's Court. Since opening its doors in 1954, the Troubadour had attracted a loyal following of anti-establishment types: drummer Charlie Watts was discovered there by Alexis Korner two years before he joined the Rolling Stones; Bob Dylan played his first UK shows there (as Blind Boy Grunt); and *Private Eye* began life in a darkened corner of the café, which was the first place in the UK to sell copies of the satirical magazine. The Troubadour was also handily situated right next door to the Coleherne, where Robinson would go to drink and where he would find further inspiration for his best-known song.

Robinson saw first-hand the harassment that the Coleherne's customers had to contend with: punters were routinely hassled outside the pub and often arrested on spurious charges such as loitering or blocking the pavement. Further incidents occurred in other pubs: after turning up in drag and being refused service in the Champion, a pub popular with Notting Hill Gate's gay community, 20 members of the GLF were taken into custody, strip-searched and subjected to both verbal and physical abuse by the arresting officers. In retaliation, *Gay News* set up a fund to help pay the legal costs of any readers affected by the arrests, including taking legal action against the authorities.

Café Society would record a demo of 'Glad to Be Gay', but their version would not be released at the time (an earlier and entirely different song, also called 'Glad to Be Gay', credited to Tom, Rose and Annie, had been released on a CHE fundraising EP in 1974); however Robinson would record the song in 1977 after disbanding Café Society and forming a new group, the Tom Robinson Band.

After several years as a prominent – but not exactly financially successful – member of New York's emerging punk scene, singer Jayne County decided that her career prospects might improve on the other side of the Atlantic, where a similar musical movement was beginning to make waves. County, who had been present during the Stonewall riots, could not have picked a better time. 'I moved to London in 1976,' she explains. 'I had been over before, first in 1971 to appear in *Andy Warhol's Pork* [at the Roundhouse, Camden]. On that first trip the producers set me and my manager up in an apartment in Earl's Court, and we used to go to the Coleherne and the other one across the street, the Boltons. We had a ball there. It was a kind of trashy gay bar, and we loved anything we considered trashy. The Coleherne was more reserved; it didn't have the reputation as a leather bar at that time. The gay places in London were very subdued, very different to what we were used to in America. The people there were acting like they were scared, weren't sure they wanted to be there or weren't really comfortable with being gay. You would hear people talking about this poof or that poof; I didn't even know what a poof was!'

Despite their reputations as safe havens for homosexual men, both the Coleherne and the Boltons (and the nearby Lord Ranelagh) were regularly raided by police, as Peter Munday, advertising manager for *Gay News* discovered for himself. Munday was enjoying a quiet drink one Sunday evening in the downstairs lounge of the Boltons when seven police officers entered. 'They studied the scene downstairs, then walked upstairs,' he reported. 'I heard one of the uniformed policemen say quite loudly, "Watch it, lads. Backs to the wall and fingers up your arse with this crowd." I protested, saying that while they had a job to do, they could do it a little less offensively. He asked who I was, and I replied that I was an innocent bystander. He said, "Good, make sure you stay that way, because I'm looking for someone just like you."' When Munday went to Kensington Police Station the following day to complain, he was interviewed by 'a uniformed inspector who was disturbed and surprised to learn that his force did not enjoy good relations with the gay community and said if the conduct of his force could not stand up to public scrutiny something was amiss'. Deciding to press forward, he was asked to go to Chelsea Police Station the following week to give a statement. There he was interviewed by Superintendent Leighton, who told him, 'If I had my way, we would close down the Coleherne and prosecute the licensee for conspiring to corrupt public morals.'[5]

The capital's gay pubs proved easy pickings for police officers eager to boost their arrest numbers. 'If somebody was a closeted stockbroker from Surrey, dressed up in leather and chains and drinking beer in the street outside the Coleherne, and they arrested them for obstructing the pavement, they'd be most likely to plead guilty and not appear in court so that their picture would not get into their local newspaper,' Tom Robinson explains. 'The editor of *Gay News* was trying to photograph the police doing this, and he was arrested on suspicion of having stolen the camera. They took the film out of the back, bundled him into a police van and beat him up. It was clear that the police were our enemy, as they were for other oppressed minorities at that time.'

Paul Southwell agrees: 'I was at the Coleherne when it was raided in in the mid-seventies. This was a regular thing with the Coleherne and other gay venues. I can remember the police arriving and closing the bar, so we all congregated outside. There was some jostling and some raised voices, but we held our ground and eventually it all calmed down before we dispersed to either the Boltons or the Catacombs. The police didn't treat gay men very well at all in the seventies: there was a lot of homophobia. They used to lie about events all the time and generally harass gay men regularly. Entrapment was also very common in this era. Overall, it didn't foster trust or credence in gay and police community relations. As a gay man I didn't trust them and even to this day I have a deep mistrust of the police and authority in general.'

Trouble came with the territory, and the Earl's Court regulars were used to it. More than a decade earlier, in May 1965, the *News of the World* ran an article entitled 'This Show Must Not Go On', about the weekly drag nights at the Lord Ranelagh, which would later change its name to Brompton's. So many people had gone to see what all the fuss was about that the tables and chairs had to be removed from the pub to make room, and the police turned up to close the place down after dozens of customers spilled out onto the street. With live music provided by local teenagers the Downtowners, and visits from then-closeted sixties celebrities including Brian Epstein, Dusty Springfield and their friends, the 'Queen of the Month' shows at the Lord Ranelagh were some of Britain's earliest, and most visible, nights for trans people and cross-dressers. Back then, there was an ingrained respect for the law, and few, if any, of the Lord Ranelagh's customers were up for a fight. But by the mid-seventies things had changed. The discovery that the Metropolitan Police's Obscene Publications Squad was riddled with corruption, with some officers receiving backhanders of thousands of pounds, only added to the distrust between the authorities and the LGBT community.

Basement drinking den the Masquerade Club on Earl's Court Road (which, in 1975, became the Pink Pig) had been attracting no end of trouble for years, with reports of sex and violence taking place both inside and outside the club, door staff being assaulted by drunk customers and the occasional stabbing. With Earl's Court Road branded 'the wickedest street in Britain' by *The People*, where 'homosexuality abounds in the most blatant of ways,' and 'male prostitutes openly put themselves up for hire',[6] it's little wonder that Bernard Brook-Partridge, local resident and member of the Greater London Council, described his own neighbourhood as 'degraded, sleazy, nauseating and generally filthy', and complained that his two sons, aged three and seven, were being 'bombarded by photographs of sex organs while walking in the street'.[7]

After years of persecution, and spurred on by an oppressive heatwave, few of the Earl's Court regulars were in the mood to simply kowtow to authority any longer. On 2 June 1976 a 'near-riot' broke out in the street outside the Coleherne after two customers were involved in a brawl with police officers from the local Chelsea force. One of the men, Roy Lea, was arrested for wilful obstruction. When he argued with the arresting officers, claiming that because he was in the immediate vicinity of the pub he was actually on private property, one of them, PC Day, became abusive and attempted to bundle him into the back of a police van. Lea's friend, Peter Greggan, remonstrated with the three officers, and one, PC Baker, claimed that Greggan tried to get him in a headlock. According to Lea, Greggan was punched by the three officers and bundled into the back of a police van, unconscious. A fourth policeman, the driver, then kicked Greggan in the face. A large, angry crowd of drinkers from the Coleherne and the Boltons surrounded the police van, but no further arrests were made that night. The Boltons had, until now, received less attention from the police because although it was on the opposite side of the road it was served by a different force – Kensington police. That September, after a hearing at the Horseferry Road Magistrates' Court, Greggan – still bearing some of the scars from his beating– was fined £65 and Tony Lea was fined £15. Both men were ordered to pay a further £20 costs each.

A few days later, a further three men were arrested outside the pub for obstruction and for being drunk and disorderly. Far from being an end to the trouble, that incident was simply a foretaste of what was to come. Another spate of arrests targeting gay men doing nothing more than drinking together was the final straw, and every weekend from then on the Coleherne's regulars were on pins, waiting for trouble to kick off. Then, on Saturday 26 June 1976, almost seven years to the day from the start of the Stonewall riots, it did. Fighting broke out between customers and police after, once again, arrests were made at the Coleherne.

It was a hot night: the heatwave enveloping the country would continue for more than two months, leading to a drought and water rationing. It was also the first night of a week-long Pride festival that began with the obligatory march through the centre of London and a picnic in Hyde Park. Three men were arrested outside the pub and one plain-clothes police officer was treated in hospital for injuries resulting from a scuffle, adding assault to the charge sheet.

Like the customers of the Stonewall Inn, the Earl's Court patrons had had enough; only days before, David Seligman, Gay Switchboard volunteer and an original member of the *Gay News* collective, was beaten unconscious by queer bashers on Hampstead Heath. A large number of the Coleherne's regulars were ready and waiting when, at 11.12 pm, the Chelsea police arrived en masse, car tyres screeching and blue lights flashing. One arrest was made. Having moved from the Coleherne, a large angry crowd now stood outside the Boltons, where they thought they were safe. They were not. Men in leather were screaming 'fuck off' at the police, and a chant of 'we've had enough' broke out. From within the crowd, two men started a fight, attacking a man who had walked over from the Coleherne. The two attackers turned out to be plain-clothes policemen, one of whom, in his fury, picked up an orange plastic milk crate as a weapon. Louis Eaks, whose arrest for cottaging in 1970 had sparked the first ever demonstration by the Gay Liberation Front, was there that night, and told *Gay News* what he saw take place. 'Everyone was jeering and booing,' he explained.

'Then one of the policemen picked up a wooden box, the crowd moved forward and he fell through the glass in a shop window. Then he went berserk.'[8] The reaction was markedly different to the one that Eaks encountered the previous summer, when he had been attacked outside the pub. At that time, the 60 or so men who had congregated outside the Coleherne quickly vanished, leaving him to fend off two assailants on his own, until the police arrived and chased them off. The attack resulted in Eaks needing hospital treatment and receiving 14 stitches to three wounds after being punched in the face, dragged to the ground and kicked in the head.

As the window shattered and shards of glass flew across the pavement, the crowd, some of whom had been obstructing traffic by kissing in the middle of Old Brompton Road, surged. The officer, still holding the crate, managed to struggle free and brought the weapon down on a man's head, knocking him unconscious. The man he had floored turned out to be another plain-clothes police officer. 'We rose up, like Stonewall,' says musician Steve Swindells. 'I went and spoke to one of the senior officers. I said, "Why are you doing this? Is this because you are being told to, or because you get points for easy arrests?" and he looked embarrassed. I said, "Can't you just call off your hounds? This is ridiculous. It's totally unnecessary."'

Tom Robinson frequently witnessed the provocation, and the first verse of 'Glad to be Gay' graphically illustrates this abuse of power, when Robinson sings of policemen 'raiding our pubs for no reason at all, lining the customers up by the wall' and of customers accused of 'resisting arrest as they're kicked on the ground'. Another Coleherne regular, Dave Wainwright, remembers that night clearly. 'It was quite outrageous the way they behaved,' he says today. 'They weren't expecting the violent reaction; milk crates went flying everywhere in the struggle to free the guy they had detained in the doorway of the shop, opposite the Coleherne. About half a dozen of us marched up Earl's Court Road to Kensington Police Station in order to make formal complaints regarding the two plain-clothes police officers who started the whole thing. I believe they were acting as agents provocateurs when they attempted to bundle the guy off without being seen, which is why I started to make a noise and draw people's attention to what was happening. I can still remember being alone in an office with the chief inspector, and him angrily saying, "I have two officers in hospital", and me retorting that they deserved it. I was outraged at what I had witnessed, outraged and angry. I can still see the look of disbelief in the eyes of the chief inspector whilst I was giving him a piece of my mind.'

With attacks occurring during Pride week, the community might have been expected to rally, but thanks to a schism within the LGBT community, with the remnants of the GLF attempting to take control of the festival and other factions making their own demands, this did not happen. The 1976 Pride march, which was eventually organised through the offices of Gay Switchboard, was poorly attended: it did not help matters when the CHE announced plans to hold their own Gay Pride Week in London that year from 1 August, with a march held on 7 August attended by around 2,000 people. At the same time, the Lewisham CHE enclave were making a documentary film, *David Is Homosexual*, with a soundtrack from Paul South and Handbag. The film captured the run-up to Pride and some fascinating footage of the march, including a few seconds of Tom Robinson performing an acoustic version of 'Glad to Be Gay', the first public performance of the song.

It did not take long for news about the arrests and raids on gay venues to spread around the capital's gay community. For those outside of London, *Gay News* was the best way to keep up with events, so long as you had the bottle to buy a copy and walk around with it in your pocket. Of course, not everyone who visited the Coleherne enjoyed the notoriety the pub was attaining. The following year, when residents of nearby Wharfedale Street – an area much used by rent boys to ply their trade, and another street lambasted by the *People* for its 'homosexual vice trade' where 'every night up to 50 male prostitutes troop the pavements or lounge insolently against the garden walls'[9] – petitioned the local council to help clean the place up, many of the Coleherne's customers signed a petition of their own backing the move.

11

Better Blatant Than Latent

'Tom Robinson, signed to EMI Records in England, is using rock and roll to further his own political cause, gay liberation. The company doesn't seem to fear the potential for controversy, contending that the artist handles his issue with "taste".' – Cash Box[1]

The Catacombs, the popular gay club in Earl's Court, had been running since the end of the 1960s. Made up of a series of interconnected rooms in a rather dingy basement, the Catacombs had featured in a 1971 exposé of Earl's Court's gay scene by the *Sunday People,* which described the area as 'a place where decent people fear to tread', and the club as 'packed with men and youths – all male. Some sat around at tables talking and drinking soft drinks [the club was not licensed for the sale of alcohol]. Others danced on the crowded dance space. In the darkened corners [the reporter] saw couples holding hands. When our investigator left, a young man with long fair hair approached him in the street and said: "Are you looking for business? I can do almost anything. I charge £5."'[2] Steve Swindells recalls it as 'the most amazing gay club in London. The music they played was astonishingly good. Tallulah [Martin Allum] started there – he was a soulful DJ, with a great love for proper music.'

147

Outside of members-only venues or unlicensed clubs like the Catacombs, the only gay discos that existed in London in the mid-seventies were transient: crowds would follow Tricky Dicky and others like him as they moved from place to place. Then, in 1976, the Sundown in Charing Cross launched a new night, Bang!, and for the first time the capital had a licensed disco with a permanent home advertised to, and catering for, a primarily gay audience, and you did not have to be a member (or the guest of a member) to walk through the door.

'I did Bang! right from the start,' says London-based DJ Norman Scott.* 'I had been working in straight clubs. I put on Bob Marley at the Tottenham Royal in 1972, before anyone had heard of him. I did it as a favour to [American singer] Johnny Nash.' Scott was close to many musicians in London's reggae scene, and Nash had been working hard to help promote the Wailers and to get them signed, but the management of the theatre assumed that the DJ must have been paid to book the unknown act. 'They accused me of taking a backhander and sacked me! But he did me a favour because a month later I got a job at the Sundown in Edmonton, which was a huge cinema that had been converted into an entertainment complex... They kept the seats upstairs so you could still use it as a cinema but took them out downstairs and used that as a concert hall and, twice a week, as a disco. I worked as a DJ as well as putting bands on like Kilburn and the High Roads and acted as compère for lots of the concerts as well. Rod Stewart and the Faces did their Christmas show there; they had a bar on the stage and by the end we were all as pissed as farts!

'There were four Sundowns: Edmonton, Brixton, Mile End and Charing Cross Road. The DJ in Brixton, Jerry Collins, got in touch with me. He had approached the manager of Sundown in Charing Cross Road about putting on a gay night, and he wanted to know if I would be interested in DJing with him. I said, "Yeah. I've never done a gay club before, but it doesn't bother me", and that became Bang!' The Sundown in Charing Cross was situated below the Astoria, which had

---

* Not the same Norman Scott who was part of the Jeremy Thorpe scandal. The London-based DJ, who first became involved in London's music scene while working in Soho in the 1950s, passed away in September 2020 at the age of 79.

operated as a cinema since 1927, with the basement used for ballroom dancing. Bang! opened its doors in 1976, initially on Monday nights, before demand quickly had them expanding to Thursday nights as well. The popularity of Bang! and its turntable spinners was confirmed when, on 5 September 1976, Scott was invited to Elstree Studios to DJ for a double birthday celebration, for Freddie Mercury and John Reid. Freddie was 30 and Reid just 27, yet he was managing both Queen and Elton John. He was also Elton's boyfriend. 'It was an amazing gig,' says Scott. 'Imagine being the DJ playing to a room full of dozens of celebrities! It was a great night: I have never seen so many big stars under one roof.'

Bang! was different from the GLF dances or Tricky Dicky's mobile nights and heralded a major improvement in LGBT nightlife. London now had a 1,000-capacity venue that was advertised as gay, whose DJs and staff were gay and whose music policy was directly influenced by US soul and disco. Collins* and Scott were soon joined by Catacombs DJ Tallulah and, later, Jeremy Joseph.** Scott was also one of the resident DJs at the nearby Global Village, that in 1979 would become Heaven.

Other clubs would follow, including Mario's in Newcastle and Nottingham's Le Chic (which would later rename itself as Part Two), the largest gay club in Europe at that time. But as Britain's LGBT community became more visible, homophobic attacks increased: after a petrol bomb attack on Valentino's, a gay club in Shepherds Bush, one customer was taken to hospital overcome with fumes and, as if dealing with homophobia wasn't enough, in many of Britain's major cities there was the ever-present threat of becoming the innocent victim of a terror attack. On 28 January 1977, after almost a year of relative peace in the capital, seven bombs went off in and around Oxford Street and Soho, retribution, it seemed, for the trial at the Old Bailey of IRA members involved in the infamous Balcombe Street siege in December 1975. Gay disco Crackers, at the junction of Wardour Street and Oxford Street,

---

* The DJ career of Collins, who worked under the name Gary London, would come to an abrupt end when he was shot in a freak accident at a showbiz party in February 1979.

** Joseph would later take over the business and rechristen it G-A-Y in 1993.

was just yards from several of the blasts, which began shortly before midnight. 'I heard a loud bang at about five to twelve,' manager Roy Vickers told the *Daily Mirror*. 'I rushed out and realised that a car had exploded... A second bomb went off in Wardour Street a few minutes after that. I think it was in a shop. Then at 12:20 I saw a third bomb go off in Wardour Street.'[3] Vickers decided not to tell the patrons of the disco, then packed with around 500 revellers, for fear of starting a panic, until the police demanded that he clear the venue.

Crackers had been a popular haunt for several years, and on Fridays and Saturdays ran lunchtime sessions which were always well attended. Thanks to the outdated licensing laws, like many other gay clubs, Crackers could only operate after the pubs had closed by offering its customers food, like a sandwich of tinned ham. Animal Nightlife singer Andy Polaris, who initially attended shows at the Roxy and the Marquee in search of companions, became a regular visitor. 'The earliest gay clubs I went to were Bang! at the Sundown on Charing Cross Road, and Sombreros, and then Benjy's in Mile End, which was very low-key. But things started to gel at Crackers, at their soul night, though it was a Saturday afternoon rather than a night!' A few months after the bombing, Crackers would debut a new punk club night, the Vortex, that launched with a gig featuring the Fall, John Cooper Clarke and headliners Buzzcocks. 'That's where I first saw people like [designer and club promoter] Philip Sallon, and I started seeing other gay people there and hanging out with them,' Polaris remembers. 'They were the freaky people, and the music was great!'

Change was happening fast. Teens fed up with the artificiality of glam, or the histrionic keyboard noodlings of prog rock, were looking for their own sound, something cheaper, easier and, essentially, working class. Back in the summer of 1975, clothes shop owner Malcolm McLaren, an aspiring entrepreneur who had recently spent a few months in the States attempting to manage the New York Dolls, introduced his current band to a new singer, the green-haired John Lydon. Taking their lead from bands like the New York Dolls and CBGB favourites the Ramones, London's young bands started playing a faster, dirtier form of rock 'n' roll, influenced equally by this new American sound, their own poverty and disaffection with a political system that had brought the country to its knees. McLaren's group, now called the Sex Pistols (after the King's Road clothing emporium Sex, which McLaren co-owned with his then-partner, designer Vivienne Westwood) played their first gig on 6 November 1975, at Saint Martin's School of Art. Punk was born, and by the summer of 1976 it was taking over the capital.

But not everyone jumped on the bandwagon. 'Punk influenced us a little,' says Ova's Rosemary Schonfeld. 'Mostly we did not like the aggressive male element and the lack of good musicianship. That said, Jana was definitely vocally influenced by some punk women singers, particularly the German singer Nina Hagen, who came from an opera background.' Tom Robinson agrees with Rosemary's assessment. 'I didn't like it at the time,' he says. 'It went against everything I believed about music, about how you had to be respectful to the audience and play in tune, sing in tune, and play your nice, melodic songs in time.'

The birth of British punk rock (as opposed to the American version) is inextricably linked to London's gay scene. When no venue would consider hosting punk bands or allowing them to practise there, it was the underground gay clubs of Covent Garden and Soho that provided space. When every other public house refused to serve these weird-looking kids, with their spiky hair, outrageous make-up, torn clothing and safety-pin jewellery, it was London's gay clubs, including Madam Louise's on Soho's Poland Street, that embraced them. And when they needed a hangout of their own, it was a gay club, Chaguaramas, that became the Roxy, London's premier punk venue. 'People forget how important those gay clubs were,' says musician, DJ and filmmaker Don Letts. 'And not just for punk, they were also places where young Black kids could go too. Louise's, Chaguaramas... I remember seeing Freddie Burretti dancing at the Sombrero. Great times!'

Gay clubs outside of the capital also provided succour: Manchester's Ranch Bar, a straight bar that had become a Mecca for the city's LGBT community thanks to its Bowie-heavy soundtrack, was the favoured hangout of bisexual singer-songwriter Peter Shelley (born Peter Campbell McNeish) and his friends, including the Fall and aspiring musicians such as future Joy Division/New Order bassist Peter Hook. Occupying the adjoining basement to local drag superstar Frank 'Foo'

Lamar's Palace club, the former drinking den would quickly become an important live venue for punk and new wave music. Shelley's band Buzzcocks (originally formed at the end of 1975 with fellow student Howard Devoto, and named after a line in a *Time Out* review of TV show *Rock Follies*) would play there in August 1976, just two months after Shelley and Devoto had organised the infamous Sex Pistols gig at Manchester's Lesser Free Trade Hall. Buzzcocks (now without Devoto, who left to form the equally influential Magazine) would soon be racing up the pop charts with a series of sexually ambiguous, Shelley-penned anthems.

Chaguaramas had already flirted with reggae, issuing two albums by singer John Holt through an agreement with Trojan Records, and its regular live band nights drew a mixed crowd that included Charlie Harper, singer with the UK Subs, and Gene October, who fronted punk band Chelsea. When part-time gay porn actor October, his manager Andrew Czezowski and Czezowski's partner Susan Carrington managed to persuade the owners of Chaguaramas to let them take over, they brought in a young clothes stall manager, Don Letts, to spin reggae records between acts. Letts was the manager of Acme Attractions, a clothes shop in the King's Road antiques arcade, owned by John Krivine and Steph Raynor, and inspired by McLaren and Westwood's Sex store. When McLaren took on the Sex Pistols, Krivine and Raynor attempted to jump on the same bandwagon, taking on October and Chelsea (who, with William 'Billy Idol' Broad, rather than October at the helm, would morph into Generation X), before handing over management of the group to Acme's accountant, Czezowski.

Opening in December 1976, the first three months of the Roxy's life was documented by Letts in his film *The Punk Rock Movie.* Shot in Super 8 over 100 days, the movie features the Sex Pistols, Siouxsie and the Banshees, the Clash and many other notable punk acts, including Jayne County and the Electric Chairs. 'London was a culture shock in a lot of ways,' says County. 'But it was a very good one and I absolutely loved it, because the audiences were so receptive. I was taken aback: I could not believe how well we were received. We had lines around the block. I was on the cover of *Melody Maker* [in October 1973] when we came over to do [Bowie's musical spectacular] the 1980 Floor Show,

152

much to Bowie's displeasure! So people had been hearing about me before I had actually played, and the Roxy was packed.

'It was mostly young kids in their home-made clothes. I played there several times in early 1977, with bands including the Adverts, Siouxsie and the Banshees and X-Ray Spex. I got on great with Siouxsie, but [X-Ray Spex's singer] Poly Styrene kept making sarcastic remarks to me in the dressing room. She was opening for me; I was headlining. I guess she had a problem with that, but no one knew who X-Ray Spex were back then.'

Shortly before the Roxy opened its doors, at the Princess Alice in Aldgate, the first Rock Against Racism (RAR) gig took place. Coming just two months after Eric Clapton's infamous racist tirade on stage in Birmingham,[4] RAR would see musicians around the country band together to raise awareness about the rise of the far right in the UK, a cause that was near to the heart of many LGBT performers. Clapton was not the first musician to espouse support for right-wing politician Enoch Powell: as far back as 1970 Rod Stewart had told *International Times* that 'I think Enoch is the man... The immigrants should be sent home. That's it.'[5] Over the next few years, the Tom Robinson Band, Buzzcocks and other LGBT acts would share RAR stages with punk and new wave acts including the Clash and the Undertones, British reggae acts Steel Pulse and Misty in Roots, and 2 Tone stars the Specials, Madness and others. From 1977 the capital's annual Pride marches would see RAR banners, as well as those belonging to the Anti-Nazi League, unfurled alongside those of LGBT groups from around the UK.

Thanks once again to lurid and often made-up headlines in the nation's tabloids, punk would shock Mr and Mrs Middle England, and the sight – and sound – of the spiky-haired Johnny Rotten uttering a rude word on teatime television caused the nation's newspapers to go into meltdown. But Britain's punk rockers were not the only ones garnering headlines. Other musical mavericks were inciting apoplexy too, as was evidenced in the outrage caused by gender-fluid musical provocateur Genesis P-Orridge and their Arts Council-funded show *Prostitution*. Born Neil Megson, P-Orridge had been a member of the artist collective COUM Transmissions since the end of 1969. Their insistence that 'anything that makes a noise is an instrument, but also anybody who can make it make a noise is a musician' was a truly punk attitude.[6] Throbbing Gristle, the group formed by P-Orridge and fellow COUM members Cosey Fanni Tutti (Christine Newby), Chris Carter and Peter 'Sleazy' Christopherson were pioneers of both punk and industrial music, but Conservative MP Nicholas Fairbairn (who had once been honorary vice president of gay rights lobbyists the Scottish Minorities Group but had since become vehemently opposed to LGBT equality) was apoplectic over *Prostitution*, branding the show 'an excuse for exhibitionism by every crank, queer, squint and ass in the business', and he demanded that the Arts Council be abolished: 'This is another example of the Government allowing people to promote every swill-bin attitude they can.'[7] The following Sunday, in best muck-raking tradition, the *People* got in on the act, accusing Cosey of being 'one of Soho's best-known blue movie queens', even though she had only appeared as an extra in a couple of minor X-rated comedies, and claiming that she had been 'photographed in explicit lesbian scenes' for porn magazines.[8]

Despite Fairbairn's protestations, the Arts Council was not forced to close; however it did have its government funding slashed by £1 million the following financial year. With Britain's tabloids (and members of the Conservative government) fired up and on the warpath, it would not be long before the authorities would come for other LGBT businesses and organisations.

12

Cocks in Frocks

*'The two most common attitudes are to show us as camp, flapping queens,
or tragic, lonely, outcasts. The most famous play about homosexuals,
The Boys in the Band, actually managed to do both.'* – Drew Griffiths[1]

Throughout the first half of the 1970s, while pop musicians were grabbing headlines as they explored (and, occasionally, exploited) their sexuality, and gay, lesbian, bisexual and trans people in Britain struggled to have their voices heard and their rights recognised, a revolution was taking place in theatre and in cabaret.

Actors had been blurring the lines of sexuality on stage for centuries. From ancient times women were barred from appearing in front of a paying audience, and traditionally women's roles were played by men in make-up and wearing female garb. For centuries women were expected to be subservient, had few – if any – rights and those that did attempt to traverse strict social mores by appearing on stage were often assumed to be prostitutes. With a constant need for actors who could pass for the opposite sex, the theatre gave homosexual men the opportunity to express their true nature without fear of persecution, and, in the first decades of the 1700s, the country's Molly houses provided some of these men with a space to be themselves off-stage too. During the Victorian era, as women started to push for change, the British music hall saw a number of female stars emerge, dressed as fops and dandies, singing songs about the louche life, and as we moved into the 20th century, the often-flamboyant social life that extended around the theatre offered both men and women a certain amount of freedom.

The GLF's Street Theatre troupe, and the Women's Liberation Theatre Group, who had worked together on direct action 'zaps' including the Miss World protests in 1970 and 1971, provided the most radical face of LGBT theatre, and their stunts would inspire a generation of writers, actors and directors. In October 1971, the same month that GLF Street Theatre Group were staging mock abortions in protest at the paperback publication of David Reuben's *Everything You Always Wanted to Know About Sex* (*But Were Afraid to Ask)* outside Foyle's in London, a little over 50 miles away a young student training to be a teacher got the message.

'I can date my coming out very precisely, to 9 October 1971,' says Peter Scott-Presland. 'It was the beginning of my first term doing a postgraduate degree; Saturday nights would be spent going around Oxford looking for parties to gatecrash, and I came across this party in Hertford College. There were lots of people wanting to get into it, a queue going up the stairs to this tiny room, and ahead of me was a man wearing a Gay Liberation Front badge – his name was Mick Wallis. I was absolutely astonished that somebody could be so open about something that I had been wrestling with from the age of eight. So, I sort of buttonholed him and ruined his evening. We sat on the stairs and talked, and he told me about the GLF and what they had been doing in London and so on. It was a complete revelation. Oxford was its own enclosed world: people did not go up to London for the weekend like they do now, and this was like a dam bursting. I came out to all of my friends, I told my parents over the Christmas holiday, which was a big mistake, and I started wearing a GLF badge.

'I had to go off for teaching practice, and I quickly decided that teaching wasn't the thing for me! I went back to Oxford for the summer term, and Mick and I decided to do a play, which was the first thing I had been involved with that had a gay identity. It was at the Oxford Playhouse, a sort of bisexual love triangle called *And What About Me?*, written by a friend of mine. At the same time, there was a film out, *Sunday Bloody Sunday*, which came to Oxford while we were in rehearsal. We went to see it and I remember being absolutely appalled, because it was the same plot as the play we were doing! It wasn't a case of plagiarism or anything, it was just two people having the same idea at the same time: a bisexual man at the centre with a straight woman on one side and a gay man on the other. Anyway, we did it, but it was dreadful! I directed it, and I really did not know what I was doing at that stage. I had been writing revue material for a long time, and at the same time as we did *And What About Me?* I started writing gay songs. I didn't really have a concept of gay theatre as an entity, at its full potential, I was just writing things that I wanted to write.

'I premiered the first out-gay political song that I wrote, at my college ball, at about three o'clock in the morning in front of 300 drunk rugby players,' continues Scott-Presland. 'I was wearing the most appalling beige frock because, as far as I knew at that time, if you were gay and you were a performer then you had to do it in some kind of drag. The song was called "We Were in There", a three-verse song about gay history, with a verse about Oscar Wilde, one about the 1930s and a more contemporary one about the Stonewall riots. I was writing more and more gay material, a song called "Dragula, Queen of Darkness" which sounds a bit clichéd now.'

His assumption about drag was hardly surprising. At the time, British film and television was overrun with men in dresses. Camp humour was everywhere, and audiences rocked with laughter to the antics of closeted homosexuals including Stanley Baxter (who came out in November 2020 at the age of 94), Frankie Howerd, Kenneth Williams, Charles Hawtrey and Danny La Rue, and in 1972, the same year Scott-Presland decided to give teaching the boot, two new camp stars would be born. John Inman, whose portrayal of 'mummy's boy' Mr Humphreys would project comedy series *Are You Being Served?* into the stratosphere, and camp Northern comedian Larry Grayson both got their first big TV break that year, but neither man would admit to their loving audience that they loved men, let alone have been so bold as to march in a Pride parade.

Scott-Presland was determined to shake things up. 'Political action carries its own element of theatre, most obviously with things like the

GLF Street Theatre Group. We didn't do very much street theatre in Oxford, although we did once do something in support of the women's campaign against movements to restrict the 1967 Abortion Act.' The Oxford Gay Action Group (OGAG) recreated GLF Street Theatre's abortion stunt from the Foyle's protest, only on a more spectacular scale. 'I went to a local butcher and bought a large amount of offal, lungs, blood and things like that. We had it in an enormous bag and had this woman with the bag strapped to her, hidden by a white shift, and we laid her out and then did this thing with a coat hanger, ripped the bag open and the blood and offal poured out... two people in the audience fainted!' It was at this time that Scott-Presland first became aware of the potential that theatre had to reach out to an audience. 'I put on a gay cabaret,' he explains, 'And the response was absolutely extraordinary. We put it on for three nights and every night there were queues going around the block, people coming from 50 miles away, and that was a mixture of camp and exclusively gay material. That gave me the idea that this kind of thing had a place within our community, something by us and for us, which I think is the essential element of gay theatre.'

While Scott-Presland was making a public nuisance of himself in Oxford, aspiring songwriter and cabaret performer Mark Bunyan decided to try his luck in the capital. 'I had enough money to pay the rent until the end of the week, so I went to an agency and got a job working for a medical bookseller,' he explains. 'I didn't really know what I was going to do; I'd had auditions for RADA and the Bristol Old Vic and was turned down by both, and I couldn't pay for more auditions.'

Bunyan ended up moving into the basement of a house owned by artist Betty Swanwick, best known for her painting *The Dream*, which was adapted for the cover of the Genesis album *Selling England by the Pound*: 'I wanted a basement flat because I was getting a piano and I wanted to learn to tap dance! Shortly after moving to London, I decided to tell people that I was gay. I thought that if it is a phase, then I may as well enjoy it while it lasts. I thought I would tell all of my friends, and they were going to have to accept it or not. I made a conscious decision to do everything I could to prevent anyone else going through what I had.' With that in mind, Bunyan began volunteering for Icebreakers, a support group for lesbians and gay men founded as an offshoot of the GLF's counter-psychiatry group.

His life was about to take a dramatic shift: a man he had fancied but had dared not tell had realised that he too was gay. 'Someone told Andrew [Andrew Craig, Bunyan's partner], who was in Edinburgh doing his PhD, "Bunyan's done practically everything bar take an ad in the *Times* to tell everyone that he's queer!" I didn't know, but Andrew had also fancied me and had apparently kissed me the night before we graduated, although I cannot remember that as I was very, very drunk. Well, he was on the next train to London, and we've been together ever since! I told my parents. Almost immediately the money ran out and there was no more coming in, but I was so happy, and I couldn't believe that anyone would not want me to be happy. It was awful. I knew that I would have to tell Betty that my parents had cut me off; she kept asking me what was wrong, and told me that I looked terrible, and after about three days I said, "I've fallen in love... with a man." She took a step back and put her hand on the cooker, which luckily wasn't on, and said, "Well, that's wonderful! Let's have a drink!" She became the most amazing friend.'

Dr Andrew Craig was part of the Edinburgh University Gay Society, co-organisers – along with the Scottish Minorities Group – of the International Gay Rights Congress. Taking place in the city from 18 December 1974, it was the first ever International Gay Rights Conference and attracted more than 400 delegates from all over the world. 'It was an incredible crash course in sex and politics,' Bunyan explains. 'There was a word coined around 1967, sexism, and for me that was what this was all about. The idea that there are only two genders, that men should behave like proper men, and women should not be behaving like men and so on. There were people who claimed that the lesbians were trying to derail gay liberation, but I could only see it as a joined-up thing: this wasn't just about getting rights for white, middle-class gay men.'

Nineteen seventy-four had also seen the formation of Gay Sweatshop, Britain's first professional LGBT theatre company. Founding member

Drew Griffiths explained that the group was conceived 'to make a positive statement about homosexuality. We're not trying to hide behind a mask. In the straight theatre scene homosexuals are tolerated so long as they hide "it". Our philosophy is to offer an alternative to that.'[2] Demonstrating their belief that 'homosexuals in all areas of the theatre continue their collusion in putting down gay women and men',[3] and occasionally employing a young gay singer-songwriter by the name of Tom Robinson, the group were an instant success, breaking box office records for the largest lunchtime audience in any British theatre with their play *Mister X.*

After a year of sell-out shows and excellent reviews, in late 1975 Gay Sweatshop went out on the road. At that same time, Peter Scott-Presland found himself in Birmingham. 'I went initially to become the administrator of the Birmingham Arts Lab,' he explains. 'While I was there, I programmed the first Gay Sweatshop tour [Sweatshop member Philip Osment had been at Oxford with Scott-Presland], which was *Mister X*, and a women's show, *Any Woman Can.*

'*Mister X* was devised by Roger Baker, who was the membership officer of CHE at the time, and Drew Griffiths. It was a journey of a gay everyman and very scathing about the gay scene in a way I don't think we would be now. Wherever it played, *Mister X* brought people from miles and miles around; in Birmingham, the place was absolutely packed. There were discussions afterwards, which was the first time many people had talked to other gay people where the purpose wasn't just sex. It was touching in a way, almost shy; people literally had no idea how to talk to each other. No one knew what the etiquette was. The discussions generated a huge amount of energy, and I know that some people went away from there and founded their own local gay groups. That gave me a sense of how theatre can fit into a community.'

Not everyone approved. 'On the contrary,' Griffiths told a reporter from the *Birmingham Post*. 'We have had homosexuals in the audience who have hated it – some have actually said: "You gay libbers are ruining our private lives."'[4] When the Sweatshop tour reached London, all hell broke loose. With permission from the church pastor, in October 1975 *Mister X* was performed inside the Golders Green Unitarian Church.

As soon as the play began, the Reverend Edward Walton of Christ Church, Hendon, stood up and started to heckle the actors, and his family and supporters produced placards proclaiming, 'Man Shall Not Lie with Man'. Gay Sweatshop repeatedly tried to start the play, which begins with a scene involving simulated masturbation, and eventually Reverend Walton was asked to leave, although he noted with some dismay that, 'As I left there was a round of applause, not for me standing up for what I thought decent but the people turning me out.'[5] His wife stayed in her seat and continued to heckle the actors for another 20 minutes or so.

'I was inspired by Sweatshop to write my first gay play, *Latecomer,*' Scott-Presland adds. 'I sent it to Sweatshop, and they rejected it, so I thought, "Fuck it! I'd better do it myself!", which is how I became involved in gay theatre production. I'd written it as a single set piece for four people; it was a very 'talky' play. It went down very well, partly I think because people had not seen themselves portrayed on stage. Like Sweatshop, we were working in an environment where all of the images – Kenneth Williams, Larry Grayson, John Inman – were that very false, stereotypically camp image. There was no suggestion that characters could be rounded.

'After I'd left the Arts Lab, I took over the administration of the Pub Theatre Company, which had a brief to take new work around the West Midlands, performing mainly in pubs. So, we put on this play as part of that. It was an all-male play, which was a bit problematic for a mixed company, so I wrote the next one specifically for two women. I was surprised [by the response]; I was expecting more hostility. It wasn't preachy in any sense, except that it exemplified the importance of coming out. One of the interesting side effects was that two of the actors who had previously identified as straight started having a "thing" together... The play was spilling over into real life!' Bearing in mind some of the harsh criticism Sweatshop received from the good burghers of the provinces, it is little wonder that Scott-Presland expected to face some antagonism from his audience, and if you paid any attention to the media at that time you might well believe that the entire country hated LGBT people. The British press had always shown a prurient, unhealthy interest in any form of pleasure outside of sex for procreation, while happily parading semi-naked women across its pages for the titillation of their male readers.

Gay Sweatshop's performances would often be met with opprobrium, but audiences in and outside of the capital lapped them up. In November 1976 the troupe performed *Mister X* and the lesbian-themed *Any Woman Can* at Dublin's recently reopened Project Arts Theatre, before moving on to the city's Trinity and University colleges, part of a short tour co-sponsored by the Irish Gay Rights Movement (IGRM). Their performances split the critics: the show was derided as promulgating 'crudely offensive' propaganda and for being 'grotesquely obscene' by the *Irish Independent*;[6] however the *Irish Press* was fulsome in its praise, telling readers that 'acting of this standard is a rare occurrence... only the stone-hearted will fail to be moved, and only the insane will miss it'.[7] It did not matter what the critics thought: audiences packed the theatre and loved it, although several called for Project Arts Theatre to lose its £4,000 annual grant. Ned Brennan of Dublin Corporation's cultural committee ranted that 'ratepayers did not elect me to subsidise this kind of filth', and colleague Carmencita Hederman wanted the theatre and Gay Sweatshop investigated by the police on obscenity grounds: 'If it is shown that they are abusing the grant then we must make it a precondition in future that no money be given out without an agreement that only responsible productions be shown.'[8] Sean Loftus, another member of the culture committee, told reporters that 'this is a Christian country and the importation of this sort of stuff should not be tolerated or paid for by ratepayers',[9] although, after seeing the play for himself, he declared that he was not offended and that neither play should be withdrawn.

'I hadn't been allowed to listen to pop music as a child,' Mark Bunyan reveals. 'I always had to play my scales and grade pieces for my piano lessons.' But in May 1976 he got the opportunity to write his first gay-themed song. 'I said that I would write a song for Icebreakers' birthday party. I sang it twice at the party, and by the next morning people were saying, "Oh, I'm still humming your song." The following year, a couple of friends were putting on a show, and they asked if I would like to play piano and sing some of my songs. Then I did a couple of successful benefits to raise money for the *Gay News* fighting fund, and Keith Howes from *Gay News* ran a piece about me. It was that article that got me the audition at Country Cousin.'

Although Country Cousin had seen a number of police raids in its early days, it was now well established as one of the city's best-known cabaret venues, with owner Christopher Hunter happy to spend out for big names. Freddie Mercury would hold his birthday party there in 1977, with guests including the other members of Queen, gay DJ Kenny Everett and Elton John, and any night of the week you might see Shirley Bassey sitting at a table sipping champagne, escorted by her hairdresser. 'I did the audition slot,' Bunyan explains. 'All of my friends came, and we packed the place out. After my first show, Christopher invited us back that evening to see Peter Allen, who was doing three weeks there.' Australian cabaret singer Allen had divorced his wife, Liza Minnelli, two years earlier and was now living with male model Gregory Connell. 'Sitting at the next table was Barry Manilow, who was about to start four nights at the London Palladium,' Bunyan continues, 'and the whole show was Peter Allen talking to Barry Manilow: the rest of us might just as well not have been there! He made it obvious that he didn't like the fact he was playing this place at the end of the King's Road while Manilow was doing the Palladium. It was a hoot!'

Yet as Bunyan would discover, success in the performance world could have difficult personal consequences. 'The next day my mother rang to find out how it had gone, and I told her that there was a bit of barracking at some of the gay material, and she said, "The WHAT?" I told her again, and she burst into tears and put the phone down. My father rang back that evening. He said, "I'll be at Paddington Station at one o'clock on Wednesday, and I expect you to be there."' Bunyan went to meet with his father but refused to return to the family home with him. 'I thought, "I can change things with the songs I'm singing, and if I tell him that I'm not going to sing these songs it will be my fault if other fathers and sons are having rows like this in 20, 30 or 40 years' time." I thought, "He's got to know that this is who I am."

'So, there I am, depressed as hell because my parents were not talking to me. I bumped into Christopher, and he said, "I haven't got anyone to do Sunday lunchtime, could you do it?" Of course, I accepted, and my mother turned up, sat at the back of the room on her own. I got through the show, then we went out onto the pavement. She said, "Come home. I'll look after you. You don't know what kind of place this is... I saw two men kissing in there!" And I said, "No. I'll take you back to Paddington." But she wouldn't let me, so I walked back in... She had been to our home, and Andrew or David [Bunyan and Craig's lover] had told her where I was. She started screaming, "I want you out of my son's home." She said to Andrew, who was doing laundry, "And you go back to your woman's work", so they had physically thrown her out!

'A few days later, my father wrote to my work. It said, "I have sent this letter to the office because you are obviously not master in your own home. I don't want anything to do with you. I don't like queers. I don't like queer material. I don't want to hear anything that you have done", and he never spoke to me again.'

While Bunyan was taking his first steps to success, other forms of gay-dominated entertainment were hitting the big time. Drag had gone mainstream, thanks to the success of stars such as Danny La Rue, Dick Emery and Stanley Baxter, and, as a result, LGBT pubs and clubs that specialised in drag saw less interference from the long arm of Lilly Law. One such venue was Chaguaramas, on Covent Garden's Neal Street which, before its reincarnation as punk club the Roxy, featured cabaret every Tuesday and Thursday night. The Thursday spot was usually given over to drag acts, including the perennially popular Mrs Shufflewick, and Hinge and Bracket.

Played by George Logan (who replaced the original Hinge, Leslie Warren, in 1974) and Patrick Fyffe, Dr Evadne Hinge and Dame Hilda Bracket were a pair of elderly female musicians whose act dripped with innuendo, and who had been building up a name for themselves on the cabaret circuit, with regular appearances at Knightsbridge restaurant AD8, co-owned by trans actress and model April Ashley.

Norman Scott, who kept a day job to supplement his DJ work, would regularly serve Patrick Fyffe at a menswear store in Queensway. He recalls, 'A very interesting character. Before Hinge and Bracket, he worked as a drag artist under the name Perri St Claire. They met at the Black Cap: he already had a partner who couldn't make it one day, and so George Logan stood in. I used to see them at a place in Luton. They were very basic when they first started, not quite what they later became. He brought his sister in [to the shop] one day; they were both appearing in pantomime together. He was a drag artist, and she was principal boy! I said to him, "Your parents must get very confused!" He came in not long after that and was very excited. He said, "I've got a part in a film."' The role Fyffe had landed was as a drag artist in the first *Steptoe and Son* film. Hinge and Bracket would go on to huge success on radio and television and would continue until Fyffe's death in 2002. Other London pubs that specialised in drag, including the Royal Vauxhall Tavern, started to pull in curious tourists who had seen similar acts on TV or who had laughed at the comparably camp antics of John Inman or Larry Grayson.

Jayne County had seen Hinge and Bracket at Chaguaramas when she was in London in 1973, taking part in Bowie's 1980 Floor Show. 'It was amazing,' says County. 'They were just an underground drag act at the time, they didn't get big until much later. Me and Leee [Black Childers] were quite amused: these two drag queens as two very reserved, conservative old ladies. We just thought they were a hoot! We hadn't seen anything like it. Drag acts are usually sexy and outrageous, but this was something totally different. We absolutely loved it.' By the time County next stepped through the door of Chaguaramas, it would be a very different venue.

13

Blasphemy!

'It was a personal decision, but I felt this was such a gross blasphemy of our Lord that I could not live with myself if I did not do something about it.' – Mary Whitehouse[1]

On 9 December 1976, at a private hearing at the High Court in London, Mary Whitehouse, anti-porn campaigner and head of both the Festival of Light and of clean-up TV campaigners the National Viewers' and Listeners' Association, was given permission by judge Mr Justice Bristow to bring a private criminal prosecution against *Gay News*, and its editor Denis Lemon, for blasphemy. By seeking permission to bring action in this way, Whitehouse effectively denied Lemon and *Gay News* the right to contest the claims against them – an action which West Dudley MP Doctor Colin Phipps called 'preposterous', adding that 'it does seem ridiculous not to allow the magistrates an initial opportunity to throw the matter out'.[2] Whitehouse later claimed that Lemon and other representatives for *Gay News* had been invited to the hearing but had chosen not to attend. It would be the first trial for blasphemy heard by a British court since 1921.

The object of Mrs Whitehouse's ire was 'an obscene poem and illustration vilifying Christ in His life and crucifixion', which had been brought to her attention by a probation officer. Rather than raise the issue with the police, the unnamed officer went instead to the self-appointed protector of Britain's morals. The poem, 'The Love That Dares to Speak Its Name', had been written by Professor James Kirkup, yet he was not the target of Mrs Whitehouse's anger. 'My position on censorship has always been that what a person writes is his own business,' she told the media. 'One's concern arises at the point of publication.'[3] Kirkup's poem was written from the viewpoint of a Roman centurion who was present at the crucifixion and who had sex with Jesus's lifeless body afterwards. The centurion notes that Jesus had had sex with many other men before him, including John the Baptist, Judas and Pontius Pilate. 'The Love That Dares to Speak Its Name' was described in court by Mrs Whitehouse's counsel as 'so vile it would be hard for even the most perverted imagination to conjure up anything worse'.[4]

The trial began at the Old Bailey on 4 July 1977, 10 days after around 1,000 LGBT people took part in the sixth annual Pride march. Lemon and *Gay News* were represented by John Mortimer, QC, civil rights defender, and author of the play *A Voyage Round My Father*, and of the *Rumpole of the Bailey* series of books. Mortimer had previously defended the editors of *OZ* during the infamous 'schoolkids edition' trial in 1971. With £12,000 to find for legal fees, disparate LGBT groups around the country were roused into action. Some groups held fundraisers, others rattled donation buckets in their local gay pub. In Manchester, the city's Gay Alliance organised a series of discos held at the university. In Bristol, members of the local CHE and volunteers for the city's lesbian and Gay Switchboard came together to organise the first Gay Bristol Festival, which took place over a fortnight from 17 July 1977.

'We only had five weeks to arrange it all,' switchboard founder Dale Wakefield explains. 'Fundraising was fairly straightforward, and that first festival didn't cost us a lot to put on... The Oasis offered us a Sunday afternoon to hold a fundraiser for *Gay News*.' Since the closure of the Moulin Rouge, Bristol had two gay clubs left: the Oasis, hidden away in the basement of a shop on Park Row, and the King's Club, which stretched over three floors on Prince Street. In May rock group Queen had played two nights at the Bristol Hippodrome and, after one of those shows, Freddie Mercury took the band to the Oasis, where his nervous bandmates occupied a corner booth while Freddie took to the dancefloor.

The first event of the Gay Bristol Festival, a Sunday afternoon garden party, proved so popular with the local LGBT community that it became a regular fixture, raising much-needed funds for Bristol's switchboard for years to come. 'We organised a party on the beach at Brean, and a picnic on Brandon Hill, then we managed to get Romeo and Juliet's, the nightclub on Nelson Street near the Odeon. We booked a couple of acts, one was a fire-eater... And we invited other groups to get involved and put on their own events. In five weeks we pulled together a programme, and we were away!'

'Although I was involved and organised a number of events, Dale was the inspiration to get all of this going, the one who would whip us all into action. She had all the contacts,' explains co-organiser Charlie Beaton. It's little wonder that *Gay News* reporter Keith Howes claimed that 'Dale Wakefield seems to be at the centre of every positive thing that is happening in Bristol's gay community'.[5]

'I suppose the model came from what we saw happening in London,' Beaton continues. 'London Pride was such an event that we felt we should have something local, but we did want to organise a fundraiser to support the blasphemy trial. It was motivated by that.

'Looking back on it, we put on an astonishing range of stuff, including a talk from Black Women for Wages for Housework, which was quite radical, but we didn't see participation in the festival as a political act; we were simply trying to socialise, to create alternatives to the pub and club scene. But clearly there were some events that were more political than others. We were so pleased to get venues to take us because you couldn't be sure that they would; they didn't want their name to be muddied. We were worried that it might be a flop, given we had little experience... Very few of us understood anything about marketing, for example; we were just organising events and then persuading everyone we knew to come along.'

One of the highlights of that first Festival was a talk, at the Students' Union, given by Quentin Crisp. 'That was a bit of a coup,' Charlie Beaton adds. Dale recalls attending a meal given in Crisp's honour. 'I was invited to a cream tea and was entertained by the delightful Quentin Crisp after he appeared at the Students' Union,' she says. 'That was in Richard's flat, which was above the Oasis.' Midway through the festival, on the evening of 24 July, the Tom Robinson Band made their television debut, with a mesmerising performance of 'Glad to Be Gay' on *The London Weekend Show*. The singer was introduced to the audience at home as a man who 'apart from being an excellent singer and musician... Is gay and not ashamed to admit it'.

A year after the festival, Bristol's first, and to date only, Gay Centre opened. With a café, meeting rooms, a small library and drop-in health services, the centre provided a home for the city's Gay Switchboard, allowing the service to finally move from Dale Wakefield's spare bedroom. 'We were still calling [the Switchboard] 'Gay', but there was a lot of tension,' Charlie Beaton admits. 'Lesbians in the group were saying that they needed to have a bigger profile; they didn't feel represented. It was very hard to keep the right proportion of women and a lot of lesbian feminists were irritated by Dale, who found it very easy to work with men.' The service would soon be renamed Bristol Lesbian and Gay Switchboard (BLAGS) and would continue offering its services until 2012.

Despite some heavyweight names in their corner, including broadcaster and journalist Bernard Levin and author Margaret Drabble, Lemon and *Gay News* lost the blasphemy case: the last successful blasphemy trial in Britain to date. The jury took more than five hours to reach a 10–2 majority in Mrs Whitehouse's favour. Patricia Hewitt, general secretary of the National Council for Civil Liberties (Liberty), condemned the verdict as 'a dangerous new form of censorship, particularly for artists and writers who must now conform to the standards of a religion practised by only a minority of the country. The offence of blasphemy, like Lazarus, has risen from the dead.'[6]

The defendants were fined £1,500 plus costs between them, with Denis Lemon also given a nine-month suspended sentence that, he announced, he intended to appeal. Several Labour MPs condemned the sentences as 'scandalous' and 'offensive and insulting to the concept of God as a God of love',[7] and Haydn Roberts, of the Chester CHE, wrote that 'I am absolutely certain that Mrs. Mary Whitehouse did mean to sink without trace the homosexual newspaper "Gay News". What actually happened of course, is that the law has been brought into disrepute, liberal people's opinion of the Christian church has fallen, awareness of homosexuality has risen, the newspaper "Gay News" has had the kind of publicity you couldn't buy for £20 million and the organised homosexual movement has been united as never before.'[8] A new support fund – widely advertised through the underground press, feminist magazines and in punk fanzines – raised £21,000.

On 11 February hundreds of LGBT people and their allies joined the *Gay News* Defence March through London, which culminated in a rally in Trafalgar Square with a performance from the Tom Robinson Band. Two days later, the appeal against the convictions meted out to *Gay News* and Denis Lemon was heard. It would be six weeks before the three appeal judges finally announced that, although the guilty verdicts would stand, Lemon's nine-month suspended sentence would be quashed. 'I had been optimistic and thought we were going to win,' a dejected Lemon told reporters afterwards. 'It's a great relief that the suspended prison sentence has been removed. It was an incredible burden to have over one's head. But I think it's a very sad day for freedom of speech.'[9] A second appeal the following February was dismissed by the House of Lords. Whitehouse continued to equate homosexuality with child abuse, telling a packed Chester Central Hall shortly after the trial, 'I believe that homosexual relationships are wrong. The same as I believe that lustful use of children in pornographic magazines in wrong. The fact that, whenever they can, homosexuals take their leaflets and go into schools to try and influence children, is also wrong.'[10]

While the nation's self-appointed moral guardian was spreading her paranoia, local LGBT groups were becoming more visible around the country. The rights of gay and lesbian union members in the workplace were discussed for the first time during the annual TUC conference in Blackpool, and in Digbeth, Birmingham, the local LGBT community opened their own gay centre. 'It was a big place, four stories. They would hold discos in the basement, and we would put on plays on the top floor,' explains Peter Scott-Presland. 'Because Pub Theatre was a touring company, we had our own lighting rig and sound system, which we took around. Doing plays in the Gay Centre led to us setting up a gay theatre company, One In Ten. By that stage, I was living in a cocoon, and mainly knew gay people, while the few straight people in the Pub Theatre Company were entirely sympathetic.' Yet not everyone displayed such compassion. 'We did find it difficult playing places like the Fighting Cocks in Moseley, which was a music pub with a big heavy metal crowd and a lot of die-hard folkies. There was a certain amount of sneering and nasty comments from them, but we didn't get any trouble from groups like the National Front, perhaps because our publicity wasn't good enough. The Gay Centre did have a couple of attacks – a few bottles through windows meant they had to put up mesh or bars – but the theatre company itself never got directly attacked.' They were not the only target. A gay disco held on Barge Semington, Gloucester's floating arts centre, 'ended in trouble when yobs broke the windows, sending glass showering down onto the dancefloor beneath,' says Phil Booth, who had gone along with members of Hereford's CHE group.

In August 1977, Scott-Presland took the Pub Theatre Company to Edinburgh, for the annual Fringe Festival. He had been the previous year as part of an initiative called the Midlands Umbrella Scheme, which took several local theatre groups, but this time, things would prove far more fraught. 'We hired a theatre in Hill Street, and Gay Sweatshop came. We went as the Pub Theatre Company and did four different shows, which was absolutely exhausting. We didn't account for there being no back-up in terms of running the actual theatre, manning the box office and so on. You had to do all that out of the cast and any lovers or friends that came up to support you. I was doing two shows a day, running the box office and trying to write another show, because towards the end of our second week two people in the company collapsed. They each had a breakdown and said, "We can't do this anymore. We're not going to stay for the third week, we're just exhausted." So, I had four days to write a show to fill this spot. I wrote a very silly thing called *Sir Herbert Macrae: A Tribute* – and that won a Fringe First!

'At that time, the Fringe was really homophobic. The Fringe Club, which was a kind of cross between the Comedy Store and a rugby club, was so rowdy and rude; it was a nightmare to play in. You were trying to showcase things in a wider sense, and I really didn't have a sense of the local community and who would support us. There was no *ScotsGay* magazine which, when it came along later [in 1994], was really supportive and helped get people along to shows.'

171

Back in London, it was not the Fringe that people were concerned with, but fascists. On Saturday, 21 January 1978, almost a year to the day after the Soho bombings, 20 thugs from the National Front (NF) invaded popular drag pub the Royal Vauxhall Tavern. Built in the 1860s, the RVT began to develop a reputation as gay-friendly after the Second World War, and had been hosting drag acts since the late 1950s. The attack saw the bar wrecked and several people injured, including barman Dave Pegg, who needed hospital treatment for broken ribs. The NF, who made their escape from the pub via black cabs waiting for them outside, had made a point of targeting gay venues, businesses and initiatives. In March 1977, at a by-election held in the Harrow ward of Headstone, the NF fielded a candidate, a former member of the Labour Party, in direct opposition to an out-gay Labour candidate, Alex Bruce, who was also a member of the CHE.

The same month that the NF smashed up the Royal Vauxhall Tavern, organisers of the Second Gay Bristol Festival booked the Corn Exchange, then one of the city's major venues, for an advance live performance. Sadly, their plans were thwarted after the Reverend Windsor Grace, vicar of St Mary the Virgin church in nearby Leigh Woods, objected, calling homosexuality 'a maladjustment among people' and stating that organisers were 'wrong to try to press their ideas upon other people'.[11] As Charlie Beaton remembers, 'We had some local artists playing, some folk singers and the like, and the council took the booking, but then the officers were told to turn it down. It was a row that raged for a while, and we got some useful publicity out of it, but the event never took place. There was too much prevarication. Later we had Tom Robinson play, but that was much easier to organise.'

A few months later, teacher Dick Wilcox was left fighting for his life in hospital after being viciously attacked by National Front members in the bar of the Fenton Hotel in Leeds, a gay-friendly venue used by the local chapter of the GLF for their Tuesday night meetings. A group of NF members, some in paramilitary uniforms, had been waiting outside to pounce on LGBT people as they left, but after word of their presence got around, 20 NF members stormed into the bar and began assaulting anyone in the building, gay or straight, breaking chairs and glasses and injuring several people. As well as the heterosexual teacher, a young girl also needed hospital treatment for cuts. It was the culmination of a series of attacks by right-wing hate groups on student, socialist, Asian and LGBT meetings and businesses that had been taking place with alarming regularity in the city for the past few years. Similar attacks would inspire LGBT people to join the Anti-Nazi League, established in 1977 to oppose the rise of the far right. Pride became an opportunity for the community to show solidarity with other minorities, to demonstrate that they were not going to be oppressed.

By late 1977, the shockwaves radiated by the birth of punk had reached other cities around Britain, and the movement's strong ties to the LGBT community encouraged a number of LGBT musicians to take their first steps into the recording industry. In October Liverpudlian punk band the Spitfire Boys released their only 45, 'British Refugee', backed with 'Mein Kampf'. The band gained little fame, but drummer Peter Clarke, aka Budgie, would go on to play as part of Liverpool supergroup Big In Japan – whose line-up included Holly Johnson, David Balfe, Ian Broudie, Clive Langer and Jayne Casey – before joining Siouxsie and the Banshees, while the band's gay 17-year-old singer Maggot would, under his real name, Paul Rutherford, eventually join forces with Johnson in Frankie Goes to Hollywood. Hull-based band Dead Fingers Talk – whose singer, Robert Eunson, had been given the nickname Bobo Phoenix by his friend Genesis P-Orridge while both were at university – relocated to London, signed to Pye Records and recorded their first single, 'Hold on to Rock 'n' Roll', and its more outré flip side 'Can't Think Straight' with David Bowie's guitarist Mick Ronson.

In September 1977 punk band Raped, featuring Liverpool-born gay guitarist Faebhean Kwest – who had once been asked to audition for the Sex Pistols by Malcolm McLaren – recorded their first EP, *Pretty Paedophiles*. With a name like Raped (chosen, apparently, to suggest that young people were being raped by society) and a title like 'Pretty Paedophiles', a level of notoriety was bound to follow them. By the following February, the *Daily Mirror* included them in an exposé on child pornography, falsely accusing the band of being members of the Paedophile Information Exchange (as well as suggesting the group was called the Pretty Paedophiles and the disc called 'Raped'). To bolster their image, the band invited Tony Drayton, editor of punk fanzine *Ripped & Torn*, to the Coleherne to interview them. At the behest of DJ John Peel, they would soon change their name to the more user-friendly Cuddly Toys to issue their recording of the then-unreleased Marc Bolan–David Bowie composition 'Madman'.

EMI, the company that had signed the Tom Robinson band, were eager for their new hit act to consolidate the Top 5 success of their first single, '2-4-6-8 Motorway', and, in February 1978, the group issued a four-track EP, *Rising Free*, which included a live version of the band's anthem 'Glad to Be Gay'. The EP reached number 18 in the British singles charts. Despite being the only gay-identified member of the four-piece, Robinson recalls very little in the way of outright hostility. 'Danny Kustow [the band's lead guitarist] was absolutely okay with TRB being identified as a gay band... But in the world of punk rock being gay wasn't an issue, although punk became a bit of a straitjacket after the first push was over. We never really got any stick from fellow musicians, though one artist's manager was pretty homophobic. I think our manager asked him if he wanted to see the band and his attitude was, "I don't want to go and stand around with a load of queers!"' 'Glad to Be Gay' was a game changer: soon armies of straight, sweaty rock music enthusiasts were punching the air and singing alongside their queer fellow fans when Robinson and the band performed the song. It was not the first punk or new wave single about homosexuality – that honour probably belongs to obscure punk act the Luxury Item, whose sole release, the 1977 single 'Trade', is about cruising for sex in the capital's gay bars – but it helped awaken political beliefs and spur people into action, with much of the audience going on to support causes fighting fascism and oppression, including Rock Against Racism and the Anti-Nazi League.

In April the Tom Robinson Band shared a stage in Victoria Park with the Clash, X-Ray Spex, Steel Pulse and others for Rock Against Racism, which had a huge impact on its audience. 'I was this suburban boy from Essex,' Andy Polaris, who was among the estimated 100,000 people that filled the park, recalls. 'Punk made people politically active, just by being yourself. You didn't realise that at the time, but later, when people say you were one of the few Black people they saw and that you were an inspiration, you realise that's a political statement in itself.' Another person in the park that day was singer and broadcaster Billy Bragg. 'At the top of the bill there was a guy named Tom Robinson... and when he sang ["Glad To Be Gay"], all the fellows around me and my mates just started kissing each other on the lips... I'd never met an out gay man, and suddenly all these guys kissing each other. And my initial thought was, "Why are these gay men here if this event is about Black people?" But it didn't take long, five minutes, to realise that actually the fascists are against anybody who's in any way different and that their fight, these gay men, is the same as our fight against racism. It's actually discrimination that we're against.

'That was a big penny drop for me. You know, I came away from that place with my view of the world changed, and it wouldn't have happened if I hadn't been there ... What changed me was the actual experience of that audience. The Clash did a great job. They got me there. That's very important. Tom did a great job. He sang "(Sing If You're) Glad to Be Gay", which allowed those gay men to openly express their identity, which had an effect on me. But it was those guys, really, it was those brave gay men and all the other kids in the audience that first made me feel that I wasn't the only person who cared about this stuff. And I think that's one of the key things that – perhaps the most that – music can do. It can make you feel that you're not alone.'[12] The message behind Rock Against Racism would reverberate throughout the country; in the Midlands, the movement – and the increasingly high unemployment rate – would inspire disenfranchised young Black, white and mixed-race musicians to form their own bands, taking influences from punk, pop, ska and reggae. Groups including Coventry's the Specials and Birmingham's the Beat (led by bisexual singer Dave Wakeling), formed in 1977 and 1978 respectively, used their music to highlight their growing social awareness and distinctly pro-socialist politics.

Punk, new wave and 2 Tone were doing what they could to unite communities, but the 1978 Pride march, which took place on Saturday 8 July, highlighted the divisions within the capital's LGBT population. With the GLF gone, and the CHE unable to grow its numbers significantly, most of the organisation had once more fallen on the shoulders of London's Gay Switchboard. The march itself, the culmination of 10 days of events across the capital, took an unusual route, through Chelsea and Earl's Court and onto Shepherd's Bush Green. Many LGBT people were frightened to march, especially in light of the attacks perpetrated by the National Front and other hate groups, and the route chosen was a political statement, an attempt to be more visible after suffering increased harassment and outright violence. Protesters realised they had made a mistake when several gay men standing outside the Coleherne threw beer cans and stones as they passed by, their safe haven threatened by the attention drawn to them by their out brothers and sisters. As Terry Stewart, a member of the Brixton Faeries, recalls, 'Everything was going well until we arrived outside the Coleherne, where a bunch of tacky queens came out and decided to bottle the march. Handbags at dawn. If we were not going to be bottled by straights, we certainly were not going to be bottled by our own. Some queens, led by His Eminence Julian [gay activist Julian Hows], put down the revolt in a way that only queens know how. Julian came out of the pub like the Victor over the Vanquished with his booty: a great big handsome leather queen and some others who joined the march. It all ended very positively with the regulars all coming out and cheering us on.'[13]

'By that stage I had enough gay material to perform at Pride,' says Peter Scott-Presland. 'I had a very clear idea that there ought to be entertainment after the march, rather than the traditional Hyde Park picnic. I'd met a guy called Andy Rosenthal, a guitarist, who could accompany me, so we went on that march. It was a very weird route, an insane route. The only places it went past were those where people were going to be hostile, and there were no tourists around, yet one of the ideas of the march is to be seen by a lot of people. We got to the Coleherne and people were throwing beer cans at us. It ended up on Shepherd's Bush Green, with lots of traffic going around, and Andy and I just started singing some songs, going through the crowd and busking. We got a really good response, because people had not had that before. They had cabaret elements, Bloolips had formed by then and Mark Bunyan had had his first show by then, but that was about it.'

176

The LGBT rights movement in the UK was in danger of stagnating. A new Gay Activist Alliance (made up of members of different groups who had originally banded together under the rather unwieldy umbrella title of All London Gay Groups Against Sexism, Racism and Fascism) formed in the first half of 1978 to take positive action against the rising number of violent assaults against LGBT people, clubs and pubs, and this was followed in August by another attempt to bring Britain's disparate LGBT organisations under one rainbow-coloured umbrella. The Coventry-based International Gay Association of Gay Women and Men (IGA) would, after going through a number of iterations, eventually become the International Lesbian, Gay, Bisexual, Trans and Intersex Association (ILGA) and be the first LGBT rights non-governmental organisation to be awarded consultative status by the United Nations.*

The ongoing fight for civil rights was necessary, but it did not pay the bills. Luckily, by the late 1970s being LGBT was seldom a problem for musicians when it came to finding work. In 1978 Steve Swindells was asked to audition for Hawkwind and their spin-off group Hawklords, even though he had been assured by his new management company that he already had the job if he wanted it. 'There was no issue whatsoever with my being gay,' he says. 'We recorded the album [25 Years On] on the farm in Devon, using Ronnie Lane's mobile studio. On the opening night of the album tour, we had a big party. We had Hell's Angels for our unofficial security and they gave me one of their own cut-off jackets. They were brilliant, so homoerotic! Before this, when I was still in Bristol, the head of the local Hell's Angels was a gay guy who had the hots for me.

'I ended up wearing their jacket and I loved the irony. The Hell's Angels were fucking each other. One of them had a tattoo above his

---

* ILGA were suspended from the UN for having a number of groups within their membership actively promoting paedophilia, including NAMBLA (the North American Man/Boy Love Association) and Dutch group Vereniging MARTIJN. These and other groups sympathetic to paedophiles were expelled, but it would be years before the ILGA would be invited back to the UN table.

bum that said, "Pay before you enter"! So, at the after-show party on opening night, I was hanging out with the road crew – all 22 of them. I told them, "Look, you've got a gay man in your ranks, and if you don't like it you can fuck off!" They did the usual "Ohh! Get you!" stuff and I said, "Don't you dare!" I put my foot down very firmly and said, "No. You do not stereotype me." I hate that assumption that people have, when they've obviously not met any gay people, it's like we're homogenous, we're all John Inman.

'While we were on tour, I had my 26th birthday,' Swindells continues. 'When we got to the soundcheck there was a great big box on my keyboard, and an awful three-dimensional card. They knew that I loved irony and that I would make fun of myself. Inside there were all these messages like "you're the best gay bloke I've ever met" and "I'll sleep with you any time" from the road crew. After that initial camp stereotype thing, it never happened again.' It was a good time but destined not to last: 'I had an influence on how their music became far less space-rock, and punkier and more musical. We were rehearsing at Rockfield Studios, and that's where I wrote "Shot Down in the Night", which Hawkwind still do. It's about being a clone, and starts off in the queue outside a gay club. It's about rejection, and people don't get it. It's about clones and gay disco, and also about the oppression of gay people at the time, which was very real.'

Fellow artists – and road crew – might have been broadly accepting of other lifestyles, but some of the public were not. 'I lived in Notting Hill, in a little bedsit with an outside toilet,' Swindells adds. 'I was walking back there from Earl's Court, sometime in 1979, and all these gay guys came walking very fast towards me, and I stopped someone and said, "What's going on?" They were being chased by queer bashers. So, I said, "Why don't we all turn around and walk back and bash them?" I thought, "Fuck this!" I had my dog with me, and I thought, "I'm not going to be oppressed by a bunch of fucking kids." Everyone ran away, but I sat down on a bench and waited, and then I heard their voices: "Ahh, fucking queers! they've all run away." About 12 of them – 15- and 16-year-olds from Holland Park Comprehensive, which was infamous for the bad behaviour of its pupils – approached me and I asked, "What are you guys doing?" "Oh, just having a bit of fun." "Why do you think that's fun?" "Why? You're not queer, are you?" "Yeah," "Well, you don't look it!" ... I told them to sit down and I gave them some fucking education. At the end, they all shook my hand and no queers had been bashed. I wanted to prove to myself that I had the strength of character to stand up to something like that. I like to think that they went away changed people, and I'm really proud of that.'

Swindells had successfully seen off a potential beating. Sadly the men involved in the *Gay News* blasphemy trial would not be so lucky. The magazine and Lemon were instructed to pay all of Mrs Whitehouse's costs (almost £8,000), and although Lemon's sentence was suspended, a further appeal to have the ruling quashed was lost in February 1979. The offences of blasphemy and of blasphemous libel would stay on the statute books for almost three more decades, until they were finally abolished in England and Wales by the passing of the Criminal Justice and Immigration Act 2008.

14

Gay's the Word

'They just barged in, showed me a search warrant and said they were going to search the shop for obscene publications. I was formally cautioned.' – David West (Modern Books)[1]

On a quiet street in Bloomsbury, a literary revolution was taking place. Gay's the Word, a bookshop and café dedicated to providing sustenance to the LGBT community, opened for business in January 1979. Named after the last musical penned by gay songwriter Ivor Novello, the shop soon became a hub for politically active LGBT people and a meeting place for LGBT groups, although leaseholder Ernest Hole had to deal with a number of objections from the local community, the police, and the council, who refused to believe that LGBT literature could mean anything other than porn.

It was not the first bookshop to stock gay titles in Britain – Modern Books, at 283 Camden High Street, had been specialising in gay literature since opening its doors in 1972 and, in August 1975, had been raided by police who confiscated nearly £3,000 worth of gay magazines – but it was the first to use the 'G' word so blatantly, and the first to specialise entirely in LGBT publications. It also offered a performance space for LGBT artists. 'Ernest and I had joined Icebreakers the same day, and he was a neighbour of ours,' says Mark Bunyan. 'He asked for help with the shop, but we didn't have any money to put in, so we helped out with painting and things like that. Then he asked if I would play there, which I did and it was wonderful. It became a regular thing, and I learnt an awful lot there about what I was doing.'

The raid on Modern Books was part of a police crackdown on gay publications carrying contact adverts, with copies of *Gay News* seized by police in Bath in October 1973, and charges brought against *Gay Circle*, a small-circulation magazine filled with ads for men seeking men, in 1975. The editors of *Gay Circle* were accused of conspiracy to procure an act of buggery, and of conspiracy to procure an act of gross indecency, whereas Bath magistrates would eventually decide that *Gay News* was not obscene after all. In Bournemouth, in February 1975, similar action had been taken against lesbian magazine *Sappho*. At the end of March 1976, Incognito, the publishers of *Him Exclusive* magazine and owners of a bookstore in Hammersmith Grove and a shop – heralded as London's first gay department store – in Old Brompton Road, had lost a two-day court battle and saw thousands of copies of their magazines pulped. The previous June, police raided the Hammersmith Grove store and seized 5,000 copies of the latest edition of *Him Exclusive* as well as other magazines and books and one film. In a second raid, they confiscated a further 16,000 copies of the magazine from the company's printer. None of this material was obscene: the Director of Public Prosecutions had simply decided that contact ads 'were a risk to the curious and the young and sexually inexperienced'. Liberal MP David Steel (now Baron Steel of Aikwood) accused the government of 'setting homosexual laws back ten years by devising new conspiracy charges which had never been approved by Parliament'.[2] The post-Thorpe Liberal Party had committed itself to furthering the advancement of gay rights in Britain, including sponsoring a Parliament bill that would outlaw discrimination against gay people on the grounds of sexual orientation.

Eighteen months before the Modern Books bust, 6,000 copies of *Streetboy: Swinging London*, a book which dealt with the experiences of a male prostitute, had been seized by police from its printers, who were charged under the Obscene Publications Act and subjected to a trial at the Old Bailey. Consultant psychologist Doctor Lionel Hayward told the jury that he intended to use *Streetboy* in one of his courses, and that the book 'would be therapy for those with a sense of sexual guilt and of great educative value for the medical and associated professions'.[3] In January 1974 *Streetboy* was found not to be obscene by the jury, and sales of the book could continue. However, Gay's the Word was dipping its toes in decidedly murky waters, as they would soon discover.

With a jury prepared to rule in favour of gay-themed publications, on the surface it probably looked as if society's attitude towards LGBT people was changing; sadly, this was far from the truth. Doctors may have argued for better understanding from the system, but LGBT people still faced massive discrimination in the workplace and in the law, and often fell victim to unspeakably violent acts. On 7 February 1979, Peter Wells – the man who had spent 20 months in jail for having a consensual S&M relationship with an 18-year-old back in 1974 – was found shot dead in his Croydon home. At the time of his death, Wells had been involved in a legal appeal to the European Human Rights Commission against the UK government's draconian laws covering homosexuality in England and Wales.

A discharged shotgun belonging to Wells was discovered near the house. Within 48 hours, the police had arrested and charged 25-year-old William George Purton-Henderson with murder. Purton-Henderson, who had been living with Wells for five days prior to the shooting, was found guilty of manslaughter due to diminished responsibility and jailed for seven years. Purton-Henderson told the court that he was not gay, but at his trial Detective Superintendent Thelma Wagstaff revealed that her 'inquiries suggested that he was a compulsive homosexual and had had affairs with a number of men'.[4] Violence directed towards LGBT people – and towards those suspected of being LGBT – was still rampant, as it was against other minorities too. Trainee teacher Nyrup Reddi, drummer in punk band the Homosexuals, bled to death after having his throat slashed with a broken bottle by a gang of nine white thugs in a racist attack outside a party on the Speedwell Estate in Deptford. The Homosexuals would later issue the track 'My Night Out', a song that opens with a bloodcurdling scream of anguish in direct reference to the attack on their late drummer. Reddi's teenage killer was later jailed for his murder. Reddi was not gay, but the death of

182

a mixed-race musician in a band with a name as provocative as the Homosexuals sent shockwaves amongst the capital's LGBT musicians, especially those who were also involved with Rock Against Racism and the Anti-Nazi League.

In February and March 1979, the same month that Nyrup Reddi was murdered, the second Gay Times Festival took place, at Oval House (the first, held over three weeks in January 1978, had been at Camden's Action Space Drill Hall). Organised by Gay Sweatshop, who performed their highly acclaimed play about Edward Carpenter, *The Dear Love of Comrades*, performers included Mark Bunyan and women's collective Hormone Imbalance.

Bunyan was shocked at the audience reaction to his set. 'It was horrendous,' he recalls. 'There was so much hostility; I sang "The Icebreakers Song" and someone stood up and shouted, "I'll never call Icebreakers again!" Part of the problem was that no one knew what they wanted gay arts to be, but they knew what they did not want it to be. They didn't want a camp man wearing yellow dungarees; my friend [folk singer and feminist music icon] Frankie Armstrong told me that she'd never felt so much hostility from a crowd towards anyone as she did when I began my spot. But when I turned around and started singing stuff like they had never heard before, they realised that you can do this and be deadly serious but also do it with humour.'

Bunyan may have faced a hostile crowd, but Gay Sweatshop's performance went down a storm, and after the festival, they took their play on tour to cities including Coventry, Brighton and Birmingham. Audiences may have hailed their work, but once off the stage the actors were vulnerable to abuse, and in Birmingham a small gang of anti-gay thugs decided to teach them a lesson. 'Gay Sweatshop were attacked after a performance, on the way to a gay pub, the Grosvenor House Hotel,' says Peter Scott-Presland. 'They ran to the door of the pub, covered in blood, and were refused entry. You can imagine there was a furious stink about that afterwards.'

Of course, intimidation, violence and a lack of reparation was not limited to LGBT people living in Britain. On 21 May 1979 5,000 LGBT people and their allies rioted in San Francisco after Dan White was cleared of the murders, in November 1978, of gay council member Harvey Milk and mayor George Moscone, smashing windows, looting businesses, setting fire to cars, pelting police with stones and attempting to burn down City Hall. Police used tear gas and clubs to quell the riot, and dozens of protesters and police were treated in hospital. The following day, roughly the same number of people took part in a peaceful vigil on what would have been Milk's 49th birthday. Milk had been at least partly responsible for the invention of the most obvious and abiding symbol of the Pride movement, the rainbow flag, which was designed by his friend, Gilbert Baker, aka drag artiste Busty Ross (after Betsy Ross, the woman credited, erroneously, with sewing the first American flag), following a suggestion from Milk that Pride needed an enduring symbol. The original flag, hand-dyed and stitched together by a group of volunteers, featured eight stripes, but by 1979 had been simplified to the classic six-stripe version: red (for life), orange (healing), yellow (sunlight), green (nature), indigo (serenity) and violet (spirit). Baker, a former medic in the US army, insisted that he would not copyright the design, ensuring that the iconic rainbow flag would forever be free for the LGBT community to use.

Along with the usual problems of police, a hostile media and queer bashers, gay men in London had a new enemy. Scots-born former soldier and policeman Dennis Nilsen frequented the Champion on Bayswater Road, a favourite haunt of many LGBT artists, including Freddie Mercury, who would use it as inspiration for 'We Are the Champions', and, later, young punks including members of the Clash. It was at the Champion, in November 1975, that Nilsen met David Gallichan, the man who would become his live-in lover. Nilsen would eventually admit to at least 15 murders and two attempted murders, although the full scale of his crimes would not come to light until after his arrest. His reign of terror gave Britain's tabloid journalists another opportunity to attack London's gay scene. Articles focussed on seedy tales of teenage rent boys, of casual hook-ups and of innocents preyed on by dangerous sexual predators. The *Daily Star* claimed that Nilsen was a transvestite, telling readers that 'wearing heavy make-up, skirts and high heels, he would prowl the notorious Soho gay bars and clubs'. The newspaper's lies continued to feed the public's fear of homosexuals being child molesters or deviants – or both.

With a virulently homophobic media filling the nation's heads with nonsense, and the police seemingly intent on supressing any and all attempts to create any kind of social life for queer people, it was time for the country's LGBT community to put aside their differences and work together once more. In June 1979, ambitious plans were announced for a National Pride Week, the first of its kind in Britain, with music as a strong focus.

Organised by a committee of volunteers working from Gay Switchboard's Caledonian Road office and dubbed Stonewall '69: Gay Pride '79 (or simply Stonewall '79), towns and cities around Britain, from Aberdeen in the north down to Brighton on the south coast, came together under one banner. Posters, stickers, badges and 150,000 promotional leaflets were distributed nationally. In Liverpool, a week-long programme of gay-themed films and plays featured Alan Pope and Alex Harding of Gay Sweatshop, who staged their play *Double Exposure* at the city's Playhouse Studio, as part of their showcase night *A Bizarre Compendium of Madness*. In London, the week included more than 100 events and featured performances from Tom Robinson, Dead Fingers Talk, Polly Perkins and Mark Bunyan. Robinson also got involved in a new fundraising single, 'Stand Together', featuring Noel Greig, author of *The Dear Love of Comrades*, and 'A Dyke's Gotta Do' with Jill Posener, the first female member of Gay Sweatshop, that was issued by a new LGBT label, Deviant Wreckords. Although established with the grand vision of recording 'gay and feminist music for general distribution to as wide an audience as possible', it would be the company's only release.[5]

Earlier in the year, Jayne County had been arrested for trespass. 'I was making love to a young man in the Queen's backyard,' she laughs about the incident in the grounds surrounding Buckingham Palace. 'We climbed over the fence; we had no idea that's where we were!' The incident seemed appropriate for someone who, in 1973, had fronted a band called Queen Elizabeth. Jayne and her group, the Electric Chairs, were one of the many LGBT acts touted as playing in London during Pride Week. Stonewall '79 celebrated 10 years since the riots, and as someone who had been present it seemed appropriate to have her there, but despite being advertised she did not take part. 'I don't remember being asked,' she says, 'but I would have played, I would have gladly played. We were touring Europe constantly, so maybe somebody asked my manager, but we were in Holland or somewhere!'

'The first time I remember there being a stage and music [at Pride] was 1979,' says Paul Southwell. 'There wasn't much in the way of bands on before. If there had been, I would have gone. That year, I played on the Gay's the Word float. I had my guitar and we sang a few songs as the march went on through to Hyde Park. Great fun!'

'1979 was the one that got a grant from Greater London Arts,' Scott-Presland explains. 'They used part of the £1,000 to pay for a stage in Hyde Park. I remember huge numbers of police, whereas the early Pride marches would have about half as many police as marchers. Tom Robinson headlined, and I'll always remember the first thing he said on stage: "I'd like to thank all of our gay sisters and brothers in the police force for turning out today in solidarity." A huge roar went up and the police all sort of blushed and shuffled their feet. Polly Perkins got into terrible trouble because she came on in some lurex hot pants – she was never a "dyke-y" dyke although she was a very open dyke – and the cameramen, being all heterosexual men, went bananas and kept trying to shoot her from below. The lesbians and feminists were furious and they rushed the stage, and she had to go off. I had to follow her, and it was terribly difficult to get the crowd's attention after that! I had a repertoire of about eight or nine gay songs, some of them comedy songs, some more political. Again I used Andy Rosenthal on guitar although we split up not long afterwards because I was getting a bit too gay for him.'

Stonewall '79 was the largest gathering of LGBT people the country – and Europe – had seen to date. Over 10,000 people joined the march, and both the BBC and ITV covered the event with special editions of current affairs shows *Inside Out* and *World in Action*. For many outside of the capital, it was the first time they had associated the phrase 'gay pride' with a protest march; for most of the country Gay Pride was simply the name of a prizewinning racehorse.

There must have been something in the air that year. Two students at Leeds Polytechnic, Marc Almond and Dave Ball, who had been rehearsing together under the name Soft Cell, began writing the songs that would appear on their debut EP, *Mutant Moments*. In Liverpool, Pete Burns formed Nightmares in Wax who would, after a couple of line-up changes, mutate into Dead or Alive. In Edinburgh, the Associates, fronted by the bisexual Billy Mackenzie, issued their debut single, a minimalist cover of Bowie's recently released 'Boys Keep Swinging', highlighting Mackenzie's impressive vocal range. Issued on their own Double Hip Records, the disc's limited distribution meant that it stood no chance of being a hit, but it brought the group attention from the music press and from record companies. Shortly after, they signed a deal with Fiction Records, home of hit post-punk act the Cure. As the 1970s drew to a close, LGBT artists were becoming more and more visible in all areas of the arts.

The late 1970s had seen a rapid growth in the number of gay venues across London, catering to many different sectors within the LGBT community. 'There were so many things going on, and we were mopping up culture from all over the place,' recalls Andy Polaris. 'I don't think people appreciate how curious we were back in those pre-internet days, so much of it was word of mouth. We learned so much about gay culture from the discos, even from listening to bands like the Village People. Seeing that video of Sylvester performing 'Mighty Real' on *Top of the Pops*, with him spinning around and turning from a man into a woman was as revolutionary as seeing David Bowie, and that was years before Culture Club and all that scene.'

69 Dean Street, Soho, was the home of Billy's, where DJ Rusty Egan and Caerphilly-born Steve Harrington, known to his friends as Steve Strange, ran a weekly night dedicated to the music of Bowie, Roxy Music, Kraftwerk and other uber-cool artists, in the basement of the long-established Gargoyle Club. After three months, the management gave the pair their marching orders; Billy's became Gossip's (home to legendary Goth night the Bat Cave) and, in February 1979, Egan and Strange relocated to the Blitz Wine Bar in Covent Garden's Great Queen Street. Patrons included Siouxsie Sioux; a young man named George O'Dowd and his friend Peter Robinson, who would become better known as Boy George and Marilyn respectively; model, journalist and DJ Princess Julia; Andy Polaris; and Jeremy Healy, who would go on

to form hit band Haysi Fantayzee before becoming one of the biggest club DJs on the circuit. Other regulars included a young puppeteer named David Claridge (who would become famous as the voice and operator of Roland Rat) and DJs Tallulah and Mark Moore, who – after a spell at Philip Sallon's Mud Club – would become one of Heaven's star attractions and, in 1988, score a number one hit of his own with 'Theme From S'Express'. (Boy George would also get his first turn at the decks thanks to Sallon, a decade and a half before he made his professional debut as a gay club DJ at Heaven, in October 1995.) The Blitz also gave birth to the New Romantics, with members of up-and-coming bands, including Spandau Ballet and Visage (and future members of Sigue Sigue Sputnik), inhabiting its space. It was also hugely popular with a new wave of young British fashion designers, many of whom would go on to become household names.

'We started at Billy's,' Polaris explains. 'The *Daily Mail* did an article about Billy's in 1978 and I was in that. We were part of the scene, so when the Blitz came around we already knew what kind of place it was going to be. We had a squat in Kentish Town, that was me, George and Marilyn, and another friend called Myra. We moved from there down to Carburton Street in Central London. Additional people would come and go, and there were other squats around the corner, with at least 30 people from that scene. We would all stroll down to Covent Garden when we wanted to go out. It was a great, exciting time. Most of us had jobs. I was working for one of the contractors that built the Barbican, and I only left when we got the record deal.

'There was never an issue with homophobia at the Blitz. They would not allow anyone in who had an attitude; they were quite strict on the door. A lot of people thought that was snobbery, but it was because they didn't want people gawking, tourists and the like coming... It wasn't a huge club, so they could afford to be selective about who went in, and they certainly didn't want any trouble, which you would get at a lot of gay clubs. You could not get into [other] gay clubs if you were dressed a bit freakishly – in the West End, you wore a suit and tie. People forget how conservative England was back then!'

The door policy was certainly strict. On one fabled occasion, Steve Strange refused to let Mick Jagger in because he was dressed too conventionally. The Rolling Stone returned a short while later in the company of a Blitz club member and was begrudgingly allowed entry.

'After Bang!, I went to Global Village,' DJ Norman Scott explains. A cinema, nightclub and restaurant complex tucked away inside the Hungerford Arches, beneath Charing Cross railway station, 'Global Village was very, very popular: it was a straight club, but I loved it. It was on two levels with a DJ upstairs and a DJ downstairs. I talked to the manager there about putting on a gay night, but he said, "Oh, don't be silly! There wouldn't be enough gay people in London to fill the place!" He was wrong, of course, because shortly after that it became Heaven.'

Global Village closed its doors for good in late 1979. When the venue reopened that December, it had a new name. Heaven was the largest gay club in Europe and it had cost owner Jeremy Norman around £300,000 to renovate, but the New York disco-inspired interior (designed by Norman's partner – and later husband – Derek Frost), state-of-the-art light show and sound system soon had the public queueing up outside night after night. DJs included former Catacombs, Bang! and Blitz club DJ Tallulah, and Ian Levine, the former northern soul DJ who would soon become inseparably linked to Hi-NRG music, after helping found the Record Shack label and working with Bronski Beat, Erasure and Pet Shop Boys, among many others. Freddie Mercury became a regular at Heaven, usually accompanied by Kenny Everett. Jeremy Norman would sell Heaven to Richard Branson's Virgin empire in 1982, and Jeremy Joseph and G-A-Y would take over the reins in 2008.

'Heaven was great,' remembers Andy Polaris. 'That was the first big gay-only club and everyone used to gravitate there. They put on a lot of gigs too: I remember seeing Culture Club, Musical Youth six months before they were at number one [with their debut single, "Pass the Dutchie"], a fantastic concert by Bauhaus [March 1981], Throbbing Gristle... They had a lot of different people playing in that venue as well as the club thing going on. It was a great space.' Erasure was just one of a number of high-profile bands that got an early break at Heaven, playing there in December 1985, shortly after the duo – former Depeche Mode and Yazoo songwriter and keyboard player Vince Clarke and Peterborough-born singer Andy Bell – formed.

Bell had moved to London in search of a life outside his home town, and clubs like Heaven provided a major lure. 'There was zero gay scene in Peterborough when I was a teenager,' He recalls. 'There were rumours of a bar at the back of the Bull Hotel, but I never saw anyone there! One of my girlfriends at the time had a gay brother and used to tell us stories about Cha Cha's, a club night at Heaven in London, so we made plans to move there. I remember playing Heaven and being very shy about it because I'd been quite a regular at the club, so they all knew me to a certain extent.'

The 1970s had seen some improvement in the public's attitude towards LGBT people, encouraged in no small part by the increased visibility of LGBT-friendly musicians, queer-themed theatre and a burgeoning nightlife. Yet the media and the authorities still had some way to go to catch up. While the country was gearing up towards Stonewall '79, the CHE's Executive Committee set up a working party to research and campaign against harassment of LGBT people by the police and court system. Citing evidence of 'substantial differences in police methods from one constabulary to another', and stating that 'in Manchester the police tell us that all people arrested for these "offences" are automatically prosecuted',[6] their research found that 'so wide are the limits of penalties which can be imposed upon a man charged with gross indecency or soliciting that in practice a first offender may face a fine of anything between £25 and £200, depending on where and before whom he is tried.' The campaign, which aimed for 'a fairer deal from the law' resulted in a report, 'The Unequal Kingdom', being issued later that year.

One of the principal targets for the CHE's ire was the chief constable of Greater Manchester, James Anderton. In November 1980 the CHE wrote to the Home Office, demanding either the resignation or dismissal of Anderton, whose tenure as chief had seen a phenomenal rise in the numbers of gay men arrested for cottaging. In Stockport alone, the figure jumped from 12 arrests in 1979 to over 150 in 1980, and there was evidence that the police were once again using agents provocateurs to entrap men. 'James Anderton is a typical example of how homophobia was rife even right at the top of the force during this time,' says Paul Southwell, but the Home Office refused to act.

Anderton, who served as chief constable from 1976 to 1991, was a former Methodist lay preacher whose conversion to Catholicism had seen a marked hardening of his personal stance on everything from vice and homosexuality to left-wing politics and public morals. His outspoken views saw the media dub him 'God's Copper'.

The police were causing problems north of the border too. For young Sheena 'Horse' McDonald, later to find fame as one of the country's most revered singers, life in the town of Lanark was no picnic. 'I had a girlfriend who was not out, who was still sleeping with men at the same time,' she explains. 'I went out with her from when I was about 14 or 15 until I was around 21, but it was all secret. The seventies were turbulent times, and my dad was an important person in the town, as well as being quite firm-minded and tough on us. I didn't want to bring shame on the family, so although I looked a certain way and dressed a certain way, I didn't really say anything. My girlfriend and I were attacked several times, verbal and physical attacks, but I just put my head down and got on with it.

'The final straw came one day when I was going to meet my mum, who worked at the hospital. I was crossing a road, and there was a patrol car parked at the side of the street. Both windows were down and as I was crossing the road this policeman with his arm out the window shouts, "There's that fuckin' lezzie". My heart sank. What made things even worse was that the young policewoman in the car was a girl I had been at school with. I thought, "I'm not safe in this town." I was already being chased and shouted at, but now I really didn't feel safe.

'Years later my dad, who become a town councillor, saw this in an interview and said to me, "But you never told us". If only I had thought I could speak to my mum and dad, but I was laden with this shame about who I was. Some of that shame comes from outside, but some from inside. Through singing I can express all of these emotions. It's the most incredible release; it's quite cathartic. Music saved my life, growing up. I was lost, really, really lost, and it gave me something to head towards.' Stonewall '79 had seen the LGBT community in Britain gain its most positive media coverage since the passing of the Sexual Offences Act 12 years earlier, yet despite generally constructive noises being made by politicians towards furthering LGBT civil rights, as the new decade began the system was still weighed heavily against change.

15

The Shock of the New

'I don't find my sexuality odd. What I do find odd is the fact that gay women have to live in a hostile world. I'm not allowed to show any affection towards my girlfriend in public, yet men and women can neck in front of me at the cinema and walk along the road holding hands. It all seems rather unfair.' – Marje Proops[1]

As the 1980s began, LGBT representation on television was still almost non-existent. Some of the most popular characters on British television were played by closeted homosexual men, many of whom were earning a very comfortable living playing limp-wristed queer stereotypes, while openly dismissing the LGBT community in the press and swearing on the nearest holy book they could grab that they were entirely 'straight'. Heterosexual actor John Hurt had won plaudits for his sympathetic portrayal of camp icon Quentin Crisp in the TV adaptation of the stately homo's biography *The Naked Civil Servant*, and a new comedy series, *Agony*, featured the first ordinary gay couple seen on the small screen outside of a documentary, but actors who were deemed to have exploited the LGBT community for a cheap laugh were in for a rough ride. A show mooted by Granada TV about a Second World War army unit made up of homosexuals, *All the Queen's Men*, thankfully got no further than the pilot script stage, but too many TV shows were using gay or effeminate men as comic fodder. In October 1977 the CHE picketed a performance in Brighton starring John Inman, who played the flouncy Mr Humphries in the BBC's massive comedy hit *Are You Being Served?*, complaining that Inman was 'contributing to television's distortion of the image of homosexuals';[2] comedian Dick Emery faced pickets in Britain and while he was on tour in Australia over his portrayal of effeminate men, and when Inman went to the antipodes, to star in an Aussie version of his department store sitcom, he too was brought down to earth with a bump. At a cabaret appearance in New Zealand, the Auckland Gay Activists Organisation arranged a protest, denouncing his act as 'the latest in a long line of ignoble entertainers to make a very good living from holding up a caricature of the homosexual for the rest of society to mock and denigrate'.[3]

While major stars like Emery and Inman were looking to extend their careers by searching for new audiences outside of the UK, back in Britain the demand for LGBT-themed entertainment that did not denigrate its audience was growing ever greater. Like so many artists before him, Peter Scott-Presland was finding the lure of London irresistible, and in 1979 he left Birmingham's Pub Theatre Company and headed towards the bright lights. 'I had the feeling that if you want to make it as a writer then you really had to be in London,' he says. 'While I was in Birmingham I'd written and directed, I'd organised festivals and I'd done some work for television, mostly writing continuity links.

'I'd written a show called *Wednesday Matinee*, which started life as a showcase for each of the members of the company. It was a kind of portrait gallery of people who go to cinemas on wet Wednesday afternoons, very stereotypical characters, a couple of pensioners, a would-be critic, a housewife, an unemployed greaser, a cinema usherette, a schoolboy playing truant and a dirty old man, who was a problematic character that went through a lot of changes over the years. They had individual songs, but there's this piece at the end where the rocker is trying to get off with the usherette and the dirty old man is trying to get off with the schoolboy... This was seen by the commissioning producer for a TV series being made in Birmingham called *Second City Firsts* [a 1974 episode, 'Girl', featured the first lesbian

193

kiss on British television]. I was commissioned to rewrite *Wednesday Matinee* for the series. I had to go down to London for a meeting with the director, and they wanted to lose the gay element. They wanted to lose the dirty old man and any suggestion that the schoolboy might be gay. But I would not do that. The whole thing was very carefully balanced, the finale was an octet, and you couldn't lose characters without recasting the whole thing. So, I dug my heels in and wore them down until eventually all they wanted were two words changed, "pulsating" and "toilet"! There was a line in the dirty old man song that went "come with me into the toilet and I'll give you half a crown", so I agreed to do that. They started casting, and I was over the moon that they had Beryl Reid as the housewife. But then there was a Musician's Union strike and it got postponed. A new date was pencilled in, but Beryl was not available, so it was postponed again, and put off and put off and never actually made. But I still have the contract!'

Outside of the still-heavily closeted – and heavily censored – world of television, the repercussions of punk and new wave, gay and female emancipation and the anti-fascist and anti-racist movements were being felt in all of the performing arts. The stagnant world of British comedy, which had for too long relied on racism and sexism for its laughs, saw a new generation of socially aware performers, including Dawn French and Jennifer Saunders, Ben Elton and Alexei Sayle who embraced minorities, including LGBT people, as their equals. Drag also got a new face: traditional drag – men in posh frocks emulating Danny La Rue or Foo Foo Lamar, singing music hall standards or miming to Shirley Bassey and Judy Garland – gave way to a new breed of more ferocious acts, whose devastating putdowns and cutting-edge comedy replaced the fey campery of their predecessors. Former dancer Reg Bundy and care assistant Paul O'Grady would slap on the slap and destroy audiences at Camden's Black Cap or the Royal Vauxhall Tavern as Regina Fong and Lily Savage respectively. Lily would cross over into the mainstream, as would defiantly out comedians such as Julian Clary. But it would not be a smooth ride.

'In 1980 I was in Edinburgh with a load of alternative comedians, some of whom were funny, some of whom were just saying "fuzz" and "police" instead of "mother-in-law",' says Mark Bunyan. 'Alexei Sayle, who I have enormous respect for, organised an audition for me at the Comic Strip.* Andrew [Bunyan's partner] said, "Don't do too much gay stuff; we need the money!" I sang "Do Yourself In", and at the end Peter Richardson [then running the Comic Strip] said, "Yes, you're very slick, but the people who perform here are really committed." At that time, I was the only professional, out-gay cabaret performer in the country, but I needed the gig, so I took a deep breath, and I started singing heavier and heavier songs, like "Late Call" which is a song about a policeman talking to a father whose son has been stabbed coming out of a gay pub. At the same time, auditions for television started, but again I was told that I can't do the gay stuff – in fact I was told that there was absolutely no way that an out-gay comedian would ever be seen on national television. This was 1980. One particular TV show wanted me to come on and play "Late Call" and then discuss it, but they decided against it. But I did get to perform on Radio Four's *Start the Week*, and Keith Howes, a journalist for *Gay News*, later told me that when I sang my version of "The 12 Days of Christmas" and referred to "my true love" as he rather than she, nobody had ever done that before. As far as I am aware, the BBC only had one letter about it, from a mother and daughter who wanted to have the words to "that very funny version of 'The 12 days of Christmas'".'

While small steps were being made with regards to LGBT exposure in the media, politically there was little to celebrate at the dawn of the 1980s. The previous May, following years of rising tension within the country's marginalised communities, the Conservative Party, under Margaret Thatcher, had swept to victory in the general election. Thatcher was committed to reducing immigration and to taking power away from the unions, and was also firmly against sanctions that may have brought an earlier end to apartheid in South Africa. The first years of her premiership would see riots on the streets of several British cities, all-out battles between the police and striking miners, and a war over a remote archipelago in the South Atlantic Ocean that most people back in Britain had never even heard of. Her government made it clear that,

---

* A new comedy club that launched at Paul Raymond's infamous Soho strip club, the Raymond Revuebar, in October 1980.

in its eyes, the typical British family was made up of white, middle-class homeowners who were most definitely heterosexual.

This new swing towards the right politically saw a renewed increase in antagonism between the LGBT community and the authorities. After the huge success of Stonewall '79, Pride in London in 1980 should have gone smoothly. However, this was not to be: the march was unruly, and a number of arrests were made. As had always been the case, the march was accompanied by a phalanx of police, some of whom saw their role not as protecting those marching but keeping them in their place and preventing them from upsetting the delicate constitutions of the capital's shoppers, commuters and tourists. In previous years, marchers had simply put up with the harassment, but from now on things would be different: the number marching would continue to grow, as would the number of those voicing their disaffection with the government that demonstrated no intention of improving LGBT rights. By the time the parade reached its destination, the University of London Union in Malet Street, many in the crowd had become more than a little disgruntled with the overt police oppression, and 10 men were charged with misdemeanours including obstruction and minor assault. 'I didn't go to protest outside because I had a show to do,' Mark Bunyan explains. 'But I remember seeing a rugby match on television and a news flash came up saying something like "gay riot in Covent Garden: Princess Margaret stranded at Opera House"!'

One of those arrested, Frank Egan, was charged with possessing an offensive weapon: a rusty prop meat cleaver that he wore as part of his headdress. Egan, a member of the Brixton Faeries cooperative, was taken off to Bow Street Police Station; Julian Hows, a former station guard who had run into trouble when he attempted to wear a skirt as part of his uniform, and who had been involved in the Pride protest outside the Coleherne in 1978, remonstrated with police over the arrest and was also detained, and a small crowd of protesters followed them there.

But while the politically aware were clashing with the police and the government, London's gay nightlife continued to expand. The success of the Blitz brought interest from the media which, in turn, brought new customers from outside of London, eager to see what all the fuss was about. In May 1980 Rusty Egan and Steve Strange launched a new club, Hell, at Mandy's, a members-only gay club on Henrietta Street that had previously had a reputation as a safe place for a closeted businessman to bring his newly acquired rent boy, no questions asked. With Blitz becoming more popular, Hell, which ran twice a week, was specifically intended to cater for Strange's friends, the underground crowd, and those who wanted to avoid the limelight. David Claridge came too, hosting the Ancients, a club night that mixed classical music with underground electronica. Apparently someone forgot to send David Bowie the memo: on 1 July 1980, on the hunt for extras to appear in the video for 'Ashes to Ashes', the megastar went not to Hell but to Blitz. 'There was a big furore,' Andy Polaris, who was in Blitz that night, reveals. 'Everyone went a little bit scatty because he was in the room. I had already seen Bowie; I went with Boy George to see the Human League once and he was there, so I was much more low-key! I hadn't actually met him, but that didn't matter. I could be cool about it, I'd already been close to my idol. He was courting the whole scene, and some of our friends ended up in the "Ashes to Ashes" video.'

Hell's co-owner Egan had been involved in Visage, a musical project with Scots-born singer and multi-instrumentalist Midge Ure, principally put together to provide music for his burgeoning DJ career. Discovering that Strange could sing (he had been a member of the new wave bands the Moors Murderers and the Photons), Egan and Ure recruited him to handle lead vocals on a demo they were shopping around, a cover of the Zager and Evans hit 'In the Year 2525'. The track was turned down by several record companies, but producer Martin Rushent showed some interest, and the group's initial sessions with him would lead to the release of their first single, 'Tar'. Strange became the public face of Visage, but that public would first see him prancing around dressed as a nun on Pett Level beach near Hastings, in the video for Bowie's first number one hit of the new decade. Hell only lasted for around six months, and the Blitz closed the following year: Strange and Egan moved on to Club for Heroes in Baker Street, but by then Visage had clocked up their biggest hit, 'Fade to Grey', and Strange had become a bone fide star.

While some venues were closing, new ones were opening up in their place. Alongside his flourishing songwriting career, musician

PRIDE, POP AND POLITICS

Steve Swindells became heavily involved in the capital's burgeoning club scene. Inspired by a trip to New York, which included a visit to the notorious hedonistic hotspot Studio 54, Swindells' first venture was the Lift, a once-a-week gay night held on the fifth and sixth floors of an office building in Soho, so called because you could only gain entry via a lift from the ground floor. 'Paradise Garage [in New York] was the inspiration for the Lift. The DJs were John Richards and DJ Mel. Susan Sarandon showed up on the opening night! It was gay, but totally inclusive. Women were welcome, straight people were welcome, lesbians were welcome, people of colour were welcome. I was so fed up with the inherent racism in gay clubs, or with the same dull people hanging around. You would see Kenny Everett and Freddie Mercury all the time, coked off their heads; they were so boring! I met Freddie several times and thought he was boring, but maybe that's because he was painfully shy.'

The venue for the Lift would change over the next few years, but the club – and Swindells – went on to host London's first underground, all-night (and strictly illegal) rave in a four-storey warehouse in Shoreditch, three years before the second summer of love saw the country covered in smiley face stickers and A5 flyers. 'The dance floor was in the basement,' he recalls, 'which was accessed by a rickety wooden staircase. By midnight, it was a sweaty, heaving mass of wildly boogieing bodies. The other floors were chill-out areas, which I had decorated with shower curtains that I had spray-painted with abstract designs – all pretty low-fi. The atmosphere was buzzing, sexy and warm. Some plain-clothes police arrived at around 5 am, but they were really polite and pleasant and simply asked me to turn the music down, then left.'

'The Lift was great,' Andy Polaris recalls. 'That was one of the first clubs in London where Black gay people were happy to be seen. To be Black and queer at that time was tough; there was still a lot of racism in gay culture. Black people were going to clubs and being refused entry; they weren't going to let you in unless you were with a white person. Or people would not believe you could be gay or queer if you were Black – it's almost like you had to prove it, maybe kiss someone or be in full drag, before they would let you in. There was a lot of that going on, so Steve's club was quite important. And the music was great: it was playing decent, proper R&B, disco and funk, it wasn't playing all the commercial stuff.'

Alongside club promotion, Swindells continued to move forward with his solo career, releasing the 1980 album *Fresh Blood*, which he describes as 'a concept album about cruising. It's about always looking for someone new. It's about rejection, it's about unfulfillment, it's about oppression...' This led to his writing several songs for Roger Daltrey after the Who singer covered 'Bitter and Twisted' for the soundtrack to hit movie *McVicar*.

On 1 February 1981 Scotland's oppressive anti-homosexuality laws were finally brought into line with those of England and Wales, and for the first time in the country's history homosexuality was no longer a crime, although the restrictions on who could have sex, and when and where they could do the deed, were the same as those permitted under the Sexual Offences Act 1967. The following year, after legal action found that Northern Ireland's criminalisation of same-sex acts was in violation of the European Convention on Human Rights, the Homosexual Offences Order decriminalised sex between two men over the age of 21, in private, in Northern Ireland.

Change had been a long time coming. Back in July 1976, Merlyn Rees, then Secretary of State for Northern Ireland, attempted to introduce a bill to bring legislation in Northern Ireland – including laws that applied to homosexuality and divorce – more in line with the rest of the United Kingdom. His move came after a series of raids by the Royal Ulster Constabulary on gay rights organisations, where documents were seized and 23 men arrested and interrogated. Although many moderates in Northern Ireland – including some outspoken clergy – agreed that the time was right for change, the court system still treated gay men with contempt. In Derry, while summing up the case against two men, aged 20 and 24, the judge reminded the defendants that 'Prior to 1885 the penalty for this sort of offence was death', before recommending that both were sent for psychiatric evaluation.[4] Northern Ireland's Democratic Unionist Party, under the leadership of the Reverend Ian Paisley, had campaigned to 'save Ulster from sodomy' for years, but finally it seemed that the laws governing homosexual acts in the United Kingdom would be the same no matter where you lived.[5] However, the British government continued to exhibit massive hypocrisy when it came to the sex lives of its citizens. The man, or woman, in the street was still subject to ridicule and prosecution should they do anything outside of the heterosexual norm, yet if you were in a position of power you could be just about as sleazy as you liked, and Mrs Thatcher and her cabinet would conspire to protect you. In March 1981 former high-ranking diplomat Sir Peter Hayman was named in the House of Commons (by Geoffrey Dickens, a Conservative MP who spent many years campaigning for the victims of child abuse) as a member of the Paedophile Information Exchange (PIE), an organisation whose leader had recently been jailed for two years for 'conspiring to corrupt public morals'.[6] Three years earlier, Hayman had been investigated by police after leaving a package containing PIE-related material on a bus, but at the time the government insisted that although he had fantasies about sex with underage boys, he had not acted up on them, and they chose not to prosecute. Hayman had been at the very top of the diplomatic corps, attended NATO meetings and had acted as High Commissioner to Canada for four years; his sexual proclivities had made him vulnerable to blackmail, but by the time the public got to know anything about it, he had already retired. Despite the government's insistence that he not be prosecuted, following Dickens's speech, former members of PIE revealed that Hayman, using the name Henderson, had been an active member of the group. Government correspondence made it clear that 'although Sir Peter was not charged with any offence there seemed to be a good deal of circumstantial evidence of his involvement.'[7]

It would not be the last time that Hayman would cause trouble, nor would this be the only sex scandal to dog the Thatcher government. Just over a year later, one of her closest allies, Cecil Parkinson, would be forced to resign after the media learned he had not only had an affair with his secretary but she was now carrying his child; later still, one of Mrs Thatcher's staunchest supporters, deputy chairman of the Conservative Party Jeffrey Archer, would be sent to prison for perjury and perverting the course of justice resulting from his affair with prostitute Monica Coghlan. David Mellor, who served as Minister of State for Foreign and Commonwealth Affairs, Minister of State for Health, Minister of State for Home Affairs and Minister for the Arts under Thatcher, would be forced to resign following tabloid stories about his extra-marital affair with actress Antonia de Sancha.

In June 1981 the first issue of a new LGBT newspaper appeared. Not only was *Capital Gay* to be published weekly, it would also be free, with in excess of 20,000 copies distributed around London and Brighton. Founded by former *Gay News* staffers Graham McKerrow and Michael Mason, *Capital Gay* took a more hard-line political stance, supporting London's Lesbian and Gay Switchboard (which by the beginning of the 1980s was answering over 3,000 calls a week from around the country), the annual Pride festival and other socio-political ventures. *Gay News* had been in decline since the blasphemy trial of 1977, and had been slow to recognise the value and importance of London's booming new gay nightlife. The efforts of editor Denis Lemon, now the majority shareholder, to bring in outside influences to financially underwrite the business met with a furious backlash from *Gay News* staff, who attempted a coup. When that failed, Lemon sold the entire business. The *New Gay News* ran for just seven issues before folding for good in April 1983.

Gay News was not the only iconic LGBT business undergoing radical changes. Richard Branson's Virgin empire had recently purchased Heaven for £500,000, and although he claimed that he had no intention of varying the club's music or entrance policy, almost immediately Heaven changed, operating as a gay disco from Wednesday through to Saturday, and introducing live gigs and cabaret the rest of the week. Branson hoped to bring popular alternative night Cabaret Futura to the venue, curated by former Blitz regular Richard Strange, now one of London's biggest alternative club organisers. The move did not happen, but Branson ended up signing Strange to Virgin Records for £54,000.

London's Pride march, meanwhile, took an unusual year off in 1981; that summer, the UK's major Pride festival relocated to Huddersfield. Trouble had been brewing in the town for a while, and many involved in the organisation of the country's only regular annual Pride festival felt the need to travel to Yorkshire to show support. Gay venue the

201

Gemini Club was raided by police on a regular basis, at one point being described by the local police as a 'cesspit of filth'.[8] The popular gay disco drew LGBT people from Manchester, Leeds and Sheffield; the police were intent on having its licence renewal refused and so on most weekends the music would be shut off, the lights would go up and the revellers would have their names and addresses taken. It was nothing short of intimidation. Other moves to upset the local LGBT community took place: at an event to help raise funds for the town's Gay Carnival, the DJ who had been booked refused to play to an LGBT audience, leaving organisers to step in and play instead.

In a very public show of solidarity with the regulars of the Gemini Club and the Huddersfield Gay Action group, coach loads of LGBT people from around the country, including the Brighton Lesbian Group, and student groups from Halifax, Nottingham and Manchester, descended on the town. On the day of the march, there was live entertainment provided by Peter Scott-Presland's theatre troupe Consenting Adults in Public and Mark Bunyan, and the day ended with an alcohol-free Florida Orange Juice Disco, named in honour of the US anti-LGBT agitator Anita Bryant, famous for her years as the public face of Florida's orange juice producers. 'I think there were about 600 of us on the march,' Mark Bunyan recalls. 'It was very unpleasant: the thing I remember most is that there was a Black guy marching a little way behind me, and there were Asian and Afro-Caribbean people stood on the pavement, incandescent with rage at him. Their homophobia was clear.' Bunyan later performed to a packed and highly charged audience at a hall on the town's Venn Street. 'When I sang "I'll Always Remember You Sweetheart" people started crying. There were heightened emotions in the crowd anyway, and they started to react, and I started to react, and I really had to hold back the tears.'

That same year, in the town of Bushey, near Watford, two school friends – Andrew and Georgios – who had both been members of local ska band the Executive, decided to branch out on their own with a new act, Wham!. Greek Cypriot Georgios 'Yog' Panayiotou would soon become famous worldwide as George Michael. 'George Michael was warm, intelligent and fabulous,' says Steve Swindells. 'We were very good friends in the eighties. His pretend girlfriend, Pat Fernandes, was my boyfriend's cousin. The four of us used to hang out a lot, and I got to know him very well.'

DJ Norman Scott was by now well-known on London's gay scene, with residencies at Bang! on Charing Cross Road and Bolts, a weekend gay night at Lazer's night club, in Haringey. 'I didn't get to know Andrew very well, but George used to come down to Bolts quite a lot with Pat,' he recalls. 'They were at Bolts one New Year's Eve, but after a while Pat went home and George stayed. He didn't drive in those days, Pat used to take him around, so I wasn't really sure why he didn't leave with her. I wondered if he was waiting for me to ask him to come home with me! At the end of the night, while we were waiting for a cab, George and I sat in the club's restaurant and chatted for over an hour about music. There was nothing sexual at all, but apparently he wrote a song about me called "Quit the Kissing Norman" which was going to be on their first LP, but I think they were worried that people would start asking "who is this Norman?", and no one wanted to have to say that he was a DJ at a gay club! Everyone at his record company knew quite early on that he was gay, they even gave him a girly nickname, but they would not have wanted the fans to know.'

Norman and George became lifelong friends, and Norman was the first club host to have Wham! perform live, again at Bolts, in June 1982. 'The girl who introduced me to Wham! was Lorraine Trent, who worked for CBS. She phoned me up one day and said, "We've just signed this new group; would you like them at one of your clubs?". I said, "Yes, how much?", and she said, "Oh no, we don't want anything – just get them a couple of drinks!" So, they came along and mimed over their first single, "Wham Rap". I thought they were so good that I asked Lorraine if we could have them on again.

'The second time they came down, I knew they had live mics, and I flipped the record over and played the B-side, the instrumental backing track. The music started and they suddenly realised that it was not the vocal side and they had to sing live. As far as I know, that was the first time they'd ever sung live in public!'

Although shocked by Norman's cheek, George and Andrew rose to the occasion, and the band's PR representative wrote to Norman to thank him for helping to boost their confidence. A few months later,

203

Wham!, along with their backing singers Pepsi and Shirley, appeared at Bolts again, this time performing their hit 'Young Guns (Go for It)' with an excited Norman Scott joining them on stage, brandishing a tambourine that he had been given by Marc Bolan a decade earlier. George never forgot his debt to Norman, and one Friday night in August 1984, just a couple of hours after they had finished mixing the track in the recording studio, George rushed over to Bolts with an acetate of the band's forthcoming single, 'Freedom', for the DJ to play. 'George told me that I couldn't keep the single, so I stuck a cassette in and recorded it as it played.' Actor and singer Divine was performing in the club that night, promoting his new Bobby 'O'-produced single 'Love Reaction', a blatant rip-off of the recent New Order Hit 'Blue Monday'. After he had finished his set, he joined George and Norman in the DJ booth while Norman spun 'Freedom' for the ecstatic crowd. Bobby Orlando (aka Bobby 'O') was nowhere to be seen: he was in New York, working with a new English duo calling themselves Pet Shop Boys. Journalist Neil Tennant, the PSB's singer, had pursued Orlando partly on the strength of the records he had produced for Divine.

A few weeks before 'Wham Rap!' was unleashed to a largely indifferent world (it would only chart after it was reissued in early 1983, following the success of their second single, 'Young Guns'), another new group issued their debut single. 'White Boy', the first single by Culture Club, failed to chart, but by the end of October the band, fronted by former Blitz club cloakroom attendant Boy George, would be at number one with 'Do You Really Want to Hurt Me'. Although George (who had sung with Malcolm McLaren's group Bow Wow Wow prior to forming Culture Club with drummer Jon Moss, bassist Mikey Craig and guitar player Roy Hay) would not come out as homosexual for a few years, from his earliest interviews he was happy to admit that he 'falls in love with people of both sexes', and that he did not mind being called a boy or a girl as it was 'all good publicity'.[9] When Culture Club made their debut on BBC's *Top of the Pops*, George instigated a wave of apoplexy among parents across the country in much the same way as his hero David Bowie had done a decade earlier.

The UK press' had a field day with this new 'gender bending' star: 'Boy George proves she can sing', wrote reviewer Robin Eggar of the band's debut album, *Kissing to Be Clever*.[10] Eggar would later claim that American music fans were so ignorant that 'they thought that Boy George was actually Girl George and that Yazoo's Alf [Alison Moyet] was really an Alfred. Now they are convinced that Eurythmics lovely Annie Lennox is actually a HE.'[11] Audiences were never confused: despite the spiky short-back-and-sides and androgynous clothing that Annie Lennox sported in the video and on the sleeve for the latest Eurythmics single, 'Love Is a Stranger', everyone knew she was a woman, and George only had to open his mouth to dispel any misapprehensions about his own manliness. But just as they did during the peak years of glam rock, lazy journalists were using the fashion for wearing clothes that did not conform to gender stereotypes as an excuse to make veiled comments about a musician's sexuality. As Scots-born vocalist of Bronski Beat and the Communards, Jimmy Somerville would later concede, that may not have been a totally bad thing: '[Boy George] has made people aware that androgyny exists. Before he came along no one knew about it – men were men and women were women. He's brought it out into the open much more than people like David Bowie – he's made it worldwide, which is one step. It's very commercial, but at the same time we've had to be commercial to an extent. It's inevitable if you want to do what we're doing.'[12]

As well as making androgyny more palatable, in their own small way Culture Club were also helping change attitudes towards Britain's BAME LGBT community. 'Once bands, like Culture Club, with Black British musicians in started to become really popular, and [so did] people like Sade, then you did notice a slight change in attitudes towards gay Black people,' says Andy Polaris. 'I think people were quite happy, people were making money, everyone had good jobs and things calmed down a little. You saw more obvious homophobia and racism in the late seventies, when it was quite dangerous just to walk around if you were Black and people thought you were queer. I can remember skinheads waiting to beat you up when you got off a train at stations like Liverpool Street or Charing Cross; they were dangerous places. You wanted to get to your venue, but before you got there you had to run the gauntlet of people who would throw bottles at you, call you "nigger" or "queer" to your face and get away with it. You weren't going to get much sympathy from the police.'

Wham! and Culture Club may have been snapped up by majors, but the early 1980s also saw a number of LGBT artists being signed to independent labels, many of which had appeared on the scene in the immediate aftermath of punk. Soft Cell, the electronic duo led by Marc Almond, signed to Some Bizzare, as did Coil, fronted by former members of Throbbing Gristle and Psychic TV John Balance and Peter 'Sleazy' Christopherson. Brighton's lesbian new wave band Devil's Dykes, signed to local label Attrix Records, metamorphosed into the Bright Girls, several of whom would also become members of the lesbian theatre company, Siren.

The increase in visibility of LGBT (or, as was often the case, assumed to be LGBT) musicians was not limited to pop and new wave. 'In the eighties, there was a bit of a jazz resurgence,' Alison Rayner adds, 'with bands like the Loose Tubes and the Jazz Warriors. It was men and women, Black and white.' During this period, Rayner joined a new women-only band, the Guest Stars. 'The Guest Stars was more mixed [sexuality wise], whereas Jam Today was pretty much all lesbian. The Guest Stars' bass player left, and I was the last to join. Josefina and Dierdre were already in it, and there was also Ruthie Smith, Laka D [Laka Daisical, born Dorota Koc], Linda Da Mango [born Linda Malone], and they had been doing some little tours of the UK. Jam Today had a more strongly political thing: the Guest Stars were still political, but less directly so. It was political in the sense that we were all women – even in the eighties, that was quite a statement. We played at political events and benefits, but a lot of those things were beginning to disappear, and we were playing more jazz clubs and arts centres and starting to tour. It was more about the music, but we did still want to retain control. So, we had our own van and our own PA and sound engineer. The woman who managed us, and did all of our admin and the sound, Debbie Dickinson [who sadly died in 2019], was just amazing. I loved being in [the Guest Stars]. We toured all over the world and had the most amazing time.

'There was always a good atmosphere. We played all kinds of wacky jazz, but people danced to our music. It was fun, and there were a lot of

206

writers in the group. In the last incarnation of Jam Today, the one that recorded the *Stereotyping* EP, Terry [Hunt] was the writer, but in the Guest Stars nearly everybody wrote, so we had a fantastically eclectic selection of music and, with three different lead singers, excellent vocal harmonies. It had a wonderful spirit.'

'The Guest Stars did not fit any genre,' Josefina Cupido adds. 'We were self-governing, but like arts organisations we were periodically funded. We were neither pop nor jazz, nor gay nor straight; we were free of all labels, and non-establishment. We wanted to be seen and wanted as musicians, not just as "women's musicians". I still have that question in my mind: "Is there such thing as a feminist chord or rhythm?" I still don't know the answer to that one!'

Life was improving for Britain's LGBT performers, but there was no room for complacency. A new enemy, more devastating than a hostile media or immobile government, was about to wreak havoc on the community, and curtail the advancement of LGBT rights.

16

The Gay Plague

'I have a Filofax... On one of the pages all my friends have gone, and every time I try to put a pen through their names I find it impossible. This dreadful, dreadful disease that has taken so many people away. I don't think anyone in this room tonight hasn't lost a friend.' – Danny La Rue[1]

On 4 July 1982, when ex-pat Americans were celebrating Independence Day in pubs across the British capital, a young Welshman by the name of Terry Higgins died in St Thomas's Hospital. He had been working at the House of Commons, as a reporter for Hansard, and also worked occasionally during the evenings as a barman and DJ.

Higgins grew up in the Pembrokeshire town of Haverfordwest but felt constrained by life in the port and moved to London. As he became more involved in the music world, he travelled to Amsterdam and New York, but he returned to London in 1980 suffering from a baffling array of illnesses. He collapsed while working at Heaven in the summer of 1982, and died shortly afterwards. His partner, Rupert Whitaker, and friends soon established the Terrence Higgins Trust in his memory, Britain's first HIV/AIDS charity, funded entirely through donations from within the LGBT community. 'There is no money coming from the public purse,' a spokesperson said. 'We have got to finance this ourselves.'[2]

The first AIDS-related death in Britain had occurred on 29 October 1981, when John Eaddie, who ran a gay boarding house in Bournemouth, died in London's Brompton Hospital. News had been reaching the country for several months about a strange illness that was affecting America's gay community, where men were developing skin lesions and exhibiting a confusing range of debilitating symptoms, and many were dying. Between January 1980 and July 1981, 26 gay men in America had displayed the lesions, known as Kaposi's sarcoma, and around a third of them had died. The disease did not have a name, but soon attracted the acronym GRID, which stood for Gay-Related Immune Deficiency. When clinicians realised that the disease was not limited to the gay community, and that heterosexual intravenous drug users and haemophiliacs were suffering from exactly the same symptoms, the disease gained a new name, AIDS or Acquired Immune Deficiency Syndrome.

Almost a year would pass after the death of Terrence Higgins in the summer of 1982 before AIDS began to make headlines in Britain, and for many LGBT people living in London, the months before they became aware of the disease were halcyon days. The Labour-run Greater London Council (GLC), the administrative body set up in 1965, seemed as if it were intent on causing headaches for a Tory Party committed to making life miserable for LGBT people. Mrs Thatcher was openly antagonistic to the GLC's leader, Ken Livingstone, and he, dubbed 'Red Ken' by the Tory-supporting media, was a constant thorn in her side. The press fabricated stories about the extremes that the GLC were reaching, criticising Livingstone's socialist aims and branding him and his cohorts the 'loony left'.

Controlling much of the budget for Britain's biggest city, the GLC offered financial support to a number of organisations working with the capital's oppressed groups, including a women's recording studio and music resource set up by Jana Runnalls and Rosemary Schonfeld of Ova. 'We were lucky with the timing,' Rosemary explains. 'The GLC had decided to fund more music projects and fewer theatre projects.' After a year of searching, they settled on premises at the Highgate Newton Community Centre in Archway. 'We believed in the importance of empowering women, which is what led to us establishing the Ova Music Studio. We were able to employ four women: me, Jana, an administrator, Jenny Gibbs, and a sound engineer, Livvy Elliott. Livvy was the sister of a friend of mine who came to see us play and said she would be interested in learning sound engineering. When she left a few years later, it was to set up her own recording studio in Brixton, Studio 9. She recorded our last album there, *Who Gave Birth to the Universe*, for free, as a thank you for starting her on her sound engineering path. Our salaries were abysmal, but it was a salary. I don't know whether we would have been able to continue without that. We had produced two full length albums already, toured Germany and the US, but I doubt we could have kept up the momentum without the financial support the GLC gave us.' When Thatcher abolished the GLC, Greater London Arts and Camden Council took over funding.

As part of their agreement with the GLC, Runnalls and Schonfeld had to present workshops and put on performances for community and social care groups. 'To fulfil the requirements of the grant, we had to offer more variety, and Jana and I worked out what other skills we could use. Jana started running singing workshops, and I offered percussion ones. Livvy offered sound engineering workshops, using the eight-track mixing desk we used for our gigs. Jana and I started providing tea dances in community centres and homes for older people. I cannot remember how many workshops we were supposed to provide, but it was dozens if not over one hundred. It was important for us; we felt we could put our politics into practice by empowering women and girls, and all of our workshops in vocals, drumming, and sound engineering were well attended.'

Workshops and schools were an important part of the women's music movement. From the very beginning, musicians were keen to share their skills and ideas with other women, encouraging them to produce their own music and write their own songs. 'I always felt that we were a little bit out on a limb compared to the London girls,' says Manchester-based Angela Cooper. 'I would go to these jazz summer schools and people like Deirdre Cartwright and Alison Rayner would be there leading workshops in their chosen fields, and clearly in London there was a whole load of people who were fluent, and moving between different bands and doing sessions... They were professional musicians, and none of us were.'

The GLC began discussions about opening a Lesbian and Gay Centre in London in late 1982: 60 people attended the first open meeting, with the GLC pledging to pay for two part-time workers to help move plans forward. This was followed by the publication of *Changing the World: a London Charter for Lesbian and Gay Rights*, which came with a letter from Ken Livingstone that acknowledged that 'the lesbian and gay community experience discrimination in every sphere. The Council is committed to tackling this'.[3] Located at 67–69 Cowcross Street, Farringdon, the London Lesbian and Gay Centre (LLGC) eventually opened at the end of 1984, with the GLC donating £750,000 to its establishment. Gay centres had been opened in other cities years prior, including the Edinburgh Gay Centre in 1974, Manchester's evenings-only centre in 1975 and their first full-time centre in 1981, the Birmingham Lesbian and Gay Community Centre in 1976 and Bristol Gay Centre the following year.

The LLGC ran into problems almost immediately. Local Government Minister Kenneth Baker, one of Mrs Thatcher's staunchest allies, refused a grant of a further £100,000 to the centre less than six months after opening. But despite this setback the centre flourished: for a couple of years, a weekly women-only disco was held in the centre's basement, while meetings, film screenings and live concerts took place on the floors above. The centre continued after the abolition of the GLC, finally closing in 1991.

The GLC was keen to fund other projects that would appeal to London's LGBT citizens and visitors, as Peter Scott-Presland recalls. 'In 1982 I'd come across this wonderful story from an old edition of *Come Together* about Camden GLF and how they had gone up to Hampstead Heath at midnight with a tea trolly in order to engage with the men cruising there.* In order not to frighten people off, they decked their tea trolly out with fairy lights – if I had seen that coming towards me, it would have sent me running off screaming into the bushes! But I thought this was a great basis for a play, so I wrote a parody of *A Midsummer Night's Dream* called *Tea Trolly, or A Midsummer Night's*

---

* Camden GLF, 'About Us', *Come Together 13*, April 1972

Scream and we did it in London and Edinburgh. Later, I thought, "Hang on. This is set at midnight on midsummer night, on Hampstead Heath, so we should do it on Hampstead Heath at midnight on midsummer night." The GLC had control of the Heath then, so I wrote to Ken Livingstone and he said, "Yes, sure... why not?" We went out and bought a load of garden flares, and on the Heath just down from [Grade II listed pub] Jack Straw's Castle and past the cruising area there is a natural amphitheatre, so we decided to do it there. As we were setting up, a couple of policemen came along asking what we were doing there and if we had permission, and I was able to show them my letter from Ken Livingstone.

'The first year we did *Tea Trolley* on the Heath was 1983, and that was really successful, so we decided to repeat it again the next year. We also did it on Clapham Common, because there was a cruising ground where people were getting arrested. At that point, I conceived the idea of a regular sequence, so we did four years in total. We did a play the year after called *Lord Audley's Secret*, a sort of gay Victorian melodrama. We had a grant from the GLC from '82 onwards; Ken Livingstone's deputy, Andy Harris, phoned me and asked me to come into City Hall and have a talk with them, and so I went in and sat down, and they turned to me and said, "Tell us what you want"! It was as simple as that. In retrospect I should have been far more ambitious and asked for a lot more, but I asked for the money for one paid worker, Neil Bartlett. He had just finished his degree, and he would use this a springboard to establish himself in London and get his own company off the ground.

'The third one we did was called *It's an Unfair Cop, Guv* which was the first purely political show that we did on Hampstead Heath and Clapham Common. It was a diatribe about the Police and Criminal Evidence Act, which was coming up as a bill at the time, which had a lot of restrictions and could have been used quite destructively against LGBT people. There was lots of stuff about the powers of search and the powers of detention, and we did a kind of political cabaret revue for that. I've always liked doing things in spaces that are not traditionally theatre spaces, and we got about two or three hundred people along, including Tom Robinson, who loved it.'

The Gay London Police Monitoring Group (which would soon become the Gay London Policing Group, or GALOP) had formed in June 1982 to expose the systematic harassment of the gay and lesbian communities by the police and to educate them about their rights. Initially a voluntary grouping of lawyers and interested parties providing a free service to the LGBT community, funding from the GLC subsequently allowed employment of two core workers; GALOP's first major achievement was to prove that the police were using agents provocateurs to entrap, arrest and convict gay men in Earl's Court. Yet, despite this ever-increasing resistance against them, the police showed no signs of change. On 3 October 1982, police raided a birthday party at a home in Chiswick and arrested all 37 men there. The men were forced to spend the night in police cells, with 15 men in one cell with only one bench and one blanket between them; another of the cells had no working toilet. Quizzed about their sexual habits and as to why one of the men had been found naked in one of the bedrooms (he lived there), it was not until late November that the men were told no charges would be pressed, due to insufficient evidence of any wrongdoing.

Coming in off the back of the 1981 race riots, the Police and Criminal Evidence Act enshrined in law new powers governing arrest, the seizure of goods and in many other areas. *It's an Unfair Cop,* highlighted the threat to marginalised communities posed by amendments to the rules around 'stop and search', which now meant that an officer was legally allowed to stop and search a person without suspicion, in other words without reasonable grounds to believe that the person detained had committed any crime... something that the LGBT community had long become accustomed to. But for Scott-Presland, success came at a cost. 'The last one we did on the Heath was called *Campfire,*' he recalls. 'A pure farce about two adjacent summer camps, one peopled by a group of leather queens and the other by boy scouts. Today there would be a huge outcry about that, although none of the boy scouts have sex with the leather queens in the play! By 1986 we were getting over a thousand people on the Heath. We didn't have such sophisticated things as radio mics... It was absolute bedlam and impossible to make yourself heard. It was becoming an excuse for a load of people to get together and have a wild old time. The play became incidental and at that stage I stopped it.'

The careers of Scott-Presland and Ova were in the ascendant, thanks in part to the GLC's largess, yet others involved in the LGBT music scene were finding the current atmosphere oppressive. After years of trying to make it in the music industry, Paul Southwell played the last of more than 40 gay benefits, for the East London CHE, in October 1982. He had had enough. 'By then AIDS had reared its ugly head, and I put my energies into looking after my friends,' he says. 'That's the reason I veered away from music. London at that time, in '83 and '84, was just terrible. That's when I went back to university; I signed on and did my degree and went into teaching and academia.

'I'd done more than a decade of campaigning and we had made a little headway with gay liberation: the gay scene was kind of getting there... Then AIDS comes along and puts everything back.' AIDS was not the only problem the LGBT community were facing: a new wave of anti-gay hysteria was on the rise. On 23 October 1982, a gay disco at the Pied Bull pub, run weekly since June by London Gay Workshops, was broken up by skinheads hurling abuse towards the function room from the public bar. The skinheads proceeded to throw missiles, including bottles and pool cues, at men attending the disco and at bar staff. Management called the police, who brought the trouble to an end, before around thirty of them entered the function room and threw everybody out onto the street. Several attendees reported hearing the police using homophobic language, with one policeman accused of shouting 'I'm standing with my back to the wall with all these queers around'.[4]

On 8 December 1982, Consenting Adults in Public held a fundraiser for the London Gay Switchboard at the Albany Theatre, which also heralded the birth of a new openly gay-owned and gay-run record label, Gayn. 'One of the things I wanted to do, as part of Consenting Adults in Public, was start a record label,' Scott-Presland explains. 'We produced an album of our first benefit concert, *Coming Out – Ready or Not*. Everybody was really excited, but the problem was that they all wanted to get their material out, but no one wanted to do the donkey work in the office, or deal with distribution and all that sort of thing.

214

But one good thing that came from that was a roadshow featuring some of the acts who appeared on the album, people like Toby Kettle and Chris Ransome, who had written some very good songs. Toby was accompanied by a young pianist from the Gay Youth group called Richard Coles, and subsequently Richard became my cabaret pianist.

'When [the roadshow] got to Stoke-on-Trent, we discovered that there was a furious row going on. A local Evangelical vicar had written to the local paper to say how disgusting it was that council premises were being used to promote homosexuality, so the newspaper got in touch with Mary Whitehouse, who came out with the line "I haven't seen it, but I'm sure I would disapprove of it"! This was publicity you could not buy, and as a result there were queues all around the block. Richard and I arrived in the afternoon to do the show, and I decided to write a song for the occasion, to tell the story of what had happened. Richard and I wrote it between us, to the tune of "Ghost Riders in the Sky", and we called it "Travelling Gay Cabaret"... It's just a little example of how you can use cabaret to reflect things back on the detractors. The Terrence Higgins Trust had just been set up; it had no authority or funding from anywhere, it was all done entirely through voluntary donations, and at that stage it didn't have any celebrity endorsement either. People would not start doing benefits for AIDS causes for a few years; that really started after the [HIV and AIDS hospice] Lighthouse opened [in 1986]. The benefits that were being done at the time were mainly things like the Pretty Policeman's Ball at the Piccadilly... The benefit that we did at the Albany, where the first Gayn album came from, that was the first large-scale benefit and in many ways that laid down the format for what would follow.' A fundraiser for London Gay Switchboard, over the next few years the annual Pretty Policeman's Ball would feature gay acts including the Communards and Tom Robinson alongside LGBT actors, comedians and several big-name straight allies including Billy Connolly, and French and Saunders.

On 24 February 1983, in the South London constituency of Bermondsey, Liberal-SDP Alliance candidate Simon Hughes was elected as Member of Parliament after orchestrating a bitter and violently homophobic campaign against Labour candidate Peter Tatchell. Hughes's win overturned a Labour majority of 11,000, with many dyed-in-the-wool

Labour supporters refusing to recognise Tatchell, the party's official candidate. In 1975 Hughes's party had been the first UK political party to openly support LGBT rights; thanks mainly to groundwork prepared by the CHE and members of the Young Liberals, at their annual conference, held in the seaside resort of Scarborough, LGBT members lobbied MPs to include LGBT rights in any forthcoming Liberal manifesto. The following year, the party passed a motion to support 'full equality for homosexuals', including equalising the age of consent. Clearly the candidate for Bermondsey thought otherwise.

Taking a page from the Liberal Party's playbook, many in the Labour Party had also decided that it was time to embrace LGBT rights. In party newspaper *Labour Weekly*, they set out a series of suggestions for inclusion in the party's manifesto, and for the first time, homosexual rights – and law reform – were included on the agenda, and specifically 'the age of consent for male homosexual relationships'.[5] However, that September, at the annual Labour Conference in Blackpool, despite a large Gay Labour Group presence, James Callaghan, the party leader, made no mention of gay rights in his speech. The old guard would take some persuading, but many were ready for change: Bryan Gould, the New Zealand-born MP for Southampton Test, made an appearance at the CHE conference, and in his speech urged CHE members to continue to campaign for equality, particularly within political parties and trade unions.

'I went down to help campaign for Peter,' says Lord Smith. 'It was, I have to say, a really disheartening experience. I can remember on election day itself going around Bermondsey knocking on the doors of lifetime Labour voters, and it was very clear from the look in their eyes, the shiftiness in their body language, that they had no intention at all of voting Labour at that by-election. I remember coming away from that thinking we were not going to win. And indeed, that proved to be exactly the case.' Called 'the most written about and vilified Westminster contender for years',[6] Labour's veterans did not want an openly gay man representing them, especially not one as vocal as Tatchell. However, newer, younger and more militant members of the party saw a need to bring Labour into the modern era.

'We fought this election with honesty and honour,' Tatchell told reporters shortly before the results were announced. 'But I would not want to repeat the sneers that have been made against me. It only gives them credibility. The people who voted for me have resisted 15 months of hostile campaign[ing].'[7] Among many dirty tricks used to discredit Tatchell, Hughes had distributed leaflets to voters, describing the election as 'A STRAIGHT CHOICE' between the two candidates. Tatchell received hate mail and more than 20 death threats after the *Sun* printed his address; a 'small, unmarked brown envelope' containing a live bullet was shoved though his letter box, and he was attacked in the street, leading police to shadow him while he was out campaigning and keep a close watch on his flat.[8] 'Most of them have been from cranks,' he said of the threats to his life. 'The only thing is that one of these days one of these cranks might do something.'[9]

Bob Mellish, the constituency's previous MP, had campaigned against Tatchell in support of John O'Grady, who was standing for the unofficial 'Real Labour Party'. Both men were also on the board of the London Dockland Development Corporation (LDDC), set up by the Tory Party in a bid to gentrify the poverty-stricken area. Tatchell wanted money to be spent on making Bermondsey better for the residents already there: the LDDC wanted a marina, expensive new houses and shiny new office developments. An anonymous leaflet which asked the question 'which queen will you vote for?' was later attributed to Mellish, MP for the borough since 1946, by Lord Smith.[10] Tatchell himself believed that the Liberal Party was behind the leaflet, which 'invited local voters to have a go at me by listing my home address and phone number'.[11] Whoever did pen the leaflet knew that Liberal candidate Hughes was a closeted bisexual who, despite rumours to the contrary, denied on a number of occasions that he was anything other than completely heterosexual. Simon Hughes came out, after the *Sun* discovered he had been using gay chatrooms, in January 2006.

'Bob Mellish's campaigning against Peter was really homophobic,'* says Lord Smith, 'and that was overlaid with the row within the Labour Party about what was then called "extra Parliamentary activity", creating

---

* Tatchell would later claim, in a 2003 BBC interview, that Mellish's personal campaign against him was, in part, because Mellish was a closeted bisexual who persistently propositioned him.

the notion that Peter was some kind of wild-eyed extremist. The two of those things together combined to create a disaster.' The campaign was a wakeup call. 'By the time the Bermondsey by-election happened, I was already the candidate for what became the Islington South and Finsbury seat. I had never made any particular secret within the local party of the fact that I was gay, everyone knew. I had a conversation with my agent as we prepared for the election campaign. She said, "What are we going to do if we're holding a public meeting, you're giving a speech and someone in the audience stands up and says, 'We don't want to hear this from him, he's queer'?" She was all for having a burly, working-class member of the party standing on the sidelines ready to leap in at that point to say, "We're not interested in that. We want to hear what he has to say about unemployment!" But I said to her that if this comes up there's only one way of dealing with it, and that's for me to say, "Yes, I am. So what? Next question, please!" Fortunately, during the election campaign that never came up.'

Unlike Tatchell, who had built a reputation as a voluble and visible campaigner for LGBT rights since his arrival in the UK back in 1971, Smith's sexuality was not widely known to voters in the constituency. His chief rival at the election was George Cunningham, the incumbent MP who had recently defected from Labour to the recently founded SDP. 'I was elected in April 1983 by the skin of my teeth, with a 363 majority,' he explains. 'I decided very soon after that I needed to say something in public about my own sexual orientation. That was partly because I had seen one Labour colleague who was already an MP being hounded by the press. He never publicly came out, although I thought that he should have done, and I just thought, "I don't want to go through what he's going through." The only way to remove the problem was to remove the story, and you do that by standing up and telling it yourself.' Smith would do exactly that the following year.

Had the election been held a couple of months later, it is likely that Smith would not have won, for by the summer of 1983 AIDS hysteria was building, and the situation in London between the police and the gay community had become intolerable. More than two dozen men were arrested in the Earl's Court area, all charged with importuning and all victims of entrapment by two plain-clothes police officers who

218

became so well known in the area that locals at the Coleherne and the Boltons began to refer to them as the Beverley Sisters, others as the 'pretty police'. Regular drinkers began staying away from the area on Tuesday, Wednesday and Thursday evenings, the nights when the two police officers in question were most active. The National Council for Civil Liberties (NCCL, later to become Liberty) and GALOP, discovered systematic abuse of the system by the police, with threats to expose the arrested men to their family and work colleagues, and refusal to let arrested men contact solicitors. GALOP's David Wilson-Carr told *Capital Gay*, 'I don't think it is any exaggeration to say importuning is the gay Sus law. [The police] know that if they stick a couple of attractive young hunks outside the Coleherne at closing time and they are dressed provocatively someone, not unnaturally, is going to smile back and get arrested.'[12] The police, naturally, denied using such underhand tactics and said that any arrests made were always after their attention was drawn to the area by complaints from members of the public. They used the same excuse the following summer when, in a two-week period, more than 40 men were arrested for cottaging in East London. The force was under pressure to get their arrest figures up: according to Sam Jenkins, of the National Council for Civil Liberties, the arrests were 'a convenient way to improve the crime statistics.'[13] More arrests meant more money from central government, and arresting gay men who would usually plead guilty – often without having committed a crime in the first instance – was an easy way to tick boxes.

The Pretty Police soon found their way into popular culture. After a spell in Berlin, Tom Robinson was back in London to make the most of a recent resurgence in his career. In 1982 'War Baby', a song he wrote while living in Berlin and experiencing first-hand the difference between life in East and West Germany, had become his first Top 10 hit since '2-4-6-8 Motorway'. That same year he met Sue Brearley, who he would marry three years later. 'Tom got very disillusioned with the music scene here and went to live in Berlin for several years,' Scott-Presland adds. 'When he came back, he started getting a lot of flak because [some LGBT] people would not accept the fact that he was bisexual and that he was very honest about it. But he was getting asked to do things, and he got in touch with me and said, "I think 'Glad to

Be Gay' needs updating, can you give me a verse for it?" We had just done *It's an Unfair Cop*, which included the story of the Pretty Police... You would see things in the papers and think, "That's a gift; I can do something with that", and I had seen a story in *Capital Gay* about how the pair were nicknamed the Beverley Sisters. Of course that was a cue to do parodies of Beverley Sisters numbers as part of this show; one was "A Cottage for Sale". So, I did him a verse about the Pretty Police.'

As bothersome as the Pretty Police were, they were hardly the main scourge attacking the LGBT community. By October 1983, more than 2,000 people were known to have died from AIDS in Europe and America. Around the same time, scientists discovered that the disease was caused by the HIV virus. Even though the number of men reported to have contracted AIDS in the UK was still tiny compared to the USA (by December, 27 AIDS cases had been reported in the UK compared with over 3,000 in the States), in December the first play about the crisis debuted on the London stage. *Anti Body* initially ran for a fortnight at the Cockpit, Gateforth Street, and was written by Louise Parker Kelley, an American lesbian residing in London, after a friend had been diagnosed with AIDS the previous year. The play was directed by Peter Scott-Presland. It would be another two years before anyone staged a similarly themed play in the United States.

'I was sent *Anti Body* by Louise,' says Scott-Presland. 'She had come over on a six-month visitor's visa with her lover, a high-flyer in some big commercial company who had been transferred over here, even though at that time there was no formal recognition of partnerships. She sent me this play, which was about HIV, and I really liked that it was set in a community, in an LGBT community, around the people that worked on the local switchboard. She came from Baltimore, so it was about the Baltimore experience. There were no other plays about HIV or AIDS, at all... At that stage I think we knew of about 10 cases in this country in total. I saw great potential in the play because obviously HIV/AIDS was something that we were just beginning to become aware of. I worked for *Capital Gay* as a columnist, and they were the first paper to take the whole thing seriously and have a regular column about this disease. At that point, it was the Gay Plague or LAV [Lymphadenopathy Associated Virus] or GRID; it didn't even have a name. I wanted to do it, but at that stage the safe-sex advice that was going around was "don't sleep with Americans"; in other words it was seen as an American phenomenon. So, I anglicised it and made it relevant to the British experience. At that stage, Lou's visa was going to run out, so I married her so she could stay for the play!

'Looking back on it, it stands up fairly well; I was really strong on safer sex and protection. At that stage, having an HIV diagnosis was a death sentence, there was no question. The central character has had an AIDS diagnosis and the play follows him through to his death, and it's about the reactions of the people around him. Louise turned it into something positive in the sense that one of the last things he does is make a safe-sex video, as a kind of warning. He's basically saying, "Do you value yourself enough to take care of yourself properly? If you don't, then you think you're worthless," which I certainly did, but I know now that I'm not. It's one of the things I am most proud of. I know that there were 14 cases when we went into rehearsal, I think there were 28 by the time we were actually on stage. It caused a furore because it was saying things that people didn't want to hear. It was accused of being alarmist. One of the characters is a bit of a stereotypical Irishman, and that got picked up on by some very vociferous Irish queens who accused it of being racist – Louise's roots were Irish Catholic. People were claiming that HIV was all a conspiracy, but we had good audiences, and I'm quite convinced that putting that on helped to shift opinions about safer sex. I think people started to understand that this was not just an American problem and, hopefully, we might have helped save a few lives.'

17

Out!

'Do homosexual lawyers get legal AIDS? Do gay orange growers get marmalAIDS and do teetotallers get lemon AIDS?' – The Daily Star[1]

While *Anti Body* may have been the first AIDS-related show, others would follow. It was at this point that Phil Booth joined Bette Bourne's theatre co-operative Bloolips, who had already attempted to address the AIDS crisis with their song 'Tap Your Troubles Away'. 'I was in my early 30s, broke and living in London,' he recalls. 'I got a phone call asking me to audition for *News Revue*, a topical comedy [which began at the Gate, Notting Hill but by now had moved to the Canal Café Theatre, Maida Vale] and I got that job. I was the musician, but I also had to fill in some small parts, and do the occasional monologue while everybody was off changing for the next sketch. I enjoyed doing that: I had done theatre before, but not professionally, and one or two people saw me doing that. I was living in an artist's housing cooperative, paying something like six quid a week rent at first, and one of the other guys in the co-op said to me, "I hear that Bloolips are auditioning for a musician. You should try it; you'd be a shoo-in." I had never heard of Bloolips, I hadn't the faintest idea what they did, but I said, "Yeah, I'll do that!" And then I immediately went down with the flu!

'I thought, "I can't do it", but this guy had already phoned Bette Bourne and said, "I know someone who would be really good for you", and Bette rang me, so I said, "Yeah, alright, I'll come and do it." I auditioned without the least idea what I was getting myself into, but Bette had photographs and some of the scripts, so by the time I left I'd got a pretty good idea of what the job involved, and that was how I got into the 'Lips. I'm glad I'd never seen them, because I might have thought that I couldn't possibly do it. But it was amazing.'

Adopting the stage name Phil Harmonia, Booth quickly became an important member of the collective. 'I gradually adapted to the ethos of the group. A lot of the early Bloolips members had been involved with the GLF and their street theatre group, so it was obviously political from the outset. It worked on the same principle as an anarchist group in that everyone's opinion had the same value as everyone else's, everyone was paid the same, with a share set aside for the kitty. It was very simple as a structure, but very difficult to pull off. The only exception was that Bette reserved a right of artistic veto; he referred to himself as artistic director, but he never used it.

'My personal political journey had come through anarchism, but I was also interested in Green politics and gay politics, and I took a lot of that into Bloolips, but I guess I also brought a less metropolitan view. Bloolips had spent a lot of time in New York, and had a tremendously urban focus, but Stuart [Feather], who was from Yorkshire, and I brought something that was, in a way, less aggressive... Which must have been rather irritating in a context of radical, aggressive, left-wing politics!'

Like all LGBT theatre, Bloolips had to work beneath the ever-present shadow of AIDS. 'Bloolips had grown out of defiance and celebration, not out of this need to hunker down and deal with a collective crisis,' Booth continues. 'You could hear a grinding of gears in the company after the first 10 years: "We've got a profile, but maybe something else is needed." Jon Jon [Bloolips member John Taylor] took real risks at times. He had a very dark vision of toxic masculinity which he wove into *Teenage Trash*, a show about the history of the suit. The whole show is about AIDS, but without ever mentioning it. It was much darker than anything Bloolips had done before, and that was because of

AIDS. It was a contribution to the politics of the time and to why AIDS wasn't being responded to rationally by the government and health professionals. He included an incredibly bitter number called "Daddy Is Dangerous", which was a solo for me while everyone else was off changing into something fabulous, which ended with a list of names of children who had been abused or murdered. You could have heard a pin drop; it was immensely powerful and effective.

'It was a very daring thing to do. People had not come to the theatre expecting that, and it came just minutes after the most frivolous song in the show, "Let's Scream Our Tits Off"! A complete stranger to subtlety was Jon. It was very shocking for audiences, but that was part of the appeal. Previously he'd used music that he'd found in the mainstream and repurposed it, but having a composer to work with, like me, he found that he could create structures, effectively use the tools of the musical which he'd never done before. Rather than dumping the audience with the confrontation of "Daddy Is Dangerous" we were able to use music to carry them through that, through other images and ideas, to the final number, "The Bloolip Blues", which again was very, very powerful, a statement of strength and maturity, which is not something we did very often, because we were about being very, very silly. The lyrics and the setting are a massive reaffirmation of gay desire, at a time when the media were intent on eradicating it as something not just abhorrent but also lethal. The effect on gay audiences was very powerful – they instantly recognised what they were seeing. It was saying to people, "We can cope with this; we can come through this", but without saying that. That was the politics of that show: "This is what we're up against, but we can face it."

'It was an extraordinary time to be alive. It was like being in a war because it was so awful, and you were forced to live it: you couldn't take a back seat. It formed you and shaped you for the rest of your life. I think most of us who were very tied up in all that are still living it; it was a trauma.

'Because of the way we made the shows,' continues Booth, 'it wasn't really my place to decide how political these songs were going to be. But people have different ideas about what constitutes political, of course. Later, when I had left Bloolips but was still writing for them it was not quite the same collective enterprise. Bette and Paul went to New York, where they were working with a writer called Ray Dobbins, and I came along, in the instance of *Get Hur*, when they needed to expand the show, and I added half a dozen songs to make it a full evening. Then I did have the opportunity, because I was also the lyricist, to decide what kind of songs needed to be done. But in the context of a Bloolips show, the best kind of politics is the total phenomenon of the song, rather than what the lyrics say. For example, it always seemed to me that there were not enough gay love duets out in the world. Dancers were doing duets for men at that time, which you had not seen before, but you did not see two men on stage singing a love song. So, I said, "Can we put a love duet in this?" It was going to be Bette and Paul singing it, and they were not sure if they'd be able to do it vocally, but I told them, "You'll be fine." So, I wrote a love duet for Bette, who was playing the Emperor Hadrian, and Paul was his lover, Antinous – so it's very much two guys in some sort of drag, but it's clearly a love song for two guys. That was the sort of politics that was going to work best in this context. Bette and Paul, as Bloolips, did a couple of co-productions with [New York-based lesbian theatre collective] Split Britches – they did a show called *Belle Reprieve*, a reworking of *A Streetcar Named Desire*, and again I was brought in to write a few songs for it. I adopted the policy that Jon used to adopt, going around asking everybody in the troupe what was on their minds at that time, and I said to Bette, "You're going to have a solo at some point in the evening. What do you want to talk about in it?" It was when AIDS was absolutely wreaking havoc, an absolutely terrible time, and he said, "I want to talk about the grief of losing the bathhouse culture in New York, and the ambivalence towards that." So, that's what I wrote a song about. That's not an activist's approach to the AIDS crisis, it's about doing a piece of psychological work through having somebody, like Bette, voicing a collective grief and sense of loss.'

While LGBT theatre was highlighting the dangers of casual sex, in the pop charts the opposite was happening. On 24 November 1982 five young men from Liverpool, whose 'outrageous live performances have had everyone in a lather about leather'[2] entered the BBC's Maida Vale studios to record their first session for the legendary John Peel show, a programme well-respected within the music industry for helping to discover new and emerging acts. This particular act had already been turned down by two labels, but this session (which would air the following week), a live appearance at Peel's roadshow in Warrington a fortnight later and an appearance on prime time Channel 4 music show *The Tube* would help convince producer Trevor Horn to sign Frankie Goes to Hollywood to the newly formed ZTT Records. FGTH would become the first chart act in British history to be fronted by two out-gay men and the first to take a gay-themed record, 'Relax', to number one. Accompanied, in case you missed the message, by a video that hammered it home, 'Relax' entered the official UK singles charts at number 77 in October 1983. By the start of the New Year, it had crawled its way up to number 35. Then BBC DJ Mike Read decided that he would no longer play the song on the Radio 1 Breakfast Show, the nation's most listened-to programme.

It was hardly the first gay-themed disc to be banned by BBC radio: in 1967, shortly after Radio 1 first took to the air, the station banned Scott Walker's 'Jackie' (a cover of the Jacques Brel song, later covered again by Marc Almond) and as recently as 1981 the corporation announced that it would not play 'Homosapien', the single from former Buzzcocks frontman Pete Shelley, because of its explicit references to gay sex. If Read had hoped that a ban would stop the single from progressing further up the charts, he must have been spitting feathers when, a little over a fortnight later, Frankie Goes to Hollywood's debut hit the coveted number one spot.

In October 1983, a few weeks before 'Relax' was let loose, came the shocking news that the first British woman had died from AIDS – in Frankie's home town of Liverpool, no less. Surely now the press had to accept that the spread of this horrific disease was not limited to the gay male community? No. The press on both sides of the Atlantic tried to convince their readers that homosexuality had brought down a plague of biblical proportions: gay men were entirely to blame for what was happening, and anyone else who contracted the disease either a poor innocent or a disgusting drug user who deserved no better. Pathologists refused to carry out post-mortems on people suspected to have died from AIDS, and the ever-liberal British press screamed

'Britain Threatened by Gay Virus Plague' at anyone who would listen.[3] By July 1984, the Terrence Higgins Trust was reporting that they were aware of '51 people known to have caught the disease' in Britain, 28 of whom had died, with newspapers still insisting that 'the fatal disease AIDS' only 'attacks homosexual and bisexual men'.[4] Within 12 months, the death toll would increase to 108.

At the end of 1984, after the *Sun* ran the headline 'Blood from Gay Donor Puts 41 at AIDS Risk',[5] and the *Times* printed a story claiming that an 'outbreak of AIDS which has infected more than 40 people in the south of England' was 'known to have been started by a homosexual who was a regular blood donor',[6] a blanket ban on blood donation from gay and bisexual men, intravenous drug users and sex workers was introduced. The ban on gay men donating blood existed until 2011, when new rules allowed men who have sex with men to donate so long as they had not had sex for at least a calendar year. In November 2017 that was reduced to a three-month wait, and in June 2021 the rules were changed again, allowing anyone who had the same sexual partner for the last three months or more to donate.

Back in January 1984, at Knightsbridge Crown Court, the trials took place of a number of men arrested by the Pretty Police in Earl's Court, among them journalist Brian Palmer, accused of 'approaching men in the streets around the Coleherne public house' the previous July. PCs Shaun Quinn and Allen Bowler claimed that Palmer had 'stopped two feet from another man and put his hand over his crotch and squeezed it. He then licked his lips "in a vulgar manner".' In his defence, Palmer claimed that the only man he had spoken to was PC Quinn: it was Quinn – 'dressed provocatively in tight jeans which were split revealing part of his buttocks' – who had initiated the conversation, and after the two had walked off together PC Bowler appeared and arrested Palmer for 'persistently importuning for an immoral purpose'.[7] The jury took just half an hour to return a unanimous verdict of not guilty, the fourth such acquittal of men accused of importuning by plain-clothes police officers in the Earl's Court area in recent months.

Despite some progress in the courts, 1984 would prove to be a wretched year in the battle for LGBT equality in Britain. The media, empowered by the hysteria surrounding AIDS, went after anyone in the public eye who may have been gay. Tennis star Martina Navratilova's relationship with mother of two Judy Nelson was ridiculed, with John Junor, editor of the *Sunday Express*, referring to the world-beating sports personality as 'that hatchet-faced lesbian';[8] Bill Buckley, a presenter on the BBC's popular consumer show *That's Life* was outed by the *Sun* and Su Pollard, the star of hit TV series *Hi-de-Hi!*, was castigated in the press for having married gay Australian Peter Keogh, although as she later revealed, 'He was trying desperately to wrestle with his sexuality and do you know what, darling? I was never the first to marry a gay bloke and I'm certainly not going to be the last!'[9]

Pop stars also felt the wrath of Fleet Street's self-appointed protectors of the country's morals. A new generation of would-be Mary Whitehouses were on the rise, only these had the power of Britain's tabloids to fall back on. Unscrupulous journalists were offering thousands of pounds to people for salacious stories about anyone in the public eye suspected of being LGBT, and their sights were set on the men at the top of the pop charts. When, on Valentine's Day 1984, moments after telling the assembled representatives of the world's press that 'I know people thought I was gay, so this will surprise a lot of people, won't it?',[10] Elton John married German recording engineer Renate Blauel, the press had a proverbial field day. 'Oh my goodness, what a gay day,' wrote 'straight talking John Smith' in his column in the *Sunday People*, following that up with the phrase 'good on yer, yer pommy poofter'.[11] The 'poofter' slur was also hurled at cross-dressing pop star Marilyn. The former Blitz Kid, then at number five in the Australian charts with his hit 'Calling Your Name', was attacked in a bar in Sydney while on a promotional tour of Australia. Marilyn needed hospital treatment after being floored and then kicked in the face and groin during the attack at the Exchange Hotel, although a local policeman downplayed the incident, telling the press that 'he's not badly hurt – all he needs is a powder puff'.[12]

George Orwell must have been gazing into a crystal ball when he wrote about repressive government actions in his dystopian novel *Nineteen Eighty-Four*, for on 10 April a government hell-bent on stamping down on the LGBT community's hard-won civil rights raided Gay's the

Word, impounding 144 titles and carting away thousands of pounds worth of stock from both the bookshop and the homes of its directors. As part of Operation Tiger, the directors and staff of the store were threatened with jail terms and accused of conspiring to import and sell indecent or obscene literature, including works by Oscar Wilde, Armistead Maupin and Tennessee Williams.

Despite strenuous denials from the authorities, there could be no question that Gay's the Word was being prosecuted for selling homosexual literature: titles impounded included books from America about the AIDS epidemic, and one titled *The Joy of Gay Sex*, yet the 'straight' equivalent, *The Joy of Sex: A Gourmet Guide to Love Making*, had been readily available from bookshops up and down the country since its first publication in 1972. Books that had no obvious LGBT content but were penned by authors that customs officers considered to be gay or lesbian were also seized from directors' homes. Further raids followed: radical bookshop the Balham Food and Book Co-operative received notice that Customs and Excise had impounded a consignment of books heading their way from the United States on the grounds that they were 'indecent or obscene'. Richard Kirker, the secretary of the Gay Christian Movement, was also visited at his home and, later, issued with a seizure notice for 15 copies of *The Joy of Gay Sex* that had been purchased for resale to members through its own mail order catalogue.

Once again, the troops rallied to the cause. Independent books stores throughout the UK put collecting tins on their counters, sending hundreds of pounds to Gay's the Word, and the campaign garnered impressive support internationally. 'I had met Armistead Maupin,' says Peter Scott-Presland. 'He came to London because he was planning to set the fourth book in the *Tales of the City* series, *Babycakes*, there. One of the things I was doing for *Capital Gay* was delivering the paper all over London on a Thursday night; we would hire a van, pick up 20,000 copies of that week's issue from the printer then spend the next 12 hours delivering to every conceivable gay venue, to libraries and so on. There were 129 places on my list. Armistead came to the *Capital Gay* office and introduced himself and I said, "If you don't know London that well, I should take you out on a van run" so that's what I did, telling him about the venues as we went around. He'd had enough after about three hours and got off in Earl's Court, but that was my initial connection with him.

'His books were seized. I knew that we had to raise some serious money for this, because legal fees are always enormous, so I thought that the best thing to do was to get in touch with the individual authors involved, and say, "Can you send copies of the books that were seized by Customs and Excise, and can you sign them with a message of support for the bookshop, and we'll auction them at this event we're planning?" And everyone was great about that except for Larry Kramer, who said, "Why can't you just ask me for money? This is too fiddly! I'll give you money!" I said, "No, I want the books!" We were making a political point, so he said, "Alright". We got Gore Vidal and a few others.

'Armistead said, "I've got an English publisher, can I send you those?" But they had seized American editions and I wanted those. At that point, I thought, "Why don't we do a marathon reading of the whole series?" The fourth book was just out, and I had worked out we would need 13 people if we did it as a dramatised reading, and bless him, Armistead organised at his own expense 13 sets of the four *Tales* novels, one for each reader, shipped over from San Francisco, and he signed every single one. Then he said, "I'm going to be in London at the time, I shall come along." We held it in the upstairs room of a pub called the Fallen Angel, owned by Kelvin Sollis and his partner David Bridle, who would go on to take over the *Pink Paper* [a UK-wide LGBT newspaper, which began publication in 1987]. Chris Smith read the first couple of paragraphs. We started at midday on the Saturday and went through all four books with an hour break between each one, finishing around half past ten on the Sunday night. It was just euphoric. The pub downstairs was absolutely packed. Armistead and his partner came along and they were chuffed with the whole thing, although they didn't stay overnight. Tom Robinson turned up quite late on the Saturday night, and we had the auction afterwards, conducted by the trans magician Fay Presto. She's one of the sweetest people I know and always up for doing benefits. We got all 13 members of the cast to sign the books as well as a sort of record of the occasion, and as far as I remember we raised something like £2,700, which for a pissy little theatre group isn't bad!'

Scott-Presland sought out further performance-based fundraising opportunities. 'Louise [Parker Kelley] had gone back to the States, and I had gone over to talk about the possibility of helping her and her partner have a baby. I was in the States, and Quentin Crisp was doing a tour of the eastern seaboard. He was always terribly approachable, his number was in the New York telephone book, and I knew that he would go anywhere for a free meal, so I rang him up and offered to take him for lunch. He explained that he was about to do this tour [*An Evening with Quentin Crisp*], and I asked if I could do a little support slot before he went on to raise the issue of the Gay's the Word campaign, so I became Quentin's support act for a few nights; my pianist was George Goehring who wrote the music to the Connie Francis hit "Lipstick on Your Collar". I raised quite a lot of money, and every night my spot got longer and longer. Quentin was quite pleased with that, because it meant that he had to do less.'

Meeting Maupin would also have a huge impact on Mark Bunyan's future. 'The day after *Just Good Friends* [Bunyan's show, which ran at the Cockpit theatre in September 1982] closed, I was going to dinner with [*Gay News* journalist] Michael Mason, and he introduced me to Armistead Maupin. They started talking about this choir, the Pink Singers, and asked if I would get involved. I didn't have great faith in my abilities as a musical director, but Bryan Kennedy, the driving force behind the Pink Singers, would not take no for an answer, so eventually I said that I would do it. We had the first meeting; there were not that many people there. We sang "Frère Jacques", but the words were "homosexual, homosexual, lesbian, lesbian! I am homosexual! I am homosexual! We're all gay! We're all gay!", and a song I had written as a thank you to the Sisters of Perpetual Indulgence, who had put me up when I was in San Francisco [and who, in 1985, would canonise Mark], "Veni!", which was very simple.' Maupin had been involved with the San Francisco Gay Men's Chorus, the world's first gay choir, since its inception in 1978; they performed 'Veni!' on their radio show, *Fruit Punch*, in 1982. Established in April 1983, the Pink Singers are now the longest-running and most successful LGBT choir in Europe.

The raid on Gay's the Word was part of a crackdown on any and all homosexual activity, and as far as the authorities were concerned even members of the establishment were fair game. On 3 May 1984 Dr Keith Hampson, MP and former personal assistant to Edward Heath, had been arrested at the appropriately named Gay Theatre male strip club in Soho's Berwick Street after being accused of touching the thigh of what turned out to be an undercover policeman. The subsequent court case against him was dropped, but it ended his ascent towards the cabinet. At the time of his arrest, he had been Parliamentary Private Secretary to Tory grandee Michael Heseltine: the scandal forced Hampson to resign from this high-profile position, although he would remain an MP. The Hampson case, which came to court in October, once again brought police entrapment methods into the spotlight, the same methods that just a few months earlier had seen TV star Leonard Sachs – presenter of the long-running BBC TV show *The Good Old Days* – and Welsh MP Dr Roger Thomas both charged and fined £75 for individual acts of importuning men for an immoral purpose in public lavatories. Sachs had helmed *The Good Old Days* for 30 years; the arrest, which took place at Notting Hill Gate tube station, and subsequent court appearance brought his television career to an end.

Hampson, however, was not going down without a fight. Charged with indecent assault, the MP denied the claim made by PC Marshall that 'he put his left hand at the back of my right thigh and raised it on to my right buttock. Simultaneously his right hand went on to the front of my thigh on my right leg. He moved towards me then grasped my groin area – my penis and testicles.'[13] The MP admitted that he had been drinking but insisted that he had never visited a male strip club before, and that his only physical contact with PC Marshall had been to accidentally brush his thigh as he tried to get a closer look at the female police constable who accompanied him, who Hampson claimed to have thought was a man in drag. After the jury failed to reach a unanimous decision, the case was dismissed, and a fortnight later an attempted retrial was dropped. The case proved unusual in that, for the first time, the majority of the British press sided with the victim of gay entrapment, not the police. Marshall was ridiculed for his actions and his attire: 'surely the police and the courts have better things to do',[14] asked the *Daily Mail* and even the *Sunday People* wondered if he 'went there looking like a proper poof in the hope that he would be treated like one'.[15]

The Hampson Case led GALOP to issue a 12-page briefing document to the press, outlining many instances of police entrapment, despite Home Office instructions that 'no member of the police force, and no police informant, should counsel, incite or procure the commission of crime', and instructions issued by the Metropolitan Police that 'great care must be exercised to ensure that it cannot be alleged that police or their informants have counselled, or procured the commission of a crime or have acted as agents provocateurs.'[16] At the same time, Prime Minister Thatcher was also being publicly embarrassed by the antics of Sir Peter Hayman, who was in the news again, arrested and fined £100 (plus £45 costs) for committing an act of gross indecency with a 35-year-old lorry driver in a public lavatory in Reading. This time the diplomat was warned that if he were involved in any further scandals, he would be stripped of his knighthood. The married father of two, who had earlier been implicated in a paedophile scandal, was pressured into seeing a psychiatrist by senior members of the civil service; after his death, it was revealed that he had been a long-standing officer in MI6, the UK's secret intelligence service.

It was in this volatile political era that, on 10 November 1984, a sitting Member of Parliament addressed a rally in Rugby. 'My name is Chris Smith,' he announced. 'I'm the Labour MP for Islington South and Finsbury, and I'm gay.' With those few words, the opposition spokesperson for National Heritage became the first male MP to publicly come out while still sitting in Parliament.

'I had decided in my mind that I needed to do this at some point,' Lord Smith explains. 'The only question was when and where.' Smith was in the town that day to join a protest against Rugby Borough Council; the town's burghers had recently (by 20 votes to 19) removed the phrase 'sexual orientation' from their Equal Opportunities policy, erasing any protection for LGBT people against discrimination. 'The rally was happening because there had been a change of political control in Rugby council and the new Conservative leader was effectively saying, "I do not want LGBT people coming to work for Rugby council".

So, there was a big march called for a Saturday lunchtime, followed by a rally in a community hall and, because I had said supportive things about LGBT rights before, they asked me to go up and speak.' The council denied that it was its intention to discriminate, yet councillors were reported as having made inflammatory comments including 'we are not having men turn up for work in dresses round here', and describing the LGBT community as 'queers, perverts and other trash'.[17]

'On the train going up to Rugby, I was writing this very boring speech, but when I arrived at the hall the meeting had already started, and as I walked up to take my seat on the stage, I just suddenly thought – and there were a thousand people in this room – this is the place to do it. The issue was all about the ability of anyone, no matter what their sexual orientation happened to be, to do an equally good job working for Rugby council. And exactly the same principle applies to MPs. Having made that decision, the next 10 minutes, before I stood up to speak, were amongst the scariest of my life. I was absolutely terrified, but I stood up and I began my speech.' He received a five-minute ovation from the crowd which, in the wake of the death threats issued against Peter Tatchell the previous year, was quite astonishing. 'The entire audience got to its feet,' he adds. 'It was a huge surprise, and a moment of real pride. The rest of my speech didn't matter after that! And I have not regretted that moment for a single minute ever since.'

The rally was one of a number of protests that took place in Rugby against the council's new policy, and on the day that around 1,000 people heard Smith's words, 18 people were arrested in the town in clashes with police. A poll by local newspaper the *Rugby Advertiser* found that the town was split roughly down the middle: 54 per cent of those who responded felt the council was in the wrong to alter the wording, while 46 per cent agreed with what, for many, amounted to a ban on gay people working for the council.[18] Protests would continue until the following February, when the council bowed to pressure and reversed its decision.

'It was not only a time when HIV and AIDS were beginning to surface as a big public issue and the source of a lot of prejudice – we were about to go into all the adverts with tombstones and icebergs and things – but also there was a lot of anti-gay feeling anyway,' Lord Smith recalls. 'The offices of *Capital Gay* newspaper were firebombed, Gay's the Word was raided by Customs and Excise, the Pretty Police were using entrapment down in Earl's Court... There was a lot of really nasty, homophobic stuff going on, so that was all really worrying, but I thought, despite that, "I've got to do this." I have to say, apart from occasional articles and a very nasty homophobic cartoon in the *Sun*, most of the reaction, and the reaction in my constituency, was remarkably positive. The Friday following the rally, the *Islington Gazette*, which went through 20,000 letter boxes in my constituency – it was the most important paper as far as my profile locally was concerned – came out with the banner headline on their front page, "I'm Gay Says MP", next to one of the worst photographs of me that's ever been printed. That evening, I was doing my constituency surgery, which I did every Friday seeing 30 or 35 different constituents about a variety of different problems, and I thought, "Oh, my God! What are they going to say?" Not a single one of them mentioned a word about it.'

'I was the first person to interview him after he came out,' says Peter Scott-Presland, then writing for *Capital Gay*. 'I interviewed him on the train on the way back from the demonstration in Rugby. He was so high afterwards, not on drugs but on adrenaline. It was lovely because he was not normally a very demonstrative man.'

'There was a lovely moment the following week,' Lord Smith continues. 'I was at the opening of a new housing estate, and we had a nice little ceremony, with sausage rolls and cups of tea, and this woman who was about to move into one of the new flats asked me if I could help her. She needed assistance from social services to move in, because she had absolutely no belongings, no bed, no cooker, no fridge, no table... nothing. I took all the details down and I said, "Yes, of course; I'd be very happy to help." I took the address she was moving from and the address she was moving to, and then I said, "Please can you let me have your name?" She suddenly got terribly embarrassed, and she said, "Oh, Mr Smith, I don't really know what to say, I'm so embarrassed. I've read all about you, you know. My name is Mrs Gay!" She endeared herself to me forever by adding, "and I think you're wonderful!" I'm pleased to say that she went on subsequently to become a member of the Labour Party and a stalwart campaigner.'

Lord Smith's own positive experience sadly did little to change things in Parliament, and it would be almost a decade before another MP would come out. 'I had hoped that some others might follow me,' he says, 'but for nine years no one did. Through all of the campaigns against Section 28 [which prohibited local authorities from 'promoting' homosexuality], and through all of the equal age of consent issues and so on, I sort of wished I had some backup. I had people who were prepared to talk and to march and to make speeches, make arguments in the House of Commons, but no one else came out. Because I fundamentally believe that coming out voluntarily is the thing we need people to do, rather than people being outed against their wish, I did not want to push anyone into saying anything. I might have tried suggesting once or twice, but it had to be their decision.'

His bravery in coming out was overshadowed by the media's obsession with HIV and AIDS. With no legal protection, scaremongering in the press saw people suspected of being HIV-positive losing their jobs and their homes as well as their families and their friends, and although cases were increasing – 275 by the end of 1985, with 144 of those having already died – it would take years for the government to react decisively. Despite the AIDS-related death of former Conservative Party whip Nicholas Eden, the son of former Prime Minister Anthony Eden, Margaret Thatcher fought against a press campaign highlighting the dangers of unprotected sex in 1985, telling ministers that she felt that 'it would be better in my mind to follow the VD [venereal disease] precedent of putting notices in doctors' surgeries, public lavatories, et cetera. But to place advertisements in newspapers, which every young person could read and learn of practices they never knew about, will do harm.'[19]

18

Pride, Pits and Perverts

'At the Bronski Beat benefit the other week there was this lone Yorkshire miner standing there, and I got chatting to him. He said something like... "I had no idea you people supported us. I'd never even thought about you people." I think he was genuinely moved and also terribly confused, because he didn't even think that lesbians and gays had any connection to working-class struggles.' – Mike Jackson[1]

Along with their reluctance to deal with the AIDS epidemic, it seemed obvious that Mrs Thatcher and her all-male cabinet were intent on waging a war against the advancement of LGBT rights.

Back in April 1983, Education Minister, and former school headmaster, Rhodes Boyson had launched a stinging, unprovoked attack on LGBT teachers, calling into question the teaching of 'deviant practices' in schools. 'Most parents do not want their children taught by proselytising homosexuals,' Boyson announced. 'They do not want any persecution of homosexuals, but they do not want deviance, or anti-life treated as normality.'[2] Boyson had form: a year earlier, he had objected to the London Borough of Brent advertising for school governors in the gay press, accusing the council of 'threatening the moral standards of the classroom', and calling their plans 'an affront to the decencies of the vast majority of local families.'[3] It was the start of a long, orchestrated campaign by the Conservative Party against any and all mentions of homosexuality in the classroom, a campaign fuelled by the mania surrounding AIDS.

As well as attacking LGBT rights, the Tories also wanted to neuter the country's trade unions, which wielded huge power. The government was intent on breaking up the country's many publicly owned utilities – under Thatcher, Britain's gas, electricity and water industries would leave public ownership and be snapped up by independent owners – and top of the list was the National Coal Board (NCB) and the thousands of members of the National Union of Miners (NUM). The government first announced its plans to shut 23 collieries – mostly in Scotland, Wales and the North West of England – in 1981, but at that point the threat of a strike was enough to make them rethink their strategy. However, by early 1984 Thatcher was in a stronger position: she parachuted in Ian MacGregor – who had previously halved the workforce of British Steel – to head the NCB, and he announced the closure of some 20 pits with the loss of around 20,000 jobs.

Headed by NUM leader Arthur Scargill, miners went on prolonged, expensive and at times violent industrial action. Pitched battles took place between police and pickets as workers (referred to as 'scabs') broke the strike and crossed picket lines. Families across Great Britain suffered as union pay ran out and welfare benefits were denied to the striking miners and their dependents. Over a 12-month period, more than 11,000 arrests were made, almost 200 people were imprisoned and two picketers were killed. The strong-arm tactics used by the police caused a national scandal.

Mark Ashton, then aged 22, started working as a volunteer for the London Lesbian and Gay Switchboard in 1982. The following year, he appeared in the Lesbian and Gay Youth Video Project documentary *Framed Youth: The Revenge of the Teenage Perverts*, alongside Jimmy Somerville and Richard Coles, which won the Grierson Award 1984 for Best Documentary. With his friend Mike Jackson, Ashton formed Lesbians and Gays Support the Miners (LGSM), after the two men collected donations for the miners on strike at the 1984 Pride march. 'There was no group in existence at that stage,' he told Brian Flynn of *Gay Community News*. 'We went to the Gay Pride march with buckets and collected 180 quid. It bowled us over. Unbeknownst to us, the Labour Committee for Gay Rights had organised a meeting, a fringe meeting after the Gay Pride March, in Malet Street, and they had a striking miner there, who was talking... So, we were able to hand the money over and that was the first link we made.'

Making close personal contacts with people from the Welsh mining town of Dulais, LGSM began to raise funds specifically to help them. 'The majority of the money we raise goes directly to this one mining community,' Ashton explained. 'We basically pay, I think, a quarter of their bills every week for food, paying off debts and stuff like that... We've taken miners to gay bars and we've gone down to Wales. Lesbians and gay men have danced in a miners' welfare hall, which was outrageous.'[4] Similar groups were set up around the country. 'I think the first group outside [London] was Glasgow... then Edinburgh... and then there's Brighton, Liverpool, Manchester, Bournemouth, Southampton, Leicester, Cardiff, Swansea. And there's a women-only group... Lesbians Against Pit Closures.'[5]

In a half-hour documentary filmed by LGSM, *All Out! Dancing in Dulais*, the impassioned young socialist explained why he had to get involved. The group began, Ashton said, 'so that one community could give solidarity to another... It is quite illogical to say, "Well, I'm gay and I'm into defending the gay community but I don't care about anything else." It's ludicrous. It's important that if you're defending communities then you defend all communities, not just one.'

Initially based at Gay's the Word, LGSM's success necessitated a move to a larger venue, the gay-run Fallen Angel pub in Islington. On 10 December 1984 LGSM organised a fundraising concert at Camden's Electric Ballroom: 'Pits and Perverts' was headlined by Bronski Beat. Their story would later be immortalised in the award-winning film *Pride* (2014), which would also focus on the 1985 Pride march, led by banner-carrying groups of miners. With support from electronic duo Oppenheimer Ransom, the show helped raise £5,650 for striking miners and their families in South Wales, funds that were much needed in the run-up to the festive season, as Somerville himself noted: 'The miners' benefit we did brought a good Christmas and presents for a lot of families in South Wales. Doing benefits, it's really important – we do a lot of gay ones because the gay community is quite small and a lot of money's needed for defence costs and things.'[6]

Just six months previously, on 7 June 1984, Bronski Beat had been the first band consisting entirely of out-gay members to appear on *Top of the Pops*. That weekend their debut single, 'Smalltown Boy', jumped from number 13 to number four in the singles charts. A second appearance on the BBC's flagship pop show saw the single enter the top three. Shortly afterwards, the band played a miners' benefit concert at the University of Liverpool, along with fellow hitmakers the Style Council and Madness.

The group's influence was far-reaching. Just as a generation of fledgeling LGBT performers had swooned over David Bowie's performance of 'Starman' on *Top of the Pops* more than a decade earlier, a new generation of would-be pop stars would draw influence from 'Smalltown Boy' and its accompanying video, both of which recounted the hard-hitting tale of a young gay man forced to leave his home and his family to avoid abuse. 'I remember back in the early eighties, from afar in Australia,' says Gary Cosby of Britpop band Lick, 'Bronski Beat were totally out and political, and I thought that was so brave and amazing.'

'I saw Bronski Beat perform at a club called the Daisy Chain at the Fridge sometime around 1983,' says Steve Swindells. 'I thought, "They are going to be massive." They already had "Smalltown Boy" in the act, and I remember thinking, "This is going to be a fucking hit."'

'I loved Jimmy and Bronski Beat,' adds Andy Polaris. 'I thought they were fantastically brave, I really admired what they were doing. They made great records, they were out there, but they must have got a lot of shit. Those records have stood the test of time. "Smalltown Boy" was such an important song for young, queer people; it still is now.' The tale of a young man forced to leave home following years of homophobic abuse, it was a song that countless LGBT people could personally identify with.

The three men – two Scots and a Londoner – had come together the previous year and, almost before they knew it, were fighting off advances from major record companies. Somerville had left his native Glasgow on his 18th birthday, heading to London for the weekend but deciding never to return. Landing a job as a display assistant in a department store, he lived precariously, moving from squat to squat and for a short time sharing a flat with future Pet Shop Boy Chris Lowe. Although he had no experience as a singer, in 1982 he came up with his first song, 'Screaming', for the soundtrack of *Framed Youth: The Revenge of the Teenage Perverts*, a documentary film made by the Lesbian and Gay Youth Video Project and issued in April 1983; in the film Somerville can be seen performing the song with multi-instrumentalist Richard Coles. Shortly afterwards, Somerville met gay couple Larry Steinbachek and Steve Bronski (born Steven Forrest), and moved into the house they were sharing with friends in Brixton. With music by Bronski and Steinbachek, 'Screaming' became the first song by a new trio, Bronski Beat. The mighty international Warner Bros corporation offered them almost half a million pounds, but they turned that down to sign with the recently reactivated London Records. 'They're very flexible, and they're not just capitalising or chasing in on the gay angle,' Somerville told *Out* magazine. 'Of course, they know that they've got a formula and it's working at the moment, but they're still really flexible... If they did decide that they weren't going to let us do what we wanted any more, then Bronski Beat really wouldn't exist anymore, because we couldn't exist on those terms. It has to be under our terms.'[7]

Somerville was becoming increasingly aware of how he could use his status as a pop star to affect change, especially through his lyrics. Less than a fortnight after their first appearance on *Top of the Pops*, on 16 June 1984 Drew Griffiths, co-founder of Gay Sweatshop, was murdered in a homophobic attack. Despite police issuing a photofit of a man wanted in question with the fatal stabbing, no one has ever been charged with causing his death. Released in September 1984, and reaching number six in the UK singles charts, the second Bronski Beat single, "Why?", was dedicated to Griffiths.

'I write about things that upset me because there's so many divisions in the world,' Somerville revealed. 'A lot of people say that's the way the world is. Okay that's the way it is, but that's not the way it should be. The point is everybody should be equal, nobody's got the right to be better than anybody else, 'cos when it comes down to it all we are is feeble human beings. Nobody's got the right to suppress or be more powerful than anybody else.'[8]

241

'Pits and Perverts' marked a pivotal point in the relationship between LGBT people and the Labour movement. From the stage, miner David Donovan told the audience that 'You know what harassment means, as we do... we will support you. It won't change overnight, but now 14,000 miners know that there are other causes and other problems. We know about blacks, and gays, and nuclear disarmament. And we will never be the same.'[9] Coming just weeks after Lord Smith had outed himself, the Labour movement and the Labour Party itself would no longer simply pay lip service to their LGBT members. By Christmas 1984, LGSM had raised £11,000; the group would end up raising more than £22,000 to help the families of striking miners.

In early 1985, Somerville left Bronski Beat, forming a new duo (originally called the Committee) with multi-instrumentalist Richard Coles (who became the Reverend Richard in 2005) Coles, his friend from the Lesbian and Gay Youth Video Project. A spokesman for his record company, Forbidden Fruit/London Records, told the *Melody Maker* that 'Jimmy's decision to leave was brought on by his reluctance to accept the pressures of the business of success, and he felt that the business was taking over from the sheer fun of singing,' although that was only part of the story. In February Somerville had been arrested by a plain-clothes policeman and charged with gross indecency while cruising in Hyde Park, putting a potentially lucrative US tour in jeopardy. After arresting the singer, the officer apparently asked Somerville for an autograph for his daughter. It would not be Somerville's last run-in with the law.

All three members of Bronski Beat had been looking forward to the US tour: 'I cannae wait', he told Karen Swayne of *No.1* magazine. 'We're not worried about getting the same reaction as Boy George got – being called the Devil incarnate – I think it'll be a squeal!' But the other members of the band were becoming increasingly at odds with the singer's political agenda. With a new single to promote, a cover of the Donna Summer disco classic 'I Feel Love' featuring a duet between Somerville and Soft Cell's Marc Almond, they kept up appearances for a few weeks, performing at the Montreux Festival in May with both Almond and Coles (who played tenor saxophone on stage during 'I Feel Love'), but it was all over. The rest of the band wanted to distance

242

themselves from politics and take advantage of their new-found fame; Somerville wanted to exploit his status but did not feel comfortable being a pop star. The trio split: Steve Bronski and Larry Steinbachek found a new singer, John Foster, and Somerville moved on with Coles.

In July, having adopted the name the Communards, the pair performed their debut gig at Heaven. Joined on stage by singer Sarah Jane Morris, who Jimmy first met at a miners' fundraising gig in Brixton, the new group helped raise £2,000 for the Defend Gay's the Word Fund. Court proceedings against the bookstore had commenced at the end of June, with Geoffrey Robertson, the QC who had previously acted for *OZ* and *Gay News*, called upon to represent Gay's the Word in its battle with the authorities. Finally, in 1986, the court would find in favour of Gay's the Word, and all charges against the nine men and women involved were dropped.

Back at the end of January 1985, the Reverend Gregory Richards, aged 38, died at Chelmsford Hospital, becoming the fifty-second AIDS fatality in Britain. 'We are getting phone calls from respectable church ladies who have sipped wine from the same cup as the Rev. Richards at Holy Communion,' said medical officer Doctor Tony Kirkland. 'They are worried they may have picked up the infection, but I can assure them there is absolutely nothing for them to worry about.' Despite this reassurance, the press went into meltdown, claiming that his parishioners, as well as inmates and guards at Chelmsford jail, where he served as chaplain, 'believed there was a possibility Richards could have transmitted the disease by shaking hands if he and the person he was greeting had cuts'.[10] Tory MP Robert McCrindle demanded that there be a government inquiry into why hospital officials had kept Reverend Richards' illness a secret until after his death. Any advances that had been gained by the LGBT community were soon lost as Terry Sanderson, writing in *Gay Times*, noted: 'The British press has declared war on homosexuals. "The renewed open season on gays" was how Susan Hemmings described it in a letter to the *Guardian*, and it has gone well beyond the spiteful sniping we are used to. This month has seen one of the most concerted, sustained, and vindictive attacks ever launched on our community. Day after day the Big Guns have been

243

firing off volleys of misinformation and distortion on the subject of AIDS. With apparent glee, papers like the *Sun* and *Daily Star* have been allotting acres of space to bigots who seem to have been waiting patiently in the wings for this opportunity.'[11]

Fear bordering on hysteria was rife: Liverpool businessman Joe Farley, who owned several pubs and clubs in the city, put up signs barring homosexuals from his establishments.[12] The virulently homophobic Kelvin MacKenzie, editor of the *Sun*, quoted widely discredited American psychologist Paul Cameron (listed, as of June 2020, as an anti-gay extremist by the Southern Poverty Law Center) who announced that 'all homosexuals should be exterminated to stop the spread of AIDS. It's time we stopped pussy-footing around'.[13] The quote was, in fact, invented. He should have waited 12 months: a year after MacKenzie liberally 'adapted' his words, Cameron published the book *Special Report: AIDS*, which encouraged the US government to set up concentration camps for 'sexually active homosexuals'. In May 1985, at the annual Prison Officers' Association conference, delegates demanded a national register of drug users and homosexual inmates to make it easier to monitor incidences of AIDS. The gloves were off, and a backlash against the LGBT community began, with dire descriptions in the tabloid press about the evils of the 'gay plague'. Writing in the magazine *7 Days*, LGSM's Mark Ashton voiced everyone's concerns when he stated that 'AIDS... is frightening because unlike all the other threats, trials and tribulations which are part and parcel of our daily lives – we aren't yet sure how to respond. We could be infected by the virus from our lovers; should we be infected we could go on to develop AIDS, and if we develop AIDS we will probably die.'[14]

On 25 July 1985, while receiving treatment in Paris, the world learned what many had suspected: Hollywood A-lister Rock Hudson was dying of AIDS. He had been looking gaunt for a while, and recent appearances on TV soap *Dynasty* and at a press conference with his on-screen partner Doris Day showed the world just how frail he had become. Britain's tabloids became hysterical, speculating that the brief kiss he gave Linda Evans on the set of *Dynasty* could have exposed her to the killer disease. However, there was a marked shift in attitude from a number of media sources: if a man as manly as Rock Hudson could get AIDS then suddenly we were all vulnerable. He died, at his home in Beverly Hills, on 2 October. He was 59.

Hudson was a bona fide star: his death sent shockwaves through the entertainment industry, and he was written about as 'the first international celebrity to reveal he suffered from AIDS... his courage and generosity gave hope to millions'.[15] But the music world had been feeling the sting of AIDS for three years, having already lost disco superstar Patrick Cowley, Hibiscus (of US radical drag troupe the Cockettes, both in 1982), Klaus Nomi and Jobriath (both 1983) and others. Ten days after Hudson's death, Ricky Wilson, guitarist and co-founder of influential new wave act the B-52's, would also succumb to the disease. The entertainment industry was being ravaged, yet none of the big pop stars of the day – aside from Tom Robinson, Jimmy Somerville and the Frankie frontmen – were prepared to come out and talk openly about their sexuality. More deaths would follow, including those of music icons Sylvester, Liberace and Tom Fogerty of rock band Creedence Clearwater Revival, but it would take until the death, in 1991, of another superstar musician to finally turn the tide.

With many in Britain's media blaming the rapid advancement of AIDS on promiscuous gay people, it was important that the LGBT community show a united front. Lesbian and Gay Pride 85 would be the biggest Pride event in Britain to date, yet it might not have happened at all if it had not been for a determination within London's LGBT community to ensure the event's future. The masses gathered in Hyde Park before marching on to Trafalgar Square and then to Jubilee Gardens, Pride's new, albeit temporary, home. For Erasure singer Andy Bell it was his first Pride experience. 'I was both nervous but exhilarated at the same time,' he remembers. 'The attendance numbers were grossly undercounted by the national media. It gave me my first insight into how politics worked.'

'The whole of the staff of *Capital Gay* were instrumental in Pride 1985,' Peter Scott-Presland explains. 'Pride had almost not happened the previous year, because nobody had thought to organise it. The Gay Youth Movement stepped in and organised something with about two weeks' notice, but come what may at the end of June thousands of people are going to turn out onto the streets to celebrate. We didn't want to

245

lose the politics, but we did want to get some kind of involvement from the commercial scene. In '85 that mostly took the form of sponsorship in kind. There had been a meeting in Jubilee Gardens in September 1984, with people from *Capital Gay*, people from Switchboard, [author and activist] Lisa Power, the chair of the Gay Business Association, and a representative from Heaven, and we all agreed that this must not happen again, that we must try and get it onto a secure footing that not only brought people out onto the march, but also provided something attractive to happen at the end of the march.

'We had had the open-air festival in Hyde Park in '79, didn't get Hyde Park again in '80 so from then on – apart from Huddersfield – after the march we had finished at the University of London's Students' Union. But we decided that the next Pride would be too big for that. We were going all-out to make this the biggest one ever, and the commercial scene people offered to help with that. We got in touch with Ken Livingstone [then still leader of the GLC] and asked if we could use Jubilee Gardens. We got the thumbs up and spent a lot of time persuading the commercial scene that it was worth being involved, because we'd always been banging our heads against a brick wall trying to get floats on the march. They never allowed more than two floats until well into the nineties; we were always told that it was on safety grounds, which was absolute bollocks, of course... The major sponsorship was from Heaven and Richard Branson, and what they offered was to bring Divine, who was enormous at the time, and have him coming up the Thames on the Virgin paddle steamer to sing to the crowd in Jubilee Gardens from the middle of the river.

'There were about 12,000 people on that march. We ended up in Jubilee Gardens, then at about five o'clock there was this buzz that ran through the crowd, and everyone rushed over towards the railings on the Embankment. This paddle boat came along and all you could see – unless you had binoculars – was this fat pink blob on the top of the roof of the paddle steamer dancing up and down. You couldn't really hear what was being sung, but the fact that it happened was enough.' Most in the audience struggled to hear the songs being relayed over the boat's tannoy, but several claimed to have heard Divine screaming 'fuck you very much' as the steamer sailed past. 'We had the Beverley

Sisters on the main stage there. I'd decided that even if we were to have this commercial element, we still had to have performers that would be part of our community, so I programmed about seven hours of music for that. And for better or for worse, that was what set Pride off on its course for the next few years.'

The choice of a singing trio whose greatest fame came in the 1950s may have seemed a strange one, but the Beverley Sisters' career was enjoying something of a resurgence; they had recently played at the gay-friendly nightspot the Hippodrome, and had built up a large and loyal camp following. 'The Beverley Sisters were booked to play on the main stage,' Alison Rayner recalls. 'Crissy Lee was playing drums, and they needed a bass player. I was recruited on the day!'

'Every year, I programmed the cabaret tent. I would also compère with a lesbian performer called Viv Acious [Ova studio's sound engineer, 1983–85], and provide the catering,' continues Scott-Presland. 'It was knackering! I put up a lot of resistance to doing drag on the cabaret stage, partly because I associated drag with miming, and I really wanted people doing their own material. But with the arrival of people like Lily Savage and [Black Cap resident] Lee Paris, who used to do a recreation of Mrs Shufflewick's act,* I gradually started introducing drag. Eventually, there was a separate drag stage, which I rather regretted as it split the audience.'

LGBT people in music and the theatre were continuing to be a thorn in Mrs Thatcher's side, as was the Labour-led GLC. With its progressive gay and lesbian policies, the GLC was keen to award grants to projects that supported minority groups, which included LGBT and BAME initiatives... And sometimes both. In 1982 the Gay Black Group approached the GLC to request funding for a centre which would provide advice and counselling, a helpline, a library and other

---

* Famous on TV and radio during the 1950s, Mrs Shufflewick was the drag persona of comedian Rex Jameson. A mentor to Danny La Rue, by the early 1960s, due to his increasing alcoholism, his career was on the slide; however in the 1970s Jameson re-emerged, as Mrs Shufflewick, and became a firm favourite at the Black Cap in Camden.

resources. The Black Lesbian and Gay Centre finally received funding in 1985; however, the following year, the GLC was abolished by the government after a two-year battle to get a new Local Government Act through Parliament. The powers once held by the GLC were devolved to the various London boroughs, and the Centre – as well as for other LGBT and BAME groups – would have to rely on donations, membership subscriptions and grants from other bodies for its funding.

Even without the GLC, with more and more politically active LGBT people taking up roles in public life, they would continue to be seen as a threat to the status quo. The Tories had won two successive general elections and it looked as though they were on course to win their third. Something had to happen and, as 1985 morphed into 1986, Somerville and Robinson both became involved in a new political initiative involving musicians: Red Wedge. Trumpeted with a launch at the House of Commons in November 1985, by the following January the first Red Wedge national tour was underway. Intended to help politicise left-leaning young music fans against the Thatcher government and, hopefully, push them towards the poll booths to vote Labour, Tom Robinson and the Communards joined a tour bus that also included the Paul Weller-led Style Council and Billy Bragg, and at different venues around the country would be joined by acts including the Special AKA, Prefab Sprout, Elvis Costello, Madness and dozens of others. In January 1986 the Smiths made an impromptu appearance in Newcastle-upon-Tyne, years before the self-professed celibate Morrissey became the poster boy for right-wing nationalists, playing four songs on instruments borrowed from the Style Council.

While Red Wedge were wowing audiences in the north of the country, back in London a new group, Lesbians and Gays Support the Printworkers (LGSP), was formed. Taking its lead from the successful Lesbians and Gays Support the Miners (who, along with several miners' groups, had led the march at Pride 85), LGSP came together to add weight to the dispute between unionised employees of Rupert Murdoch's giant News International and the company itself, which wanted to move its operations from its traditional home in Fleet Street to Wapping Wharf, downsizing its workforce in the process. Unlike LGSM – whose members had no direct experience of coal mining –

some of the people involved in LGSP were printworkers themselves. Once again, the government used the police to intimidate striking workers and to break up legitimate industrial protests, and once again the LGBT community was spurred into action, organising weekly meetings at the London Lesbian and Gay Centre, joining picket lines and protest marches and holding regular fundraising events at venues including Gay's the Word, in spite of the fact that the British media was often seen as the enemy.

The fight against LGBT oppression continued. In December 1986 the Home Office again received complaints about Manchester's Chief Constable, James Anderton, only this time those complaints came not from the CHE but from the leaders of both Manchester City Council and Salford City Council, and from the members of the local police authority. Anderton, councillor Graham Stringer wrote, had 'just gone too far', when making 'prejudiced and discriminatory remarks' at a conference on policing AIDS in the city. Calling the disease a 'self-inflicted scourge', in a speech given in front of more than 100 representatives of the emergency services, Anderton blamed the spread of AIDS on 'people at risk, swirling around in a human cess-pit of their own making', going on to claim that the 'alarming spread of AIDS is being hastened and facilitated in my opinion by our increasingly degenerate conduct. Why do homosexuals continue sleeping with each other? Why do they still engage in sodomy and other obnoxious practices?'[16] On the same day as Anderton launched his inflammatory polemic, the Catholic bishops of England and Wales issued a statement which claimed that 'the most effective method of containing this epidemic must consist of a substantial change in moral and social behaviour. This means accepting that sexual love is reserved for marriage.'[17] After a series of high-level meetings at the Home Office, Anderton kept his job, thanks in no small part to the intervention of Margaret Thatcher who, through her private secretary, made it clear to the Home Office that she considered 'that it would be outrageous if the Chief Constable were required to seek clearance for all his public speaking engagements'.[18]

Anderton's attitude towards the LGBT community was reflected across the country. Eight days before Christmas, the Royal Vauxhall

249

Tavern was raided, and bar staff were arrested for selling poppers (amyl or butyl nitrate, sold in small bottles and used as both a muscle relaxant for sex and as a high for dancing). Just over a month later, in the early hours of 24 January 1987, the police raided the RVT yet again, shortly after that night's headline act, acid-tongued drag queen Lily Savage (Paul O'Grady) had left the stage to return to his dressing room. Nothing new there, but this time, for the very first time, the police – reacting to AIDS hysteria – wore rubber gloves and face masks. One of the three dozen or so policemen and women who infiltrated the bar stormed into the dressing room and demanded that O'Grady leave. Eleven people were arrested on drunkenness charges, even then a ridiculously spurious reason for detaining people in a venue where alcohol was openly, and legally, on sale. All were later released without charge, although one announced his intention to sue the police for 'wrongful arrest, wrongful detention and assault'.[19]

Violent attacks on gay men continued to increase, especially in London. This second raid on the RVT took place while police were investigating the brutal murder of a gay man, John Knowles, who had been stabbed in the neck with a broken bottle before being beaten to death in a popular cruising area of Kennington Park. The raid made many in the local gay community both angry at, and wary of, the police, and any help they had been giving to their enquiries dissipated, hampering efforts to find the killer. The London Apprentice, a gay pub in Shoreditch, was singled out on a number of occasions, with GALOP reporting at least five separate incidents involving gangs of youths attacking men as they left the pub. In one of those incidents, in March 1987, two men were attacked with broken bottles. When police arrived on the scene, 'officers were unhelpful and failed to arrest any of the attackers who were only yards away. One officer told one of the victims "stop spitting blood at me or I will arrest you." The second man was told by another policeman: "shut up you queer bastard." No arrests were made.'[20]

Six days after this latest raid on the RVT, Mark Ashton was admitted to hospital. Diagnosed as HIV-positive, he died 12 days later. Jimmy Somerville and Richard Coles would dedicate their song 'For a Friend' to him. 'Mark was a close friend of both of us and my best friend,'

Somerville later told *Record Collector* magazine. 'He was the first friend of ours to die from AIDS and it really thumped us, really brought it all home and I suppose this is a way of getting it off our chests.'[21] Ashton's friends set up the Mark Ashton Trust in his memory; within two years, the Trust had raised over £20,000 for HIV/AIDS research. That same year, journalist Louis Eaks, whose arrest for indecency in 1970 had helped spark Britain's first public demonstration for LGBT rights, conducted a survey of dentists' attitude towards HIV-positive patients. Publishing his findings in *Man Alive* magazine, more than two-thirds of the dentists approached said that they would refuse to treat patients suffering with AIDS. Eaks would succumb to AIDS a few years later.

Other industries were implementing new policies in the wake of the crisis. Firemen, for instance, were told not to give the kiss of life in case they catch a deadly disease. It was not until after Princess Diana had grabbed headlines by meeting patients at the country's first dedicated HIV ward that the government began to take notice. After Diana shook hands with patients (on 9 April 1987) at Middlesex Hospital in London, it was hoped that the resulting press coverage would help dispel the myth that healthy people could catch AIDS through social contact. The Princess spent the longest time with Shane Snape, a 28-year-old HIV-positive nurse, who told reporters that 'the Princess shook my hand without wearing gloves and that meant more to me than anything'.[22] But the government's media campaign, with television adverts full of crashing tombstones and John Hurt's stentorian warnings about how sex can kill, fuelled panic. Health minister Norman Fowler was keen that people be warned about the devastation that AIDS threatened, but his boss was not convinced. When an advisor warned Margaret Thatcher that 'Fowler is proposing to place explicit and distasteful advertisements about AIDS in all the Sunday papers',[23] she balked at the idea of discussing sex in a government-sponsored leaflet. 'She had the view that if you told young people about HIV and unprotected sex, you'd be telling them about things they didn't know about, and the implication was that they'd want to go out there and do it. I always thought that was an eccentric view. We were warning people, not urging them,' Fowler later revealed.[24] Thatcher saw herself as the country's moral guardian, a Mary Whitehouse with actual power, but her aversion to discussing aspects of sex that she herself saw as distasteful could have done untold damage to Britain's LGBT population. It was a position diametrically opposed to her support for the decriminalisation of homosexuality in the 1960s, but her stand on LGBT issues had become more conservative as her career progressed.

19

The Kiss

'Parents certainly came to me and told me what was going on. They gave me some of the books with which little children as young as five and six were being taught. There was The Playbook for Kids About Sex *in which brightly coloured pictures of little stick men showed all about homosexuality and how it was done. That book was for children as young as five. I should be surprised if anybody supports that.'* – Dame Jill Knight[1]

At the beginning of 1987, Frankie Goes to Hollywood imploded in spectacular style. Success in the States came with record-company-mandated orders for singers Paul Rutherford and Holly Johnson to dial down the gay and crawl back into the closet, something that neither man was prepared to do. 'We weren't very good at being told what to do,' Rutherford explains, 'so we ignored all that. Frankie was an exercise in being really honest. That's why we split up in the end, because we were very honest with each other!' Johnson was travelling separately to the rest of the band and barely acknowledging them on stage. By mid-January, rumours were circulating that he was making plans to leave the band, and when a charity pop concert to raise funds for AIDS patients was announced in February, the line-up included a now Frankie-free Holly Johnson, although the singer would be prevented from signing a solo deal for the next year due to a hotly contested court case instigated by Frankie's label, Zang Tumb Tuum.

The benefit concert was held at Wembley Stadium on 1 April 1987, a date set aside for a new global awareness campaign, International AIDS Day,* and featured a stellar international line-up including Elton John (who that week had announced that he had split from his wife, Renate), George Michael, Boy George, Tom Robinson, Holly Johnson and the Communards. This would be Boy George's first live appearance since his battle with drug dependency had been splashed across the tabloids and his US work visa had been revoked.** The following day, the Communards headed a second benefit concert at Edinburgh's Usher Hall, organised by the Scottish AIDS Monitor, with all proceeds going towards a new hospice for AIDS patients in the region. In an interview later that year, the still-closeted George Michael commented that he took part because 'a few of we heterosexuals were free to perform', while berating other stars for not getting involved: 'There are some stars paying lip service. We're all keen to show how socially conscious and protective we are, but come the time for action that changes, and most are suddenly busy... I do think we have a role to play, but the caring ought to be genuine.'[2]

A couple of weeks before the show, at a press conference in London to announce his own upcoming tour, David Bowie apologised for not being able to take part in the International AIDS Day concert but told the 300 members of the media gathered there that he thought it was 'a marvellous, worthwhile and important thing to do'.[3] Over the previous 15 years, Bowie's attitude towards his own sexuality had

---

* International AIDS Day was replaced, just one year later, by World AIDS Day, held on 1 December annually, and now recognised as the first ever global health awareness day.

** In July 1986 it was revealed that George was dealing with a £200-a-week heroin habit, and his friend, Michael Rudetski, who had co-written a song for the recent Culture Club album *From Luxury to Heartache*, was later found dead at George's home. Five days before Christmas, George was again arrested over suspected drugs offences; one of the men with him, Mark Golding (aka Mark Vaultier), died the following day from an overdose.

been, at the very least, confusing, and when he announced, in 1972, that he was 'gay and I always have been', it is arguable that he was simply using the language of the day to express his own thoughts on gender fluidity. Irrespective of his own thoughts and predilections, he understood that he had a huge gay following and that, as a media personality, he had a responsibility to that fan base. On 20 March, the very day that a new drug, AZT, was approved for use in treating AIDS patients in the United States, Bowie stunned reporters when he admitted that 'I have taken an AIDS test. I would take an AIDS test every time I change a partner and I suggest everybody takes an AIDS test if they change partners. I also suggest they wear a condom – ok? AIDS is one of the most frightening diseases that this planet has ever faced.'[4] His announcement was met with spontaneous applause. Meanwhile, at a meeting of the Conservative Central Council in Torquay, Christian lobby group the Conservative Family Campaign were advocating for AIDS patients to be isolated until their inevitable death. The group, whose leader, Dr Tony Dale, insisted were not 'gay bashing', also wanted public funding withdrawn from HIV/AIDS charity the Terrence Higgins Trust, as it 'actively supports homosexuals'.[5]

Despite attention-grabbing superstar support, in the wake of the AIDS crisis, the public's attitude towards LGBT people was worsening. In 1987 the British Social Attitudes Survey found that 75 per cent of the population felt that homosexual activity was 'always or mostly wrong'. This was a massive increase in negativity towards LGBT people: just four years earlier, when the annual survey first began, it found that just half of the public believed that 'sexual relations between two adults of the same sex' were 'always wrong'. Homophobic violence soared: the 1987 GALOP report makes for shocking reading. There were more reports of homophobic attacks in the first three months of 1987 than during the whole of 1986, although an untold number of incidents would never come to light, the victims of gay bashings having no confidence in the police force to investigate their cases sympathetically.

There can be little doubt that much of this shift in attitude was down to the way LGBT people were portrayed in the press. With AIDS still a hot topic, and another gay serial killer on the loose,* Britain's tabloids pounced on any story with an LGBT theme. Elton's failing marriage made international headlines, with every story casually reminding readers that the singer was a 'self-confessed bisexual', and despite the fact that Boy George had yet to come out, Britain's media constantly made snide comments about him and his friends, as singer Andy Polaris recalls. 'This was the eighties; there was a lot of homophobia in the press, and I was very, very wary of them, even before Animal Nightlife got signed,' Polaris admits. 'There were always people hanging around the Blitz, and the squat, and then when George was starting to make it, a lot of press came to me because I was part of that scene, but I was very aware of how they could twist things. I remember one article that called me "Sade with a dick"!

'I didn't want to be known as "the gay singer", because I had to respect the rest of the band. I knew that they would get branded as a gay band, and I realised very quickly that would be all that the press would want to talk about. If we were all gay that would have been fine, but I didn't think that it was right that my sexuality would be the focus as the only gay person there. [The band] were all cool about it... But there was also the issue of safety. You had to think about racism and homophobia and your own safety. We saw what had happened with Peter Tatchell in Bermondsey, we saw the lies they were printing about Elton John and underage boys, so there was no way I was going to talk to the media about it. But obviously all of the band and all of our friends knew, and it was never a problem at all, and there were also a lot of code things in the lyrics, so people who knew would see that. The

---

* In July 1987 Michael Lupo was sentenced to life imprisonment for the murder of four men and the attempted murder of two others. He had infiltrated the very heart of LGBT glitterati; his address book featured the names of Kenny Everett, fashion designer Bruce Oldfield and photographer Norman Parkinson, alongside others. Police were unable to identify him initially because one of his victims, Anthony Connolly, was suspected of being HIV positive, and the coroner refused to work on the body until it could be confirmed that he was not infectious. This led to accusations of the police not treating the death of a gay man seriously, just as they had failed to treat the disappearance of several gay men from the capital seriously during Nilsen's reign of terror.

only time there was any drama was once, when we were recording, our producer looked at the lyrics, and said, "Oh, you're singing about a guy, not a girl!" And I said, "yes, that's right", and after that I felt a lot of attitude from him. It's weird when you meet people who are really straight in the creative arts; they don't really understand that queer thread that goes all the way through.'

Polaris was right to be wary, but it was not just LGBT musicians that the press were baying for. On 19 February 1985, the BBC had aired the first episode of its new soap opera *EastEnders*. A direct assault on the stranglehold held on serial dramas by rival channel ITV, *EastEnders* courted controversy from the off: the very first episode began with a death, and early storylines covered interracial marriage, domestic violence, the effects of alcoholism and, in a first for a nationally screened show on British television, a thoroughly believable gay relationship between two men of different backgrounds and different generations. Played by Michael Cashman, Colin Russell was not the first out-gay man on British television: Thames Television's 1979 sitcom *Agony*, starring Maureen Lipman, had been the first British TV show to feature a gay couple (teacher Michael and trainee doctor Rob) and not treat them as outmoded stereotypes for cheap laughs; in 1981 ITV franchise Southern included a gay couple – rail steward Trevor Wallace and nursing assistant Peter Hunt – in its daytime soap *Together*, and the following year Channel 4 soap *Brookside* introduced an out-gay character Gordon Collins; one of the scriptwriters on *Together* was Phil Redmond, creator of *Brookside* and, later, *Hollyoaks*.

Colin may not have been the first gay character on television, but he was one of the earliest to be portrayed as enjoying an active sex life – and to be played by an out-gay actor. Joining the cast in August 1986, Cashman soon became the bête noir of the British tabloid press, no more so than when, three months later, his character found himself a boyfriend, Cockney barrow boy and local ne'er do well Barry Clark, 15 years his junior. It would not be long before their on-screen neighbour and resident gossip Dot Cotton (played by actor June Brown) started to spread rumours that the couple had AIDS, giving programme makers an ideal opportunity to explore the issue and to spark debate in the press about how people with HIV were treated by the media. Barry was also under 21, making his relationship with Colin illegal.

For the first year of their on-screen relationship, Colin and Barry were treated in much the same way as any fictional characters by the tabloid press, but in November 1987 all that changed. After Colin gave his boyfriend a small peck on the forehead, all hell broke loose, and the BBC's switchboard received a record number of complaints. Heralded as the first time a kiss between two gay characters had been seen on British television (it was not: that took place in August 1970 between actors Ian McKellen and James Laurenson, in Christopher Marlowe's *Edward II*), the tabloids went into meltdown. Britain's redtops had already rechristened the show after a furious front-page story headlined 'It's Eastbenders' appeared in the notoriously homophobic *Sun* in April 1986. Writing in the *Sunday Sport*, TV columnist Howard Sounes dismissed the show as a parade of 'punks, pansies, perverts and pinkos... would-be incest cases and Yuppie queers'.[6]

In January 1989 the character of Colin made front pages again when he kissed another character, Guido, full on the lips. Typically, the *Sun* reacted feverishly, claiming on its front page that 'Furious MPs last night demanded a ban on *EastEnders* as the BBC soap showed two men kissing full on the lips. The homosexual love scene between yuppie poofs was screened in the early evening when millions of children were watching.'[7] The article had been penned by *Sun* staffer Piers Morgan, who had previously been responsible for an article entitled 'the Poofs of Pop', which he later admitted 'involved me and a colleague Peter Willis giving our totally ill-informed verdict on whether endless male pop stars were gay or not, and telephoning their agents for a confession or furious denial'.[8] Strangely, not one of the predominantly male journalists who had been consumed with moral outrage by Colin and Barry's brief show of affection had uttered one word when the BBC screened British television's first lesbian kiss – in the army drama *Girl* – some 13 years earlier.

The ire of the newspapers had far-reaching effects, and Gary Hailes, the heterosexual actor who played Barry Clark in the show, was subjected to horrific homophobic abuse. Hailes was attacked several times by members of the public: on one occasion he was harangued in a supermarket by a woman who threw a melon at him. More seriously he was physically assaulted by a man at a petrol station, and for years after leaving the show he found it difficult to find work in television, stigmatised for playing a gay character.

The 'loony left', a term first coined in a September 1960 issue of the *Tatler*,[9] was, by the mid-eighties, being used to describe anyone who dared to criticise Tory policy or who supported such unpopular causes as LGBT rights, women's rights or equality for the country's BAME communities. In the summer of 1985, when Hackney Council dared to suggest that LGBT ratepayers deserve the same rights as their heterosexual counterparts when it came to local council services such as fostering or adoption, the *Sun* announced: 'If it were not such a dangerous idea it would be laughable. Impressionable youngsters have enough difficulty coping with adolescence as it is. We can only assume that the Hackney loonies have taken over the asylum.'[10]

Many of the stories that appeared in the press, including the banning of certain literature or changing the words of nursery rhymes in schools, were made up or blown out of all proportion. The widely reported story that a nursery in the borough had barred children from singing 'Baa Baa Black Sheep', or had insisted that the words be changed to make them less racist, was completely false, but that did not stop the media using the phrase 'loony left' to scare potential voters as to the cost to the country should they elect Labour at the next general election. On 4 March 1987, shortly after Labour lost their formerly safe seat at Greenwich, the *Sun*'s front page screamed 'Gays Put Kinnock in a Panic – Secret Letter Lashes Loonies'. It quoted from a leaked letter written by Neil Kinnock's press secretary, Patricia Hewitt, to MP Frank Dobson in which Hewitt stated that 'the "loony Labour Left" is now taking its toll; the gays and lesbians issue is costing us dear amongst the pensioners and fear of extremism and higher taxes/rates is particularly prominent in the GLC areas.'[11] It was as if she had handed the press Kinnock's death warrant.

However Lord Smith, then still Labour MP Chris Smith, found that his homosexuality was not seen as an issue by voters on the doorstep. 'I remember when we got to the 1987 election: I'd had a majority of

363, and I was now the top target seat in the country for what was then the SDP, now the Liberal Democrats: they felt that I had their most winnable seat,' he explains. 'They threw absolutely everything at their campaign, they brought busloads of people in to knock on doors, and I'm pleased to say that we had busloads of people coming in to help us as well. We got lots of reports coming back, not of Tories campaigning homophobically on the doorsteps, but of the SDP using the fact that I was gay. We trained our canvassers. We said that if this issue comes up, you have got three lines to use. Line number one was "isn't it good to have an MP who is honest for a change?", number two was "but you know that Chris Smith works for everyone no matter who or what they are", and, if neither of those two worked, number three was "you don't mean to tell me you're prejudiced, do you?" And interestingly, through the entire campaign, no one ever got to line three! And I more than doubled my majority!'

It was in this febrile atmosphere that newly elected Conservative MP David Wilshire decided to take a stand against the onslaught of permissiveness. Wilshire, who was adopted as MP for Spelthorne in Surrey in June 1987, had recently heard about a book, *Jenny Lives with Eric and Martin*, which concerned the lives of two gay men and their daughter, that was stocked by an Inner London Education Authority (ILEA) teachers' resource centre. The book, translated from the original Danish *Mette bor hos Morten og Erik*, was only available to teachers, had not been distributed to libraries and was not available to pupils in any school, but that did not stop the fervently reactionary Wilshire and his co-sponsor, fellow Tory MP Jill Knight, from claiming that the book was harming children. Knight, who had previously campaigned for gay men to be refused roles within the probation or social services as she claimed they would be open to being blackmailed, must have blown a gasket when, in 1988, Denmark became the first country in the world to officially give legal recognition to same-sex couples.

Published in Britain in 1983 by the Gay Men's Press, *Jenny Lives with Eric and Martin* had been making blood boil for years: 'Vile Book in School: Pupils See Pictures of Gay Lovers'[12] tabloid headlines screamed over inoffensive black-and-white photos that showed Jenny, her father and his boyfriend Eric shopping and reading books together and even having a run-in with a neighbour... Although they reserved most of their ire for an image which depicted the three of them sharing breakfast in bed. Tory grandee Geoffrey Dickens was commanding column inches even before it hit bookshelves, telling reporters that 'there is a determination in the Home Office and among parents that offensive material involving children is going to be stamped out. If there is a corrupting influence in this book, the publishers can expect hell from me', before admitting that he had not actually read the offending publication.[13] Predictably, Mary Whitehouse raised her hateful head. Talking about another book published around the same time, *The Playbook for Kids About Sex*, the veteran anti-LGBT campaigner once again compared homosexuals to child molesters when she claimed that the book was 'pandering to the paedophile'.[14]

Education Secretary Kenneth Baker told the ILEA that *Jenny Lives with Eric and Martin* – which he described as 'propaganda for homosexuality' – should be removed from its lists and not used in schools, while the editor of the *Liverpool Echo* felt that 'In view of the disease AIDS, which is spreading within the homosexual community, [the ILEA was] criminally irresponsible to be promoting this book among children', despite the fact that the ILEA had done no such thing.[15] 'The ILEA never puts books into our libraries,' said Brian Haylock, principal of Victoria School in Shepherd's Bush. 'My staff and I choose books and we consider them on their merits.'[16] Schools and library services in most parts of the country had already decided not to stock or display the book, yet parents still picketed Tottenham's Devonshire Hill Junior School over plans to teach positive images of LGBT people and their refusal to withdraw the book. The parents were outnumbered by gay rights supporters from the Socialist Worker's Party, but in August 1987 the ILEA acquiesced and removed the book from circulation.

A number of Tory MPs became convinced that left-wing councils were intent on indoctrinating Britain's children with homosexual propaganda. The arrival of a free gay newspaper, the *Pink Paper*, earlier that year hardly helped to smooth the ruffled feathers of the establishment. Unlike *Capital Gay*, this new weekly was available nationally, distributed for free through LGBT bars and clubs across Great Britain, with correspondents in major cities covering news in their areas. It would continue to provide a vital service to LGBT people outside of London until 2009, when the paper printed its final issue, although it would continue online until 2012.

In the House of Lords, Lord Halsbury chose the week before Christmas 1987, when little opposition would be offered, to table a Private Members' Bill, an amendment to the Local Government Act of the same year, entitled 'An act to refrain local authorities from promoting homosexuality'. Halsbury, a former government scientist and chairman of Decca Records, had form when it came to denying LGBT people their rights: in June 1977, when Lord Arran had attempted to pass a bill through the House of Lords recommending a reduction in the gay age of consent from 21 to 18, Halsbury claimed that homosexuality was a disability, and that any changes would lead to 'the growth in activities of groups and individuals exploiting male prostitution and its attendant corruption of youth, debasement of morals and spread of venereal disease'.[17]

Halsbury's wrath was directed entirely at gay men, who the ignoble Lord saw as 'corrupting the fibre of our children and ultimately of our society itself'. Lesbians, he reasoned, 'do not molest little girls. They do not indulge in disgusting and unnatural practices like buggery. They are not wildly promiscuous and do not spread venereal disease. It is part of the softening up propaganda that lesbians and gays are nearly always referred to in that order. The relatively harmless lesbian leads on to the vicious gay. That was what I thought then and what I still in part continue to think, but I have been warned that the loony Left is hardening up the lesbian camp and that they are becoming increasingly aggressive.'[18] With these stern words of warning, and the support of Mrs Whitehouse's friend Lord Longford, the amendment sailed through the Lords and, although the Tory government decided not to promote the bill at that time, Conservative MP Jill Knight took up the challenge to have Halsbury's bill passed into law at the earliest opportunity.

After much petitioning from Wilshire and Knight, Section 28 was introduced into the Local Government Act 1988, the same act that saw the implementation of the reviled Poll Tax. The then-Local Government minister, Michael Howard, rushed the legislation through; he was rewarded by being promoted to the Cabinet two years later, and would be made Home Secretary in 1993, before finally becoming leader of the party a decade later. Wilshire would also vote against extending LGBT rights, against lowering the age of consent for gay men and against the introduction of civil partnerships. He would later be caught up in the parliamentary expenses scandal for claiming more than £100,000 for expenses syphoned through a company that he and his partner owned. Knight, who also opposed marriage equality, and stated that she believed that 'in many schools, children as young as four and five were being taught how to do the homosexual act'[19] and that her promotion of the bill had been fuelled by a fear of the GLF – which had all but ceased to exist by the time she became embroiled in her campaign – would eventually apologise for the damage caused by her role in promoting the legislation, but for now, the New Year would begin with a new war to be won.

20

No Clause 28

'Homosexuality can't be promoted... you can't persuade
people to be homosexual any more than you can persuade
white people to become black.' – Claire Rayner[1]

Initially known as Clause 28, Section 28 of the Local Government
Act 1988 stated that local authorities 'shall not intentionally promote
homosexuality or publish material with the intention of promoting
homosexuality', neither should they 'promote the teaching in any
maintained school of the acceptability of homosexuality as a pretended
family relationship'. It was what Labour councillor Jane Rose-Williams
called 'the biggest attack on minority civil liberties seen in Europe
since Nazi Germany'.[2]

'The principal damage it did was twofold,' Lord Smith explains.
'One was that it visibly, on the statute books, labelled LGBT people
as second-class citizens, and secondly it led to huge amounts of
self-censorship, especially by teachers and care workers and so
on. If they had nervous kids who were worried about their own
sexuality, who were going through a really difficult time, then
instead of enveloping them with love and reassurance, they had to
say, "No! Sorry, that's something I can't talk about." In fact, as we
now know, not a single prosecution was ever brought under Section

28 against anyone, but the impact that it had was entirely in terms of self-censorship.'

'Just before Section 28 came out there was yet another attempt to produce a platform for lesbian and gay rights that could command some kind of universal agreement,' Peter Scott-Presland adds. 'It was the last gasp of the CHE, which had for a variety of reasons run out of steam but still had some money, so they convened this conference, but it was wildly over-ambitious. It was in the Camden Centre, over a complete weekend, with 26 workshops, each of them trying to deal with a different aspect of the law, or social situations and so on. It didn't really work because people soon started arguing and there was a real destructive intervention from the Revolutionary Gay Men's Caucus [a splinter group of the Gay Noise Collective]; we were infiltrated by people who didn't believe in what we were trying to achieve, and the weekend ended without a charter.

'I was in the CHE office in Upper Street, Islington one morning,' Scott-Presland recalls, 'And the phone rang. There was a guy on the other end, a Labour peer, Douglas Jay. He said, "I think there's something you ought to know about. There's this bill coming up, you should look at it. There's a clause, just after the dog licences..." So, I phoned *Capital Gay* and asked if they knew anything about it; they said, "No, but we'll get a copy." They found this clause that eventually became Clause 28 and then Section 28. This was the end of November, beginning of December 1987; Parliament had gone into recess, the gay press were going to be out of action over Christmas and the New Year, but we knew that we had to mobilise... Everybody understood how pernicious, how dangerous this could be to the gains we had made, and so we decided that we were going to have a demonstration on 9 January. Again, *Capital Gay* – as an example of a newspaper embedded in the community combining politics with education and entertainment – was absolutely exemplary. They pulled out all the stops: they had two issues coming out before Christmas, and then one just before the actual demonstration, and they printed the text of the clause in full, had people analysing it, and they gave pages and pages of publicity to the march.'

Capital Gay would pay a heavy price for its crusading reportage, for shortly after the newspaper began raising awareness of the evils of

265

Section 28, its offices were firebombed. Two days later, Labour's Chris Smith mentioned the attack on *Capital Gay* during a furious debate in the House of Commons. 'Quite right too,' was Conservative MP Elaine Kellett-Bowman's response. When Labour MP Tony Banks – who had earlier branded the new law a 'bigot's charter' – called her out on this, she responded by saying that she was 'quite prepared to affirm that it is quite right that there should be an intolerance of evil'.[3] A month later, Margaret Thatcher made her a dame. During that same debate, around 100 LGBT protesters were forcibly removed from the Strangers' Gallery, the Speaker of the House suspending business for five minutes while they were taken outside. There could be no question that the Thatcher government wanted to see the LGBT community's hard-won rights rescinded.

'I was working at Morley College [near Waterloo in Central London] when Section 28 came out,' Paul Southwell explains. 'There was a big march then and I went on that. We took the Morley College banner, and lots of us from the college walked and demonstrated; it didn't do much good, but you felt better, like you were doing something. All along, I thought that the people on the marches were gelling and "getting" it, but Section 28 did a lot of damage to education. We had just got to the point where teachers could come out, where teachers could talk about gay things, and then suddenly you could be sacked for it. The funding went: a gay youth service suddenly had its funding withdrawn... I was disappointed. I was never a fan of Margaret Thatcher for obvious reasons, but when she started Clause 28, which was blown out of all proportion by the gutter press, how we were promoting homosexuality, it was a nightmare. I did feel that it was an affront. Clause 28 gave the homophobes and bullies a green light to stop any gay youth work, removing positive role models and taking away any chance of our voice being heard in a school setting. This stopped kids seeing that being gay was good and normal and you could lead a happy and fulfilled life. It did push back the cause years and of course happened during the height of the AIDS epidemic, adding even more stress to the LBGT community.'

'You just had to get involved, didn't you?', asks Lick frontman Gary Cosby. 'I was bullied for being gay at school. I was brought up to feel horrible about myself. There was absolutely no educational material that could have helped me realise it was okay to be me. Luckily, I had a strong sense of self-awareness and didn't cave in. This was one of the most insidious laws ever. I remember the meeting point was at the Embankment and there was a real atmosphere of solidarity. It was a good day.'

As the march progressed towards Downing Street the atmosphere changed. Protesters blocked the entrance to the street, where the Prime Minister and the Chancellor of the Exchequer had their London residences, and dozens of arrests were made. Columnist Terry Sanderson told reporters that he 'saw a woman being dragged by her hair and a disabled man was knocked flat' by the police. 'People were literally flying through the air. It really was very frightening.'[4]

'The march ended on a bit of waste ground opposite the Imperial War Museum in Kennington,' Scott-Presland continues. 'Chris Smith gave a speech, as did Jenny Wilson, who was chair of the Pride Committee at the time, and I was compèring along with American lesbian performer Robin Tyler.' The 9,000 who gathered were not there to listen to music that day. 'We did not have anyone performing: we didn't have any money for sound equipment, and we were all so incensed that I think we would have regarded performing as a bit frivolous. The most important thing about it was the police presence, which was the most intimidating of anything I have ever been on. Not only were there thousands kettling* people in on the actual march itself, but there were a lot of mounted police, and they ringed the crowd and the stage, and you could see off in the back a whole fleet of Black Marias. It was clear that they were expecting trouble, possibly even intending to initiate it. There were certainly some in the crowd that wanted to defy the police, and not disperse afterwards, and it was one of those really difficult moments... I had a lot of sympathy with that, but I looked at this ring of police and then looked at the crowd with children in it, and I thought, "No. This is not the place to cause that kind of disturbance; too many people are going to get hurt if we do that." So, I asked Chris

---

* Kettling is a police tactic used to control crowds during demonstrations, with officers containing protesters within a particular area.

to read an appeal for people to go, and we did disperse. We got about 10,000 people on that in three weeks, from nothing, over the Christmas period.'

After the *Capital Gay*-publicised rally, the first people to actively campaign against the clause were actors: their livelihood was under threat, and there was a very real possibility that works penned by LGBT writers could be banned from the stage. On 27 January 1988, two days after a number of well-known actors, writers and producers held a meeting to denounce the Local Government Bill before marching to the House of Lords to lobby Peers who were debating the act, Ian McKellen went on Radio 3 to discuss his reaction to the clause. McKellen who, the previous Sunday, had appeared on a televised awards show giving an impassioned speech against the clause, took the opportunity to publicly out himself. McKellen recalled how 'until then I had not defined my sexuality in public, nor told my blood family.

> Everyone else knew. At work being openly gay seemed to have no disadvantages and my live-in partners and I never disguised our relationships. I wish I had completed the coming-out journey long before I was 49 years old. My fear that honesty would harm my career was ill-founded. My family and I have never been closer. I have discovered a multitude of new friends and the lesbian/gay/ bisexual movement, its literature, research, and politics. I don't get angry with my colleagues who persist in equivocating about their sexuality, because I remember for how long it seemed to me more comfortable to accept society's judgment on homosexuality and dodge its disapproval. When a famous actor lies about his homosexuality you just have to feel sorry for him. Remember no one ever had to lie about his heterosexuality.[5]

Later, visiting Michael Howard to lobby against Section 28, McKellen was asked by the MP for an autograph for his children. The actor, whose visit had made no difference to Howard's promotion of Section 28, scribbled 'fuck off, I'm gay' on a piece of paper.

On 20 February McKellen – one of the men involved in the first gay kiss on British television – and *EastEnders* actor Michael Cashman lead more than 20,000 people on a march through Manchester city centre protesting both Section 28 and the strong-arm tactics of the local police. The James Anderton-led police force had, according to march organiser Paul Fairweather, become 'very hostile and were raiding gay bars and clubs. I had experienced some harassment on the street and in the gay village, but no one would report hate crimes because of the attitude of the police. We certainly felt they were becoming more aggressive, encouraged by Section 28.'[6]

This increased police aggression included targeting the sex lives of LGBT people. Over a three-year period, from 1987, approximately 100 gay and bisexual men were questioned by police who were compiling a report into same-sex male sadomasochism across the United Kingdom. Investigations began in Manchester after police were sent a videotape featuring a man undergoing consensual genital torture but were soon handed over to Scotland Yard and included input from 11 provincial forces. Operation Spanner would result in the arrest of 16 men, 15 of whom ended up in court in October 1989 facing more than 100 charges between them, from assault on their co-defendants, to running or aiding and abetting the running of disorderly houses at which numerous persons resorted to 'acts of sadistic and masochistic violence and in accompanying acts of a lewd, immoral and unnatural kind'.[7] The sixteenth defendant was remanded in his absence on charges of conspiring to send, and possess, indecent material, and aiding and abetting an assault on himself.

The thousands who massed upon the city's Albert Square in 1988 to witness an impassioned performance of 'Glad to Be Gay' from Tom Robinson may not have all been aware of Operation Spanner, but they knew that Anderton's force – and others around the country – felt empowered by the introduction of Section 28. That evening, Robinson, along with other out-gay artists including Jimmy Somerville and Erasure's Andy Bell, took part in a benefit concert to raise awareness about the attempt to stifle gay and lesbian freedom, dubbed 'Never Going Underground' at Manchester's Free Trade Hall. 'I didn't have to think about it,' says Andy Bell. 'Along with people like Jimmy, Paul O'Grady, Ian McKellen and Michael Cashman, we all just clubbed in and did our part wherever we could.'

'Section 28 appeared out of the blue,' says benefit co-organiser Angela Cooper. 'I don't remember knowing that it was coming. Maybe people in London had some sign that this was on the way, but it seemed to suddenly happen and everyone was freaking out, because we felt that we were done with all that. This was like a generation later: we had been activists when we were younger, and now we were almost 40. I went down to the march in London, and I remember standing there, watching people go by, and I was just in tears thinking, "My god, here we are 18 years later [following the formation of the GLF]; how has this happened?" Perhaps we had become a little bit complacent. I decided, whatever anybody else thought, I had to do something about this. So, I went back to Manchester, and a group of us got [the benefit] together within a very short period, something like six weeks. I went to all of the meetings. I felt as if I was being regarded with some suspicion by some of the men there – "Oh, here we go, the feminists have arrived!" But I didn't care; I had to get involved.

'I was given the Free Trade Hall to organise, along with another woman, so we did most of the work behind the scenes. I did perform as well [along with Luchia Fitzgerald and three others as Five Famous Women]. There were 2,000 people in the Hall, and all these famous people jostling backstage, using the two dressing rooms. I wasn't able to go on the march because we were busy preparing for the evening, but I did go to the gathering in the Square – that was incredible. We were very lucky: Manchester City Council got behind us. They facilitated [the gathering], but we never thought we would get 20,000 people... People sometimes look back at that as having had a role in making Manchester this gay focal point. We proved that people would come, and it has made such a difference to the pink economy. The gay village has become an integral part of Manchester's finances now.'

'One of the reasons for going to Manchester was because the city had a socialist council,' explains Peter Scott-Presland. 'We didn't have the GLC in London anymore, so Manchester organised a march. The CHE still had a little bit of money, so they hired a train to go up, which we dubbed "the Pink Express", and it sold out in a matter of days. We ordered lots and lots of pink champagne, which was meant to be sold on the train back down, but unfortunately somebody cracked it open on

270

the way up; when we got to Manchester, there were all these reporters waiting for us at the end of the platform, banks and banks of cameras, and this drunken mob poured out of the train and into the station. We were trying to line them up to have some photos taken, but it was like herding cats!

'We had busking on the train; people, including drag queens like Regina Fong, went around the carriages doing little shows as they went. Fay Presto was doing close-up magic, I went with a guitarist and sang a couple of songs... We were entertaining the troops. I felt like the gay Vera Lynn!' One week after the Manchester march, the House of Lords confirmed its support of the legislation. Immediately after the vote had passed, three members of activist group the Lesbian Avengers threw ropes down into the chamber from the public gallery and abseiled into the history books. They, along with two of their colleagues, were instantly arrested.

The Thatcher government was baying for blood, and the legislation passed into law in May 1988. The evening before, the BBC's flagship *Six O'Clock News* bulletin was interrupted by four lesbian activists, who stormed the studio just as the programme went on air. One woman handcuffed herself to a camera, another was rugby-tackled to the ground by co-host Nicholas Witchell, who sat on her while Sue Lawley attempted to carry on with the programme despite the calls of 'Stop Section 28' from the protesters. 'We've got a song specifically about this on our last album, *Who Gave Birth to the Universe*,' says Ova's Rosemary Schonfeld. 'It's called "Abseil Away", and it is a tribute to the heroic lesbians who abseiled in the House of Lords and invaded the *Six O'Clock News* in protest against Section 28.'

The following year, McKellen and Cashman would be among the 14 founding members of Stonewall, a charity dedicated to fighting for the repeal of Section 28, to lifting the ban on lesbians and gay men serving in the armed forces (a campaign won in 1999), and to lobbying parliament on behalf of LGBT people. Stonewall is now the largest LGBT rights organisation in Europe.

Mrs Thatcher was not going make a U-turn on policy because of a few thousand people on the streets of Manchester. In October, at the annual

PRIDE, POP AND POLITICS

Conservative Party Conference, in Blackpool, she took to the podium to announce that 'children who need to be taught to respect traditional moral values are being taught that they have an inalienable right to be gay... all of those children are being cheated of a sound start in life.'[8] A member of Thatcher's government, Peter Bruinvels (MP for Leicester East) simply toed the party line when he announced that 'I do not agree with homosexuality. I think that Clause 28 will help outlaw it and the rest will be done by AIDS, with a substantial number of homosexuals dying of AIDS. I think that's probably the best way.'[9] After two decades of improvement, LGBT people were being forced back into the closet.

'At the time you're just living these things and you're partly in reaction mode,' says former Bloolips member Phil Booth. 'Those two things – the AIDS crisis and Section 28 – are so closely related in British politics; Section 28 really sprang out of something the Tory Party thought they could get away with because of AIDS. I went back into activism a bit. I was still living in London but spent months in Bristol from 1988, and I was with a "Stop Clause 28" group there.'

A national network of similar groups sprang up, and many in the entertainment world rallied to support the fight against this attack on artistic freedom. On 5 June McKellen, Cashman and others brought together a cast of around 60 fellow actors and friends, including Pet Shop Boys for only the fifth live performance of their career, for what they originally called the *Clause 28 Show*, but which was eventually christened *Before the Act*. Other theatres openly defied the new law by staging controversial works: the council-funded Theatre Royal in Stratford put on Spanish playwright Federico García Lorca's *The Public*, which included homosexuality, bestiality, pederasty and paedophilia amongst its themes. Three days after the show, television presenter and chat show host Russell Harty died. Harty, who had made a name for himself interviewing the biggest names in the music industry, including David Bowie, Marc Bolan, Ringo Starr, Grace Jones and countless others, died in hospital in Leeds from hepatitis, yet the media, especially the *Sun*, went to great lengths to suggest that the bachelor (his long-term partner, Jamie, was simply dismissed as a 'close friend') had not only been dallying with underage rent boys, but that he had contracted AIDS as a result. Reporters and photographers camped outside the hospital as he battled against the liver infection. After his death, he was tarred as a 'master of hypocrisy and sleaze queen of the rent boy trade' by one journalist despite there being no evidence that he had paid for sex.[10] But the truth mattered little when it came to making wild accusations against LGBT celebrities. In December 1988, Elton John would be awarded £1 million in damages after the *Sun* accused him of using underage rent boys and of having the voice boxes removed from his guard dogs so that they would not disturb his sleep. Despite this expensive slap on the wrists, Britain's tabloids would continue to hound LGBT celebrities, emboldened by the government's anti-gay stance.

A coalition of comic book artists, illustrators and writers, including Alan Moore, Robert Crumb, Charles Shaar Murray, Posy Simmonds and Neil Gaiman, produced a comic anthology called AARGH (Artists Against Rampant Government Homophobia) that raised over £17,000 for the fight against the legislation, and, following Pet Shop Boys' lead, other pop acts got involved too. Boy George recorded a hard-hitting, acid-house-influenced song entitled 'No Clause 28', which was accompanied by a video that featured a female impersonator (Steve Nallon) voicing the part of Margaret Thatcher. Boy George, who previously had either flatly denied his sexuality (telling the *NME*'s Paul Morley 'I'm not a gay or anything like that...'[11]) or who had coyly inferred that he might be bisexual, finally came out of the closet and would never go back in again, issuing several records that reflected his newfound confidence and growing awareness of the political scene. He criticised South Africa's apartheid regime in 'Sold', and it was a headline in the *Sun* – 'Tell the Gays to Shut Up' – that prompted him and several friends to write 'No Clause 28'. 'I'm not political,' he told interviewer BP Fallon, 'but I'm not semi-conscious either. Homosexuality is not the real issue here, and this is just the thin edge of the wedge. Wait until the amendments start.'[12]

'Of course quite a number of musicians were on the frontline campaigning,' says Lord Smith. 'The likes of Jimmy Somerville, Billy Bragg and Tom Robinson were part of the whole movement against Section 28, and I think that was important. Then elsewhere in the arts, with actors like Ian McKellen and Michael Cashman setting up Stonewall and doing their bit, the fact that this wasn't just a handful of politicians arguing about this – it was musicians, actors, people involved in the cultural field – really made a huge difference. It made it much more of a popular movement than just something that related to politics.

'[Section 28] was a really big wake-up call for everyone,' Lord Smith adds. 'And the fact that we had thousands of people outside the Imperial War Museum in London, thousands of people in Albert Square in Manchester, absolutely had a galvanising effect. A lot of gay men particularly, but LGBT people generally, were used to getting on with their lives and having fun, building relationships and enjoying themselves, and suddenly there was this thing happening and it was about them, and they needed to get off their backsides and join with others in protesting.'

Agitprop band Chumbawamba issued their own single, 'Smash Clause 28! Fight the Alton Bill!' which raised funds for the London Lesbian and Gay Switchboard and the Women's Reproductive Rights Campaign; the Alton Bill was an attempt to make abortion far more restrictive in the United Kingdom. In Bristol, an awareness-raising rally was added to that year's Pride week, on College Green in front of the city's Council House. 'That cost me a blooming fortune! A thousand quid, I think it was,' says organiser Dale Wakefield. 'It rained. It was pretty dire. I had to cash in some of my investments to pay off some of the debt we had run up for the hire of tents and things, because I didn't feel right raising funds to cover what I had invested after the fact. It was a disaster. I remember that the *Evening Post* wrote that the Pride festival had split into two, and the good lot were on College Green while the bad lot were marching... But no, we were the same lot!' In Exeter, the city council threatened to withdraw funding from the local arts centre if they staged a performance from Gay Sweatshop. The management of the Devon and Exeter Arts Centre decided to carry on regardless, and the council retaliated by cutting their annual grant by £10,000. In open defiance of the government's aims, the North London boroughs of Camden, Hackney, Haringey and Islington came together to organise a month-long LGBT arts festival, dubbed Lesbian Strength and Gay Pride.

The changing political landscape provided gay singer and bass guitarist Patrick Fitzgerald, one third of indie band Kitchens of

Distinction, opportunity to express his dismay with the prime minister in the song 'Margaret's Injection'. Fitzgerald was walking a lonely road as one of the only out-gay men on the UK indie scene, and despite being feted by critics and fans alike, the band, which formed in Tooting in 1986, were unable to make the crossover into the mainstream. After the band split, Fitzgerald began a new musical endeavour under the name Fruit, recording a single 'The Queen of Old Compton Street' about life on the gay scene around Earl's Court. Some LGBT artists were prepared to pin their political allegiances to the mast, although not that many. 'AIDS sapped everybody's energy,' says Paul Southwell. 'It was just so devastating, but we fought through and we got through and, eventually, we got through Section 28 as well. The thing is a lot of people did not stand up to it. People like Elton John, Freddie Mercury, they did nothing. Now Elton's the Queen Mother and we're always being told about how he has done so much for gay liberation, and we're told how Freddie Mercury paved the way for gay musicians but that's bollocks. They did fuck all... and that pisses me off!'

Mercury, who a few months earlier had told the press that he had given up sex and 'almost become a nun'[13] following an AIDS test, was still flitting around London's best known gay night spots, often in the company of Kenny Everett – another gay man who had been hiding in plain sight, camping it up for years on radio and television while married to former pop singer 'Lady' Lee Middleton. Everett and Mercury had been friends since 1974, and Everett had been the first DJ to play Queen's international hit 'Bohemian Rhapsody' on radio, weeks before the disc was issued by a less-than-enthusiastic EMI. One Friday night in 1988, Everett, Mercury, Everett's friend and comic foil Cleo Rocos and Princess Diana were knocking back martinis at Everett's London pad when it came time to move on. 'Freddie told [Diana] we were going to the [Royal] Vauxhall Tavern – a rather notorious gay bar in London,' Rocos revealed in her 2013 book, *The Power of Positive Drinking*. 'Kenny said, "It's not for you, it's full of hairy gay men. Sometimes there are fights outside"... But Diana was in full mischief mode. Freddie said, "Go on, let the girl have some fun."' Diana, dressed in leather baseball cap, bomber jacket and jeans, disappeared in the crowded RVT, although the foursome only stayed for 20 minutes or so, just long enough to knock back a drink before anyone started asking questions about the anonymous chicken in the company of three well-known faces.

There was little chance that stars of the stature of Everett or Mercury – neither of whom were publicly out at the time – would say anything in response to Section 28; however for many LGBT people in the arts there was no option but to battle against its implementation. Leaving Consenting Adults behind him, Peter Scott-Presland began a new theatre project. 'I started Homo Promos as a direct response to Section 28,' he explains. 'I got the name from that line about not promoting homosexuality. I thought that we could sail into the eye of the storm. We were doing shows in local authority venues, and we only ever had one problem with that, at the Oval House, which was funded by Lambeth Council or Greater London Arts, and they said, "No, you can't bring a company here called Homo Promos... we could lose our funding." We got around that by simply changing the logo to "Not" Homo Promos!

'No one was ever prosecuted under Section 28; I'm sure that we lost a lot of bookings because of it, but they never said as much. The real danger was self-censorship. People were worried about what they could teach and what they were going to say if pupils ever asked questions about homosexuality... Would they get any support if they answered honestly? The ridiculous thing of course was that it was completely tokenistic: sex education had been taken out of the hands of local authorities two years earlier with the Education Act of 1986, which transferred control of sex education to school governors, and although the Department of Education was sending around circulars to say you must not teach homosexuality as a valid lifestyle, it wasn't down to local authorities anyway. It was a tokenistic sop to the right wing of the Tory Party, with no practical value at all.'

'As a child at school under Section 28, I was always told that homosexuality was "unnatural". Subsequently, I thought that there must be something terribly wrong with me,' says queer singer Oli Spleen. 'I was spat at daily throughout secondary school, and as a teen I was repeatedly beaten up on Hastings' streets. Looking androgynous as I did back then, it wasn't safe to go out at night. If I wasn't attacked by gangs of youths, I would often be stopped and searched by police who bizarrely thought I was trying to solicit clients as a male prostitute whilst wearing a dress. Throughout those years, I was deeply unhappy and repeatedly attempted suicide. I would write poems and songs as a child and teen, but it was a near-death brush with AIDS on the millennium that drove me to feel compelled to express my pain and frustration through music,' he adds.

In late 1988, while LGBT people and their allies around the country were protesting the pernicious Section 28, Act Up London was formed, a year after the original Act Up (the AIDS Coalition to Unleash Power) was established in New York by LGBT rights activist Larry Kramer. The 30 or so people at that first London meeting included Peter Tatchell and Lisa Power, author and one of the founding members of Stonewall. The group specialised in direct, non-violent action to help bring about the end of the HIV pandemic; Jimmy Somerville was a keen fundraiser and took part in several demonstrations, including one in which he chained himself to the railings of the House of Commons.

In Worcester, aspiring musician Melanie Rosatone had just completed her teacher training and was about to start her first job at a local school. 'I was angered by the developing oppressive climate fuelled by Section 28,' she explains. 'I went to London with my partner for a Pride march, to celebrate being gay, and yet I remember becoming very worried because there were helicopters filming for the evening news... Not that I would be among all the thousands of people, but I did not want to be seen on the news because I was not openly gay at the school where I taught. It would have been extremely difficult to be out as a primary school teacher in those days.'

On Valentine's Day 1989 Channel 4, the UK television station with a reputation for pushing boundaries, introduced a new series, *Out on Tuesday*, aimed specifically at LGBT people and openly challenging the intent behind Section 28. Series producer Mandy Merck, an out-lesbian, told the press, 'The question we are asking is "can homosexuality be 'promoted'?"... I hope that eventually this clause will be shown to be illegal and against the Bill of Human Rights. I am outraged by it and most thinking people would agree.'[14] Twenty years later, and despite a history of voting against the repeal of the pernicious law, at a Conservative party fundraiser during Pride Month, then-prime minister David Cameron apologised for Section 28. 'We got it wrong,' he said, adding that he now believed that the legislation was 'offensive to gay people'.[15] As welcome as those words were, for those forced out of the jobs they loved, or prevented from following their true vocation, they came two decades too late.

21

A Death in the Family

'I'm so powerful on stage that I seem to have created a monster. When I'm performing I'm an extrovert, yet inside I'm a completely different man.' – Freddie Mercury[1]

In the early hours of Sunday 30 April 1990, Michael Boothe, an actor and singer with a wealth of screen and stage credits behind him, was viciously attacked by a gang of queer bashers outside a public lavatory in Elthorne Park, West London, just 10 minutes' walk away from his home. The 49-year-old, who had appeared in the Alfred Hitchcock film *Frenzy* and was a leading light in the campaign to save London's historic theatres, died in intensive care eight hours later. He was, as a police spokesperson put it, 'kicked to death and suffered the most appalling injuries. The main cause of his death was internal bleeding. It was an absolutely merciless killing.'[2] There was little doubt within the local gay community that his murder had been exacerbated by the rise in homophobia since the arrival of AIDS and the implementation of Section 28.

The murder of Michael Boothe was the bitter icing on an ugly cake. Recent months had seen the death of gay barrister Christopher Schliach, stabbed more than 40 times in his London home in September 1989, followed, three months later, by another stabbing, this time of gay hotelier Henry Bright. Bright also died from his wounds, inflicted again at his home. Just a few weeks after that, gay hotel porter William Dalziel was discovered unconscious on a patch of wasteland in West London. He had been bludgeoned around the head by the young man he had picked up in a public convenience in King Street, Acton, and the anguished screams of the 61-year-old man had been heard by the residents of a nearby care home. He died in hospital of his wounds. 'There were numerous instances of homosexuals being attacked and robbed,' said Detective Inspector David Stone, acknowledging that victims were often blackmailed and seldom came forward to report their assailants. 'They are an easy source of revenue for determined people.' Several men 'known to attack gays were quizzed after the attack; one man even boasted to police about the money he made from frightened gay victims. But they were all eliminated from the inquiry.'[3] Although a number of arrests were made, Michael Boothe's murderers were never brought to justice. At the time, the Metropolitan Police found that Boothe's lifestyle was 'destined to bring him into contact with his murderers'.[4] Many years later, the investigation into his murder was highlighted as having been blighted by the 'institutional homophobia and transphobia' within the police.[5]

A community already battle-weary from protesting against Section 28 and trying to combat ignorance surrounding HIV and AIDS had to act again. In May 1990, the same month that the World Health Organization finally declassified homosexuality as a mental disorder, a candlelit vigil was held in remembrance of these men, murdered within months of each other, which saw hundreds of LGBT people march from the scene of Boothe's attack to Ealing Town Hall. Shortly afterwards, at a meeting held at the London Lesbian and Gay Centre in Farringdon, a new, louder, angrier group was formed. If Stonewall was the natural successor to the Campaign for Homosexual Equality, then OutRage! took up the cudgels set aside by the Gay Liberation Front. The 35 activists who attended that first meeting had been spurred into action by two things: an escalation in violence against LGBT people and the enormous rise in the number of gay and bisexual men arrested and convicted for cottaging. In its mission statement, OutRage! made clear their demands: 'OutRage! is a broad based group of queers committed to radical, non-violent direct action and civil disobedience to: ASSERT the dignity and human rights of queers, FIGHT homophobia, discrimination and violence directed against us [and] AFFIRM our right to sexual freedom, choice and self-determination.'[6]

Founded by a group including Keith Alcorn and Peter Tatchell, over the next two decades OutRage! would become infamous for a series of direct-action stunts, from trying to arrest Robert Mugabe, the despotic President of Zimbabwe (then still a member of the Commonwealth), to invading the pulpit of Canterbury Cathedral on Easter Sunday to interrupt Archbishop George Carey in protest of his position on same-sex partnerships and opposition of gay priests in the clergy. High-profile supporters included Jimmy Somerville (who had been among the 10 people arrested the previous October during a demonstration in Central London against Australia's ban on HIV-positive people travelling to the country) and film director Derek Jarman, who had worked with Pet Shop Boys on several projects and who was one of the very few public figures to talk openly about being HIV-positive at that time. Their involvement would help OutRage! become the longest-running LGBT direct-action organisation in the world.

'OutRage! was equivalent to the suffragettes, campaigning from outside and against the political system, whereas Stonewall was more akin to the suffragists, working within the system,' Peter Tatchell explains. 'We needed both. OutRage! protests got media coverage, which raised public awareness about LGBT+ discrimination and hate crime. They also prompted public debates and put the authorities under pressure to act. This opened doors not only to OutRage! but also to Stonewall and other LGBT+ organisations.' One of the group's first actions took place on 7 June 1990 at the public toilets in Hyde Park, almost 20 years after the first ever gay protest, outside a public convenience in Highbury Fields. In protest against Metropolitan Police entrapment of gay men cruising, the group distributed leaflets informing men of how to act if approached by the police, and who to call if they needed legal advice. That September, they organised a 'kiss-in' at Piccadilly Circus to protest against the arrests of gay men for kissing in public, with Tatchell announcing that 'we demand that lesbians and gays should have the right to kiss and cuddle in public without fear of arrest or conviction'.[7] Their demand that gay clergy be honest about their sexuality was not popular with the media nor with many more conservative members of the LGBT community, but the campaign resulted in the Church of England issuing its strongest condemnation to date of homophobic discrimination. OutRage! gained a reputation for its fierce denunciation of double standards, and the politically motivated 'zaps' (as they, like the GLF before them, called their stunts) that OutRage! pulled helped see the number of men convicted for consensual gay behaviour between 1990 and 1994 fall by two-thirds. Some of their stunts were hysterically funny: in December 1995 two dozen drag queens – in sequinned ball gowns and tiaras – arrived at the gates of Buckingham Palace, brandished glitter-studded pennants emblazoned with slogans including 'what's a ball without fairies' and demanded entry to the annual Royal Household Christmas Ball. As guests arrived at the Palace, the activists sang 'Hark the Herald Fairies Shout' and queer versions of other traditional Christmas carols and, at a mock tribunal near the Palace gates, 'Queen Betty' was denounced as 'the Wicked Witch of Windsor'. 'We were protesting against a decree from the Queen that forbade gay male Palace staff from bringing their partners to the Ball, whereas no such ban applied to the partners of straight employees,' says Tatchell.

The remorseless criticism of the police began to pay dividends; the drop in convictions for cottaging coincided with the formation of the Lesbian and Gay Police Association (LAGPA), Britain's first LGBT police group. Finally, it seemed, the police were beginning to take homophobic attacks seriously. In 1990, after 64-year-old Kenneth Rothwell was brutally murdered in his Highgate home, the two men responsible, who had picked him up in a gay pub with the sole intent of robbing him, were sentenced to life imprisonment.

By 1990 a pop star's sexuality had become so passé that the revelation by the Who's Pete Townshend that he was bisexual barely caused a suburban curtain to twitch. The songwriter and guitarist admitted that the song 'Rough Boys', from his solo album *Empty Glass*, was his coming out song and 'an acknowledgement of the fact I'd had a gay life'.[8] Music fans may have been more accepting of LGBT artists, yet management and record labels were still convinced that any major star would do irreparable damage to their careers should they come out. Scots singer Horse McDonald, an artist who was used to confusing people with her gender-defying look, was on the cusp of signing to Capitol Records imprint Echo Chamber with her band, also called Horse. 'I was incredibly androgynous,' she explains. 'We did a show on the south side of Glasgow, and there was no toilet backstage, so I had to sneak to the toilet in the hall. I was in a cubicle, and a group of young women came in and one said, "That singer's fucking gorgeous, isn't he?" And some political lesbian shouted out, "Hey! That's not a man! It's a woman!" I was sitting in this cubicle thinking, "What the hell is going to happen here?" Finally, they went and so I left.

'[Later], this little gang came up to me and got me up against the wall, going, "What are you? Are you a man or are you a woman?" They were so determined to pin me down. I'm just me; I'm not going to be one thing or the other, because for a long time I didn't know myself who to be or what to be. And this went on and on, and then I said, "Look, it's up to you. You decide for yourselves what you want to call me. I'm just me, okay?" And this girl burst into tears, crying, "I'm so sorry. I'm so sorry that I did that." I ended up sitting down and comforting her! People need you to be a man or a woman, and I didn't put myself into either of those boxes, and at that point in time that was really bucking the trend. When I was starting out there was no one. In fact, the only person I had heard of was [self-styled 'All-American Jewish Lesbian Folksinger'] Phranc, who people talked about as this dodgy, butch thing. That's the only name I had. People we now know about, like Melissa Etheridge or k.d. lang, were not publicly out. I'm patently, obviously a butch lesbian, and I was signed by a company who knew I was lesbian. They didn't know what to do with me, but at least they were interested in trying to do something.' Sadly, they seldom got it right. The band were taken on by the management team behind Prince and Sinead O'Connor, but they too struggled with how to market the act. Their debut album, *The Same Sky*, was issued that year. 'I got a real awakening; it was one of the worst things that happened, it was awful,' Horse recalls. 'We were on a major tour of the UK, and I found a flyer. I picked it up and it said, "Horse. What is it? A man or a woman?" And this was the record company! I had no idea at all, I was completely and utterly shocked. It was tactless and hurtful.'

Throughout the late seventies and into the eighties, British pop music fans had become more accustomed to seeing – and accepting – women in prominent positions in rock bands. Pioneers such as Siouxsie Sioux and Chrissie Hynde had gained as much press interest and as many column inches as their contemporaries in America, like Patti Smith and Debbie Harry, and singers with Black, Asian or mixed-race ethnicity, including Poly Styrene of X-Ray Spex, Pauline Black of the Selecter and Rhoda Dakar of the Bodysnatchers, encouraged a new generation of BAME women to pick up guitars and make their voices heard. Yet although the audiences were more accepting, record labels and management were often slow to react, as Horse recalls: 'They had no idea. Just because you sign somebody that doesn't mean that you know what to do with them. The guy who signed the band recognised a unique quality in my voice but wanted rid of the band so that he could do anything he wanted with me. But I stuck with the band, which I'm glad about, because that album, *The Same Sky*, was about the input from everyone, their experiences, everything.

'They were trying to market me as a very unapproachable, severe butch lesbian in suits, which is the antithesis of me. Once, when we were doing some promotion in America, the record company was missing out states, Texas and so on, because there was a real negativity towards gay people. The company was quite anxious... Their anxiety was for my safety but also it could have been about damaging the product.'

After placing an advert in *Border Women*, a feminist and lesbian magazine covering the west Midlands and Welsh border area, in 1988 teacher Melanie Rosatone began to piece together a new band, the Fabulous Jam Tarts. 'It was a conscious decision to form an all-woman, all-lesbian band,' she explains. 'I got a response from Carol, so she and I started off as One Goddess Too Many, an acoustic, slightly folky sounding duo performing our own songs. Then she brought in a bass player, who stayed for a little while but moved on, and our drummer, Suzanne, who knew Wendy, who became our bass player.

'We all had quite different influences. Mine were folk, opera and classical; Carol came from punk and heavy metal, and Suzanne and Wendy had more of a jazz background. But when you put us together, we sounded more like the Pretenders or Blondie... Sassy, fun, feel-good music. We all wrote songs. Carol, our lead guitarist, was much more political. She had a real anger which would come through in the music and that was helpful and healthy. She definitely drove that side of things. I was more interested in having fun, but she really wanted to make a statement. Wherever there's an angry lyric that I wrote it was fuelled by the oppression of Section 28. It was appalling; you would come across homophobia in some areas of education, little jokey comments rather than real aggression, but that was hard. I had to stay quiet about it; it would not have felt at all safe to be out in school, even though I was happily out to all my friends and family.

'Carol and I were both based in Worcester. The women's music scene was just evolving around the Midlands at that time; I was only aware of one other all-lesbian band locally. I wanted to hear women playing music that spoke to women; I think that was needed and there were so few at the time. I know we had the girl bands of the 1960s, but I thought they were less feisty. Until you got to women like Suzi Quatro, things were quite flaccid. She was a big influence on me. We were doing gigs around local clubs, in Birmingham and so on. There wasn't a lot in our community; women's music was a lot more London-based then. We did not come across much sexism, apart from at our practice studios, a very male-dominated space. In some ways, I think things were better for women then than they are now, but we did encounter quite a bit of homophobia. We played at some straight clubs, and we would have to change some of our lyrics, take out some of the gay words or phrases. There was homophobia around, but we were able to handle it or anticipate it. We never got attacked but we did get a sense of the hostility aimed at us, but because we were not an aggressive band – our music was much more light-hearted, feel-good; the politics in our music was with a small 'p' – it wasn't too bad. We played one particularly tough straight venue, the Robin Hood club in Stourbridge. Carol used to be in a punk band, so she was used to dealing with hostile audiences, but most people just wanted to dance and have a good time.

There was one incident, at the Magazine club in Leicester, where I was being heckled by a guy, and I just walked out into the crowd and sang at him. He was inoffensive; he just wanted attention.'

Rosatone was lucky: audiences were not always so easily quelled, as singer and activist Angela Cooper recalls. 'I got punched once. We were playing in a pub in Lancaster, and we were moving our enormous speakers in; there were guys there and one said something to me and I, foolishly, said "fuck off" back. The next thing I knew he punched me in the face. That was a real shock: I'd never really been hit before. Then everything went crackers... There was an uproar. It was a timely reminder that you had to watch what you were doing. We were putting on women's discos in Manchester, in the rooms above pubs, and you'd be walking through the bar with everyone making comments, seeing all of these women with dungarees on. We were kind of out there. Sometimes we would only play women's music, women singing... It wasn't easy. We were experimenting, and making it up as we were going along, because really no one in history had been in that position before, of being able to live an 'out' life.'

'I moved to London in 1995,' says Melanie Rosatone. 'Suzanne had moved there the year before, so it became easier to do more gigs in London. I was living around the corner from the cabaret singer and comedienne Lorraine Bowen, who had a big gay audience, and she managed to get us a few good gigs, like Hackney Empire and, in 1997, the cabaret stage at London Pride on Clapham Common. We did a few other Pride gigs, one in Reading went down very well and had a good audience, but we did one in Oxford where the people started leaving... That was a very depressing night!

'We didn't have a fear of homophobia at all in London: we didn't feel we had to be careful, we didn't have to change any of our lyrics, and I think that emboldened us a little. All of the places we had played in Birmingham were gay clubs or bars, but in Leicestershire and Worcestershire we had to be more cautious. Malvern was a bit more alternative and artsy, but the reaction in places like Leicester was more mixed.'

There are untold numbers of individual stories that highlight the horrors, the hopelessness and the injustices meted out during the HIV/

AIDS epidemic. In 1990 there were approximately 3,000 new HIV-positive diagnoses, and more than 1,000 AIDS-related deaths in the UK, including that of a young history graduate, David Nickson, whose short life would have a lasting effect on cabaret singer Mark Bunyan. 'Andrew had started a relationship with David back in Edinburgh,' Bunyan explains. 'David had never been to London, so he came down and stayed at my flat, where I only had one narrow bed, but we managed. We lived as a trio for about four-and-a-half years. He would spend all of his vacations with us and come down for weekends.' With gay sex only legal for two consenting adults in private, any or all of the threesome could have faced jail should their situation become public knowledge.

David, who spent the last four years of his life in a committed relationship with another man, contracted HIV in 1985 and finally succumbed to AIDS in May 1990. His last wish was that much of his estate go to the National Secular Society, which he had joined in 1977, and that he have a non-religious funeral. His mother, a devout Christian who had not been left a penny in his will, took his executors – Mark and his partner Andrew – to court to challenge the will. It was a long and bitterly contested case, but at the end of October the judge found in David's favour, and Mark and Andrew were able to carry out his interment more than six months after his death. The legal battle convinced Mark that he should investigate the possibility of joining the judiciary. 'If we had had a decision in favour of his mother, I would have been doing voluntary work for Liberty,' he says. 'But we had a decision in David's favour, which made me think, "Well, there is justice."' He was appointed as a magistrate in 1992.

Although David's story made the newspapers, the coverage was nothing when compared to the massive headlines that followed the death of Freddie Mercury, in November 1991, and the shabby way in which Britain's tabloids treated the ailing star in his final days heralded a further relaxing in the public's attitude towards LGBT people, especially those living with HIV/AIDS.

Earlier celebrity deaths, including those of Liberace and Rock Hudson, had done nothing to stem the tide of hatred and bile in the press, and right up until he finally succumbed, Mercury's own life –

and the lives of his family and friends – was made impossible thanks to his being doorstepped by the media. The red tops were filled with lurid tales of his debauchery, with paparazzi photos of the now-frail musician wandering around his garden or snapped on visits to clinicians, and stories about how he was now being visited at home by an AIDS specialist following the death of his former personal assistant (and erstwhile lover) Paul Prenter. Stories based on supposition, rumour and conjecture filled front pages, the press desperate for any crumb that might help destroy the reputation of the King of Queen. Then, the day before his death, Mercury released a press statement confirming his fans' worst fears: 'Following the enormous conjecture in the Press over the last two weeks, I wish to confirm that I have been tested HIV positive and have AIDS. I felt it correct to keep this information private to date in order to protect the privacy of those around me. However, the time has now come for my friends and fans around the world to know the truth and I hope that everyone will join with me, my doctors and all those worldwide in the fight against this terrible disease.'[9] Within 24 hours, he was gone.

It was an enormous blow to the group's fans, who at that time were celebrating the band's 20th anniversary, but Mercury's illness was hardly a well-kept secret. The press had been after him for more than five years, with a furious Freddie forced to deny he had AIDS to a reporter from the *Sun* as early as October 1986, six months before his diagnosis. For more than a year before his death, the band had kept away from the limelight, turning down opportunities to appear on television to promote their most recent album, *Innuendo*, and its related hit singles. Mercury's last appearance of any sort with his bandmates was in the video to the single 'These Are the Days of Our Lives', filmed six months before his death. Mercury looks painfully thin, despite wearing several layers of clothes in an effort to bulk up his body.

In the immediate aftermath of Mercury's death, Britain's tabloid press speculated about the number of men Freddie may have infected. Kenny Everett (who Mercury had shared partners with) had been diagnosed as HIV positive two years before Mercury's death but only his closest friends knew at the time; Everett would outlive his friend by four years. Others who had come into the star's orbit had already

The launch of
Red Wedge,
November 1985.
Mirrorpix
▼

Bronski Beat ►
with Marc
Almond, 1985.
Mirrorpix

Boy George at the Stop the Clause ►
march, April 1988. *Mirrorpix*

Michael Cashman, Chris Smith and
Peter Tatchell at the Stop the Clause
march, April 1988. *Mirrorpix*
▼

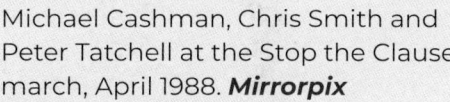

Diana, Princess of Wales, visits
HIV patients at Middlesex
Hospital, April 1987. *Mirrorpix*
▼

Here is The Six O'Clock News . .

'One dead' as fire hits cargo ferry

BEEB MAN SITS ON LESBIAN

..while Sue reads on with woman chained to her desk

▲

Crowds gather in Manchester for the Stop the Clause march, February 1988. *Mirrorpix*

▲

Stop the Clause protestors interrupt the BBC *Six O'clock News*, May 1988. *Mirrorpix*

◄ Jimmy Somerville in an Act Up shirt, 1989. *Shutterstock*

1990s

◄ The Pride march in front of the Houses of Parliament, 1990. *Mirrorpix*

OutRage!
supporters on
a gay rights
demonstration,
February 1991.
Mirrorpix

Elton John and ▶
Axl Rose perform
together at the
Freddie Mercury
Tribute Concert,
April 1992.
Mirrorpix

▼

◀ George Michael
performs
with Queen
at the Freddie
Mercury Tribute
Concert, April
1992.
Mirrorpix

◀ OutRage!
activists
march at Pride,
London 1993.
Getty Images

Debbie Smith,
guitarist with
Echobelly, 1997.
Mirrorpix
▼

Lesbian ▶
activists on
the march,
1995.
*Getty
Images*

▲
Pet Shop Boys
play Pride, 1997.
Shutterstock

◀ Tom Robinson
and Holly
Johnson,
Pride 1998.
Shutterstock

◀ Boy George addresses the crowd at the reopening of the Admiral Duncan, 1999. *Shutterstock*

Peter Tatchell ▶ joins protestors following the bombing of the Admiral Duncan, 1999. *Getty Images*

◀ Elton John and David Furnish at their civil partnership, December 2005. *Getty Images*

◀ GLF veterans mark the 40th anniversary of the first Pride march, 2012. *Alamy*

Skin, singer ▶ with Skunk Anansie, at the *Attitude* magazine Pride Awards, 2016. *Alamy*

▲
Peter Scott-Presland stands up for solidarity, 2017. *Alamy*

Pride in ▶ London, 2017. *Alamy*

Protestors ▶
outside
Anderson Park
School, 2019.
Mirrorpix

▲
Sonic Yootha, Kitchen
Street, Liverpool, 2019.
***Photo by John Appleton,
used by permission***

◀ Horse
McDonald
at the *DIVA*
magazine
Hall of Fame
awards, 2018.
Getty Images

◄ Veterans celebrate the 50th anniversary of the founding of the GLF in London, 2020. *Alamy*

Oli Spleen live ► in Brighton, 2020. *Photo by Kirill Nikitin, used by permission*

▲

John Grant on stage in Bath, October 2021. *Photo by Darryl W. Bullock*

died from the disease, and the *Daily Star* reported that Freddie 'was tangled in a lethal web of disease involving 500 people or more', going on to say that: 'The showbiz mafia must NOT be allowed to turn Freddie Mercury into a saint. An angel on stage, he was a sinner in the alleyways of his private life away from the spotlight. He debauched his enormous talent by pressing his own self-destruct button.'[10] The media frenzy, and comments from politicians including Labour's David Blunkett, who accused the singer of indulging in a 'bizarre and, in my view, quite unacceptable lifestyle',[11] discouraged others from coming forward with their own diagnosis. Shortly before Mercury's death, Holly Johnson discovered that he too was HIV-positive, leading to what he later described as 'moments of black despair'. Johnson was offered counselling but, as he revealed, 'I was in such a state of panic... I could hardly hear what was said to me.' He would not talk about his diagnosis for several years because he was scared of 'what [the media] would do when they got hold of the story'.[12]

Shortly after Mercury's death, the band's global number one hit 'Bohemian Rhapsody' was reissued, as a double A-side with 'These Are the Days of Our Lives'. Mercury's mini-opera topped the charts once again, raising £1,000,000 for AIDS charity the Terrence Higgins Trust. The following April, 72,000 people crammed into Wembley Stadium for an all-star tribute concert, featuring Metallica, Guns N' Roses, Robert Plant, David Bowie, George Michael, Annie Lennox, Elton John and (by live video link) U2 amongst others, many of them sporting red AIDS-awareness ribbons. Profits from the concert were used to launch the Mercury Trust, a new AIDS charity set up in Freddie's name.

Mercury's death forced the pop and rock business to re-examine its attitude towards LGBT artists and audiences, although the inclusion of Guns N' Roses on the bill was seen by many as perverse. Why was a band that had issued the homophobic and racist polemic 'One in a Million' celebrating the life of a gay man from Zanzibar? Despite the sheen of acceptability, homophobia was still rife in many musical genres. Ted Brown, the early GLF convert who had been fighting homophobia within the Black community, was attacked in his own home after campaigning against homophobic lyrics in songs by Jamaican singers including Buju Banton and Shabba Ranks. The assault came after he appeared on Channel 4 music show *The Word* and resulted in Brown being hospitalised for the best part of a month. The Stop Murder Music campaign would see shows by reggae stars cancelled and sales slump as more and more music buyers responded to the call to ban hate speech in music.

Public opinion towards the LGBT community may have been softening, but governments are notoriously slow to act. On 6 February 1992, 45 people, including Jimmy Somerville, Peter Tatchell and Derek Jarman, were arrested as they attempted to march on the House of Commons with hundreds of other OutRage! supporters to present a letter to Prime Minister John Major demanding a citizen's charter that would extend civil rights for LGBT people. Protest marches within a one-mile radius of Parliament were forbidden while MPs were sitting and, when police impeded the marchers' progress, Somerville, Jarman and others began a sit-in in the middle of the road, before they were arrested, physically manhandled into police vehicles and taken to the cells.

Despite the perceived change in the police's attitude towards LGBT people following the murder of Kenneth Rothwell, like the government they too were dragging their feet. In March 1993 vulnerable men from within London's LGBT community were once more falling prey to a serial killer. In a grim echo of the Dennis Nilsen case, another murderous sadist was on the prowl, terrorising regulars of Earl's Court. Colin Ireland would commit five murders after making a New Year's resolution to become a serial killer, picking up men at the Coleherne, whose colour-coded handkerchiefs indicated that they were into taking the passive role in sadomasochistic sex games. He accompanied his victims to their homes, where he restrained and then killed them. As had happened previously, institutional homophobia within the Metropolitan Police hampered the hunt for Ireland. He telephoned police on several occasions during his killing spree and left clues – including fingerprints – that should have helped identify him more quickly. A 2007 report from the independent Lesbian Gay Bisexual and Transgender Advisory Group found that homophobia, and a lack of interest or understanding of LGBT culture and lifestyles, had impeded several police investigations in the past, including those into the murders of Michael Boothe, trans sex worker Robyn Brown, and Ireland's victims.

While the LGBT community was dealing with the twin threat of HIV/AIDS and yet another serial killer, in 1991 actor and activist Ian McKellen was knighted in the Queen's annual New Year's honours list. It may have seemed as if LGBT people were finally being accepted by the establishment, but this did not always sit well with other members of the community. Gay film director and OutRage! member Derek Jarman objected to his accepting the award, principally because the Tory Party had stigmatised LGBT people. Eighteen notable actors, writers, artists and broadcasters including Stephen Fry, *EastEnders* star Pam St Clement and West End producer Cameron Mackintosh, publicly outed themselves in support of the new knight, calling the award a 'significant landmark in the history of the gay movement'.[13]

In spite of this very public acknowledgement, and the ousting of Margaret Thatcher as party leader and prime minister in November 1990, the New Year also saw a renewed offensive by the Conservative government to crack down on homosexual acts in Britain. Parliament's Criminal Justice Bill outlined 11 new 'serious sexual offences', containing several that Jarman saw as taking 'important steps towards recriminalising homosexuality', including any show of affection between two men in public.[14] Two men kissing, or simply holding hands, in the street would now be committing a serious sexual offence rather than a minor infraction of the law. Courting controversy, the film clip accompanying Pet Shop Boys' new single, 'Being Boring', featured two men kissing, a first for a pop video. On 16 February, a protest march against the bill saw 15,000 people descend on London, snaking their way from the Embankment to Hyde Park Corner, the original site of the Tyburn Tree where so many homosexual men had met their death in the past.

It was a major setback, but the move to equalise the age of consent continued unabated. Prominent members of the Labour Party had been lobbying its MPs to put pressure on the government to bring an end to the disparity and, in April 1993, Stonewall backed a campaign by three young men – couple Hugo Greenhalgh, 19, and William Parry, 24, and Ralph Wilde, also 19 – to take their fight to the European Court of Human

Rights, claiming that the law banning homosexual acts for men under the age of 21 in Scotland and England was a breach of their human rights. By coincidence, their first appearance in court took place on the anniversary of Oscar Wilde's 1895 arrest. All three men had suffered homophobic abuse, with Ralph Wilde falling victim to a gay bashing in his hometown of Stockport while still at school. Emboldened, other young men came forward to take their own grievances to court. It was expected that it would take years for the court to come to a ruling; in the meantime, some MPs had decided the time was right for change.

Introducing her amendments to the Criminal Justice Bill, Conservative MP Edwina Currie argued that the law at the time was 'not only prejudicial and discriminatory; it is painfully effective. Honourable Members on my side of the debate cannot argue that the law is ignored. On the contrary, it is widely, if erratically, employed.' In a heated and often fractious debate in the House of Commons in February 1994, Currie stated that:

Between 1988 and 1991, there were more than 2,000 arrests for offences involving consensual sex with men under 21 years of age. Even in 1992, as the research of the House of Commons Library shows, men were still being committed to prison for consensual acts with other men. The fear of being arrested and questioned, and perhaps cautioned or charged, is real and ever present. Last year, three young men – Will Parry, Hugo Greenhalgh and Ralph Wilde – announced that they were to take their case, on equality grounds, to the European Court. Two of them – Hugo and Will, who are lovers – spoke openly on television. I understand that they were promptly reported to the police by a self-appointed guardian of public morality, Mr. Stephen Green. The police may have been deeply embarrassed about the whole affair, but because the complaint had been made it had to be investigated. The young men found themselves in Rochester Row police station for several hours, and they were subjected to the most intimate and intrusive personal questioning. Eventually, they were released, and no prosecution has been brought. Had such an episode occurred to a heterosexual couple, we should all have been appalled. We ought to be just as disgusted that in 1994 this can still happen to gay men.[15]

Green, the leader of religious extremist group Christian Voice, was a former advisor to the Conservative Party and a virulent homophobe who advocated the death penalty for homosexual acts.

Dawn Primarolo, Labour MP for Bristol South, agreed, and argued that the then-current laws were also sexist: 'It is totally unacceptable that the Committee should take the view that young men ought to be protected longer than young women. If young women, with the age of consent set at 16, are suitably protected, there is no reason whatever why the same age should not apply to men, whether heterosexual or homosexual.' Currie was shouted down by members of her own party: Tim Devlin (Stockton South) continued to equate homosexuality with child abuse, while Tony Marlow (Northampton North) berated her for 'seeking to persuade honourable Members to vote to legalise the buggery of adolescent males. Does she think that that is what our constituents have sent us here to do?'[16]

Behind the scenes, senior members of the Conservative Party were conspiring to keep a clear distinction between the age of consent for homosexual and heterosexual sex. Although Currie lobbied for the age of consent to be equalised, Tory MP Sir Anthony Durant suggested that the age of consent for homosexual sex should be reduced to 18 instead and Major, acting on advice from Home Secretary Michael Howard, preferred the latter option. Party whips were convinced that, if the House of Commons was offered the chance to 'vote on the more extreme option first, i.e. a reduction to 16', that had 'a fair chance of winning,' and lobbyists would ensure that MPs would not be given the opportunity to vote for equality.[17]

On 14 March during a protest against the inequality in the age of consent, Jimmy Somerville, alongside several other protesters, was arrested yet again when police removed a number of OutRage! activists from Haymarket in Central London. In an attempt to thwart a march on the House of Commons, more than 250 officers used vans to impede the 1,700 LGBT people and their allies as they advanced towards Westminster. When it became obvious that they could go no further, protesters lay down in the road, partially blocking traffic, and the police stepped in. After a tense stand-off, an uneasy compromise was reached, with the police allowing dozens of splinter groups of up to five people each to carry on towards Parliament. The following November, the government reduced the age of consent for gay men to 18; an improvement, but still two years beyond the heterosexual age of consent. It would take a change of government to finally bring about equality.

22

This Is Britpop

'A girl of 16 can marry and do all sorts of things. But a boy who wants to get involved in a homosexual relationship, he can't choose whom sleeps with. He can join the Army and die for his country, but he can't make a choice about his personal life. I think that is now out of date.' – Edwina Currie MP[1]

The end of the eighties and beginning of the nineties brought a new set of fey, androgynous musicians to the charts, who fused different threads, including 1960s Carnaby Street cool, seventies glitter, eighties indie and a healthy dose of nineties nihilism. Paying homage to the flamboyant narcissism of Morrissey, Brett Anderson of Suede purposely included gay references in many of his band's songs and who would later claim, in a statement that could easily have come from either David Bowie or Marc Bolan two decades earlier, that 'I see myself as a bisexual man who's never had a homosexual experience. I've never seen myself as overtly heterosexual, but then, I didn't see myself as gay. I sort of saw myself as some kind of sexual being that was floating somewhere.'[2]

Anderson's right-hand man, the Marr to his Morrissey, guitarist Bernard Butler left Suede in 1994 and soon hooked up with out-gay singer David McAlmont, formerly singer in the band Thieves. Their album, *The Sound of McAlmont and Butler,* which included the Top 10 single 'Yes', was issued the following year, the same year that McAlmont played Pride for the first time. Damon Albarn, of Britpop pioneers Blur, whose Mockney vocals masked his decidedly middle-class upbringing, echoed Alice Cooper when he claimed that he had dabbled: 'I like the idea of bisexuality. It's just that I'm not physically capable of coming up with the goods. I'll say this though – I'm more homosexual than Brett Anderson. Always have been. As far as bisexuality goes, I've had a little taste of that particular fruit, or I have been tasted you might say.'[3] Others were far less coy. In January 1993 Roddy Bottum, keyboard player in US indie metal band Faith No More, used an interview with British pop magazine the *New Musical Express* to come out, and become the first out-gay man in hard rock.

The big difference this time was that many of the artists adopting this new androgyny were female, including Elastica's Justine Frischmann (former partner of both Anderson and Albarn), and even Spice Girl Melanie C, whose tomboyish, sports gear look was purposely designed to appeal to young girls just as her bandmates' looks had been constructed to appeal to different sections of Britain's male youth. As the 1980s indie scene slowly splintered into various subgenres, including the introspective shoegaze and pill-popping Madchester rave culture, the music press started to take notice of women such as Skin, the bisexual lead singer with Skunk Anansie, and Debbie Smith, out-lesbian guitarist with Curve and, later, Echobelly.

After years of cajoling from her father, at the age of 14 Smith bought an inexpensive acoustic guitar from her local branch of Argos and taught herself to play. Inspired by Siouxsie and the Banshees, and by art punk collective Crass and feminist punk band the Poison Girls – who both recorded just around the corner from her family home in Haringey – Smith's immersion in music went hand-in-hand with her growing awareness of politics and her own sexuality. 'It blew my mind that the Poison Girls had been around the corner from my house,' she explained in a 2015 interview. 'Going to their gigs was absolutely amazing. Me and my best friend at the time, Josh, would go to every Poison Girls gig we could, and get really pissed and throw ourselves about at the front. And the Poison Girls were really nice to us... They'd say hello and make sure we were alright, because we were pretty young. The Poison Girls and Crass were kind of my musical political awakening. They talked about issues of class, race, sexism... which you didn't hear in early 80s pop music at all.'[4]

Labelled a 'butch, lesbian, Amazonian woman who spits venom at the press',[5] Skin admitted that she had not considered she might be bisexual until she was at university. 'Being bisexual didn't occur to me. I didn't know any gay people and I was one of those straight people with a terrible gaydar. I had grown up in a straight Christian household, so it never occurred to me that I could be gay. I thought I was just going through a phase. Then towards the end of the year it dawned on me that I would really like to kiss this girl and I might be gay. Then once I realised it, it was a bit of a relief, really. I was at university by this point too, so I was becoming wise to different types of people.'[6] The singer was also well aware of how her image may have held the band back: 'I think we would have been supported a lot more and we would have become a far bigger concern had I not been bisexual... we've always had a lot of opposition and got up a lot of people's noses in the process.'[7]

Having arrived in Britain almost a decade earlier, by the middle of 1994 Australian émigré Gary Cosby was fronting hotly tipped Britpop band Lick, formed in time-honoured tradition through an ad in *Melody Maker*. Early shows were notable for the presence of Britpop glitterati, with members of both Suede and Elastica spotted in their audience, and early support slots with Skunk Anansie saw them draw plenty of interest from the media. On hearing the buzz, Seymour Stein, founder of Sire Records, whose roster included the Ramones, Talking Heads and the Pretenders, flew into London to see Lick perform at queer indie night Up to the Elbow, at the Bell, King's Cross, a venue that had such an impact on Debbie Smith that she ended up sharing a squat with members of the bar staff. 'It was pretty much the only gay, alternative mixed club in the whole of London,' she recalls. 'The gay scene was extremely segregated, and lesbian clubs were, music-wise, not very good... They would play Top 40, and the boy's clubs would play Hi-NRG; the Bell would play that, but they would also play Danielle Dax, or Siouxsie and the Banshees, or New Order, Echo and the Bunnymen,

Grace Jones.... All that alternative stuff. And it was mixed: men and women would go there. It was a one-of-a-kind place.'[8]

'I came to England just as that amazing new romantic period was burning out,' Cosby explains. 'A whole new era was dawning with the arrival of Pet Shop Boys, acid house and dance music generally. The whole gay scene was fracturing in a positive way. Up until the mid-nineties, it seemed like the only choice for a gay boy was the muscle Mary tops-off dance clubs or the leather scene. I thought I was the only skinny gay boy who liked bands, and suddenly there was a whole new tribe on the scene. It was like, "What?! Gay men and women actually like indie guitar music?" It turns out loads did, actually. It's not that surprising I suppose. Gays have always been part of rock 'n' roll, but they never really congregated as a group around it until the mid-nineties and Britpop. There was the odd gay alternative night at places such as the Bell as far back as the mid-eighties, but it wasn't until around 1994 when nights like Marvellous, Duckie, Up to the Elbow, Vaseline and, of course, Popstarz came into existence. They were full of skinny, floppy-fringed boys who just did not fit in at the huge gay clubs, where it was all about dance music and having huge biceps.

'The Bell was my kind of place. That's where the classic eighties ripped 501s, flight jacket and DMs look originated, later adopted by Bros. Erasure did one of their very first shows there [March 1986]. I lived for every Thursday and Sunday when you could go there to meet boys and hear indie music alongside more clubby stuff. A good mix. That led me to Pyramid at Heaven, and the Black Cap in Camden. I was all over the place. This was just prior to G-A-Y, which replaced Bang! at the Astoria 2. I remember seeing Suzi Quatro, the first pop star I ever loved, perform at Bang! on a glam-themed night. It was quite bizarre to see a rock icon appear in a gay club!

'I met my partner in 1988 at Ciao Baby [a club night at the Fridge] when I was living in Brixton. Whereas G-A-Y had all the pop PAs [personal appearances], Ciao Baby presented the cooler acts. I remember seeing fantastic performances there by the Beloved, S'Express and Amanda Lear. Take That did a PA there with their first single and Jason Orange mooned at us. I thought that was pretty cool. I was never really into acid house and the gay clubs or nights that played it. I liked a club called FF which was at the same place as Trade, but on a different night. Then, in 1989 Kinky Gerlinky came along [at Legends, in Westminster], which was awesome. I was up for experiencing it all.'

Stein was suitably impressed with Lick's performance at the Bell, telling his British team that 'I couldn't get the music out of my head... this is certainly the best band you have been involved with since I have known you and we would love to have them for the US... we would make their release a major priority.'[9] It did not faze Stein that Cosby was gay (although closeted, Stein was gay himself: he came out in 2017) and that, outside of McAlmont, Skin or Smith, few of this new generation of musicians were willing to be as open about their sexuality. 'I felt like the only out gay on the block during Britpop,' Cosby recalls. 'You had Brett Anderson who in essence was merely living out his Bowie infatuation by declaring himself a "bisexual who had never had a homosexual experience", and I suppose there would have been quite a few gay – and straight – lads willing to help him out, but I somehow doubt he genuinely desired it. Martin Rossiter from Gene was open about being bisexual. Debbie from Echobelly was very obviously a dyke and a very, very cool one at that. I wasn't prepared to hide it. The downside was it became the focus of interest in the band press-wise. That sounds ridiculous now but back then simply being gay got you a headline. We decided to be very blatant about it by including a song called "Shirtlifter" on the B-side of our debut single. Probably a little too blatant!

'I can't recall experiencing any homophobia in the music industry though. I know for certain it was talked about at the label when they were considering signing us. I was never asked to hide who I was, by anybody, and I would not have listened to them if they did. However, when that was becoming the focus on us as a new band, I did put the brakes on it a bit. I was proud to be gay and fronting an indie band, but we certainly did not promote ourselves as "the indie band with a gay singer". I didn't mind being asked about it, though, and the guys in my band were 100 per cent supportive. They were cheeky and flirty with it. Totally comfortable in their own sexuality to be tactile, protective and unfazed over the media attention of me being gay sort of overshadowing the most amazing thing about Lick – the fact that, actually, we were a really good band. It was at the height of 'laddism' though, when magazines like *Loaded* and *Nuts* were huge, and everyone was looking to sign the new Oasis; Lick were not a safe bet in terms of a band that would appeal to "Noel-Rock" Britain. Ironically, Suede had paved the way for a gay indie rock star to come along, but that happened quite a bit later with Kele Okereke of Bloc Party and Beth Ditto with the Gossip.'

Thrust into the spotlight, the group may have had the support of their management and label, but the press was not so kind. While some media outlets praised Cosby and the band for their 'barbed wire tunes, irresistible cool, and choruses with hooks big enough to land a great white shark',[10] others simply dismissed them as a 'faggot-fronted loud guitar' act.[11] It was because of this negative attitude that Faith No More's Roddy Bottum had been reticent about coming out to a British publication. 'The tabloids over there are notorious for sensational junk,' he told US journalist Lance Loud. 'I was afraid I'd end up cast in this inflammatory light. I didn't want them talking about me being gay like it was anything to be ashamed of, or something that I'd been hiding.'[12]

The four singles that Lick issued in Britain failed to chart, yet bizarrely they became big news in Thailand. 'Bands like Suede, the Manic Street Preachers and especially Shed Seven were massive there,' Cosby explains. 'And unlike here, where Lick failed to get the radio play required to reach the mainstream, our singles were being played constantly on Thai radio. We were sort of scratching our heads when we were invited to play a headline show there. This was the days before the internet, so we had absolutely no idea we were popular... [We were used to playing] 20-minute support slots around Camden, so we crapped ourselves when they told us we'd have to play for at least an hour and fifteen minutes. But we did it. It was very surreal arriving to screaming fans at an airport when you are not already famous, but we'd all been rehearsing for that since we were like 5, so we instinctively knew what to do!'

When sales and interest abroad proved encouraging, Sire's parent company, Warner Brothers, forged ahead with plans for an album. *Turbulence* was recorded and mixed, sleeve shots were taken, promos were sent out, but the lack of chart success for their singles meant that the record would never hit the stores and, although initially supportive, the music press soon turned on the band. 'There were a lot of knives out for Lick,' says Cosby. 'They didn't like the image. We were definitely at odds with the prevailing laddishness at the time. It seemed we came out of nowhere. And to be fair, we formed in July and had a major record deal by December. It just wasn't the done thing for a band to sign that quickly, let alone directly to a major. You were expected to at least release a few independent singles, be discovered by the indie press who would then champion you and be part of the glory when you signed, or preferably licensed your music through a major. Lick's failure to break through was pretty much down to lack of exposure, which is absolutely crucial for any new band.'

Despite not having experienced any homophobia from his management or record company, Cosby is unsure if the press were ready for a Britpop band fronted by someone so unapologetically gay. Neil Tennant and George Michael had yet to come out publicly, and even though Boy George, Holly Johnson, Jimmy Somerville and Andy Bell were very vocal about their sexuality, the press still treated LGBT people as freakish oddities: Brett Anderson's throwaway comment about his supposed bisexuality would haunt him forever, that one phrase quoted by almost every reviewer and interviewer over the next two decades.

'I don't think my being gay held Lick back, but others disagree,' Cosby admits. 'I doubt many people in the music industry then were homophobic: it's not the sort of industry that attracts conservative types. Things may have been different if we started getting more well-known and had reached the mainstream. It must have been hell being a closeted gay mainstream celebrity back then. That was a guaranteed front page.

'In the beginning we had quite a feminine-looking image. We were into wearing cool make-up like Richey Manic and Lou Reed: rock 'n' roll make-up. That was in our DNA from when we were kids. We all loved Duran Duran and the new romantics. I was heavily inspired by female artists. We were all wearing make-up long before Lick. It was a very natural choice for us. We also *wanted* to look like pop stars. All our influences were bands with strong images. It was pretty obvious just in

301

our look and how we carried ourselves that something was going on. We weren't what you would call camp in the traditional sense, but as soon as we put out "Shirtlifter" people were obviously going to ask. And it made us unique I suppose, so it was a natural angle for journalists to go with. The double-edged sword was that it started getting more attention than the music. I even started turning down interviews with the gay press because we thought it was starting to become all about me being gay; a decision I regret because any press is good press and would have got us noticed more.'

Britpop may have taken over the hearts and minds of the country's cool kids and been dominating the music press, but a series of lookalike and soundalike boyband acts, put together by aspiring songwriters or managers (or both), were raking in a fortune for their handlers. Several had been purposely pitched to appeal to a potent mix of mums, screaming schoolgirls and young gay men. Take That, the biggest of the lot, began their career playing gay clubs, as DJ Norman Scott recalls: 'Take That played at Bolts in the old Hammersmith Palais. I was doing the meet-and-greet on the door. They had hardly been heard of then, and when their agent asked me if I wanted to have my photo taken with them, I didn't bother!' The band played gay club nights up and down the country on their ascent to the top, prancing around in studded leather jackets and tight Lycra shorts, and it would not be long before others followed suit. Ireland's Boyzone, who debuted in 1993, were a carbon copy, but unlike Take That they had a gay member in their ranks, singer Stephen Gately, although he would remain firmly closeted until 1999, outing himself after a former friend threatened to sell his story to the press. Westlife, another Irish boyband formed the year before Gately's revelations about his personal life, also included a gay singer, Mark Feehily. Although he too would not come out for several years, when Feehily went public it was of his own volition, and once the band already had 13 British number one singles behind them. Had it come a few years earlier, Feehily's revelation could potentially have caused irreparable damage to the band's career, but by 2005, the world had moved on, and he could happily tell the press that there had been no negative reactions to his coming out. 'I am so much happier

302

now and I think our fans can see that,' he told the *Sydney Morning Herald*.[13]

Not every boyband jumping on the bandwagon made the grade, but before either Gately or Feehily had built up the courage to come out, on 22 March 1996 a Dublin-based five-piece called 4Guyz debuted at Wonderbar, the city's newest and biggest gay nightspot. The five young men, all aged between 18 and 21, had put up with cameras, TV crews and newspapermen following them around the city all day, and that evening's performance, singing anthems including 'I'm Coming Out' and 'I Am What I Am' to a largely appreciative audience, was no different: national and local media had been primed that there was a story here. The big reveal, perhaps not so shocking to readers outside of an Ireland where the church was still an integral part of everyday life, was that, unlike other boy bands, 4Guyz were all unashamedly gay.

On the same day that 4Guyz were whipping up a frenzy at their debut gig, Bob Mellors, one of the founders of the Gay Liberation Front, was murdered at his home in Warsaw, the apparent victim of a violent burglary. Mellors, whose bloodied body was discovered two days later, had moved to Poland a few years earlier, telling friends that he was drawn to the local gay scene. Perhaps Gately and Feehily were right to keep their lips zipped for now.

23

Pride in Crisis

The vitality, passion and spectacle of Pride, the huge numbers of out lesbians and gay men, bisexuals and transgendered groups and individuals all coming together [is] the most eloquent testimony of how far the movement for lesbian and gay rights has come in the last twenty years.' – Angela Mason[1]

By the mid-1980s several cities outside of the capital had already established their own regular Pride events. In Bristol, following the success of the 1977 and '78 Gay Festivals, Avon Pride ran for more than 15 years until the mid-1990s; several attempts would be made to relaunch the festival over succeeding years, with gay pubs and clubs banding together to hold a bank holiday weekend Mardi Gras until a new, fortnight-long Pride Festival arrived in 2010. In 1985 Manchester held its first gay carnival (later to be rechristened Mardi Gras) over the August Bank Holiday, an event that began as 'a few trestle tables outside a pub... selling bits and pieces,' but that quickly became 'a four-day extravaganza with a parade, three-day fun fair, two-day market, cabaret and much, much more'[2] and had become the biggest annual fundraising initiative for the Village Charity, helping support HIV/AIDS patients in the North West. Over the same weekend, beginning in 1983 and running for over a decade, Birmingham's LGBT venues got together for their own charity project, Five Days of Fun, which saw a mix of male strippers, karaoke nights, live music and drag performers take over the city's gay village.

By the beginning of the 1990s annual Pride festivals outside of London were becoming far more commonplace. Brighton, which had staged a Pride march in July 1973, re-established its own annual event in 1991, the inaugural GlasGay, headlined by Horse, took place in Glasgow in 1993, and Edinburgh would hold its first Pride in 1995; Cardiff would have to wait until 1999, but by then Pride festivals were taking part right across the UK. Other smaller gay days, marches, protests and proto-Prides took place around the UK, while subsects of the LGBT movement, including the bear, leather and trans communities, also took advantage of the growing acceptance of alternative lifestyles, holding their own annual events in different cities around Britain.

In London, in February 1994 a new company, the Pride Trust, had been created to steer Pride forward. Board members and stakeholders included actors Michael Cashman, Simon Callow and Sir Ian McKellen, all of whom had been involved with the previous organisers, the Lesbian and Gay Pride Weeks Committee; out-gay businessman Ivan Massow; Chris Smith MP; Lily Savage; and G-A-Y owner Jeremy Joseph. In 1995, following two years in Brockwell Park, where the event had moved to after becoming too big for Jubilee Gardens, Pride found a new venue in Victoria Park. This would allow better access for wheelchair users, but it was also necessary because the post-march party had once more outgrown its home.

The Pride Trust had grand ambitions, chief of which was to grow Pride into a much bigger event. Things began well: in 1995 the march brought a massive 60,000 people to the streets of London, and the official figure for the festival in Victoria Park was 197,500, making it one of the five biggest LGBT events in the world that year. Liverpool also held its first Pride in 1995. Things had been improving for the local LGBT community for a number of years, partly thanks to the successful growth of Manchester's gay scene and partly because the early nineties dance resurgence had seen a revitalisation of the city's nightlife. DJ John Aggy had been playing in gay clubs in the North West since the early 1990s, and in 1994 he secured a residency at newly launched

Liverpool club Garlands. 'Garlands really took off and for the first few years was amazing,' he says. 'It was a place where people just got on, it was a little community. It really helped change attitudes around here, when straight people were coming in and being welcomed, and then going home after having the best night out of their lives. It was well-known citywide, not some scary place stuck down a side street.'

While at Garlands, Aggy spearheaded the club's first LGBT all-nighter, Queer, and in 1996 became one of the first to play at Liverpool's newly opened G-Bar. Soon after, he began a residency at Manchester LGBT superclub, Legend. 'Liverpool was a bit late off the mark,' he explains. 'I put that down to the fact that it's a very Catholic city, it has that religious yin-yang: you're either in Paddy's Wigwam or you're in the Anglican.* You pick up a lot of guilt by osmosis, and people were very paranoid about being seen to be gay; it's a relatively small place, and people were frightened. Pride was a lot slower to get off the ground, but Manchester was the catalyst. Manchester's gay scene emboldened people who were going out dancing for three days non-stop over a weekend then coming back home to Liverpool and having nowhere to go.

'The first Pride I ever went to was in Manchester, around 1990, and there was nothing: a few trestle tables outside the Rembrandt, like a bring-and-buy sale... A picnic in the park and then people went to the bars at night, then went home. But it became a big deal very quickly, and every year they were raising money for charities. By 1995 it was just incredible: Danceteria opened on the Friday night and didn't shut until the Monday... It just kept going. Manchester was seeing hundreds of thousands of pounds spent there over the three days and Liverpool City Council saw that they could make money; that's what drove Pride here.

'The first one was 1995 in Pownall Square. I was DJing in the afternoon, and the organisers expected maybe a couple of hundred

---

* Liverpool's two cathedrals, the Catholic Metropolitan Cathedral of Christ the King, known to locals as Paddy's Wigwam, and the more austere Liverpool Cathedral on St James's Mount, immediately in front of John Lennon's former student hovel in Gambier Terrace.

people, but we had 1,500 turn up. The God squad turned up as well, the first time I had seen that in Liverpool. People just laughed at them.'

With more and more people forsaking London for regional events, by the early part of 1997 it was obvious that it was all over for the ambitious Pride Trust: the new organisation was £100,000 in debt and needed a lifeline. Sponsors had not come through with their promised contributions, expensive equipment had gone missing and there was massive, unauthorised overspending of the festival budget. After much anxiety over a 'straight' company coming in and taking over Pride, a new concern – Pride Promotions Limited – came to the rescue. Fronted by lesbian publisher Linda Riley and business partner Jean T, the pair coughed up £30,000 of their own money to secure the rights to Pride, on the strict understanding that the regenerated festival would be promoted as an LGBT event, LGBT businesses and organisations would be prioritised and that not-for-profit and community LGBT groups would not be excluded. The new company even agreed to clear the Pride Trust's debts over a three-year period. However, for the first time, the idea that people may have to pay to attend was suggested.

These lofty ideals did not last long. The commitment to pay off the previous company's debts proved too big a millstone to carry; Pride was broke, and by the following year, 1998, yet another organisation, Pride Events UK Limited, was at the helm of the festival, with LGBT charity Stonewall organising the march itself. The board of this new company was staffed mostly by concert and venue promoters, including veteran live concert supremo Harvey Goldsmith and Kevin Millins, managing director of club promoters the Pure Organisation. This time, the post-march festival would take place on Clapham Common. Radio 1 would broadcast highlights of the festival to its millions of listeners across the country, but entry would cost £5 and only those who had bought tickets in advance would be allowed in.

'I think it lost that balance because it no longer came from the community, in the way that it did throughout the eighties and into the nineties, before Pride went bankrupt,' says Peter Scott-Presland. 'But Pride was always bankrupt... What you always did was start paying last year's bills out of next year's revenue, the advertising money as it came in... Someone new came in, said, "You can't do that", and we lost Pride, in any meaningful sense, in 1997. I remember the year that Sinead O'Connor played: all the artists were doing it for expenses, and Sinead's expenses were £25 to pay the babysitter! But over the next few years it just grew and grew.

'It got too big for Jubilee Gardens so then it went to Kennington Park, and then it became too big for there so we went to Brockwell Park in Brixton, which was a bit difficult because it was such a schlep from the city centre and it was hard to get people there after the march. Transport for London would not lay on extra trains for the purpose, so trying to get 60,000 people from Central London to Brixton fast was a real nightmare, but that was a shame because the park was on a hill and you could look down on the whole thing, which was delightful. Then it went to Clapham Common and that's when they started to fence it in, at Lambeth Council's insistence, and that killed the spirit of it.' Thankfully, most of this would have gone unnoticed to the tens of thousands of revellers who were turning up each summer.

Following the Christopher Street Liberation Day in June 1970, the Pride movement has spread around the world, and in more recent years LGBT communities in some of the most oppressively religious, or most fervently anti-civil rights, countries have ensured that, for at least one day a year, LGBT people's stories are highlighted. 'When I appeared at those early Prides, I felt it was a political statement,' says Horse McDonald. 'I felt I had to stand up. When Section 28 came out, I was worried about what would happen, but there were more and more people who were not willing to be silenced. There are people who go along to the marches for the party. Not that I'm saying it's wrong to party, but they're not looking at why people actually marched in the first place. Times do change, and there's a lot of people who are quite happy to go with the flow, because they don't really have to stand up and be counted. But there are places in the world where you don't have that freedom, and that's something we should all be aware of. When you're walking down the street with your backside hanging out of your chaps, or whatever, you have to remember that there are people in the world who do not have that luxury.'

In 2006, 13 years after the decriminalisation of homosexuality in Russia, LGBT activists in Moscow organised the country's first official Pride festival. Although the event was banned by the mayor's office and the leader of Russia's Central Spiritual Governance for Muslims told Christians and Muslims to join together and attack revellers, dozens – including veteran gay activist Peter Tatchell – took to the streets to protest and celebrate. Despite violent opposition, organisers pressed on with a second Pride the following year. At a press conference to launch the event, several people were attacked by anti-LGBT thugs; the Russian police did nothing to stop the attacks and instead arrested several of Moscow Pride's high-profile supporters, including Tatchell and Italian MP Marco Cappato.

In 2009 Moscow Pride was scheduled to take place on the last day of the Eurovision Song Contest, also being held in the city, and several contestants threatened to boycott the event should the parade not go ahead. The march would also take place on the eve of the International Day Against Homophobia, Transphobia and Biphobia. Despite this, riot police charged a group of around 30 LGBT people holding a peaceful protest in the city and bundled several – Tatchell and Russian gay rights movement leader Nikolai Alexeyev among them – into the back of waiting vehicles. In 2010 the European Court of Human Rights fined Russia $40,000 for human rights violations and damages for the authorities' actions against the LGBT community since 2006. However, a year later, at the last Pride event to take place in Moscow, the event was once again broken up by police within minutes, with more than 30 people arrested. In the same year, feminist art punk collective Pussy Riot was formed. Within 12 months, three of the women, including out-lesbian Yekaterina Samutsevich, were in prison, serving two years each for crimes against religion after a performance in a Moscow cathedral. Outspoken proponents of LGBT rights, in November 2020 two members of Pussy Riot were fined for hanging Pride flags on public buildings in Moscow.

24

21st-Century Boys and Girls

*'As we approach the 21st century, there is no room for complacency.
Looking back over forty years we have chalked up some
impressive gains. But none of them has been easy to achieve,
and much is still depressingly negative.'* – Anthony Grey[1]

In May 1997 the Labour Party, under its charismatic new leader
Tony Blair, brought an end to 18 years of Tory rule, producing the
biggest electoral defeat in almost a century and a half, and making
great use of the D:Ream anthem 'Things Can Only Get Better'.
Blair's PR machine went into overdrive, photographing him at every
opportunity with the musicians, models and artists at the forefront of
an optimistic resurgence of British pop culture. For many, Blair was
seen as the young, hip, guitar-slinging leader of Cool Britannia; you
could scarcely open a magazine or turn on a television without seeing
the new PM and his wife rubbing shoulders and sipping champagne
with Noel Gallagher of Oasis, the Spice Girls, artists such as Damien
Hirst or TV scriptwriter Richard Curtis, a man who appeared to have
singlehandedly resurrected British cinema.

Younger politicians, like Blair and his closest advisors (including gay
MP Peter Mandelson, constantly emasculated in the press as 'Mandy'),
understood the power of the pink vote. They were also far more likely to

be influenced by the positive changes in attitudes towards LGBT people being shown in other countries within the European Community. British politicians were keen to distance themselves from the Thatcher years of LGBT persecution, and a full year before Labour took power, at a press launch in Nottingham, the Liberal Democrats launched their 'gay guarantee', which promised an end to police entrapment, and also assured lesbian and gay couples the same adoption rights as heterosexual couples. The Lib Dems also promised an end to the ban on LGBT people serving in the armed forces, at a time that the Ministry of Defence revealed that they were still using surveillance techniques and agents provocateurs on suspected LGBT people in the military, and that chaplains and doctors were being coerced into informing on gay colleagues.

Britannia may have been cool, but where were the LGBT musicians who had been fighting the cause for the last three decades? Photographs of Blair supping champagne with Mick Hucknall of Simply Red were splashed across the press, but where were the queer Red Wedge founders and supporters, like Jimmy Somerville and Tom Robinson? Somerville, Billy Bragg and Paul Weller, the three men who shepherded Red Wedge and who had previously expressed staunchly socialist views, had all turned their backs on the newly branded New Labour before the election, with Somerville admitting to *Gay Times* that 'I don't really want to be involved with [New Labour] or have my face used by them for their own purposes... I really can't stand the man [Blair]. He gives me the creeps.'[2] Bragg complained that New Labour were too elitist: 'If we're going to commit ourselves to a society that has equality in it, then the leaders of the party that bases its ideology on equality have to experience it. New Labour won't come out of the closet and tell us what they are: a democratic socialist party, a social democrat party, a Christian democrat party – they don't seem to have decided.'[3] Just about the only visibly LGBT musician to pass through the door to Number 10 in those early days was Neil Tennant of Pet Shop Boys. The duo would headline London's biggest Pride event to date that summer, when they performed on Clapham Common on 5 July, but even he would walk away from Blair before too long.

Blair's ascendancy may have provided mixed blessings, but at least the newly appointed Secretary of State for Culture, Media and Sport,

Chris Smith, finally had an ally: four months after Labour's victory – and 23 years after Maureen Colquhoun was forced out by the press – Angela Eagle, Labour MP for Wallasey, became the first MP to voluntarily come out as a lesbian. As Junior Environment Minister, Eagle was also the first serving cabinet member to out themselves. Both Eagle and Smith were keen to ensure that the new premier did not backslide on his commitments to the party's LGBT members, including the repeal of the hated Section 28, and first on the agenda was the delivery of an equal age of consent. As Lord Smith recalls, 'When we came into government in 1997, there were a number of us in the Labour Party, people like [actor and LGBT rights activist] Michael Cashman*, Waheed Alli [who as Baron Alli, in 1998 became the first openly gay Muslim peer in Parliament] and me who were arguing virtually from day one that we needed to start the process of bringing in legislative equality for LGBT people: an equal age of consent, getting rid of Section 28, equal access to goods and services, the armed services, the diplomatic service, the civil service and eventually civil partnerships, and so on. We started with the equal age of consent, because that was the most visible bit of discrimination on the statute books. Tony Blair's office, at that point, in 1997–8, was really nervous about doing anything about it. They were saying things to us like, "How is this going to play with the voters?", "What are the pensioners who vote Labour going to think about this?", "Surely there are more important things we have to be getting on and doing?"'

It seemed as if New Labour meant new hope for the UK's LGBT community. Just four years earlier, Edwina Currie and her supporters had managed to reduce the age of consent for homosexual acts to 18, but Smith and his allies would be happy with nothing less than full equality. Blair came to power while the European Court of Human Rights was already hearing an appeal against the lack of parity in the UK. 'Blair's office agreed that if the European Court found that UK law was discriminatory [as they had in 1993 when the age of consent for gay men was still 21], then the Government would be able to say, "We are

---

* In 2014 Michael Cashman, after serving as an MEP for 15 years, was given a life peerage, becoming Baron Cashman of Limehouse.

being made to do this, we have to bring it in,"' Lord Smith recalls. 'And that is, of course, precisely what happened. Those young men won, and we got the Government to bring in an equal age of consent on the back of that, and of course the roof didn't fall in.' After a free vote on the subject a year after Labour came into power, MPs agreed to reduce the age of consent for homosexual acts to 16, the change coming into effect in England, Wales and Scotland with the passing of the Sexual Offences (Amendment) Act of 2000. 'There wasn't a riot from Labour voters,' Lord Smith continues. '[Most] Pensioners couldn't have cared less – they were rather pleased that people were being made happy for a change. After that, because public reaction was, on the whole, rather positive, it became easy to persuade the prime minister that this was the right thing to do. The whole succession of things, including getting rid of Section 28, happened as a result of that initial success. Now, of course, Tony Blair talks about all of this as being one of the great achievements of his administration! And, fair do's, once he got it he pushed it through. But it did take him a little while to get there.

'It was a rather remarkable series of success stories,' Lord Smith continues. 'Particularly because this was happening only 20 years or so after the atmosphere had been so poisonous, so homophobic. If you had told me we were going to have that degree of success over that relatively short time period I would have said, "No... That's for the birds!"'

But before the new law came into force, the current prejudicial rules continued to be imposed. On 12 January 1998, in the town of Bolton, Greater Manchester, seven gay and bisexual men were convicted of gross indecency under the Sexual Offences Act 1956 and age of consent offences under the Criminal Justice and Public Order Act 1994. The men, one of whom was six months under the age of consent (at that time still 18), were convicted because more than two men had sex together: the Sexual Offences Act 1967 had made it clear that consensual, legal gay sex could only happen between two men above the age of consent. Although all were willing participants, they had been arrested and videotapes of several of the men having sex together were confiscated by the police. The seven men were all given probation or community service orders, but a high-profile campaign led by OutRage! and Amnesty International succeeded in having their sentences quashed the following year – after four of the men had revealed that they were in relationships with women.

As if to prove that the new government was indeed LGBT-friendly, and having already been awarded a CBE two years earlier, at the end of 1997 it was announced that Elton John was to be knighted in the Queen's New Year's Honours list. Earlier that year, his re-recording of 'Candle in the Wind', dedicated to the late Diana, Princess of Wales, had become the biggest-selling single of all time and had raised tens of millions of pounds for charity. 'Elton's already a queen,' sniped Boy George, 'so isn't this a bit of a comedown?'[4]

Elton, who first came out as bisexual in an interview with *Rolling Stone* in 1976 and outed himself as gay after splitting from his wife in 1988, had proved that being gay did not necessarily mean that you would lose your audience, yet the fear of ridicule and rejection had prevented Judas Priest vocalist Rob Halford from coming out for years. Finally, in February, on hiatus from Priest and about to debut his own solo act, the singer decided the time was right for him to discuss his sexuality. Talking to MTV, he made it clear that he was coming out on his own terms: 'This is the moment to discuss it,' he said. 'A lot of homophobia still exists in the music world, in all kinds of music. I wouldn't say it's any more phobic in metal or rap or whatever this music is that I'm doing now, but that's just something that I think we all have to address in our own lives. If we have a problem with it, I think we should seek help and find out why we do have a problem with it.'[5] The singer later revealed that his decision to come out was 'the greatest thing I could have done for myself... the record sales didn't plunge, the show attendance didn't plunge. Unconditional love will accept you for who you are, and I think that was the blessing I had from the fans.'[6]

Halford was lucky to be able to choose the timing of his coming out: in April, George Michael was very publicly outed after he was arrested in a public lavatory in Los Angeles. He was fined $500, had to undergo five hours of counselling, and was told that he would be jailed if he was caught a second time. Up till then, George had fiercely guarded his private life. His name had been linked with supermodels,

314

actresses, female singers and dancers, but rumours about his sexuality had circulated for years. As early as 1985 the *Daily Mirror* suggested that then-girlfriend Pat Fernandes was 'a decoy... she's there to keep the female fans away'[7] almost a year to the day after the same newspaper had labelled her as 'the girl he calls his soulmate'.[8] In 1991 Michael met Brazilian designer Anselmo Feleppa, and their relationship sparked a change in Michael's attitude. In a 1993 interview, he claimed that he did not care what people thought about him or his sexuality: 'If people look at me and they think, "This is a gay man", fine. If they look at me and think, "This is a straight man", that's fine too. It makes no difference.'[9] Sadly, their relationship was brought to an abrupt end that same year, when Anselmo died of AIDS. Michael dedicated his 1996 album, *Older*, to the man he would later refer to as the love of his life; his death signalled the beginning of Michael's spiral into depression and drug use.

At the time of Michael's arrest in 1998, his management and record company knew that he was gay, and that he had a live-in boyfriend, Kenny Goss. It was finally time for George to admit to his adoring public what many already suspected. Taking control of the situation, George – who insisted that he had been the victim of entrapment – retaliated by first coming out and then releasing a video for his next single, 'Outside', that poked fun at his arrest, featuring public toilets that turned into discos, male and female same-sex couples getting hot and steamy, and ended with two cops locking lips. Mary Whitehouse, now retired as the head of the National Viewers' and Listeners' Association, was not amused: 'I hope no one will buy this video or broadcast it. That is the best way of showing Mr Michael we do not think his behaviour is funny.'[10]

'I have been waiting a long time for George to admit he had a boyfriend,' Boy George said at the time of Michael's arrest, adding that 'Pat Fernandez [sic] was my "girlfriend" for three years. When I read a newspaper story "How Pat Broke My Heart", I was tempted to write one called "How Pat Broke My Hoover". The idea of her and George having a relationship is as likely as me having sex with a door.'[11]

Michael's new-found audacity would also manifest itself in his politics. In 2002 he would release the single 'Wag the Dog', which took pot shots at Prime Minister Blair's close relationship with US President George W. Bush. The title came from Blair's nickname: Bush's Poodle. The video ended with Michael – in cartoon form – as all five members of the Village People. Pet Shop Boys would also find inspiration in Blair's sycophantic backing of Bush and in the prime minister's support for the introduction of personal identity cards. Two tracks on their 2006 album, *Fundamental*, would document the band's disillusionment with New Labour and Blair in particular: 'I'm With Stupid' is a damning indictment of the relationship between Bush and Blair, while 'Integral' highlights Tennant's concerns over ID cards. 'Neil has always been a Labour Party supporter, but at the last election [2005] he voted Liberal Democrat because he is completely against the idea of ID cards,' a spokesperson for the band told the *Evening Standard*. 'The Pet Shop Boys think we should try to increase our freedom, not limit it. They don't believe ID cards are an effective way of countering terrorism.'[12]

On the cusp of the millennium, it felt for many that advances in LGBT rights were reaching their apogee; there were still a couple of big boxes to tick, but LGBT musicians who had been previously guarded about their sexuality were becoming less inhibited. Via the pages of his 1999 autobiography, *A Cure for Gravity*, Joe Jackson came out as bisexual. The singer, whose hits included the new wave classic 'Is She Really Going Out with Him?' and the defiantly queer 'Real Men', wrote that he had struggled with his sexual identity since he was young: 'As much as I liked girls, I began to wonder if I was gay. People were always calling me a poof or a queer. I was somewhat effeminate, but not a pretty boy. Rather, I was awkwardly androgynous, and open to just about anything short of sexual congress with beasts of the field.'[13]

Then, on 30 April 1999 a nail bomb exploded in the heart of London's gay village, destroying the long-established gay pub the Admiral Duncan, killing three people and injuring 30 more. It was 6.30 pm, a Friday evening and the start of a long bank holiday weekend; the pub was packed with customers when the bomb went off. Those murdered were a young woman, Andrea Dykes, who was four months' pregnant, and her friends Nick Moore and John Light. The three met that evening, along with Andrea's husband Julian (who survived the blast but was seriously injured), to celebrate the news of Andrea's pregnancy; the couple also wanted to tell John that they would like him to be the unnamed baby's godfather. Landlord Mark Taylor suffered 75 per cent burns as well as injuries from nails, shrapnel and flying glass. In shock, he told people surveying the devastation that 'I can't believe this. I've just paid £30 for a facial'.[14] Bar manager David Morley also received burns in the blast, but despite his injuries he spent the weeks following the explosion visiting other victims in hospital. In a sad twist of fate, although he would recover from his injuries, David was murdered by a gang of teenage thugs in October 2004, 'kicked in the head like a football as he lay on the ground', by a 14-year-old girl.[15]

The incident followed similar events over the previous two weekends, with those bombs targeting Black and Muslim communities in Brixton and Brick Lane respectively. The attack on the Admiral Duncan is the worst single act of violence committed against the LGBT community in Britain in the modern age. The bomber, David Copeland, was identified from CCTV footage taken in the vicinity of the Brixton bombing, which took place 13 days before the assault on the Admiral Duncan. 'A day before, I had received an e-mail from the gay organisation OutRage! which said I should be a little more vigilant about my personal security because people who were known to be gay, especially well-known gays, were possible targets for these right-wing groups,' Jimmy Somerville revealed in an interview given just 10 days after the fatal attack. 'It has turned out to be that the attack wasn't initiated by an organisation, rather a 22-year-old man. To have so much hate for so many different kinds of people and to be so young is very, very disturbing. It was so sad for me, not only because of the act but also because the people in the bar had to suffer this attack.

'It could have been any of us and we are all victims of the attack, however they paid with their lives and injuries. Although I didn't personally know any of these people, I felt a connection and a sympathy there. It shocked us all so the next day there was an emergency gathering. We marched from Leicester Square to Trafalgar Square, about 200 of us. The people there were angry, confused, and sad. It was a strange feeling. Times have changed and it's scary because when one person does this, it opens the door for others to do the same. It's frightening times really.'[16]

A week after the attack, hundreds of people – including Tom Robinson, Peter Tatchell and Ken Livingstone – gathered outside the pub for a vigil: hundreds more attended a memorial service at the nearby St Anne's church. One of the men present, Peter Orrin, had been in the Admiral Duncan when the bomb went off, and had only been released from hospital on the day that the vigil took place. 'My first reaction after being let out today was to come down here,' he told reporters. 'I am overwhelmed by the number of people who have turned out.'[17]

As Lord Smith says, one of the most important items on Labour's gay 'wish list' was for openly LGBT people to be able to serve their country and, after years of lobbying, in January 2000 the government finally allowed out-LGBT men and women in the armed forces. Before then, men and women of all ranks serving in the army, navy, merchant navy or air force had been subject to ridicule, open to exploitation by blackmailers and forced out of their jobs should their sexuality become known. Stonewall had been pushing for change through the British court system, but when judges at both the High Court and the Court of Appeal refused to overturn the ban, they took their fight to the European Court of Human Rights, who ruled that servicemen and women had a right to privacy which was compromised by investigations into their sexuality. The Labour government immediately overturned the ban; however, Iain Duncan Smith, a former army officer who would become leader of the Conservative Party the following year, insisted that allowing LGBT people to serve would run the 'risk [of] undermining the operational effectiveness of our armed forces',[18] and pledged to roll back the decision as soon as the Conservatives were next in power.

While LGBT people serving in the forces had cause to celebrate, others were still weighing up the potential cost that coming out could have on both their public and private lives. Sean Dickson, leader of hit band the Soup Dragons, came out in 2001. Married, and with a child on the way, he admits that his journey was 'very messy and personally destructive. I still bear the scars mentally to this day. It was not all rainbows and unicorns, believe me.' However, he would find some solace in Record Playerz, a club night he established, with co-organiser

Alan Miller, at the Glasgow School of Art as he transitioned from indie idol to star DJ, under the name Hifi Sean. 'Record Playerz was like our own family; we had our own anthems that seemed to only belong within our four walls. It was an education in the power of playing music in a different way. Up until then, I had played music live in a band; this was a completely different extension to the power of sound and rhythm and energy.'

Spending time in New York during the final years of the Soup Dragons' career had a huge impact on the music Dickson was playing. 'It was an influence culturally and emotionally. My favourite clubbing experiences were in New York City in the early nineties, although at the time I was not aware of how iconic some of the venues and parties I went to were. It was also my first foray into the world of after-hours parties, which I would DJ at a lot in later years. You would meet a lot of the same people on the NYC scene back then, some wonderful characters that became good friends. There was a very friendly, family camaraderie. It was my playground and influenced the Soup Dragons hugely, not just musically but in attitude and aesthetics too: the video for 'Divine Thing', which was nominated for an MTV award, starred many of the club kids from the parties in downtown New York and the Meat Packing District. The whole colour of downtown New York City heavily coloured the album *Hotwired*, which was mainly written in the USA on tour.'

Despite decades of improvement in the treatment of LGBT people, the advances in legislation and the increasing openness and acceptance shown towards LGBT culture, Britain's newspapers still had some way to go to catch up. In March 2002, with his debut single at the top of the official UK charts, TV talent show winner Will Young came out. His sexuality had hardly been a secret; if the viewers of *Pop Idol* had missed the clues then they must have been blind, but he was forced to talk about his sexuality after discovering that, once again, a national newspaper had planned to out him. 'It's totally no big deal, just part of who I am,' he said. 'For me it's normal and nothing to be ashamed about. I'm gay and I'm comfortable with that. I really don't know what the fuss is about.'[19] Young's single not only remained at the top spot, it became the fastest-selling debut of all time; he would go on to score 11

Top 10 singles, including three further number one hits. As if to show the media just how far the LGBT community had come, the following summer a defiant Jimmy Somerville headlined Pride in Hyde Park, 18 years after he had been arrested there for cottaging.

25

Celebrate!

*'It is remarkable to have a Conservative leader standing
on a Gay Pride platform. Five years ago, not many
gays would have turned up.'* – Andrew Pierce[1]

Way back in 1989, Denmark had become the first country in the world to introduce officially recognised registered partnerships for same-sex couples, but it would be 12 more years before another country, the Netherlands, first allowed civil marriage for same-sex couples.

For many, same-sex marriage seemed little more than a pipe dream, something that would never happen in Britain thanks to the power of the church and the institution's unbreakable grip on Parliament. Twenty-six Anglican Bishops have an unopposed, automatic seat in the House of Lords, and many more current and former members of the church qualify for a seat in the House as a result of obtaining a peerage. Many of these are (or were) vocal opponents of LGBT rights, unwilling to relinquish their vice-like grip on the country's morality.

Although there were many involved in the early years of LGBT liberation who found the idea of assimilating the mores of heterosexual society abhorrent, for others full equality, including same-sex marriage, had been the goal since the very beginning. Not only did there need to be parity in the age of consent, but LGBT people had to enjoy the same civil rights that heterosexual members of society took for granted.

Fear of same-sex marriage had been present for decades. In 1971 the *People* ran a feature on churches in New York, California and Kansas that were conducting ceremonies for same-sex couples under the headline 'They Call This "Gay", But We have Another Word for it... UGH!'[2] With no legal standing, these unions were described by former Catholic priest Robert Clement (who had undergone a similar ceremony with his own partner 11 years earlier) as 'a blessing of the love of two people sacramentally in the eyes of God and the church'.[3] When Clement was accused of performing ceremonies at the Church of the Beloved Disciple illegally, members of the Gay Activists Alliance occupied the New York Marriage License Bureau in protest.

The *People* called these unions 'nauseating', gloated that the ceremonies had brought about 'a fair amount of healthy revulsion', and branded the men involved 'sickening', but changes were afoot. The LGBT-friendly Metropolitan Community Church established its first church in London in 1972, and by the mid-1970s other churches in Britain were welcoming same-sex partners, including the church of Christ the King, near Redhill, where the Reverend George Nairn-Briggs began offering blessings to gay and lesbian couples. Nairn-Briggs told reporters that 'it would be unloving to reject these people on the grounds of their sexuality. I am not prepared to throw them out of the door and discard them because they are homosexuals.'[4]

Marriage seemed a world away from what many of the pioneers of gay liberation had been looking for when they began campaigning. 'We wanted to change society, not conform to it,' says Peter Tatchell, and Frankie Green agrees: 'What I liked about GLF was radicalism, revolutionary politics with transformational aims, not the assimilationist, equality-orientated move to rights within the existing society.' Yet in fighting for the right for same-sex couples to marry, activists also wanted to secure them other rights enjoyed by heterosexual couples, including job security, pension rights, the right to be recognised in law as next of kin, and the ability to adopt or have children. None of these secular activities need involve the church, but that would not stop self-appointed moral guardians offering their views on the country's decline. As recently as October 2008, the Reverend Peter Mullen – who had once been forced to resign his ministry after committing adultery with a parishioner – was ordered by his current diocese to remove a personal blog he had penned which called for gay men to have their backsides tattooed with the slogan 'Sodomy can seriously damage your health', and for 'obscene' Pride parades to be outlawed.[5]

The church, and religion in general, has had a difficult relationship with same-sex attraction, and LGBT people of faith are often conflicted. Fourth century Christian martyrs Sergius and Bacchus were venerated for centuries as 'brother saints' and, it has been suggested, as a homosexual couple, but over the years elements of the Christian church have promulgated the idea that being LGBT is at odds with having a religious belief. It is not just Christianity that has an issue: in several Islamic countries, the death penalty still exists for homosexuality.

Often the loudest voices against LGBT equality are from cults with small followings, noticeably the Westboro Baptist Church, infamous for organising hate rallies and pickets of the funerals of American service personnel and LGBT people. The 'church' (despite the name, it is not affiliated with any Baptist denomination) gained notoriety picketing the funeral of Matthew Shepard, a young gay man who, in Colorado in 1998, was abducted and pistol-whipped before being tied to a fence where he was beaten, tortured, set on fire and left to die. In 2009, members of the Westboro Baptist Church were banned from entering the UK; their sole reason for coming to the country was to picket a play, *The Laramie Project,* about Shepard's murder. Sadly it is not just US hardliners making a noise. Based in Carmarthen, Christian Voice, a tiny lobby group with an undisclosed membership led by former chairman of the Conservative Family Campaign, Stephen Green, actively campaigns against LGBT rights. Arrested handing out homophobic literature at Cardiff Mardi Gras in 2006, two years later Green told out-gay singer Ian 'H' Watkins, of the pop group Steps, that being a happy homosexual was akin to being a mass murderer.

The innate wish to conform and please one's parents or church can have devastating effects that last a lifetime. Having been raised within a deeply religious family, as he got older, Michigan-born singer, songwriter and musician John Grant's upbringing came back to haunt him. 'I was always so conflicted about sexuality and how I should feel about my homosexuality,' he explains. 'I think there was a lot of homophobia inside of me because it was quite ingrained in me growing up, which leads to self-loathing. You can see that in a lot of gay people and a lot of groups who are marginalised; it seems to be a human reaction. I think a lot of groups that have been marginalised internalise what has been done to them and then can inflict it on each other. That happens a lot.

'Maybe it's because it was drilled into me or beaten into me when I was young about the church rejecting homosexuality, but it was never my goal to be accepted in the same way. I suppose there was a lot of anger about the way I was treated, as being seen as psychologically weakened, an inferior specimen of a human, and that was quite damaging for me because I was quite sensitive, and I believed what people were telling me. I believed my parents and trusted them. The people that were teaching me at church were supposed to be telling the truth and being kind; it was about love, so a lot of the things that were happening didn't make a lot of sense.

'It's quite amazing to me to see how many people out there don't even think twice about [homosexuality] these days, don't seem to have any trouble with it at all, but I think that's the younger generation. But the suicide rates seem to indicate that there is still a big problem. It's not over with; it's not like we had it rough and now it's easy. There are still issues.'

With an increasing number of countries and states legislating for same-sex marriage, in 2004 the Labour government unveiled the Civil Partnership Act. First introduced in the Queen's Speech the previous November, the same month that Michael Howard, one of the architects of Section 28, became Conservative Party leader, it would allow same-sex couples to enter into a legally binding, and legally recognised, partnership which offered many of the same rights and protections as marriage, including pension and property rights, and the right to be recognised as next of kin. Prior to the change in law, several local councils had already introduced same-sex blessings, held on council-sanctioned premises by registrars (a mass 'wedding' of 70 gay and lesbian couples took place in Manchester in August 2004), but once the Act became law every council in the United Kingdom would have to comply. There were crucial differences to heterosexual marriages: ceremonies could not take place in churches or include any religious sacrament. Prime Minister Tony Blair refused to go up against the church, although he would later support plans to introduce same-sex marriage despite his own religious belief. Partnerships would not be known as marriages, and should a partnership break down, lesbian and gay couples would have to match different criteria to obtain a dissolution to heterosexual couples seeking a divorce. UK law did not recognise that adultery could take place in a same-sex partnership, so a couple could not bring a legal end to their relationship if one of them had been unfaithful.

The first same-sex civil partnerships took place in December 2005, with the 21 December set as the earliest day they could take place in England. However, the first ceremony occurred 16 days earlier at St Barnabas Hospice in Worthing, West Sussex, when Matthew Roche entered into a partnership with Christopher Cramp. The statutory 15-day waiting period between registering for a partnership and any ceremony taking place in England and Wales was waived as Roche was suffering from terminal cancer: sadly, he died the following day. On 19 December, Belfast – which had a shorter registration period – became the first city in the UK to hold civil partnership ceremonies. The following day, ceremonies took place in four Scottish constituencies – Aberdeen, Dumfries and Galloway, Edinburgh, and Glasgow. Almost 700 ceremonies had taken place around the UK by the end of 21 December, with a further 1,200 scheduled before the start of the New Year.

One of the first high-profile names to take advantage of the change in the law was Sir Elton John, who entered into a civil partnership with David Furnish at Windsor Town Hall on 21 December. In March 2004 he revealed to the *New York Daily News* that he was looking forward to the day when same-sex civil partnerships became recognised in law in Britain and he could wed his partner of 11 years. 'I'm totally for it,' he said. 'In this day and age, if people who want to make a life commitment can't have protection, then we live in a pretty sick world. I would like to commit myself to David. I already have in my mind anyway.'[6] Former Communards keyboard player Richard Coles would also enter into a civil union with his partner, Reverend David Oldham, with both men adopting the surname Coles. The pair were both serving Anglican priests and agreed to abide by Church of England rules that allowed two men to enter into a civil partnership so long as they remained celibate. Coles would find out exactly how Christian his flock was after his husband died, in 2019, after a long illness. Posting on Twitter, Coles revealed that he had received 'a small but lively correspondence from Christians who wish me to know that [David] is in hell and I will follow. It's like the Khmer Rouge suddenly popping up in a stream of condolence', and that another wrote 'Dear Mr Coles, I can't begin to tell you how happy I am to hear of the death of your partner...'

Although, as the Reverend Coles saw for himself, the church still had a long way to go, the introduction of civil partnerships may have been seen by many as proof that LGBT people had been assimilated into most strands of British society. However, just two months before those first ceremonies took place, one of the most shocking and brutal attacks against a gay man on British soil took place. Jody Dobrowski, a 24-year-old bar manager, was walking home across Clapham Common when he was set upon by two men, who beat him so severely that, following his death in hospital from severe head, neck and facial injuries, his family were unable to identify him. His murderers, who had attacked another gay man a fortnight earlier, were jailed for a minimum of 28 years each in June 2006. It was the first time in British legal history that the length of a sentence had been influenced by the victim's sexuality, after sexual orientation (or the presumed sexual orientation) of the victim was added to the list of hate crimes with the Criminal Justice Act 2003.

Following the sentence, Jody's mother condemned his murder as 'a political act. It was an act of terrorism. Jody was not the first man to be killed, or terrorised, or beaten or humiliated for being homosexual, or for being perceived to be homosexual. Tragically, he will not be the last man to suffer the consequences of homophobia which is endemic in this society. This is unacceptable. We cannot accept this. No intelligent, healthy or reasonable society could.'[7] In 2006, the city of Gloucester held its first ever Pride march, dedicated to Jody, who was originally from Stroud, in Gloucestershire.

The media continued to promulgate stigma attached to being LGBT, and scandalous stories about the private lives of LGBT celebrities still sold newspapers. In a move designed to deny sensationalist headlines, shortly before Christmas 2004, Erasure's Andy Bell had confirmed, via the group's website, that he was HIV-positive. He had been aware of his status since 1998. 'It did take me a while,' he admits, 'but I'd had enough of feeling that I had a sword hanging over me, and I didn't want the press to put it out there before I had. I think the most important thing is being honest about who you are.' Shortly afterwards, rumours began to circulate that Andy Fraser, co-founder of legendary rock band Free, had died from complications due to AIDS. Fraser had not previously discussed his sexuality but broke his silence to refute the stories. Yes, he was gay, a fact he had realised more than 20 years previously, and yes, he was HIV-positive, but the bass player was very much still alive, issuing a press release to inform the world that 'while many may have considered me dead long ago (artistically or otherwise) and I do confirm I am living with AIDS, I am still very much here, and wish to let my friends and supporters know that I intend to be for quite a while.'

In an interview with Tom Guerra of *Vintage Guitar* magazine, Fraser elaborated on his decision to talk: 'When you see yourself through thousands of other peoples' eyes, you're sort of made aware of many of your shortcomings, and you either have to change them, or accept them, or some people try to drown them and that never worked for me. So I really could not see how I can be outwardly gay, and publicly gay... it was really quite a mountain. I remember at school, the way "faggots" were treated was not a good thing, and it was nothing that I wanted to be treated like. So that helped with the self-denial. I do believe things have gotten better for gays, but we still need to get to the point where it's not even thought about and I think part of my mission is to present a normalcy.'[8] At the time of writing, Andy Bell has been living with HIV for more than 20 years; Holly Johnson for more than 30. Being HIV-positive is no longer a life sentence, and Fraser would not succumb to AIDS: he died in March 2015 of a heart attack caused by atherosclerosis, a vascular disease.

'I was diagnosed in 1999, but in 2000 I was hospitalised with AIDS-defining complications,' says Brighton-based Queercore singer Oli Spleen, whose 2020 album *Night Sweats and Fever Dreams*, documented his journey with HIV. 'I remember being reassured by the doctor that I might go 10 or so years without needing to start on the antiretroviral medication. I wasn't very happy living in London though: I was 21, my parents had just divorced, I wasn't enjoying university where I felt my creativity was being stifled and my art was misunderstood, and I was struggling with drug and alcohol problems. I had attempted to come out to my mum aged 17. She didn't want to confront the psychological turmoil I was going through, so I kept things to myself and my self-destructive behaviour escalated. It was only when I ended up in hospital, fighting for my life, that I felt able to open up a dialogue with the rest of my family about my sexuality and I realised that they were just glad I was still alive. The thinking back then was that I'd be lucky to live another year or two; I don't think anyone expected me to be here 20 years later.

'I've been on the same antiretroviral combination since I first took the medication back in 2000. Whilst I had ongoing complications in the first years of the millennium, my medication was deemed to be effective enough not to change the combination.

'Since then, the availability of PrEP [a drug taken by HIV-negative people before and after sex that reduces the risk of getting HIV] has prevented a whole generation from succumbing to the infection and HIV is no longer perceived as a death sentence [for those with access to the medication]. Also, the awareness that someone with an undetectable viral load is incapable of passing the infection on is a weight off my mind. I have been undetectable for the majority of the last 20 years, but it was sometimes problematic explaining to a partner that my HIV status wasn't a risk to them.'

Times, and attitudes, change, but sadly, despite the major advances made in the UK, prejudice can still rear its ugly head, and in 2009 several high-profile media professionals proved that they were still remarkably out of step with their readers and listeners. In January, BBC Radio 1 DJ Chris Moyles, the presenter of the UK's most listened to breakfast show, mocked out-gay singer Will Young on air in a way that had, thankfully, gone out of fashion a generation earlier. After several listeners contacted the BBC and broadcasting watchdog Ofcom to complain, Moyles was criticised for 'promoting and condoning certain negative stereotypes based on sexual orientation'.[9] However, the BBC sprang to his defence, telling the press that 'there are no plans to take Chis off the air'.[10] Just three months earlier, there had been uproar, followed by suspensions, resignations and sackings when comedian Russell Brand and presenter Jonathan Ross had telephoned actor Andrew Sachs and made lewd implications about his granddaughter. The hypocrisy was palpable. Fortunately, over a decade later, it would be impossible for any broadcaster to stay in their job if they ridiculed an LGBT performer in the way that Moyles did, affecting an effeminate voice and claiming that Young wore dresses.

However offensive Moyles' comments may have been, nothing could have prepared readers for the vitriol spewed by *Daily Mail* columnist Jan Moir following the sudden death, at just 33 years old, of Boyzone singer Stephen Gately from a pulmonary oedema, the result of a previously undiagnosed heart condition. Gately, who had come out a decade earlier to pre-empt a story about his personal life in the press, died at the home he shared with his husband in Port d'Andratx, Mallorca on 10 October 2009. Less than a week later, while thousands of Boyzone fans – as well as Gately's family and friends – were mourning their loss, Moir insisted via a particularly spiteful column that the singer's death was due to his lifestyle and sexuality. Titled 'Why There was Nothing "Natural" About Stephen Gately's Death', the article brought over 25,000 complaints to the Press Complaints Commission (PCC) that day, making it the most complained about article published by a British newspaper. On 17 February 2010 the Press Complaints Commission, whose chairman at the time was Paul Dacre, the editor of the *Daily Mail* and Moir's boss, confirmed that although it was 'uncomfortable with the tenor of the columnist's remarks',[11] it would not uphold the complaints made.

Moyles' and Moir's homophobic attacks, and their respective employers' refusal to censure them, was hardly news. Unbelievably, as far as the law was concerned, it was still perfectly acceptable for people, and businesses, to discriminate against LGBT people. Hotels could refuse to allow a same-sex couple – even if they were in a civil partnership – a bed for the night. Then, finally, the passing into law of the Equality Act 2010, which consolidated already-existing anti-discrimination laws in the UK and added new legislation against discrimination on the grounds of sexual orientation, made denying services to LGBT people illegal: for the first time, if a business owner attempted to treat someone differently because of their sexual orientation, even if they insisted that their religious beliefs justified their prejudice, they were breaking the law.

Thankfully, the rampant homophobia displayed by Moyles, Moir and their ilk was no longer preventing LGBT artists from coming out. In 2010 gay actor and singer Olly Alexander joined a new band, Years and Years. In 2012, the same year that Years and Years issued their debut single, the country first heard of another exciting new singer, Sam Smith, who originally identified as gay and has since come out as non-binary. Both Smith and Alexander have faced their share of homophobic abuse, but the music industry and the public have embraced both artists. It seems people have woken up to the idea that an artist's sex life is less important than the art they create: Smith would go on to reach number one in the UK charts no less than seven times, including with the James Bond theme 'Writing's On the Wall', and *Communion*, the debut album from Years and Years, would also go to number one. Alexander has become a powerful campaigner for mental health issues within the LGBT community and has talked openly about the abuse that caused him to self-harm. In 2021 he starred in the TV drama *It's a Sin*, a series about life for LGBT people during the early years of the AIDS crisis, written by *Queer as Folk* creator Russell T. Davies.

26

Pinkwashing

'Being an arse bandit [is] nothing to be proud of.' –
Geoffrey Caton, UKIP candidate for Wallasey[1]

All of the recent progress in legislation for LGBT people had happened under a Labour government, and when, after 13 years in opposition, the Conservatives were returned to power, there were fears that advancements were about to be rolled back. Yet in 2014 the new Conservative government went where Labour had not dared: introducing same-sex marriage. For a party to take such a step, having shown little commitment to LGBT rights over the previous half century, was a major commitment towards progressiveness and equality. Only four years earlier, in their Contract for Equalities, the furthest leader David Cameron would go was to say that the party would consider recognising civil partnerships as marriages if they were to be elected. Once Cameron and the Tories came to power, they entered into a coalition with the Nick Clegg-led Liberal Democrats, who had campaigned for full equality, and for the legal status of British same-sex marriages to be recognised internationally. Finally, in Great Britain at least, same-sex couples would receive exactly the same recognition as heterosexuals. You still could not hold ceremonies in Church of England or Catholic churches (although more liberal sects, including the Quakers and the Metropolitan Community Church, would allow services and ceremonies in their chapels), but for the first time in British history, same-sex couples could legally marry.

Couples who had previously entered into a civil partnership were able to convert it into a full marriage if they wished to do so, having their marriage back-dated to the date of their partnership, and, on 21 December 2014, the ninth anniversary of their original wedding, Sir Elton John and David Furnish converted their civil partnership into full marriage. Couples in Northern Ireland would have to wait before they could enjoy the same rights as the rest of the UK, but thanks to infighting between the different political factions in the region, in 2020 Westminster was able to usher through not only same-sex marriage but also, finally, abortion rights, bringing to an end laws that would only allow a woman to have an abortion if her life was at risk.

By securing the right for same-sex couples to marry, Britain's LGBT community seemed to have finally achieved equality, and that was something for everyone to celebrate. Yet the community's annual flagship party, the Pride march through the streets of London, was once again in trouble, not for running up debt this time but for straying too far from its political roots. By 2015 Pride had become a huge corporate behemoth, with the movement's original political message lost in a sea of supermarket-purchased rainbow tat, alcohol branding and a desperation to be all things to all people. This pinkwashing strategy, with political parties, corporations and other groups jumping on the gay bandwagon for as long as it suited them (which was often no longer than Pride season itself), was exemplified perfectly by the decision taken by Pride in London to allow members of right-wing political party UKIP to join the march.

Frankie Green, drummer in pioneering lesbian groups the London Women's Liberation Rock Band and Jam Today, and one of the many women who took part in that first Pride march back in 1972, took umbrage with many of the assertions made by the chair of LGBT in UKIP, Flo Lewis, including her claim that the earliest Pride marches 'almost entirely comprised of gay men'.[2] In an open letter to Ms Lewis, she stated that 'I assure you that many women were amongst those "few hundred men who marched, years before my birth," who faced "serious abuse and threats when they set off from Hyde Park. They were pioneers and must be celebrated for their courage." Those women, of whom I was one, went on to work in hundreds of organisations working for the rights of lesbians because of what we had experienced including losing custody of our children, our jobs and housing, being stigmatised and ostracised or incarcerated as mentally ill.

'Some of us have worked in coalitions with gay men and others and in Trades Unions against class exploitation, racism, ableism and sexism. We have also worked in the overlapping causes of justice for those, including LGBT people, seeking refuge after fleeing persecution elsewhere in the world... combating racism in its myriad forms... and the principles of human rights, feminist and anti-racist causes – and continue to do so... We were well-aware of the traditional practice of scapegoating immigrants, and anyone regarded as "other" by racist mindsets (as if Britain was not a nation formed by migrants), by the political establishment, as a means of turning people against one another and diverting attention from real common enemies, such as unjust systems of power, economic greed and mean-minded notions of nationalism.'[3]

UKIP were dedicated to eroding hard-won LGBT rights, had campaigned against same-sex marriage and allowed a leaflet to be handed out at their annual conference that compared LGBT people to Hitler and the Yorkshire Ripper. Lewis eventually resigned from her role, claiming that she could 'no longer, in good conscience, represent the party that no longer represents me'.[4]

'You can see in today's political climate the way certain LGBT people – mostly white – are positioned differently from others,' says Frankie Green. 'How they are granted relative legal protection and citizenship, while others – migrants, people of colour, asylum-seekers – are in a very different category. As ever it's dualistic: one group legitimate, the other not. To keep the "other" precarious and denied safety, the state's strategy manipulates citizenship rights in a racialised, nationalistic manner. I think it's important to recognise that it's not only corporations and commercial interests which use the tactic of pinkwashing, but states too: Israel uses enormous official PR resources to cover up its crimes against humanity in Palestine, for example. Right-wing groups taking part in Pride is retrogressive in my view, although this maybe an inevitable result of identity politics, and the pinkwashing needs to be opposed. As a whole, Pride marches and events are positive, celebratory, necessary statements against the right-wing attempts to shut us up which are currently bedevilling many places in the world. Threats to power structures are always met with strategies to confine and co-opt them, to defuse the radical potential of movements and constrain them with the promise of pseudo-equality.

'You can't control the meaning or form of what develops over time from a movement, of course, nor should we try, but we can continue to be present in that ongoing process and contribute to debate, challenge or support others.'

Pride in London already had a ban in place on other right-wing groups, including the British National Party and the English Defence League, but for several years the Pride march had been led by the Mayor of London, Conservative politician Boris Johnson, a man who referred to gay men as 'tank-topped bumboys'[5] in a 1998 article for the *Telegraph*, castigating the recently outed Peter Mandelson. Although the decision to allow UKIP to join the march was eventually reversed, around 15 UKIP members crashed the parade, waving placards that announced, 'some gays vote UKIP: get over it', adapting the Stonewall slogan 'some people are gay, get over it'.

Lesbians and Gays Support the Miners (LGSM), reunited in the wake of the success of the movie *Pride*, had been asked to lead the parade, which took place on the thirtieth anniversary of LGSM and members of the mining unions heading the 1985 rally. Obviously, LGSM were honoured: 'In 2015 we feel there is a greater need than ever for solidarity between those fighting against all forms of oppression and injustice, and for the liberation of LGBT people. When Pride in London asked us to lead the parade we naturally welcomed the opportunity to replicate not only the actions but also the spirit of the 1985 parade, and to become a point of attraction for trade unions, student and youth groups and other campaigning organisations. Over the last few years many people have become concerned about the increasingly higher profile of major private corporations on Pride, both in terms of sponsorship and their prominence in the parade itself, and were excited by the prospect of this Pride having a different atmosphere and focus because of LGSM's role in heading the march.'[6]

However, that was not to be. Pride in London would not allow the miners and other trade union groups to join LGSM at the head of the parade, awarding that prime position to corporate sponsors instead and insisting that political groups and unions had to join the march further back. Feeling that Pride in London were only using LGSM for publicity purposes, the group chose instead to march further back, alongside their union comrades. 'I think it's our duty to stand up and do these things,' says Horse McDonald. 'When we're marginalised within the community, like when I played Pride in London previously, and was told I could only be in the Community Tent, I think, "No. I belong on the main stage. I've worked very hard to be visible, for you, for all the people out there and for myself, and now you're telling me I have to be part of the non-professional community section." It's patronising.

'It's terrible when you do so much but you still feel like you don't belong. I did Pride in Milton Keynes [in 2019] because the people running it spoke to me about what they were trying to achieve, and I thought that was incredible. They wanted to gather people from all around, they didn't want big bucks coming in which obliged them to use chart-orientated artists who are only there to get attention.' Andy Bell has also been put off by the changing scale of Pride in London: 'I don't enjoy it so much now that it has become corporate sponsored, but I suppose it's inevitable. That's why it's nice to be invited to play in some of the smaller towns across the globe.'

Despite Pride in London growing in numbers year by year, by the 2010s the focus for the LGBT community continued to shift towards other cities round the country. Between 2004 and 2018 Brighton's Pride festival grew from bringing 100,000 to almost 500,000 people to the streets of the city over the first weekend in August and, after a couple of false starts, in 2010 Bristol had relaunched an annual fortnight-long Pride festival and march which quickly became one of the biggest free LGBT events in the country. In October 2020 Daryn J. Carter, the man who had led Pride Bristol for the previous decade, was awarded an MBE for his work on behalf of the LGBT community. And in Liverpool a new monthly club night was launched that would soon see its DJs playing on some of the biggest stages in Europe with superstar Kylie Minogue.

'I had been DJing in Manchester for years, but I'd gradually become less and less interested in it,' John Aggy explains. 'It seemed that the clubs were just full of people in a k-hole* or on their phones. The euphoria had gone. I retired in February 2015 and started a proper job.' Things were no better in his hometown. 'The scene at the time in Liverpool was all based around one area, like lots of cities, and it was predictable. It was tired: it was Rihanna and Madonna videos; it was pop tosh. It was the same records people had been listening to for years with maybe a couple of Top 20 ones thrown in. People always complained that the scenes were better elsewhere, that there was more going on, but whenever you tried to put on anything [new] no one came. They were all stuck in the same place, waiting for the miracle to happen.'

That miracle was Sonic Yootha, a new club night that eschewed hard dance and chart tunes for a random mix of sixties soul, seventies glam, eighties indie and nineties cheese. 'We could see that there were enough people who felt they were not part of the local scene, and we wanted to see if we could make something happen,' Aggy continues. The first few nights of Sonic Yootha, which took its name from the band Sonic Youth and actress and camp icon Yootha Joyce, were staged at a warehouse venue on Liverpool's Baltic Triangle in July 2015. Only 20 people turned up for the first night. 'We wanted to do a social for people around our own age and whoever else was interested, but it wasn't the right venue, so, Ian and Shaun [Yootha founders Ian Usher and Shaun Duggan] and I decided to see if we could find somewhere else. Ian just happened to be walking past this old brick garage, and he heard music coming out of it, so he stuck his nose in. He explained what we had been doing; they liked the idea, but they had no openings for a few months. Ian was about to leave, and their phone went; the manager turned around and said, "What are you doing this Saturday? We've just had a cancellation; do you want it?" And that was it. It was

---

* High on ketamine.

meant to be. As soon as I walked in, I thought, "This is it." The best venues have got a feeling, as soon as you walk in there's a feel about the place. There was just something about it.'

Liverpool, just like the rest of the country, was in desperate need of an injection of feel-good factor. For the music world, 2016 proved to be an awful year, with the deaths of LGBT icons David Bowie, George Michael and Prince, and the city's own queer superstar Pete Burns. Bowie had been battling cancer for some time, although few apart from those closest to him were aware, and Pete Burns's body gave up after being put through years of abuse. Body dysmorphia had caused him to begin a series of radical plastic surgery modifications 20 years earlier, and he admitted to having had 300 operations over the intervening years to fix botched procedures, at one point almost dying under the surgeon's scalpel. But it was George Michael's death, on Christmas Day, that was particularly shocking, the international superstar dying from a previously undisclosed heart condition and liver complaint at just 53.

It was not long before the *Liverpool Echo* was heralding Sonic Yootha, now at its new home 24 Kitchen Street, as 'the club night that saved Liverpool's gay scene'.[7] As Aggy recalls, 'It was word of mouth; it just grew and grew over the next eight or 10 months. The crowd liked the place: it's a nice space run by nice people, and they liked the music and the daft visuals. It's fun, and that's all we wanted it to be. It wasn't designed to be anything other than a big, daft piece of pop... And it worked. And it's done something really unexpected, in that a lot of young kids flocked to it, because they said that they felt safe. People coming up and say, "Thank you for doing this. There's nowhere else in town I can go out and not get abuse," especially some of the trans kids. We were the antidote to that.'

Soon people outside of Liverpool started to take notice, and in August 2018 the Sonic Yootha DJs were invited to play in Ibiza. 'We were booked to go to Pikes; we were on two nights after Fatboy Slim. It's gorgeous, a magical place. The room I was given had a giant portrait of Freddie Mercury on the wall – it's all very rock 'n' roll,' Aggy reveals. Pikes, a 25-room luxury hotel in the San Antonio hills, had been established in the late 1970s by Tony Pike, and had been a playground for his many friends in the pop industry. In 1983 Wham!'s manager

337

Simon Napier-Bell took them to Pikes for 10 days to film the video for their chart-topping single 'Club Tropicana'; Tony Pike appears in the video as the straw-hatted barman. Labelled 'the Hugh Hefner of Ibiza' by Boy George, Pike claimed to have bedded both George Michael and Freddie Mercury, and his hotel hosted Mercury's 41st birthday party.

Mercury is said to have first performed his hit 'Barcelona' in the bar of Pikes, now fittingly renamed Freddie's. It was at that party (in 1987) that Mercury first told his friend, journalist David Wigg, that he was HIV-positive. Like the others in his circle that knew of the diagnosis, Wigg was sworn to secrecy: 'The secret had to be kept because he was still hoping that there could still be some kind of a cure or the drugs he was taking for this illness would help him get through it.'[8] One of the other guests at Mercury's birthday party, according to the *Sun*, was a young actress who was due to fly to London the following month to record what would become her first British hit, 'I Should Be So Lucky'.[9] In his memoir, Pike himself makes no reference of Kylie Minogue being present that night, although he met her on several occasions, and she did stay at the hotel at a later date. And it was because Kylie had stayed at Pikes that Liverpool's Sonic Yootha crew were invited to join her on her 2018 *Golden* tour.

'In the reception were these printed curtains, with pictures of people who have stayed there, and one of these was Kylie,' Aggy explains. 'Ian photographed it and sent it to Steve Anderson, who is Kylie's arranger and producer, just saying something like, "Look who has popped up on the curtains." Steve happened to be with Kylie at that time; she saw the picture, asked who had sent it, and said to him, "I've been thinking about having DJs on the tour. Are they any good?" He said that he thought we'd be perfect. That's how we got the gig. Because Ian Instagrammed those curtains we ended up playing the O2!'

The Australian singer is a long-time LGBT ally, and Kylie and her management made sure that the Yootha DJs were well looked after. 'It was a fantastic experience, and everyone in her team was supportive and nurturing,' John Aggy adds. 'I came away from that tour with a lot of respect for her: she sang every note, never mimed once, and when she wasn't performing she was in rehearsals or sound checking, or she was doing press... It literally didn't stop.'

In 2016, a conference attended by delegates from around 60 different British Pride events came up with the idea of establishing a new network to share information and experiences. With over 100 Pride events taking place each year (by 2019 that number was up to 150, ranging from small, community-driven events for a few hundred people to massive parades featuring tens of thousands), it seemed sensible for the individual organisers to try and work together. To highlight the fact that there was more to Pride than the annual London march and party, each year a team from the UK Pride Organisers Network (UKPON) would also take part in events outside of the usual LGBT hotspots, marching in Hull in 2017, on the Isle of Wight the following year, in Newry, Northern Ireland and, before the Covid-19 pandemic put paid to plans, 2020 would have seen UKPON banners unfurled in Newcastle.

'It was an opportunity to connect Pride organisers across the UK,' says UKPON board member Stephen Ireland. 'Things were very disjointed: people knew of one another's events but weren't able to effectively coordinate things like Pride dates, for instance, and we were now talking about the challenges that face the LGBT community across the UK, Ireland and, of course, across the world. So, it was a really good opportunity for Prides to start connecting. It started off very small and now we have over 200 members registered to the UK Pride Organisers Network – that's Pride events that are established, have held their first Pride this year or are looking at setting up their first event next year.

'We're connected to the EuroPride organisation [a pan-European annual Pride festival, began in 1992], we're connected to InterPride [a global network of more than 400 Pride organisations from more than 70 countries], and we work closely with the LGBT Consortium [the largest network of LGBT groups, projects and organisations in the UK]. What that does is give you a fantastic pool of resources: it gives you the experience of Prides that are focussing on specific matters or subjects, for instance Bi-inclusion and Trans-inclusion. The BAME community is often under-represented but UK Black Pride [co-founded by queer Black feminist Phyllis 'Lady Phyll' Opoku-Gyimah in 2005] are members of UKPON, and they share their knowledge and understanding of the community and help create an even more diverse, welcoming and

339

inclusive network. There's so much diversity and there's so much pride, passion and determination, and there is strength in numbers. Prides working together can share costs, get discounts and reap those rewards as a collective.

'Each Pride is responsible for their own funding. UKPON doesn't get involved in that, but we can offer training on how Pride organisers can effectively present bids for funding and show them how they can provide the relevant evidence. Every LGBT community in every area is different, but the premise is the same for each event: how to set up an organisation, how to remain financially stable... Prides take a lot of time and a lot of resources and, of course, cost a lot of money to put together. Through us they can come together, and new events can call on the experience of more established Prides.'

Corporations are never going to miss an opportunity, and sponsorship is now an inextricable part of making Pride happen. As Britain's LGBT community became more visible – and more influential – businesses aware of the power of the Pink Pound were wondering how to align themselves with Pride events. For many in the LGBT community, corporate sponsorship was a dirty phrase, and many of these businesses have been accused of simply pinkwashing. Yet financial backing would be essential for many of these events to continue. Pride events were drawing larger and larger crowds, and incurring greater costs: security, policing, advertising, barriers, public liability insurance, even things as mundane as portable toilets and street cleaning all have to be paid for. Costs were rising, and new restrictions meant that organisers had to apply to their local authority for road closure notices, public events licences and more.

Someone had to foot the bill. Money from sponsors helps to keep costs down for people attending Pride events, but not everyone is happy with businesses getting involved with the LGBT community. Barclays Bank, UKPON's principal sponsor, saw a backlash from customers for using the colours of the rainbow flag for its logo during Pride month (nominally June/July, although Pride events now take place throughout the year). Barclays, the first UK bank to promote a transgender woman to the position of branch manager, took part in more than two dozen Pride events in 2019 and are recognised for

340

championing LGBT rights in the workplace, but not all companies who jump on the Pride bandwagon are as committed to the cause.

Pinkwashing has become endemic in the corporate world, with businesses keen to be seen to be supportive of LGBT rights, especially as it is broadly accepted that members of the LGBT community are big spenders. Since 2005, LGBT charity Stonewall has published an annual list of the 100 best employers for LGBT people, and while hotel chains, alcohol brands, airlines and sundry other companies have proudly waved the Pride flag, few of them have withstood closer examination. Arne Sorenson, the CEO of the Marriott International hotel chain until his death in 2021, was a vociferous defender of LGBT rights, openly criticising Indiana's Religious Freedom Restoration Act which would give businesses in the US state the right to discriminate against LGBT employees, yet the Marriott Marquis in New York City was happy to host a Brazilian-American Chamber of Commerce gala in 2019 that honoured Brazil's president Jair Bolsonaro, a man who would 'rather have a son who is an addict than a son who is gay', and who has gone on record saying that he is 'proud to be homophobic'.[10] When the Sultan of Brunei decided to introduce new laws making gay sex and adultery punishable by stoning to death, the Dorchester Hotel in London (and other venues in the Brunei-owned Dorchester Collection group) faced a severe backlash from high-profile clients including Sir Elton John and actor George Clooney.

'I feel a bit sad about it,' singer and activist Angela Cooper sighs, 'but I think the seeds were there from very early on; it quickly became a commercial event. When we were organising Pride in Manchester and meeting in the village with some of the bar and club owners, it was clear that there was a "what's in it for me" element. For them it was going to be a money-maker. I suppose there's an inevitability about how Pride has evolved; they're like big parties now. But people are coming out all the time, so they still have an important role.'

In August 2017, as part of the filming for *Invisible Women*, a documentary about their lives as activists, Angela and long-time comrade-in-arms Luchia Fitzgerald joined Manchester's Pride march. 'I hadn't been on one for a while,' Angela says, 'but it was really quite moving. We had this big banner, and we were walking along with rainbows painted on our cheeks and this band behind us, and I can

341

remember just looking at the crowds. We never thought that there would be such a thing as gay marriage, that there would be such a thing as a parade where the people of Manchester and their children would be waving and smiling at us. I definitely think that it still has a role. People do get quite cross: do we want the banks on the march, do we want the police on it, but what are you going to do? Companies have realised that there is kudos to be gained. The Pink Pound is massively important, and the scene will cater for wherever it can make a profit.'

Musician and club DJ Sean Dickson agrees: 'Pride is about money first and politics second these days; you only need to see the amount of sponsorship injected into the marches by corporations feeling the need to be inclusive. It's great in a way, but there is something very sad in seeing HIV charities having to walk half a mile behind a convoy of expensive and loud advertisements for brands adding a rainbow flag and gaying it up for the one day. I sometimes DJ at Pride events, but only if I feel like they are being run for the right reason, and it's not some cash machine trying to generate rainbow-branded dollars.'

So has Pride become too big and too commercial, and are LGBT artists being overlooked in favour of crowd-pleasing, big-ticket headliners? 'I don't know to what extent an artist playing a Pride event thinks about it,' musician John Grant admits. 'It's hard to strike a balance, but it's on the people promoting and curating these events to think about a good mixture and think about a good representation because, as artists, we're all trying to pay the bills as well! I'm sure there are people out there who think, "No, I don't want to play for a bunch of faggots. I don't want that fucking crowd liking my music." I'm sure there's some of that in the world, but mostly I think that people want to do it. They want the pay cheque but also they would be flattered that they are wanted, and that people want to hear their music.

'Artists are just trying to make it through the day, to survive and make their art and a lot of people don't want to be political, so I do really feel that it's important that the people who are curating and organising these events are thinking specifically about how to get a good mixture of political moves, showing support for the queer community, and also mixing communities and bringing people together... helping build new relationships.'

'It's a tough one,' Stephen Ireland admits. 'Some Prides are there to make money; they are run more like events companies. However, they do make a big contribution to their local LGBT community. Brighton Pride isn't a member of UKPON: they charge a significant price and focus on real high talent... They're run like a business. But what they also do – and this is something that we recognise as being really positive – is make a significant contribution to LGBT charities. Is there anything wrong with that? Not really, but perhaps they have lost that political feel. We're standing up against a government where half of the cabinet voted against same-sex marriage,* and unfortunately that message is perhaps lost on the likes of Brighton and other Prides like Manchester.' Other artists have expressed their dissatisfaction with this type of set-up. 'In 2017 my band, Pink Narcissus, got to perform at Brighton's Trans Pride but the regular Brighton Pride has shown no interest in what I do whatsoever and doesn't seem to support and nurture local live music at all,' Oli Spleen explains. It was this lack of acceptance that led him and a friend to launch Fag Machine, an LGBT club night in Brighton, in September 2013, showcasing acts that fall outside of the mainstream, or that have been marginalised by the commercialisation of the city's gay scene. 'The trans community seem to intrinsically understand the importance of giving a platform to authentic local talent,' he says. 'Fag Machine was a big hit with that crowd.' It would be another two years before London would host its first Trans Pride.

'There are so many variables that come into it,' John Grant explains. 'People ask for what they like, what they're really into, but I do think there should be a mixture of things that support the queer community as well as what's popular, what everybody seems to be listening to and loving, clamouring for, desperate to hear. I don't really think it matters where they come from if that's what people want to hear, but then

---

* Of the 22 ministers in Boris Johnson's July 2019 cabinet, five opposed the introduction of same-sex marriage in England and Wales during a final House of Commons vote in 2013 and a sixth, Alun Cairns, who had opposed the bill, was absent for the vote. Sixteen of the cabinet members, including Johnson himself, were absent when the House of Commons voted to allow same-sex marriage in Northern Ireland.

there is that more political side to it and I do believe that Pride should be more inclusive.

'When I did my festival in Hull, for example, we were bringing artists from Iceland... I was curating a festival based on what I liked, but I was cognisant of the fact that if we're coming to Hull we should be asking people from Hull to play as well. You need to acknowledge the pool of talent you've got in your own community as well, and give people a chance to be seen ... The gay community is so varied, it shouldn't be just Cher. There are a lot of gays who love industrial goth, or heavy metal or country music, and there are gay people who play that music. There should be a great mixture of different styles, from different communities.'

'I think we need to continue to challenge and fight those who are trying to supress us,' says Stephen Ireland. 'Whether that be our Parliament or in Commonwealth countries where people would face persecution or a lot worse if they were open about being LGBT. We absolutely still need to challenge that. We need to do something, go back to grass roots and stand positively together. We need to celebrate inclusion and diversity but the message still needs to be very clear, and you're seeing this a lot more. But you also have to understand that a lot of people who are going to Pride events now are younger; they've not seen the challenges that people have had to fight over the last 50 years and it's not until some challenges come along, like hate crime, when they stand tall. I still think we've got a fight on our hands.'

'We played a number of Pride events in Brighton and in London,' Alison Rayner adds. 'I remember getting ready to play the main stage at Brockwell Park and Lily Savage and Regina Fong were also getting ready... They had these industrial tool chests with the most unbelievable collection of make-up and they were just plastering it on... The Pride gigs were great; I really enjoyed them. I'd been going to Gay Pride for years and years, and going on the marches, and I remember feeling quite funny about their dropping the 'gay' from Gay Pride and turning it into a much more commercial event. It was not what I thought it was... I don't go on the marches now. It's too commercial for me, but things have changed. Maybe Pride has changed because it had to? I liked it when everything was more political, but I come from another time, I suppose.

'I think it will always be relevant because as things have become more liberal in our part of the world, they're getting worse in many other parts. I'm very glad that I've had that experience, to go from a time when you were scared to mention that you were gay to anybody because you had no idea how they would react, people could be very hostile and unpleasant, and to be now in a time where you can be out with everybody and be completely accepted. A lot of young people make nothing of it, and I'm very glad for that. I got married a few years ago and it felt fantastic! I was so happy. I know some people don't want that, which is fair enough and they reject all of the straight stuff, but it was the right thing for me. I'm very glad that we no longer have to be in a ghetto, we're part of the world, but God, it's not like that everywhere... Maybe along the way we have lost some of that political thing, but we have to keep an eye on the fact that other parts of the world are very different. How fortunate we are.'

'I take a rather more relaxed view than many of my contemporaries on the commercialisation of Pride,' says Lord Smith. 'I take the very pragmatic view that if you can get big donations from big companies then for heaven's sake milk them for everything you can in order to put on the best possible Pride, the best possible show, the best possible party that you can! Having said that, don't forsake or forget your political edge.'

Putting on an event for thousands of people is expensive, but there is a simple solution for the organisers of Pride in London, according to Peter Tatchell. 'Revert to a political carnival parade for LGBT rights, like the first one in 1972. If it is a political march there would be no fees payable to the police, the council, etc. Political marches are not charged, so there would be nothing imposed by Westminster Council, the Metropolitan Police or the Greater London Authority, saving around £60,000 in fees to Westminster Council alone. The anti-austerity and anti-Brexit marches [in 2019] were not subject to any of the draconian costs and restrictions on numbers that have been imposed on Pride.' Removing the corporate sponsorship from the parade itself would, ironically, save thousands in fees. There are already several cities that host post-parade live events separate to the Pride parade itself, and London did this previously, when Stonewall organised the parade and

Pride Events Limited and Radio 1 hosted the live event in 1998. Sadly, since the Covid-19 pandemic, additional legislation has been passed in the UK which makes it an offence for groups to assemble.

'Yes, it should get back to its political roots because, even though within the UK we have achieved a huge amount of legislative progress, there is still quite a bit of homophobic sentiment. Also of course around the rest of the world there is still a huge amount of legislative discrimination, and in some cases group violence and death,' Lord Smith adds.

'I like the way that Pride has developed,' says Paul Southwell. 'I remember going to a Pride and seeing Pet Shop Boys [Clapham Common, July 1997], and it was huge, it was massive. It was a really good atmosphere, and you could see that it was a nice, happy medium between the commercial side and the gay liberation side of things. But after that it did get a little bit too much. I've seen a lot of criticism about people jumping on the bandwagon, but I think we should embrace that if people want to align with us. I'm a great believer in the idea that if you can get big business behind you, and if you can do it with integrity, do it wisely, then that can be very useful. Granted, I realise that there are some big businesses that are exploiting us, but hey; we're going to be exploited anyway. It's good that there is a little bit of the old political element coming back though, because there is still such a long way to go. In Britain things have advanced, it's a lot further down the road than Australia [where Paul and his partner now live], which is a little bit hick really when it comes to gay liberation!'

'I've only been to Pride twice,' admits John Grant. 'Isn't that terrible? I went in New York City down to the parade – I was at a friend's house and they were celebrating – and I also went to Icelandic Pride in 2019, which was really nice. It was a good experience. In the past I felt like it's lost its way politically, but I think maybe it's coming back round. To me Pride events seemed like another excuse: a sex, booze and drugs thing which, you know, if that's what you're doing then great, but I didn't want that.

'Pride has always been a difficult issue for me,' continues Grant, 'because it was deeply ingrained in me that "pride comes before a fall". Nobody ever explained to me what they meant when they said 'pride'.

Because there are different types of pride... Prideful behaviour usually means arrogance, but when we talk about having 'pride' it's about having self-confidence and believing in yourself. It's about thinking of yourself as a human being, and all I've ever wanted was to be a human being that was no better and no worse than anyone else.'

Over the course of more than four decades, Pride had strayed far from its roots, and the need to fund increasingly large public events meant that there was little room left for political sentiment. However, it would not be long before the veterans of the LGBT civil rights movement would join the fray once more, reminding younger members of the community of the ongoing need to make their voices heard.

27

Where Are We Now?

'Pride began as a protest and should remain a protest until all discrimination and hate crime is ended. It is the duty of Pride organisers to keep Pride political. Otherwise it is not really Pride any more – just a party.' – Peter Tatchell

In November 2020, America elected a new President and Vice President who both put LGBT rights at the front of their campaign; not only that, but the run-up to the election had also seen the country offered the chance to vote for its first openly gay presidential candidate, Pete Buttigieg. Here in Britain, after years of campaigning, in January 2017, thousands of gay and bisexual men who had been convicted of now-abolished sexual offences had been given posthumous pardons,* and coming on the back of rights including marriage, adoption, and work and pension equality, you could be forgiven for thinking that the

---

* Anyone still alive could apply to the Home Office for a statutory pardon under a clause in the new Policing and Crime Bill. The clause was dubbed Turing's Law, in honour of Alan Turing, a man whose brilliance helped bring an end to the Second World War, but who was hounded by the authorities for his homosexuality and eventually took his own life, aged just 41, after being forced to undergo chemical castration.

war was over. But despite our elected lawmakers responding to the call for LGBT equality, the rights we have now – that LGBT community elders fought so hard to achieve – could so easily be lost. 'In some ways things are better, but in other ways they're not,' says Jayne County. 'Things seem to be getting worse for trans people. TERFs:* God, I hate those people, they are absolutely horrible. It feels like we've taken two steps forward and one step back. The anti-trans movement has picked up. Violence against trans people in America, particularly Black trans women, is on the rise and people are getting murdered. I'm sure it's happening in other countries as well, where it's really frowned on and you can be put to death.

'I keep up with the British news, and I'm shocked by the anti-trans bias in the press. I think in a lot of ways, the more "out" people have become the more dangerous it is. Now that things are so open – you read about it, see it on the TV and in the news, at the movies and everything – people see more of it and can form their opinion, and there's a lot of anti-trans opinion out there. It's like the more people know about you the more they have to use against you.

'It's tied to the move to the right politically, but anti-trans stuff comes from the far left as well. A lot of these TERFs are radical femme lesbians calling themselves "gender critical", which is just stupid: it simply means that they hate trans people. They even want to take the "T" out of LGBT. They are trying to take over a lot of Pride marches with their anti-trans hate, it's just awful. There is a lot of hatred for trans people in the gay community. It's crazy.'

John Grant agrees. 'There's a lot of homophobia and transphobia inside the gay community. It's all there, and people like me should quit acting so surprised when they run up against it. It is ridiculous: one would have thought that we had been through enough, that we'd have more compassion. But there's a lot of pain involved in what we go through in our individual experiences, and I think we also do need to have compassion with the fact that we find that within our community. People are dealing with that trauma in different ways –

---

* Trans Exclusionary Radical Feminists, a term applied to both men and women who seek to deny trans rights.

they are dealing with it with non-stop chemsex, and with homophobia towards the self and also towards others. There's all sorts of variables; different personalities can be subjected to the same things and not have the same outcome and not have that trauma, due maybe to support at home or having a constitution that allows for constant mental beatings without succumbing to that. But I do believe that [the LGBT community is] becoming more political again, especially as the trans question is addressed and is brought to the fore. I do think people are warming to the idea of more compassion.'

'Look at Hungary, Poland, Russia, Brazil and the US,' says Erasure's Andy Bell. 'Look at the high number of trans people being killed. It is all too easy to become complacent and think that just because it's not happening in your back garden then it's okay, because it isn't. We should never take these rights for granted because someone will come and snatch them away before your very eyes.'

'In terms of self-determination and creativity I think it is slightly easier here in the UK,' adds Josefina Cupido. 'But there are still pockets of prejudice deep within the established world of the arts, the media and in music organisations. You can still get beaten up by people and by the tabloids if you are LGBT, with or without a guitar, despite discrimination and human rights laws.'

In 2019 Lucia Lucas became the first trans woman to perform in a leading role with the English National Opera, when she debuted as Public Opinion in Offenbach's *Orpheus in the Underworld*. 'I think that trans artists still meet resistance,' she explains. 'But I hope with some good experiences, opera houses and opera audiences won't let trans people's identities be a restriction to their career. It is clear larger houses such as ENO and the Met are taking notice, but this has been a slow build of constantly proving myself.

'Things are definitely easier now. I think the biggest problem since the beginning of my transition was that many people didn't think it would be possible to continue my career while out. Even people who were supportive couldn't understand how it would work and tended to doubt that the business was actually accepting enough to embrace a trans artist.'

Lucas, who describes performing with the ENO as 'the smoothest experience I have ever had', says that 'audiences as a whole have always been supportive. Individuals who don't like me just don't engage with me. One audience member after a *Madame Butterfly* said, "I was ready to hate your performance, but it was really good." The admission that my performance was good despite my identity is enough for me. If you like my art, that is enough.'

Lucas realised what many artists had accepted before her, that audiences rarely care about an artist's gender or sexual identity. Sadly, the media still has a long way to go to catch up. When singer Sam Smith came out as non-binary in March 2019, later choosing to use they/them pronouns, that bastion of understanding Piers Morgan mocked Smith on television and continued to do so for months afterwards via Twitter. Australian radio presenter Kyle Sandilands preceded an interview with Smith by telling listeners that he should 'be allowed to use the N-word then, because I identify as a Black woman'.[1]

'Trans people are under the heel now, with some of the things these people are coming out with,' says Andy Polaris. 'It all trickles down. You would think that we would have moved on from that. Trans people have been admired within the creative world for a long time; look at Romy Haag with David Bowie [the transgender singer and actress had an affair with Bowie during his Berlin period]. There were two trans people living in the squat I shared with Boy George and Marilyn, and they used to come to the Blitz. We didn't think anything of it, but then it wasn't such a political issue. We were learning. Gay people are always learning about other parts of gay culture that are not necessarily part of our own experience. We were more open-minded. Maybe that's because Bowie did it, and Andy Warhol had trans actress Holly Woodlawn [mentioned in Lou Reed's Bowie-produced classic 'Walk on the Wild Side'] and so we thought it was okay. I'm shocked that in this day and age, after so much has happened, that people are still getting upset about this stuff. There should be room for everybody.'

Clearly there is still a long way to go. As Brexit loomed and Great Britain was faced with leaving the European Union, the body behind so many of the recent changes in LGBT legislation, the government lurched steadily further to the right; LGBT asylum seekers were refused leave to stay in the UK, in one case because the judge decided that the man in question did not have a gay 'demeanour' and did not 'look around the room in an effeminate manner'.[2] Figures published in November 2018 revealed the surge in the number of LGBT asylum claims rejected by the Home Office, with 78 per cent of claims refused in 2017 – a rise of 52 per cent in just two years – resulting in many asylum seekers left with little option but to return to their home country and the very real threat of facing homophobic violence, ostracisation, prison or – in countries including Pakistan, Nigeria, Afghanistan and Somalia – death. 'The system has definitely become harsher in recent years. The quality of decision-making has reduced,' barrister Rehana Popal claimed. 'You come across decisions that are genuinely absurd. The Home Office do not abide by their own policy guidance. If they followed them we wouldn't have a problem. But they don't.'[3]

'When I was in government we were concentrating on getting our own house in order,' explains Lord Smith. 'LGBT rights in other countries has emerged more as an issue as the 2000s have moved on. Now of course it's a very live issue and recognising our responsibility in all of this, as the former colonial power that put most of this stuff on the statute books out there, is really important. But we can't go in with heavy boots and start telling other countries what they ought to do because that would be counterproductive. What we can do is support local activists on the ground in countries trying to secure their own rights and I hope we will continue to do that, as well as shine the spotlight of international publicity on it all. Yes, there are still things that need to be done and campaigned for, and I hope that the Pride movement will campaign for all of these things.'

'There are people who are constantly working away, trying to effect change,' adds Horse McDonald. 'The Kaleidoscope Trust, which works with people from other nations who could be killed for being gay, they are brave people. I don't think I've ever felt brave, I've always felt afraid for my own safety, but sometimes you just can't help but be yourself and stand up and talk. Talk to people on the same level; don't dictate to them. I don't know anyone who has not been won over by that.'

It is easy to become complacent: in the UK, despite the sweeping changes in legislation, homophobic hate crimes almost trebled in the five years between 2015 and 2020, with 18,465 reported crimes in the year 2019/2020 as opposed to 6,655 in 2014/15 but, as Stonewall's chief executive Nancy Kelley admitted, 'We know that 80 per cent of LGBT people don't report hate crimes. So, this is really just the tip of the iceberg.'[4] And, despite major positive moves towards inclusion for all marginalised communities, in March 2019, 600 children aged between 4 and 11 were withdrawn from their school in a Birmingham suburb by their parents after protests over LGBT-inclusive lessons. Sixteen years after Section 28 was erased from the statute books, Andrew Moffat, the assistant headteacher of Parkfield Community School was verbally and physically threatened over the implementation of his award-winning No Outsiders lessons, aimed at promoting inclusion, and 400 parents signed a petition calling for them to be dropped from the school's curriculum.

Abuse was hurled at Moffat, awarded an MBE for his work in equality in education and shortlisted for the $1 million Global Teacher award in 2019 (the only UK teacher to make the list of finalists), and protests took place at the school gates. The lessons introduced by Moffat, who had been forced to resign from his previous school following similar protests, were in line with government guidelines on inclusion, yet more protests – often faith-based – followed at other schools in the area and further afield. Homophobic literature was distributed at school gates and megaphone wielding-protesters verbally abused members of school staff as they went about their work. Anderton Park Primary School was forced to take out court injunctions to stop parents – and others not connected with the school – from congregating outside after 12 weeks of non-stop abuse.

In October 2019 the government – now headed by a prime minister who just a year previously had described women wearing the burqa or niqab as looking like 'letter boxes' or 'bank robbers',[5] who had castigated the Labour Party for their 'appalling agenda, encouraging the teaching of homosexuality in schools'[6] and who had compared same-sex marriage to bestiality in his 2001 book *Friends, Voters, Countrymen* – finally issued guidelines on how schools should tackle the issue, after more than 50 MPs wrote to the Education Secretary, requesting stronger support for schools teaching about same-sex relationships. Relationships education was due to become compulsory for all primary school pupils in September

2020, yet the government's response was mealy-mouthed, placing any comeback to the protests in the hands of the schools and local councils, and informing teachers that, under the Human Rights Act 1988, parents had the right to withdraw their children from lessons that did not conform with their own religious and philosophical convictions. In March 2020, the government quietly withdrew their funding for anti-bullying programmes aimed at helping LGBT kids, despite earlier assurances that they would continue to invest in programmes that targeted homophobic, biphobic and transphobic bullying. It was as if Section 28 had never been repealed. The previous month, when Woodside High School in North London had its zebra crossing painted in Pride colours to mark LGBT History Month, the school received more than 200 abusive messages in a four-day period. 'I am hugely proud of our students in their successful campaign to have the first rainbow crossing outside a school in the UK,' said headteacher Gerry Robinson. 'This rainbow crossing stands for our commitment to championing equality, for our children's rights to be respected and able to thrive as themselves, in school and beyond. The hundreds of abusive messages regarding Woodside's work on equality will not deter us from continuing our work.'[7]

On the evening of Monday 17 June 2019, a fortnight before the fiftieth anniversary of the first bottle being thrown in the Stonewall riots, a handful of veterans of the GLF – including Ted Brown, Bette Bourne, Stuart Feather and Peter Tatchell – gathered in London. Joined by a new generation of Gay Liberation Front activists, their mission was threefold: to recreate the first ever British Pride march, to celebrate the anniversary of the founding of the GLF and to remind people that Pride began as a political act, not a party. Original GLF member Nettie Pollard said that '2020 brings the fiftieth anniversary of the start of gay liberation in London, the moment everything changed in Britain by giving us coming out, Gay Pride and the first Gay Pride March in 1972, making 2022 the fiftieth anniversary of that political demonstration and celebration. GLF stands for liberation: the choice is always there – liberation or slavery. We did what we did to rescue ourselves, but we always thought of you as well – you who would come out after us and will come out until the world ends.'[8]

After years of being side-lined, activists used this opportunity to launch a brochure on the group's history and issued a new manifesto. In it they insisted that Pride marches should always remain free and that no one should be denied entry because they did not have enough money, that the idea of Pride as protest be central to all events, and that corporations who trade in arms or that violate the UN International Charter on Human Rights are never again to be allowed to sponsor or have floats at Pride marches. It wasn't a big ask, as veteran activist Ted Brown acknowledged: 'We are taking to Trafalgar Square to remember and reinvigorate the fires that fought back against centuries of oppression and seemingly overwhelming odds. We gather to remember and acknowledge those who had their rights stripped from them in the past and to ensure that doesn't happen to generations now and in the future.'[9] Although the gathering was low-key and spoiled somewhat by wardens trying to move the unauthorised gathering on, it was a small step on the road to re-politicise Pride, after years of crass commercialisation. As Peter Tatchell says: 'There is a big difference between the first Gay Pride march and today's Pride marches. Back in 1972, there were no calls for equality; our demand was liberation. Our radical, idealistic vision involved creating a new sexual democracy, without homophobia and misogyny. Erotic shame and guilt would be banished, together with compulsory monogamy, gender roles and the nuclear family. There would be sexual freedom and human rights for everyone – gay and straight. Our message was "innovate, don't assimilate".

'We had a beautiful dream, but it's fading fast. In the decades since, there has been a massive retreat from the ideals and vision of the early gay liberation pioneers. People no longer question the values, laws and institutions of mainstream society. They are content to settle for equal rights within the status quo. In contrast, the first Gay Priders saw the family as a patriarchal prison that enslaves women, gays and children. The focus on safe, cuddly issues like gay marriage and adoption indicates how gay people are increasingly reluctant to rock the boat and more than happy to embrace traditional heterosexual aspirations. This political retreat signifies a huge loss of confidence and optimism. It also signals that even the gay movement has finally succumbed to the mainstream politics of conformism, respectability and moderation. Perhaps it is time to revisit the radical ideals and values of the gay liberation pioneers? We can, surely, learn from their imaginative, spikey, irreverent and defiant vision of what society could be – rather than settle for assimilation into society as it is. Innovate, don't assimilate: that slogan was relevant in 1972 and it remains just as relevant and inspiring today.'

The GLF founders had wanted to organise a series of high-profile events to mark the fiftieth anniversary of the founding of the group, but sadly like many other events due to take place in 2020, their plans had to be downscaled. The Covid-19 pandemic also caused the cancellation or postponement of Pride events around the world throughout 2020 and 2021. Some organisers faced the crisis by moving celebrations online, while Peter Tatchell led a socially distanced Pride March through London, joined by many of those same veterans of the first GLF marches. The 12 men and women, all of whom had been involved in the GLF from its earliest days, marched to mark the anniversary, and in solidarity with the Black Lives Matter movement, recently in the news thanks to international outrage over the murder, in Minneapolis, of George Floyd by a serving policeman.

The death of George Floyd sparked Village People singer Victor Willis to demand that Donald Trump, then still President of the United States, stop using their songs at his rallies. Despite rolling back LGBT rights, Trump insisted on using the gay anthem 'Macho Man' at his public events; Willis initially declined to get involved, saying that Trump 'has remained respectful in his use of our songs and has not crossed the line; if he or any other candidate were to use any of our songs in a manner that would suggest our endorsement, or in a promotional advertisement, that would cross the line.'[10] However, after Floyd's death, and the worldwide condemnation that some of Trump's comments elicited, Willis stated that 'If Trump orders the U.S. military to fire on his own citizens (on U.S. soil), Americans will rise up in such numbers outside of the White House that he might be forced out of office prior to the election. Don't do it Mr. President! And I ask that you no longer use any of my music at your rallies especially "Y.M.C.A." and "Macho Man". Sorry, but I can no longer look the other way.'[11]

Fifty years on, the core principles at the heart of the GLF remained intact. 'Homophobia did not defeat us, so we're not going to let the Covid-19 pandemic stop Pride,' Tatchell announced. 'We GLF veterans confronted anti-LGBT+ bigots 50 years ago. We faced down police harassment, far right extremists, and homophobic political and religious leaders. We are marching as Pride was planned, with face masks and social distancing. We support Black Lives Matter and the just demands of Black communities, just as we did in the early 1970s. GLF did not seek equal rights within a flawed, unjust status quo. It campaigned for the transformation of society to end straight supremacism and stood in solidarity with all other oppressed communities. This same agenda of radical social transformation is needed now as the UK faces the quadruple whammy of Covid-19, economic meltdown, endemic racism and climate destruction.'[12] In October 2020, to mark the fiftieth anniversary of the very first GLF meeting in Britain, Tatchell led a candlelit vigil at the London School of Economics to honour the heroes and heroines of the movement. Plans to mark the fiftieth anniversary of the Highbury Fields demonstration were scuppered by a second national lockdown in November, but in 2021 Tatchell – a patron of Pride in London – led a group of activists in renewed calls for Pride to return to its roots. On 24 July Reclaim Pride, a community-organised event devoid of corporate sponsors and commercialism, saw thousands march to demand civil rights for LGBT people, in the UK and abroad, to bring about an end to conversion therapy, and to proclaim solidarity with Black Lives Matter.

The Covid-19 pandemic may have brought Pride events to a halt, albeit temporarily, but it offered opportunities for others. On the other side of the Atlantic, Roddy Bottum, formerly of Faith No More and Imperial Teen, formed a new duo, Man On Man, with his partner Joey Holman. The enforced lockdown gave the pair time to produce their first album together, and to rehearse before commencing a live tour in October 2021. Back in Britain, Horse McDonald had been about to embark on a tour to celebrate the thirtieth anniversary of her debut album, *The Same Sky*, before the pandemic hit in 2020. Like many other artists, she was forced to cancel or reschedule dates and, as Christmas approached, it looked like there would be little to celebrate.

Then, something happened that helped convince her that her decades of hard work had not gone unnoticed. 'I was in London doing *The Songs of Dusty and Shirley* with David McAlmont, and I met an artist, Roxana Halls, who asked if she could paint my portrait. Of course I said yes. Months later I get a call from her. She tells me that someone saw an exhibition she had in Manchester and told her that they would love to have her work in a gallery in Scotland, but it would have to have a Scottish connection. "Well," she said, "I'm doing Horse's portrait." It's been acquired by the Scottish National Portrait Gallery – how fucking amazing! This lesbian is now going to be in a gallery alongside all of these bloody blokes!

'It's a real big thing, not only for me as an artist, but for Roxana too because she's also lesbian, and of course it will be there long after I'm dead. It's an incredible compliment, and for all of the boys' club members, it's a big "fuck you"! For someone who for a long time had very little idea of self-worth it's a big thing. Society is changing, and this decision by the gallery is very important, because it bucks the trend.'

The Covid pandemic has forced us to look at the world in a different way. Politicians constantly talk about 'the new normal', but what will be normal now? And what is the future for Pride? Events were cancelled in 2020 and 2021, but in the year of the fiftieth anniversary of the first Pride march on British soil people will again be out celebrating in their tens of thousands. 'The fiftieth year is going to be a huge year,' says Stephen Ireland of the UK Pride Organisers Network. 'It's going to really put the UK on the map as far as Pride worldwide goes. There are more and more people wanting to do things in their local community. It's going to continue to grow, and I think it's going to become more localised, which is great because it means that those local people are more connected, but we have to keep an eye on the things that challenge us as a community, and hopefully tackle them as they come along.'

In Liverpool, to accompany their sets, the Sonic Yootha DJs project a series of fun, often silly but always life-affirming images onto the walls of 24 Kitchen Street. During Pride month these images are still positive, but they carry a message. 'I wanted to make sure that Pride wasn't celebrated by just showing pictures of Madonna or whatever, so I made a point of having slides showing earlier points, like Cooper Do-Nuts [the Los Angeles café that, in May 1959, became the scene of an early LGBT protest], because that was where the resistance really started,' says John Aggy. 'I want people to question what they thought they knew about our history. It didn't start with Stonewall; it started before.

'It's easy to be a bit jaded about Pride, but it's not really for us. If you are 25, it's fucking great! And that's what it should be. It's somewhere you can go, be outside with your arms around people that you care about – with no fear.'

Two decades into the 21st century, things are undeniably better for the LGBT community in Britain, as it is in most of the Western world, but things could so easily change, and homophobia is still ever-present. The summer of 2021 saw an horrific spike in homophobic hate crime in Britain, with violent attacks on men and women in cities including Birmingham, Edinburgh, Liverpool and London. 'It varies from place to place, and from generation to generation, but there is still some out there and we need to confront that and show increasingly how unacceptable homophobia is,' says Lord Smith. In December, concerns were once again raised about institutionalised homophobia within the Metropolitan Police, after inquests into the murders of four young gay men found that that police mistakes "probably" contributed to their deaths at the hands of serial killer Stephen Port.

At the dawn of the 1970s, LGBT people (and their allies) in the arts were wary of drawing attention to themselves, but today they are much more likely to stand up and challenge discrimination. Following a string of racist, anti-Semitic rants from UK Grime star Wiley, more than 700 music business professionals, including singers, songwriters, musicians, label heads, artist managers and promoters came together to speak as one against racism, as well as against homophobia and transphobia in the industry. In an open letter, using the hashtag #NoSilenceInMusic, the group pledged to work together to 'demonstrate and express our determination, that love, unity and friendship, not division and hatred, must and will always be our common cause'. Attacks on trans rights from high-profile authors, actors and writers led more than 1,500 members of the UK and Irish publishing community to add their names to a 'message of love and solidarity for the trans and non-binary community' at the beginning of October 2020.

It has now been 50 years since LGBT people took part in the first Pride march on British soil, and almost 300 years since the regulars of the Hart Street Molly house stood defiantly against the authorities, in the dock of the Old Bailey. In London, calls for Pride to return to its political roots are gaining traction, and in October 2021 Peter Tatchell delivered a letter to Sadiq Khan, the Mayor of London, asking him to step in and ensure a total overhaul of the company behind Pride in London, after they failed to answer accusations of bullying, racism and intimidating behaviour towards some of its volunteers.

The fight goes on. For 55 years, since the passing into law of the Sexual Offences Act 1967, politicians, heads of state, church leaders, self-proclaimed spokespeople for the 'moral majority' and media talking heads have done their best to impede the LGBT community's progress. Every advancement in LGBT rights had to be fought for and won. Marching alongside the civil rights activists, it has been the musicians, songwriters, composers, actors, theatre directors, playwrights and others in the arts who have stood front and centre to face the onslaught. Today, more than half a century after bricks and bottles were hurled at the police outside the Stonewall Inn, a new generation of LGBT people, their allies and their friends, still inspired by the bitter irony in the lyrics of 'Glad to Be Gay', are demanding that their voices be heard. People not even born when the clarion call of 'No Clause 28' first rang out are continuing the fight against political oppression, and lonely and scared LGBT people are still being encouraged to strike out on their own and seek better lives, thanks in no small part to the words of 'Smalltown Boy'. Britain's LGBT community owes its eternal thanks to the men and women who documented their lives in the theatre and in song, and who fought for our very existence.

Acknowledgements

A book like this relies heavily on first-hand testimony, and although not everyone I have talked to over the course of writing the book has been quoted, each and every one of them has helped shape the narrative in some way. I am indebted to everyone who took the time to answer my questions, take part in interviews, deal with my incessant emails and put me in touch with their friends and colleagues.

Thank you John Aggy, Charlie Beaton, Andy Bell, Barnaby Bennett, Andy Blackford, Richard Bolingbroke, Phil Booth, Roddy Bottum and Joey Holman, Theodore 'Ted' Brown, Mark Bunyan, Angela Cooper, Gary Cosby, Jayne County, Josefina Cupido, Gillian Dickinson, Hifi Sean Dickson, Richard Evans, Stuart Feather, Luchia Fitzgerald, Princess Julia Fodor, Fiona Glyn-Jones, John Grant, Frankie Green, Rupert Herries, Ken Howard and Alan Blaikley, Stephen Ireland, Martin Isaacs, Jimi LaLumia, Don Letts, Lucia Lucas, Horse McDonald, Jan McMillan and Ben O'Sullivan of the Postlip Community, Andy Partridge, Polly Perkins, Andy Polaris, John Porter, Alison Rayner, Tom Robinson, Melanie Rosatone, Paul Rutherford, Rosemary Schonfeld, the late Norman Scott, Peter Scott-Presland, Lord Chris Smith (Baron Smith of Finsbury), Paul Southwell, Oli Spleen, the late Ralph Stephenson, Steve Swindells, Peter Tatchell, Twink, the late Dale Wakefield, and Ken and Dede Wilson.

Thanks also to Jonno Andrews, Dean Griffith and Andy Knight, Colin and Lesley Milligan, Darren Peace, Phil Prosser and family, Georgy Ragazza, Mitchell Winn, the Woodwards, to the fantastic team at Omnibus, especially David Barraclough, Phil Harrison, Imogen Gordon Clark, Julia Halford, Rehan Abdul and David Stock; Debra Geddes at Great Northern PR, the team at the Hall-Carpenter Archive of the LSE, Stefan and the team at the LAGNA archive at the Bishopsgate Institute, and to all involved in the Women's Liberation Music Archive, an invaluable source of information on Women's music in Britain from the seventies onwards: www.womensliberationmusicarchive.co.uk

And, as ever, to Niall and the kids. Buying me a new coffee maker does not mean you no longer have to make tea, you know...

Bibliography

Avicolli Mecca, Tommi. *Smash the Church, Smash the State: The Early Years of Gay Liberation.* San Francisco: City Lights Books, 2009.

Bayton, Mavis. *Frock Rock: Women Performing Popular Music.* Oxford: Oxford University Press, 1998.

Bray, Alan. *Homosexuality in Renaissance England.* London: Gay Men's Press, 1982.

Buckle, Sebastian. *The Way Out: A History of Homosexuality in Modern Britain.* London: I.B Tauris, 2015.

Bullock, Darryl W. *David Bowie Made Me Gay: 100 Years of LGBT Music.* London: Duckworth, 2017.

Chippindale, Peter and Chris Horrie. *Stick It Up Your Punter! The Uncut Story of the Sun Newspaper.* London: Simon & Schuster, 1999.

Clerk, Carol. *The Saga of Hawkwind.* London: Omnibus Press, 2004.

Clews, Colin. *Gay in the 80s.* Leicester: Matador Books, 2017.

Clough, Brian. *Clough: The Autobiography.* London: Corgi Books, 1995.

Dee, Hannah. *The Red and the Rainbow: Sexuality, Socialism & LGBT Liberation.* London: Bookmarks Publications, 2010.

Feather, Stuart. *Blowing the Lid: Gay Liberation, Sexual Revolution and Radical Queens.* Winchester: Zero Books, 2016.

Fowler, Norman. *AIDS: Don't Die of Prejudice.* London: Biteback Publishing, 2014.

Grey, Anthony. *Speaking Out: Writings on Sex, Law, Politics and Society 1954–1995*. London: Cassell, 1997.

Harvey, Ian. *To Fall Like Lucifer*. London: Sidgwick & Jackson, 1971.

Heffernan, Richard and Mike Marqusee. *Defeat from the jaws of Victory: Inside Kinnock's Labour Party*. London: Verso, 1992.

Hodges, James. *Select Trials: At the Sessions-House in the Old-Bailey, Volume Three*. London: J. Applebee, 1742.

Holloway, Robert. *The Vere Street Coterie, Or the Pheonix of Sodom*. London: Holloway, 1813.

Jackson, Joe. *A Cure for Gravity*. Boston: Da Capo Press, 2000.

Jeffrey-Poulter, Stephen. *Peers, Queers, and Commons: The Struggle for Gay Law Reform from 1950 to the Present*. London: Routledge, 1991.

Jivani, Alkarim. *It's Not Unusual: A History of Lesbian and Gay Britain in the Twentieth Century*. London: Michael O'Mara Books, 1997.

Johnson, Paul James. *Going to Strasbourg: An Oral History of Sexual Orientation Discrimination and the European Convention on Human Rights*. Oxford: Oxford University Press, 2016.

Kersnowski, Frank L. (Ed.), *Conversations with Robert Graves*. Jackson: University Press of Mississippi, 1989.

Leigh, Spencer. *The Cavern Club: The Rise of The Beatles and Merseybeat*. Carmarthen: McNidder & Grace, 2016.

Mason, Angela (Ed.). *Stonewall 25: Making of the Gay Community in Britain*. London: Virago, 1994.

Norton, Rictor. *Mother Clap's Molly House: The Gay Subculture in England, 1700–1830*. London: Gay Men's Press, 1992.

Parris, Matthew and Kevin MacGuire. *Great Parliamentary Scandals*. London: Pavilion Books, 2004.

Pike, Tony, with Matt Trollope. *Mr Pikes: The Story Behind the Ibiza Legend*. London: MT Ink, 2018.

Power, Lisa. *No Bath but Plenty of Bubbles*. London: Cassell, 1995.

Reuben, David M.D., *Everything You Always Wanted to Know About Sex* *But Were Afraid to Ask*. New York: David McKay Company Inc., 1969.

Rigby, Andrew. *Communes in Britain*. London: Routledge & Kegan Paul, 1974.

Robb, John. *Punk Rock: An Oral History*. London: Ebury Press, 2006.

Saul, Jack. *The Sins of the Cities of the Plain*. London: William Lazenby, 1881.

Street, John. *Rebel Rock: The Politics of Popular Music*. New Jersey: Wiley–Blackwell, 1986.

Thornton, Michael. *Royal Feud: The Dark Side of the Love Story of the Century*. New York: Simon & Schuster, 1985.

Walter, Aubrey. *Come Together: The Years of Gay Liberation 1970–1973*. London: Gay Men's Press, 1980.

Weeks, Jeffrey. *Coming Out: Homosexual Politics in Britain From the Nineteenth Century to the Present*. London: Quartet Books, 1977.

Notes

Introduction

1 Author interview with Peter Scott-Presland, August 2020.
2 'Death Penalty in 2020', Amnesty International UK press release, 21 April 2021.
3 Fish Griwkowsky, 'Judas Priest's Halford on Firepower and Fantasy', *Edmonton Journal*, 6 June 2019.
4 *Evening Post*, 21 January 1725.

Chapter One: Before Stonewall

1 'Letters', *International Times*, 10 October 1969.
2 J. Robinson, 'The Women-Hater's Lamentation', Fetter Lane, London 1707.
3 Rictor Norton (Ed.), 'A Full and True Account, 1709', *Homosexuality in Eighteenth-Century England: A Sourcebook*, www.rictornorton.co.uk.
4 'London', *Ipswich Journal*, 29 July 1721.
5 *Newcastle Courant*, 28 December 1723.
6 'London', *Stamford Mercury*, 7 January 1725.
7 *Caledonian Mercury*, 2 August 1726.
8 James Hodges, *Select Trials: At the Sessions-House in the Old-Bailey, Volume Three* (J. Applebee, 1742), pp. 37–8.
9 Ibid.
10 Robert Holloway, *The Vere Street Coterie, Or the Phoenix of Sodom* (Holloway, 1813), p. 11.

11   *The Times*, 28 September 1810.
12   'Friday's Post', *Worcester Journal*, 13 December 1810.
13   'Lent Assizes', *Public Ledger and Daily Advertiser*, 17 March 1823.
14   'Assize Intelligence', *Oxford University and City Herald*, 22 March 1823.
15   Minutes of Evidence, Central Criminal Court Sessions Paper, 21 September 1835.
16   'London Sessions', *Bell's New Weekly Messenger*, 4 October 1835.
17   'Latest Intelligence', *Maidstone Journal and Kentish Advertiser*, 24 November 1835.
18   'Accidents, Offences &ct.', *Northern Whig*, 7 December 1835.
19   *Particulars of the Execution of James Pratt and John Smith* (T. Birt, 1835).
20   'Court of Queen's Bench', *Morning Post*, 10 May 1871.
21   *The Home News for India, China and the Colonies*, 6 May 1870.
22   'Court of Queen's Bench', 1871.
23   Ibid.
24   Jack Saul, 'Introduction', *The Sins of the Cities of the Plain* (William Lazenby, 1881).
25   'Mr. Fred Barnes', The *Era*, 5 August 1914.
26   'A Queen's Portrait', *Birmingham Daily Gazette*, 11 June 1927.
27   'Vile Den of Iniquity', *Illustrated Police News*, 8 November 1934.
28   'Caravan Club Case', *Coventry Evening Telegraph*, 25 October 1934.
29   'Serious Liverpool Café Case', *Liverpool Echo*, 24 January 1935.
30   Michael Thornton, *Royal Feud: The Dark Side of the Love Story of the Century* (Simon & Schuster, 1985), p. 397.
31   'Sir John Gielgud Fined, Told "See Doctor"', *Chelsea News and General Advertiser*, 23 October 1953.
32   'Sex Law Will Not Be Changed', *Daily Herald*, 21 November 1958.
33   Ian Harvey, *To Fall Like Lucifer* (Sidgwick & Jackson, 1971).
34   Ibid.
35   H. Montgomery Hyde, 'The Million Women Who Live in the Shadows', *The People*, 30 May 1965.
36   'Homosexual Bill Get Majority of 85 in Commons', *Belfast Telegraph*, 4 July 1967.
37   Ibid.
38   *Touch and Go*, August 1967.

Chapter Two: Sowing the Seeds of Liberation

1   'Gay Liberation Meets the Shrinks', *Black Dwarf*, 7 July 1970.
2   Tony Russell, 'Obituary: Dave Van Ronk', *The Guardian*, 13 February 2002.
3   'IT in Court: What Is Decency?', *International Times*, 12 February 1970.
4   'Mary Malone's View', *Daily Mirror*, 7 July 1970.
5   'J. Edgar Hoover: Black Panther Greatest Threat to U.S. Security', UPI press release, 16 July 1969.
6   Huey P. Newton, 'A Letter from Huey about Women's—and Gay—Liberation', *Berkeley Barb*, 28 August 1970.
7   'Gay Liberation', *The Beaver*, 29 October 1970.
8   Andrew Lumsden, 'Gay Liberation', *The Spectator*, 2 January 1971.
9   Jon Wilde, 'Gay Lib', *International Times*, 20 November 1970.
10 Jim Anderson, 'So Long Fag Hags', *International Times*, 24 April 1970.
11 'Young Liberal Fined in Sex Case', *Daily Mirror*, 25 November 1970.
12 Aubrey Walter, *Come Together: The Years of Gay Liberation* (Gay Men's Press, 1980), p. 12.
13 'It's All Happening At the Old Town Hall', *Sunday People*, 27 December 1970.
14 Peter Edwards, 'Gay Is Good!', *7 Days*, 1 December 1971.
15 'The Militant "Gay" People Meet for a Big Night Out', *Daily Mirror*, 23 December 1970.
16 Michael Launder, 'Who Holds the Reins?', *Gay News 22*, April 1973.
17 Maurice McKee, 'A Gay Voice Talks About "Us, the Law and Our Community"', *Kensington Post-Mercury*, 31 December 1971.
18 Ibid.
19 'NCCL Man Protests Over Visit from Police', *Birmingham Daily Post*, 26 January 1970.

Chapter Three: Dancing with the GLF

1   Jean Austin, *Reading Evening Post*, 22 May 1972.
2   'Right Then, Which One's Dad?', *Daily Mirror*, 30 June 1971.
3   Don Short, 'Dressed Up for the Bowie Life', *Daily Mirror*, 24 April 1971.
4   Ibid.

5   Peter Holmes, 'Tricky Dicky: The Gay Liberator', *Gay News 12*, 1 December 1972.
6   'Manchester Student Group (CHE)', Broadsheet No. 1, October 1971.
7   Wilfred De'Ath, 'Getting It Together', *The Listener*, 13 September 1973.
8   Andrew Rigby, *Communes in Britain* (Routledge & Kegan Paul, 1974), p. 93.
9   Maurice McKee, 'A Gay Voice Talks About "Us, the Law and Our Community"', *Kensington Post-Mercury*, 31 December 1971.
10 Maurice McKee, 'A Terrific Christmas Party, Courtesy of the GLF', *Kensington Post-Mercury*, 24 December 1971.
11 Len Adams, 'And Now Kiddies... Let's Jeer at the Police', *The People*, 9 January 1972.
12 'Punch Anti-Police?', *Kensington Post*, 21 January 1972.

Chapter Four: The Festival of Lies

1   Banner displayed at the Festival of Light gathering, Trafalgar Square, 25 September 1971.
2   'Wedding Bells for Danny La Rue', *Derby Daily Telegraph*, 27 October 1987.
3   'Gay Courting', *International Times*, 10 February 1972.
4   *Sunday Times*, 21 July 1971.
5   'The Shadow Over Platform 12', *The People*, 29 March 1970.
6   'Youth Was Ringleader, Court Told', *Liverpool Echo*, 24 January 1973.
7   David Reuben, M.D., *Everything You Always Wanted to Know About Sex* (*But Were Afraid to Ask)*, (David McKay Company Inc., 1969), p. 126.
8   Ibid., p. 127.
9   Ibid., p. 131.
10 'Liar! Oh What a Lovely Book', GLF leaflet, Hall Carpenter Archives, LSE, 1971.
11 Reuben, p. 247.
12 John Mathews and David Triesman, 'Aversion Therapy: Treating People Like Rats', *7 Days*, 1 March 1972.
13 Maurice McKee, 'It's War, Says the Gay Liberation Front', *Kensington Post,* 15 October 1971.
14 'News: Homosexuals Are a Nuisance', *International Times*, 27 January 1972.

Chapter Five: Subversives in Sequins

1   'Dr. Goodenough's Clinic Confidential', *The People*, 11 June 1972.
2   Spencer Leigh, *The Cavern Club: The Rise of The Beatles and Merseybeat* (McNidder & Grace, 2016).
3   Warm Dust press release, November 1970.
4   'Gay Convictions Soar By 160%', *Gay News 34*, 18 October 1973.
5   'Police Close "Too Gay" Dance Studio', *Gay News 25*, June 1973.
6   'You're No Trouble, It's Just These Kids with Nothing to Do', *Gay News 3*, August 1972.
7   Carol Clerk, *The Saga of Hawkwind* (Omnibus Press, 2004).
8   Michael Watts, 'Oh! You Pretty Thing', *Melody Maker*, 22 January 1972.
9   Hamish Mackay, 'Pop Talk', *Aberdeen Evening Express*, 24 January 1973.
10 'Let's Face It!', *Daily Mirror*, 4 September 1972.
11 Deborah Thomas, 'King of Rock and Rouge', *Daily Mirror*, 22 January 1973.
12 Jonathan Takiff, 'Repetition Is Making "Freak Rock" Stale', *Philadelphia Daily News*, 26 July 1974.
13 Miles, 'They Simper At Times', *International Times*, 23 February 1973.
14 Ibid.
15 Ibid.
16 'Live Ghouls', *Marylebone Mercury*, 10 August 1973.
17 Lester Bangs, 'Lou Reed: A Deaf Mute in a Telephone Booth', *Let It Rock*, November 1973.
18 Tom Robinson, 'Lou Reed Backtracked from His Implied Bisexuality. But He Didn't Let Me Down', *The Independent*, 28 October 2013.
19 Gay Liberation Front Diary, 2–8 February 1972, the Hall Carpenter Archive, LSE.
20 Maurice McKee, 'It's War, Says the Gay Liberation Front', *Kensington Post*, 15 October 1971.
21 Deborah Thomas, 'A Star Is Shorn', *Daily Mirror*, 1 October 1973.
22 www.urban75.net/forums/threads/the-brixton-fairies-1970s-gay-squat.6280/page-4.

Chapter Six: Have You Heard the News?

1   Charles Shaar Murray, 'Gay Guerillas and Private Movies' [sic], *New Musical Express*, 24 February 1973.
2   Tim Hughes and Trevor Richardson, 'Bowie for a Song', *Jeremy Magazine*, May 1970.
3   Anthony Delano, 'Going Gay', *Daily Mirror*, 15 May 1972.
4   Denis Lemon, 'Editorial', *Gay News 1*, June 1972.
5   Lemon, 1972.
6   'Seaside Uproar Over Gay Lib Get-Together', *Daily Mirror*, 21 July 1972.
7   'Jesus Loves You', *International Times*, 27 July 1972.
8   Denis Lemon, 'All Over the Rainbow', *Gay News 6*, 1 September 1972.
9   'Record Reviews', *Gay News 11*, November 1972.
10 'Gay Pride Week', *Gay News 1*, June 1972.
11 Denis Lemon, 'Believe It or Not', *Gay News 6*, 1 September 1972.
12 'Policemen Cannot Lie', *Gay News 7*, 14 September 1972.
13 Michael De La Noy, 'Attack on Police Agents Provocateurs "Society's Priorities Mixed Up"', CHE press release, 8 October 1972.
14 'Red Cap Gay Disco Raided by Police', *Gay News 27*, 12 July 1973.
15 'Gay Dancing', *Gay News*, January 1974.
16 'Red Cap Gay Disco Raided by Police', 1973.
17 Ibid.

Chapter Seven: Taking a Stand

1   John Huxley, 'Gay Lib Men Who Live in a Twilight World', *Aberdeen Evening Express*, 2 March 1973.
2   Maurice McKee, 'A Million Trade Unionists Are Gay', *Kensington Post*, 15 January 1971.
3   'Singer Mike Gives Up the Mike for Love', *The People*, 14 January 1973.
4   'The Night Men Danced with Men at the Paint Box', *Marylebone Mercury*, 2 May 1975.
5   *International Times*, 23 February 1973.
6   *International Times*, 8 March 1973.
7   'Morecambe: Paperweights, Weighty Papers, Then Great Success', *Gay News 21*, 21 April 1973 .

8   Conor McAnally, 'I Changed My Mind About Homosexuals!', *Sunday Independent* (Dublin), 17 February 1974.

9   Matthew Parris and Kevin MacGuire, *Great Parliamentary Scandals* (Pavilion Books, 2004), p. 239.

10 Tracy McVeigh, 'Heckled but Happy: The Graceful Star of Gay Marriage Debate', *The Guardian*, 26 May 2013.

11 '"Thanks for Nothing", Shouts Gay Rights Campaigner', *Glasgow Herald*, 22 February 1994.

12 'Dear Sir', *Liverpool Echo*, 15 May 1974.

13 Marje Proops, 'Teach Them All the Facts of Life', *Daily Mirror*, 17 April 1974.

14 'Spearhead Stays in Libraries', *Harrow Observer*, 24 May 1974.

15 Bob Phillips, 'The Fight for Equality', *Liverpool Echo*, 5 December 1974.

16 'Gay Libs Gather', *Belfast Telegraph*, 4 November 1974.

Chapter Eight: Sisters Are Doing It for Themselves

1   Brenda Maguire, 'She Thinks Her Boss Is a Lesbian', *Sunday Independent*, 2 June 1974.

2   The Northern Women's Liberation Rock Band Manifesto, 1973.

3   Marion Fudger, 'Stepney Sisters', *Spare Rib*, May 1976.

4   The Northern Women's Liberation Rock Band Manifesto, *Spare Rib*, April 1975.

Chapter Nine: Queer Things Are Happening

1   'Letters to the Editor', *Coventry Evening Telegraph*, 18 May 1974.

2   'DJ Takes Up Brewery Offer', *Gay News 79*, September 1975.

3   'Fangs Disco: Agreement with Charrington and Co Ltd', The National Archives, AN109/574.

4   'BBC Man Killed by Boyfriend', *Daily Mirror*, 5 April 1975.

5   Jan Iles, 'Whatever Happened to the Teenage Dream', *Record Mirror*, 1 February 1975.

6   Richard Bevan, interview with Simon Napier-Bell, 19 April 2006.

7   'Alice – A Fag?', *Spec*, August 1974.

8   Julie Webb, *New Musical Express*, 12 March 1974.

9   'Standing Up for Queen', *Melody Maker*, 28 July 1973.

10 'Solicitor Found Murdered', *Daily Mirror*, 24 June 1975.

11 'Police Swoop on Nightspots', *Gay News 75*, July 1975.

12 'Doing the Holland Park Walk', *Kensington News and Post*, 18 June 1976.

13 'Free Bill Walker!', Oldham CHE press release, February 1976.

14 'Thorpe Denies Sex Claim', *Liverpool Echo*, 29 January 1976.

15 'Thorpe Accuser: Ex-wife Tells of Fixation', *Birmingham Daily Post*, 2 February 1976.

16 Geoffrey Lakeman and Sydney Young, 'I Was Paid £5,000 to Kill Scott', *Daily Mirror*, 20 October 1977.

17 Jim Farber, 'Rod Stewart: "I Was Surrounded by Gay Men in the 70s"', *The Guardian*, 14 June 2016.

18 'Their Majesties the Queen', *The People*, 8 February 1976.

19 Cameron Crowe, 'David Bowie: An Outrageous Conversation with the Actor, Rock Singer and Sexual Switch-hitter', *Playboy*, September 1976.

20 Paul du Noyer, 'Contact', *Mojo*, July 2002.

Chapter Ten: Britain's Stonewall

1 'Debauched Life of Ex-choir Boy', *Evening Standard*, 9 August 1974.

2 'Shock Decision by Top Law Lord', *Gay News 72*, 5 June 1975.

3 'Had Enough Vengeance?', *Croydon Advertiser*, 9 May 1975.

4 'Justice with a Vengeance', *Time Out*, 9 April 1976.

5 'Weak Links in Police-Gay Relations', *Gay News 32*, September 1973.

6 'Is This the Wickedest Street in Britain?', *Sunday People*, 12 September 1971.

7 'Earl's Court Is Anti-vice Campaign's Target No. 1', *Kensington Post*, 14 October 1977.

8 Jeff Grace, 'Street Fights at the Coleherne Lead to New Arrests', *Gay News 99*.

9 Graham Ball, 'Street of Shameless Men', *The People*, 27 April 1975.

Chapter Eleven: Better Blatant Than Latent

1 *Cash Box*, 5 November 1977.

2 'Is This the Wickedest Street in Britain?', *Sunday People*, 12 September 1971.

3 'Bomb Fury Rocks West End', *Daily Mirror*, 29 January 1977.

4   John Street, *Rebel Rock: The Politics of Popular Music* (Wiley–Blackwell, 1986).

5   J. Mandelkau, 'Rod the Mod', *International Times*, 17 December 1870.

6   'The Genesis of Industrial', Genesis P-Orridge, October 2012.

7   'MPs Fury at Porn Palace', *Daily Mirror*, 19 October 1976.

8   'Cosey Fanni's Deep in Blue Movies', *The People*, 24 October 1976

Chapter Twelve: Cocks in Frocks

1   Joan Bates, 'A Plea Within a Play', *Birmingham Daily Post*, 22 June 1976.

2   Peter Sheridan, '"Gay" Folk on the Stage', *Sunday Independent*, 27 June 1976.

3   'Gay Sweatshop', *Liaison* (Trinity College, Dublin), 17 November 1976.

4   Joan Bates, 'A Plea Within a Play', *Birmingham Daily Post*, 22 June 1976.

5   'Vicar in Gay Play Rumpus – Heckling Minister Ejected During Show at Church', *Hampstead and Highgate Express*, 14 October 1975.

6   Desmond Rushe, 'Gay Group's Propaganda Offensive', *Irish Independent*, 16 November 1976.

7   Peter Martin, 'Project's Rare Double Bill', *Irish Press,* 17 November 1976.

8   Jim Farelly, '"Gay" Show May End Theatre Grant', *Irish Independent*, 17 November 1976.

9   Ibid.

Chapter Thirteen: Blasphemy!

1   'Lords Dismiss a Libel Appeal by Gay News', *Belfast Telegraph*, 22 February 1979.

2   'MP Attacks Bypass for Blasphemy Hearing', *Birmingham Post*, 23 December 1976.

3   'Whitehouse Case for Old Bailey', *Belfast Telegraph*, 21 December 1976.

4   'Blasphemy Trial Jury Told of Perverted Poem', *Birmingham Daily Post*, 5 July 1977.

5   Keith Howes, 'Gay Britain: Bristol', *Gay News 98*, 1977.

6   'Gay News Guilty of Blasphemy', *Birmingham Daily Post*, 12 July 1977.

7   'MPs Slam Sentences for Blasphemy', *Birmingham Daily Post*, 13 July 1977.

8   'Letters to the Editor', *Chester Observer*, 12 August 1977.

9   'Gay News Loses Libel Appeal', *Reading Evening Post*, 18 March 1978.

10 Brenda Hickman, 'Mary Whitehouse in Local Storm', *Cheshire Observer*, 21 October 1977.

11 'Vicar Calls for Ban on Gay Festival', *Birmingham Post*, 16 January 1978.

12 Billy Bragg interviewed by Christopher Lydon, Radio Open Source, 27 July 2017.

13 www.urban75.net/forums/threads/the-brixton-fairies-1970s-gay-squat.6280/.

Chapter Fourteen: Gay's the Word

1   'Police Seize Gay Mags Worth £3,000', *Gay News 78*, August 1975.

2   'Conspiracy: Government Inventing New Laws – MP Complains', *Gay News 78*, August 1975.

3   'Psychologist Defends "Streetboy" Book', *The Guardian*, 9 January 1974.

4   'Man Shot Homosexual Because He Feared a Beating', *Croydon Advertiser*, 14 September 1979.

5   'Stand Together' sleevenotes, June 1979.

6   *Action on Police Harassment: Proposals from CHE*, 1979.

Chapter Fifteen: The Shock of the New

1   Marje Proops, 'Our Kind of Love', *Daily Mirror*, 27 August 1980.

2   'I'm Free, for a Demo', *Daily Mirror*, 12 October 1977.

3   *Gay News 144*, 1 June 1978.

4   *Irish Times*, 6 June 1976.

5   'No Sodomy Here, Says Paisley', *Belfast Telegraph*, 19 October 1977.

6   'Briton's Friends Shocked by Paedophilia Accusation', *Montreal Gazette*, 19 March 1981.

7   Letter from Antony Acland to Sir Robert Armstrong, Secretary of the Cabinet, 27 June 1984, FOI release, published 15 May 2015.

8   Andrew Hirst, 'Remembering the 1970s Heyday of Huddersfield Gay Nightclub Gemini', *Huddersfield Daily Examiner*, 27 February 2016.

9   Gordon Charlton, 'Boy Who Doesn't Mind Being Called a Girl', *Daily Mirror*, 2 October 1982.

10 Robin Eggar, 'Rock', *Daily Mirror*, 26 October 1982.
11 Robin Eggar, 'Rock', *Daily Mirror*, 19 April 1983.
12 Karen Swayne, 'It Ain't Necessarily So', *No 1*, 19 January 1985.

Chapter Sixteen: The Gay Plague

1 Simon Garfield, 'AIDS: The First 20 Years (Part One)', *The Observer*, 3 June 2001.
2 *Capital Gay*, 26 November 1982.
3 *Changing the World*: *A London Charter for Lesbian and Gay Rights*, GLC, 1985.
4 Letter to the Commander, N Division, Kings Cross issued by London Gay Workshops, 8 November 1982, The Hall Carpenter Archives, LSE.
5 'Labour's Programme for Britain', *Labour Weekly*, 28 May 1976.
6 Philip Johnston, 'Bitter-sweet Bermondsey', *Aberdeen Press and Journal*, 23 February 1983.
7 'Bitter Tatchell Slams Liberal', *Aberdeen Press and Journal*, 25 February 1983.
8 'Police Fear for Safety of Peter Tatchell', *Aberdeen Press and Journal*, 10 February 1983.
9 'A Live Bullet for Tatchell', *Liverpool Echo*, 9 February 1983.
10 Chris Smith, 'The Politics of Pride', *Stonewall 25: Making of the Gay Community in Britain* (Virago, 1994), p. 61.
11 Andrew Grice, 'The "Homophobic" Campaign That Helped Win Bermondsey', *The Independent*, 27 January 2006.
12 'Stop This Gay "Sus" Law', *Capital Gay*, 30 September 1983.
13 Ibid.

Chapter Seventeen: Out!

1 Terry Sanderson, 'Media Watch', *Gay Times*, March 1985.
2 Peter Trollope and Jo Riley, 'Scene', *Liverpool Echo*, 21 January 1983.
3 *Mail on Sunday*, 6 January 1985.
4 'AIDS Cases Increasing', *Newcastle Evening Chronicle*, 5 July 1984.
5 *The Sun*, 21 December 1984.
6 'One Man Caused AIDS Outbreak', *The Times*, 24 December 1984.

7   'Pretty Police Lose Again!', *Capital Gay*, 27 January 1984.

8   Terry Sanderson, 'Media Watch', *Gay Times*, August 1984.

9   Michele Hewitson, 'Interview: Su Pollard', *New Zealand Herald*, 14 June 2014.

10 'Elton's Rock Marriage... Is It Rolling into Bigger Troubles?', *Evening Herald* (Dublin), 27 February 1987.

11 Terry Sanderson, 'Media Watch', *HIM*, April 1984.

12 'Marilyn Beaten up in Aussie Gay Bar', *The Sun*, 14 April 1984.

13 Guy Rais, 'Tory MP "Thought WPC in Gay Club Was in Drag"', *Daily Telegraph*, 19 October 1984.

14 Terry Sanderson, 'Media Watch', *Gay Times*, December 1984.

15 Ibid.

16 *The Hampson Case; A Background Briefing*, Galop, June 1984.

17 'Rugby's Gay Times', *The Economist*, 10 November 1984.

18 'Poll Reflects a "Split" on Gays', *Rugby Advertiser*, 18 October 1984.

19 Owen Bowcott, 'Thatcher Tried to Block "Bad Taste" Public Health Warnings About Aids', *The Guardian*, 30 December 2015.

Chapter Eighteen: Pride, Pits and Perverts

1   Brian Flynn, 'We Danced in the Miners Hall', *Gay Community News*, 16 March 1985.

2   'Minister Gets New Junior Role to Play', *Aberdeen Press and Journal*, 23 April 1983.

3   Liz Lightfoot, 'Council Drops "Gay News" Ad', *The Guardian*, September 1982.

4   Flynn, 1985.

5   Ibid.

6   Karen Swayne, 'It Ain't Necessarily So', *No 1*, 19 January 1985.

7   Maurice Cafferky and Edmund Lynch, 'The Beat of a Different Drum', *Out*, December 1984.

8   Ibid.

9   Larry Goldsmith, 'British Queers Dig Deep for the Striking Miners', *Gay Community News*, 16 March 1985.

10 'Churchgoers Concerned Over Homosexual Vicar's Death', UPI, 2 February 1985.

11 Terry Sanderson, 'Media Watch', *Gay Times*, March 1985.
12 'Gays Banned from Pub Over AIDS Fears', *Reading Evening Post*, 8 February 1985.
13 Peter Chippindale and Chris Horrie, *Stick It Up Your Punter! The Uncut Story of the Sun Newspaper* (Simon & Schuster, 1999).
14 www.mark-ashton.muchloved.com/Home.
15 'Rock and the Kiss of Fear', *Liverpool Echo*, 3 October 1985.
16 'AIDS Speech – Anderton Under Fire', *Dundee Courier*, 12 December 1986.
17 'Bishops Lash Out at BBC Theme', *Liverpool Echo*, 11 December 1986.
18 'Margaret Thatcher Saved Career of Police Chief Who Made AIDS Remarks', *The Telegraph*, 4 January 2012.
19 GALOP Third Annual report, 1986–87, p. 15.
20 Ibid., p13.
21 'The Communards', *Record Collector*, February 1988.
22 'AIDS Ward Angel Diana', *Staffordshire Sentinel*, 9 April 1987.
23 Letter from David Willits to the Prime Minister, Margaret Thatcher, 24 February 1986, The National Archives, PREM 19/1863.
24 Tim Jonze, 'How We Made the Don't Die of Ignorance Aids Campaign', The *Guardian*, 4 September 2017.

Chapter Nineteen: The Kiss

1 Baroness Knight of Collingtree, *Hansard*, 6 December 1999.
2 Jo Devon, 'My Love for Kathy, By George', *Sunday World* (Dublin), 6 December 1987.
3 'David Bowie Says: I Took the AIDS Test', *Press and Journal*, 21 March 1987.
4 Ibid.
5 'Officers Want Victims Named', *Dundee Courier*, 21 March 1987.
6 Andrew Knight, 'Sundays of Shame', *Aberdeen Evening Express*, 13 June 1988.
7 Piers Morgan, 'Scrap Eastenders Call Over Gay Kiss', *The Sun*, 26 January 1989.
8 Piers Morgan, 'No Stereotypes Were Harmed in the Making of This Film', *The Telegraph*, 18 September 2005.

9   Siriol Hugh Jones, 'Books', *The Tatler*, 28 September 1960.

10 Terry Sanderson, 'Media Watch', *Gay Times*, February 1985.

11 Richard Heffernan and Mike Marqusee, 'Defeat from the Jaws of Victory: Inside Kinnock's Labour Party' (Verso, 1992), p. 74.

12 Terry Sanderson, 'Media Watch', *Gay Times*, June 1986.

13 'Move to Ban Gay Book for Children', *Liverpool Echo*, 25 November 1983.

14 'Whitehouse Joins Kids Sex Book Row', *Aberdeen Evening Express*, 27 January 1983.

15 'Comment: Bordering on the Criminally Irresponsible', *Liverpool Echo*, 17 September 1986.

16 'Schools Lost for Words in Gay Book Row', *Hammersmith and Shepherds Bush Gazette*, 19 September 1986.

17 *Hansard*, vol 483 cc310-38, 18 December 1986.

18 Ibid.

19 'Baroness Knight: Section 28 Architect Says She's Sorry "If the Law Hurt Anyone"', *Pink News*, 25 May 2018.

Chapter Twenty: No Clause 28

1   'Claire Rayner Writes', *Reading Evening Post*, 6 February 1988.

2   Adrian Pitches, 'Gays Pay Rates Too', *Hayes & Harlington Gazette*, 9 March 1988.

3   'Prohibition on Promoting Homosexuality by Teaching or by Publishing Material', *Hansard*, Volume 124, 15 December 1987.

4   'Gay Rights Marchers Clash with Policemen', *Ealing Leader*, 15 January 1988.

5   www.mckellen.com.

6   Chris Godfrey, 'Section 28 Protesters 30 Years On', *The Guardian*, 23 March 2018.

7   '15 Charged After Operation Spanner', *Glasgow Herald*, 10 October 1989.

8   Margaret Thatcher, Conservative Party Conference speech, October 1987.

9   'Stonewall: The Reunion', BBC Radio Three, 20 September 2009.

10 Cliff Graham, 'Cursing His Memory', *Newcastle Evening Chronicle*, 13 January 1990.

11 Paul Morley, 'A Boy Called George', *NME*, 1 May 1982.
12 BP Fallon, 'Oh Boy', *Sunday Tribune*, 12 June 1988.
13 'AIDS Concern of Queen Star', *Derby Evening Telegraph*, 24 November 1987.
14 'Channel Four Gay Shocker', *Sunday Life* (NI), 29 January 1989.
15 Nicholas Watt, 'David Cameron Apologises to Gay People for Section 28', *The Guardian,* 2 July 2009.

Chapter Twenty-One: A Death in the Family

1   'Queen Star Dies After Aids Statement', *The Guardian*, 25 November 1991.
2   'Plea Over Actor Kicked to Death', *Liverpool Echo*, 1 May 1990.
3   'Gay Victim's Screams Heard at OAP's Home', *Hammersmith & Shepherds Bush Gazette*, 19 July 1991.
4   Hugh Muir, 'Officers' Homophobia Hampered Murder Investigations, Says Review', *The Guardian*, 15 May 2007.
5   Ibid.
6   OutRage! mission statement, 1990.
7   'People in the News', *Aberdeen Evening Express*, 6 September 1990.
8   'Rock Legend's Confession', *Aberdeen Evening Express*, 8 November 1990.
9   John Radowitz, '"I Have AIDS" Says Rock Star', *Sunday Life*, 24 November 1991.
10 'Fear Over Star's Legacy of AIDS', *Daily Star*, 26 November 1991.
11 *Question Time*, BBC 1, 28 November 1991.
12 'Holly Johnson Has AIDS Virus', *Evening Herald* (Dublin), 8 April 1993.
13 'Big Names in Gay Statement to Back Sir Ian', *Liverpool Echo*, 9 January 1991.
14 Ibid.
15 *Hansard*, Volume 238, 21 February 1994.
16 Ibid.
17 Letter from Mark Adams to the Prime Minister, 3 February 1994, The National Archives, PREM 19/4734.

Chapter Twenty-Two: This Is Britpop

1 'Tory Pair Attack UK Homosexual Laws as "Hypocritical Humbug"', *Aberdeen Press and Journal*, 29 May 1992.

2 'Anderson: "I'm Bisexual"', www.contactmusic.com, 3 June 2005.

3 Jon Wilde, 'Pork Life', *Loaded*, September 1994.

4 Debbie Smith Interview, *The Dukey Radio Show* (podcast), 6 September 2015.

5 Aileen O'Reilly, 'Baldly Going Where No Woman Has Gone Before', *Evening Herald*, 2 November 1996.

6 Carlene Thomas-Bailey, 'What I Know About Women', *The Guardian*, 25 October 2009.

7 O'Reilly, 1996.

8 Smith, 2015.

9 Internal memo from Seymour Stein to Kas Gold, 6 December 1994.

10 Andy Richardson, 'Live: Lick', *NME*, 14 January 1995.

11 Richard Smith, 'Tongue-and-Dance Men', *Melody Maker*, 3 June 1995.

12 Lance Loud, 'Glad to Be Gay', *Kerrang!*, 22 May 1993.

13 'Feehily Happy to Be a Gay Role Model', *Sydney Morning Herald*, 2 March 2006.

Chapter Twenty-Three: Pride in Crisis

1 Angela Mason, 'What Pride Means to Me', Pride Events UK press release, 1998.

2 'Essential Diversions', *Thud* (National Edition), September 1995.

Chapter Twenty-Four: 21st-Century Boys and Girls

1 Anthony Grey, *Speaking Out: Writings on Sex, Law, Politics and Society 1954–1995* (Cassell, 1997).

2 Cole Moreton, 'Billy Bragg Out of Tune with New Labour', *The Independent*, 26 May 1996.

3 Ibid.

4 Matthew Wright, 'Tour Gong', *Daily Mirror*, 31 December 1997.

5 'Rob Halford Discusses Sexuality Publicly for the First Time', *MTV News*, 5 February 1998.

6   Alex Petridis, 'Judas Priest's Rob Halford: I've Become the Stately Homo of Heavy Metal', *The Guardian*, 3 July 2014.

7   Gill Pringle, 'The Decoy', *Daily Mirror*, 15 August 1985.

8   John McShane, 'Gorgeous George's Soulmate', *Daily Mirror*, 23 August 1984.

9   'George Michael and Brian May: A Conversation', MTV, 20 April 1993.

10   Mark Dowdney, 'George's Sick Video', *Daily Mirror*, 8 October 1998.

11   'Boy George on George Michael's Secret Torment', *Scottish Daily Record*, 9 April 1998.

12   'Pet Shop Boy Snubs Labour with Anti-ID Cards Song', *Evening Standard*, 28 February 2006.

13   Joe Jackson, *A Cure for Gravity* (Da Capo Press, 2000), p. 56.

14   'Nail Bomb Victim Tells of Ordeal', *Aberdeen Press and Journal*, 7 June 1999.

15   'Four Guilty of Killing Bar Manager in Random Attack', *The Guardian*, 14 December 2005.

16   Jimmy Somerville interviewed in Hamburg, 9 May 1999. www.jimmysomerville.de.

17   'Hundreds Attend Vigil at Soho Bombing Site', *Aberdeen Press and Journal*, 8 May 1999.

18   'Brigadier Quits Over Gays in Military', BBC News, 27 January 2000.

19   'Pop Idol Will: "I'm Gay"', BBC News, 10 March 2002.

Chapter Twenty-Five: Celebrate!

1   Andrew Pierce, 'Cheers Ring Out As David Cameron Lays Tory Homophobia to Rest', *Daily Telegraph*, 2 July 2009.

2   Jeffrey Blyth, 'They Call This "Gay", But We Have Another Word for It... UGH!' *The People*, 16 May 1971.

3   Ibid.

4   'Vicar Who "Weds" Gay Couples', *Sunday People*, 2 March 1975.

5   'Tattoo Gay Men, Clergyman Writes', BBC News, 6 October 2008.

6   'Elton Is Hoping to Wed His Male Lover', *Irish Independent*, 4 March 2004.

7   James Sturcke, 'Barman Killer Had Been Released Early', *The Guardian*, 16 June 2006.

8   Tom Guerra, 'Finally Free', *Vintage Guitar*, September 2005.
9   'DJ Rapped For "Offensive" Comments', *Daily Express*, 23 March 2009.
10 'In Brief', *Evening Herald* (Dublin), 18 April 2009.
11 James Robinson, 'PCC Rejects Complaint Over Jan Moir Column About Stephen Gately's Death', *The Guardian*, 17 February 2010.

Chapter Twenty-Six: Pinkwashing

1   Matt Dathan, 'Ukip Candidate Referred to Gay People as "A*** Bandits"', *The Independent*, 25 April 2015.
2   Flo Lewis, 'UKIP's Brave LGBT Members Should Be Free to March at Pride', *Pink News*, 3 June 2015.
3   Frankie Green, 'Comment: Letting UKIP March at Pride Would Be an Affront to Our History', *Pink News*, 15 June 2015.
4   Flo Lewis, Twitter post, 15 May 2018.
5   'In His Own Words', *New York Times,* 23 October 2018.
6   Boris Johnson, 'Another Voice', *The Spectator*, 15 April 2000.
7   Statement from LGSM Regarding Pride 2015, 6 June 2015.
8   *Liverpool Echo*, 14 July 2017.
9   Stefan Kyriazis, 'Freddie Mercury Kept His Illness Secret for So Long Because "He Was Hoping for a Cure"', *Daily Express*, 4 April 2021.
10 George Harrison, 'Queen of Pop', *The Sun*, 23 October 2018.
11 Mariana Simões, 'Brazil's Polarizing New President, Jair Bolsonaro, in His Own Words', *New York Times,* 23 October 2018.

Chapter Twenty-Seven: Where Are We Now?

1   Emma Powys Maurice, 'Presenter Claims Sam Smith's Pronouns Means He Can "Use the N-word"', *Pink News*, 21 April 2020.
2   May Bulman, 'Asylum Seeker Told by Judge He Was Not "Effeminate" Enough to be Gay', *The Independent*, 21 August 2019.
3   Ibid.
4   Ben Hunte, 'I Thought I Was Going to Die in Homophobic Attack', www.BBC.co.uk, 9 October 2020.
5   Boris Johnson, 'Denmark Has Got It Wrong', *Daily Telegraph*, 5 August 2018.

6   Boris Johnson, 'Another Voice', *The Spectator*, April 2000.
7   Eleanor Busby, 'School Receives Hundreds of Abusive Messages Over LGBT+ Rainbow Crossing', *The Independent*, 11 February 2020.
8   Steve Brown, 'LGBT Activists and Allies to Recreate the First-ever Pride', www.attitude.co.uk, 17 June 2019.
9   Ibid.
10   Jon Blistein, 'Village People Singer Victor Willis Tells Trump to Stop Using Their Music at Rallies', *Rolling Stone*, 8 June 2020.
11   Victor Willis, Facebook post, 5 June 2020.
12   Peter Tatchell Foundation press release, 13 June 2020.

Index